Gender in the Middle Ages

Volume 24

THE QUEENSHIP OF MATHILDA OF FLANDERS, *c.* 1031–1083

Gender in the Middle Ages

This series investigates the representation and construction of masculinity and femininity in the Middle Ages from a variety of disciplinary and interdisciplinary perspectives. It aims in particular to explore the diversity of medieval genders, and such interrelated contexts and issues as sexuality, social class, race and ethnicity, and orthodoxy and heterodoxy.

Proposals or queries should be sent in the first instance to the editors or to the publisher, at the addresses given below; all submissions will receive prompt and informed consideration.

Professor Jacqueline Murray
jacqueline.murray@uoguelph.ca

Professor Diane Watt
d.watt@surrey.ac.uk

Boydell & Brewer Limited
editorial@boydellandbrewer.com

Previously published volumes in the series are listed at the end of this book.

THE QUEENSHIP OF MATHILDA OF FLANDERS, *c.* 1031–1083

EMBODYING CONQUEST

Laura L. Gathagan

THE BOYDELL PRESS

First published 2025
The Boydell Press, Woodbridge
Paperback edition 2026

ISBN 978-1-83765-068-2 (Hardback)
ISBN 978-1-83765-489-5 (Paperback)

The Boydell Press is an imprint of Boydell & Brewer Ltd
and of Boydell & Brewer Inc.
website: www.boydellandbrewer.com

Our Authorised Representative for product safety in the EU is Easy
Access System Europe – Mustamäe tee 50, 10621 Tallinn,
Estonia, *gpsr.requests@easproject.com*

A CIP catalogue record for this book is available
from the British Library

To Kevin,
for everything

CONTENTS

ILLUSTRATIONS

PLATES

MAPS

TABLES

ACKNOWLEDGEMENTS

I have incurred a mountain of debt, both professional and personal, in the course of writing this book. I am indebted to libraries and archivists around the world, especially the John Rylands Library in Manchester, UK. Special thanks go to its staff, including Rebecca Winstanley and the wonderful John Hodgson whose knowledge of its riches is unparalleled. I would also like to thank the Archives de Calvados in Caen and its knowledgeable staff. Generous support of my work was provided by the Maison de la Recherche en Sciences Humaines (MRSH) at the University of Caen. Christophe Maneuvrier deserves particular gratitude for his generosity, both with his time and his office. The entire staff of the MRSH has shown me great kindness over the years. Several other generous funding bodies furthered my work: the John Rylands Research Institute, the American Philosophical Society, the Friends of the Princeton University Library, the Haines Fund, the Karen Goodell Gift and the Myers Family Fund. I've benefitted from the largesse of Bill and Liz Sharp, who established a fund in the History Department at my university that allows our research to flourish. My university home, State University of New York at Cortland, regularly provided support for my scholarly activity. The most important resources there, of course, are my colleagues both retired and those still toiling beside me, especially Judith Van Buskirk, John Shedd, Randi Storch, Amy Henderson-Harr, Girish Bhat, Sharon Steadman, Scott Moranda, Anisha Saxena and those whose paths have led them elsewhere: John Aerni-Fleisner, Celeste McNamara and Danielle Candelora. Thanks to the wonderful Cortland students who helped with aspects of this book; Chelsea Lachman, Jessica Goon, and Brianna Gamblicher. Thanks are owed to Meg Hutchins and Peter Dohan who provided encouragement and support. There are innumerable scholars whose kindness helped move the book forward, but particular thanks are due to those whose work on Anglo-Norman history made this project possible: David Bates, Véronique Gazeau, Elisabeth van Houts, William Aird, and the late Marjorie Chibnall. Many thanks to Benjamin Pohl for his scholarship and friendship and for reading the manuscript. My gratitude is due especially to Lois Huneycutt, for her early mentorship, and friendship over many years. My support system of exceptional women also includes Kathy Krause, Miriam Shadis, Heather Tanner, Mary Dockray-Miller, Abby Thomas, Ann Burns-Thomas and the 'Godas': Amy Livingstone and Laura Wangerin. Thank you to the wonderful Catherine Letouzey-Réty, my 'sister' in the work of uncovering the women of

Holy Trinity. Warm and sincere thanks to Leonie Hicks, Charles Insley, April Harper and Joanna Huntingdon whose camaraderie and encouragement have been indispensable. Leonie Hicks and Amy Livingstone also read chapters of the manuscript; their help and comments improved it markedly. Thanks to my dear friends in the Haskins Society, especially Jennifer Paxton, Joanna Drell, Steven Isaacs, Bill North, Bob Berkhofer, Thomas McCarthy, Emily Winkler and Charlie Rozier. I would also like to thank a number of talented writers who have ensured this book did not languish forever in a desk drawer: Lauren Mossotti-Kline, David Frank, Geoffrey Bender, Katie Ahern, Teagan Bradway, Laura Davies and Matthew Lessig. Sincere thanks to the ever-patient Andrea Harbin, who was pressed to read large portions of this book. And to anyone who ever asked, 'How is that Mathilda book coming…?', thank you.

I owe an enormous debt of gratitude to Caroline Palmer, whose knowledge of our field is vast, whose clemency appears to have unplumbable depths, and whose trust in my vision for this book has resulted in its presence in your hands. She is a treasure. The entire team at Boydell were wonderful from start to finish. My gratitude goes out to the anonymous readers of my book who invested time and energy in reviewing it. Thanks also to Matthew Carnicelli for his support and generosity.

To my family, thank you for never asking me to please stop talking about Mathilda: Henry and Carole Gathagan, Lynn Gathagan, Leslie and Peter Crane, Grant Gathagan, Lydia and Louis Hamilton. To Lydia and Louis especially, who were next to me in this endeavor at every step, my undying gratitude and love. And to my sons, Will and Alex, thank you for your love and support, and for never complaining about my month-long absences in the summer, missing your elementary school graduations, Little League games, and award ceremonies. You make me enormously proud.

Lastly, to my husband Kevin, whose creative mind inspired the structure of this book. Thank you for the innumerable ways you kept our ship afloat as I scribbled throughout the house, dragging papers and books in my wake. Thank you for the annual stretches of single parenting that included all of the aforementioned graduations, games and ceremonies. Your answer was always 'yes'. This book is dedicated to you.

CHRONOLOGY

The chronology below provides important dates in Mathilda's life and, when possible, provides her location. The list is not exhaustive nor are the majority of dates precise. Some of the dates below are anchored to charters, diplomas or other documents. The others are indicated with *c.*

c. 1031–1034	Mathilda of Flanders is born, possibly in Bruges
Pentecost, May 14, 1048	King Henry convenes his Pentecost Court in Senlis, Mathilda's betrothal is probably arranged
Before July 1049	Baldwin V of Flanders excommunicated by Pope Leo IX
October, 1049	Mathilda's proposed marriage to William of Normandy is banned by Pope Leo IX at the Council of Rheims
c. 1050–1052	Mathilda marries William of Normandy at Eu, and is received as duchess at Rouen
c. 1051–1052	Mathilda bears her first child, Robert Curthose
c. 1052–1059	Mathilda gives birth to William Rufus, Richard, Adelaide, and Cecelia
c. 1058–1059	Mathilda begins construction on the Abbey of Holy Trinity, Caen
1059	Papal ban is lifted on Mathilda's marriage to William
c. 1059–1066	Mathilda gives birth to Constance and Mathilda
July 18, 1066	Dedication of Holy Trinity
c. July 1066	Norman fleet moves from Dives-sur-Mer for larger port at Valery-sur-Somme
September 1066	Norman ships leave Valery-sur-Somme for England
October 14, 1066	Battle of Hastings
c. December 1066–April 1067	Mathilda gives birth to Adela

Easter, 1067	Easter Festal Court at Fêcamp after successful invasion. William returns to Normandy
September 1, 1067	Death of Mathilda's father, Baldwin V of Flanders
March, 1068	Mathilda sails for England
Pentecost, May 10, 1068	Royal inauguration of Mathilda of Flanders
c. late 1068–early 1069	Mathilda bears her last child, Henry
Easter, April 13, 1069	Mathilda at Winchester. Mathilda and William prepare for the possible invasion of the Danes
c. May, 1069	Mathilda returns to Normandy
Easter, April 4, 1070	Mathilda at Winchester. She and William celebrate crown-wearing
July 17, 1070	Mathilda's brother, Baldwin VI dies, Mathilda's nephew Arnulf III inherits
Autumn, 1070	Robert the Frisan, Mathilda's younger brother, attacks her nephew, Arnulf III
c. Dec. 1070–February, 1071	Mathilda at Rouen. At her request, William fitz Osbern travels to Flanders with an armed company
February 22, 1071	Battle of Cassel; Arnulf III and William fitz Osbern are killed. Robert the Frisian becomes Count of Flanders
Easter, April 8, 1072	Mathilda at Winchester, signs Accord of Winchester
May 27, 1072	Mathilda at Windsor, signs second version of the Accord
Easter, April 5, 1075	Mathilda at the ducal festal court at Fêcamp; Cecelia takes final vows as a nun at Holy Trinity
Winter 1077–early 1078	Robert Curthose rebels, leaves Normandy
January 8, 1079	Death of Mathilda's mother, Adela of France
Easter, April 12, 1080	Mathilda reconciles Robert Curthose with William, the ducal family celebrates at Rouen
c. Autumn, 1080	Robert Curthose leads army to Scotland; Mathilda travels with him. Malcolm of Scotland submits through diplomacy. Mathilda stands as Edith of Scotland's godmother

Christmas, 1080	Mathilda, Robert and William celebrate Christmas at Gloucester
c. February 4, 1081	Mathilda in Salisbury with William
c. late February	Mathilda in London with William
Pentecost, May 31, 1081	Mathilda in Winchester
Summer 1081	William leaves for Wales with Robert Curthose, Mathilda remains in Winchester
c. June 1081	Mathilda adjudicates case at Winchester
c. Autumn 1081	William returns to Normandy with Robert Curthose. Mathilda rules England
c. 1081–1082	Mathilda settled in Windsor dispensing justice
c. 1082	Mathilda presides over the Four Shires in Warwickshire
c. July 1083	Mathilda returns to Normandy
Nov 2, 1083	Mathilda dies in Caen

ABBREVIATIONS

ANS	*Anglo-Norman Studies* (formerly Proceedings of the Battle Conference on Anglo-Norman Studies)
ASC	*Anglo-Saxon Chronicle*; normally cited from Two of the Saxon Chronicles Parallel, ed. Charles Plummer (2 vols., Oxford, 1892–9), with year and MS
BL	British Library, London
DB	*Domesday Book*, Phillimore Edition [ed. John Morris] (35 vols., Chichester, 1973–86)
EHR	*English Historical Review*
EME	*Early Medieval Europe*
GND	*The Gesta Normannorum Ducum of William of Jumièges, Orderic Vitalis, and Robert of Torigni*, ed. and trans. Elisabeth M.C. van Houts (2 vols., Oxford, 1992–5)
HSJ	*Haskins Society Journal*
JEH	*Journal of Ecclesiastical History*
JMH	*Journal of Medieval History*
MGH	Monumenta Germaniae Historica
AA	*Auctores Antiquissimi*
Epp.	*Epistolae*
LdL	*Libelli de Lite*
SS	*Scriptores in folio*
SSRG	*Scriptores Rerum Germanicarum, separatim editi*
SSRG n.s.	*Scriptores Rerum Germanicarum, nova series*
MS/MSS	*Manuscript/Manuscripts*
MS/MSS	Manuscript/Manuscripts
OV	*The Ecclesiastical History of Orderic Vitalis*, ed. Marjorie Chibnall (6 vols., Oxford, 1969–80)

PL	*Patrologia latina cursus completus*, ed. J.-P. Migne (221 vols., Paris, 1844–64)
Recueil, ed. Fauroux	*Recueil des actes des ducs de Normandie de 911 à 1066*, ed. M. Fauroux (Caen, 1961)
Regesta	*Regesta regum Anglo-Normannorum: the Acta of William I (1066–1087)*, ed. David Bates (Oxford, 1998)
William of Malmesbury, *GP*	*William of Malmesbury, Gesta Pontificum Anglorum*, ed. and trans. R.M. Thomson and M. Winterbottom (2 vols., Oxford, 2007)
William of Malmesbury, *GR*	*William of Malmesbury, Gesta Regum Anglorum*, ed. and trans. R.A.B. Mynors, R.M. Thomson, and M. Winterbottom (2 vols., Oxford, 1998–9)
William of Poitiers, *Gesta*	*William of Poitiers, The Gesta Guillelmi of William of Poitiers*, ed. and trans. R.H.C. Davis and M. Chibnall (Oxford, 1998)

Map 1. Select Locations, Flanders and Normandy *c.* 1030–1100. Map by Gordie Thompson.

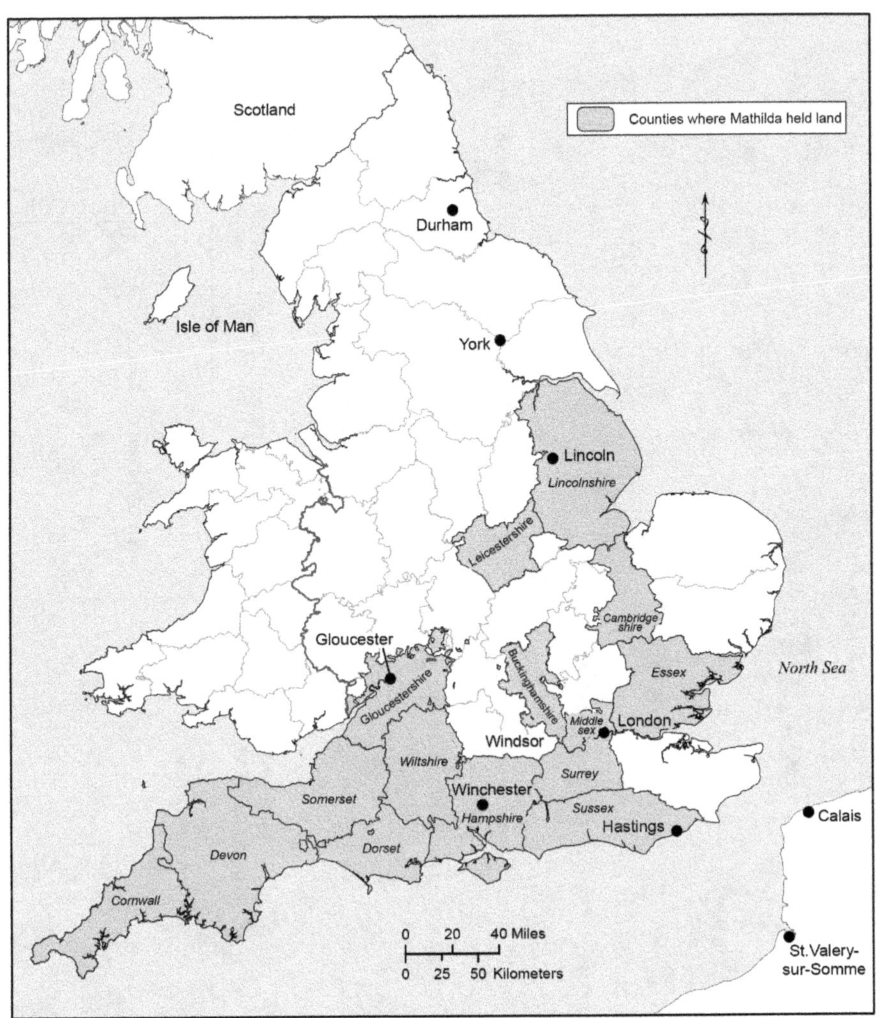

Map 2. Doomsday counties in England *c.* 1086. Map by Gordie Thompson.

Table 1. Genealogical Table of Mathilda of Flanders.

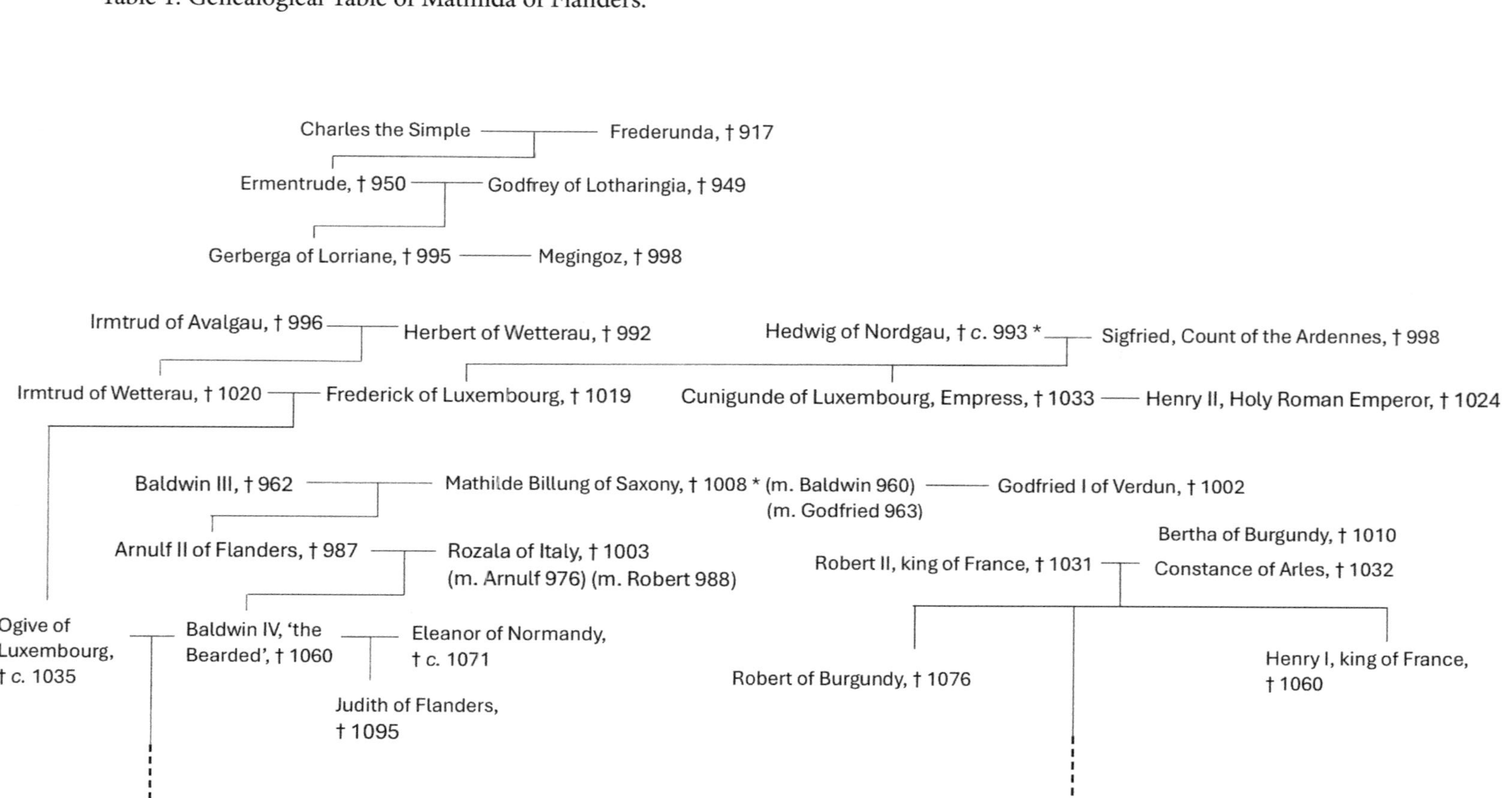

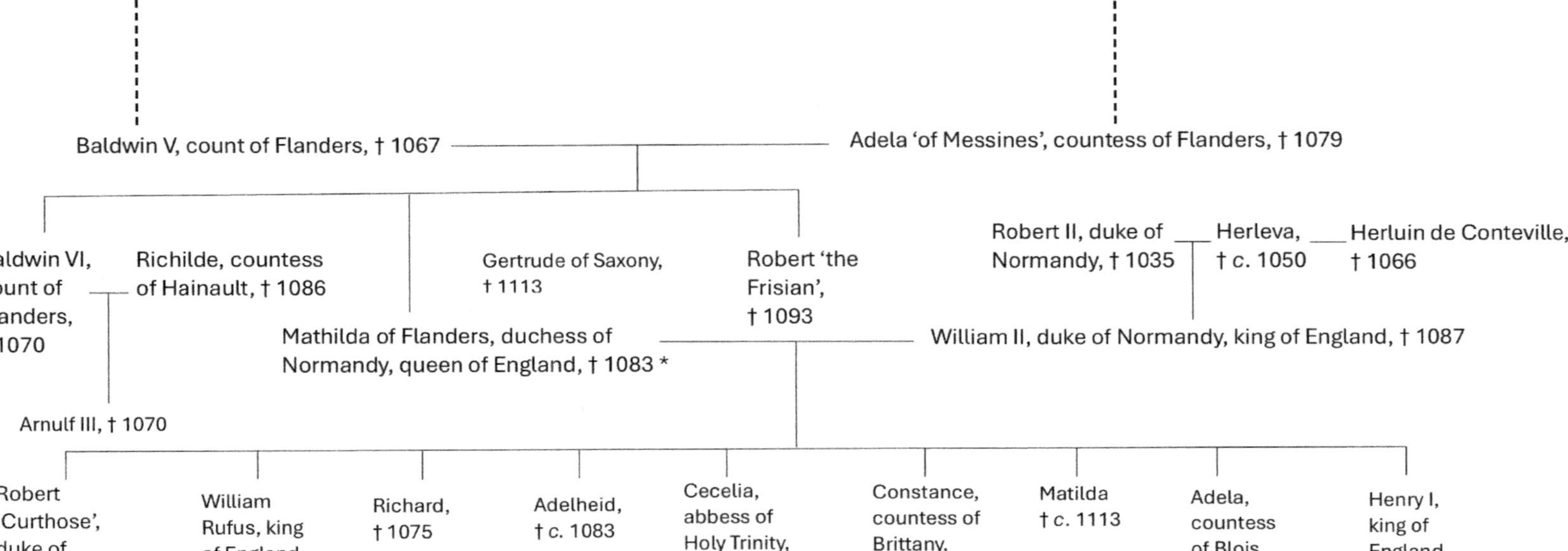
Baldwin V, count of Flanders, † 1067
Adela 'of Messines', countess of Flanders, † 1079
Baldwin VI, count of Flanders, † 1070
Richilde, countess of Hainault, † 1086
Gertrude of Saxony, † 1113
Robert 'the Frisian', † 1093
Robert II, duke of Normandy, † 1035
Herleva, † c. 1050
Herluin de Conteville, † 1066
Mathilda of Flanders, duchess of Normandy, queen of England, † 1083 *
William II, duke of Normandy, king of England, † 1087
Arnulf III, † 1070
Robert 'Curthose', duke of Normandy, † 1135
William Rufus, king of England, † 1100
Richard, † 1075
Adelheid, † c. 1083
Cecelia, abbess of Holy Trinity, † 1127
Constance, countess of Brittany, † 1090
Matilda † c. 1113
Adela, countess of Blois, † 1137
Henry I, king of England, † 1135
* = multiparous women (eight or more children)

INTRODUCTION

The structural organization of this book owes a debt to Edward E. Baptist's examination of slavery in the nineteenth-century United States.[1] It may seem a strange inspiration; the subjects of these two books are separated geographically by an ocean and chronologically by a thousand years. The center of Baptist's analysis is the black enslaved body; written on the slave is the history that would produce modern American capitalism. The harrowing experience of an American slave offers few points of contact with the biography of a medieval queen. Yet, a focus on power's interaction with the body crosses boundaries of time and space. The intimacy and viscerality of power is something medieval queens and kings would have understood. Royal power in the eleventh century was personal and individualistic. Bureaucracies of the exchequer, the treasury and representative institutions were certainly present, but were less concretized than they would be even 100 years later. Political power in the central middle ages was based on a web of personal relationships between human beings, not merely administrative structures. Power was navigated through channels of intimate relationships, whether friendly, hostile or opportunistic. Women's elite power, moreover, was regularly contextualized in terms of female bodies. Whether their power was celebrated or demonized, women's flesh was constantly evoked. Royal women, especially, were subjected to body-centered ideology and at the same time drove it. Elizabeth I's claim to the 'heart and stomach of a king' may be the most famous to modern audiences, but her claim rested on a centuries-old trope of female power drawn from bodily awareness. Thus, a study of Mathilda of Flanders, centered on her royal body, draws that viscerality back into frame; a position that reflects its centrality in medieval sources.[2]

The theme of embodiment runs through this volume as it did Mathilda's life. Embodiment was the webbing that held together belief and thought in the Middle Ages. For foundational thinkers like Augustine and Ambrose, Christ's incarnation – the concept of the 'Divine made flesh' – underpinned

1 Edward E. Baptist, *The Half Has Never Been Told: Slavery and the Making of American Capitalism* (New York, NY, 2014).

2 A later example is Marie-Antoinette: *Writings on the Body of a Queen*, ed. Dena Goodman (New York, NY, 2003) which engages the queen's body as a site of contested identity. The chapters in Goodman's collection variously address how Marie's identity was crafted, utilized and exploited.

theology, philosophy, self-consciousness, reflexivity, presence, signification. All these rested on the mystical embodiment of God into Mary's body – a woman's body – for the medieval thinker. To paraphrase Laura Saetveit Miles, Mathilda's reality was 'a world where all understanding of meaning was contingent on a girl in the distant past saying "yes" to an angel'.[3]

One can argue that this was especially true of the mid-eleventh century. It was at this time, precisely during Mathilda's reign as duchess then queen, that radical beliefs about Eucharistic piety were concretized. Not just a memorial feast, the Eucharist was Christ's actual body and blood made real at the altar. The mystery of the Divine Office henceforth required the philosophical acceptance of the intimate relationship – indeed, the identicality of – the person of Christ and the bread and wine on the communion table. That drastic change profoundly altered the distance between a thing and its referent; it shrunk to a vanishing point. The adoption of 'Real Presence,' argued by Lanfranc, Mathilda's own archbishop, reverberated through the eleventh-century Christian world. The new orthodoxy transformed many aspects of religious practice and belief, but also had consequences for society writ large, as many historians have shown.[4] Thus Mathilda's creations, those things commissioned, donated, proffered by her, had the force of her own presence, her own body. This tactic would have been well understood by the court who were her audience, entangled in Eucharistic debates.

The title of this book also reflects Mathilda as a consummate practitioner of representation through embodiment, a talent repeatedly demonstrated through the choices she made. She created opportunities to extend herself; to appear even when absent.[5] She founded a monastery, which in itself is not unusual for an aristocratic woman, but she linked it to the conquest of England, fashioning it into a monument to military victory. She used objects to transmit her presence – a cloth of gold, a liturgical chalice, a warship – to intentionally step in to places she could not be herself, claiming a place through the signifiers she created. The moveable goods she commissioned might seem disparate – a naval vessel versus the liturgical clothing of a priest – until they are viewed in situ. In each case, their materiality bore her essence, just as the incarnation was understood to have done.

3 Laura Saetveit Miles, *The Virgin Mary's Book at the Annunciation: Reading, Interpretation and Devotion in Medieval England* (Cambridge, 2020), 6.

4 Brigitte Miriam Bedos-Rezak, *When Ego Was Imago: Signs of Identity in the Middle Ages* (Leiden, 2011) remains the essential work on the subject. A more thorough examination of the issues noted here can be found below; Chapter Six: Flesh, 171–84.

5 Bedos-Rezak used the phrase 'technological extensions of a person'. Brigitte Miriam Bedos-Rezak, 'Medieval Identity: A Sign and a Concept,' *American Historical Review* 105: 5 (2000), 1489–1533.

It bears noting here that Mathilda was pregnant for at least seven of her first nine years as duchess of Normandy. Between 1052 and 1066, she bore seven of her nine children. At the most conservative estimate, including nine months of active pregnancy and perhaps another three months of churching, Mathilda's body had spent seven of her thirteen married years in some stage of pregnancy or recovery. Given that context, it is hardly surprising that Mathilda had a heightened awareness of the way her fecund royal body might be interpreted. Indeed, she utilized her physical body, even weaponized it, in a series of masterful and sophisticated strategies by which she inserted herself into all-male spaces. Pregnant, present, anointed and crowned, absent, signified, at the altar rail, on the battlefield, Mathilda pushed open the door to places not usually accessible to women, even royal women. Thus, the following chapters demonstrate both her canny ability to utilize representation through objects and that she appeared in modes that challenged and even enraged her enemies. Her pregnant body and the triumphalist elements of her coronation combined to fire the already seething unrest of the English nobility, at least what was left of them, after the Conquest disinherited them.

Positioning Mathilda's biography on her body is an attempt, paradoxically, to free her story from the constraints of the female lifecycle. Biographies feel most natural when organized chronologically and many excellent works on queens have followed this structure.[6] What could be simpler than examining a life through its natural courses? Writing women's lives, however, has too often in the past suggested that biology defined them. Even to speak of a woman's 'courses' refers implicitly to her physical maturation – her move from daughter to prospective mother – traced out in an explicit physical change of menses that marked her transition from child to adult.

The current study, by contrast, preferences Mathilda's actions, creations and speech, instead of her roles as daughter, spouse and mother. It challenges the traditional life cycle organization which too easily segues into biography by relation. Analyzing a royal woman as 'daughter of,' 'spouse/consort of' and 'mother of' can serve to elide her endeavors in ways that men in history do not suffer. Medieval elite men also derived their power from family networks, but these are rarely emphasized in male narratives of power. William the Bastard inherited the duchy of Normandy from his father; without his family,

6 Select examples include Lindy Grant, *Blanche of Castile, Queen of France* (New Haven, CT, 2016); Janna Bianchini, *The Queen's Hand: Power and Authority in the Reign of Berenguela of Castile* (Philadelphia, PA, 2012); Lois L. Huneycutt, *Matilda of Scotland: A Study in Medieval Queenship* (Woodbridge, 2003); Pauline Stafford, *Queen Emma and Queen Edith: Queenship and Women's Power in Eleventh-Century England* (Oxford, 1997); Majorie Chibnall, *The Empress Matilda: Queen Consort, Queen Mother and Lady of the English* (New York, NY, 1991). See most recently Matthew Firth, *Early English Queens, 850–1000: Potestas Reginae* (New York, NY, 2024).

he would be lost to history. He conquered England through military effort, but his birth allowed him to do so.[7] As Theresa Earenfight has shown, the rule of the 'prince' in the Middle Ages was a collective.[8] The fiction of the solitary man who wields power alone at the apex of aristocratic society was a publicly promoted construction. Networks of royal power – in which women were indispensable – were often obscured by chroniclers.[9] This elision has too often been adopted to credit men with wielding power alone, more than women who perform the same actions; medieval ruling men have power, medieval ruling women have 'agency'.[10]

Yet medieval royal power was always relational, conditional, contingent, and based on the rather spongy foundation of the aristocratic subjects' consent to being ruled. Sovereignty was an arena where gender 'plasticity' was demonstrated; royal anointing resulted in a ruler who 'whatever their biological sex' was 'neither exclusively "masculine" nor "feminine."'[11] Through anointing and coronation, medieval rulers were thought to participate in the divine status once reserved only for consecrated bishops and, historians have argued convincingly, royal abbesses.[12] It may be no coincidence that the development of sacral kingship can be traced to the Ottonian dynasty, whose daughters had already assumed such sacred personae. The development of sacral kingship may have been an answer to the increased prestige of Ottonian abbesses, the very heritage Mathilda favored, a connection explored in later chapters.[13]

7 His father's repudiation of Estrith, the resultant relationship to Edward the Confessor, the support of his mother's family and the support of the Anglo-Norman aristocracy made his rule possible. David Bates, *William the Conqueror* (New Haven, CT, 2016), 28–30 and 37–8 (hereafter Bates, *William*).

8 Theresa Earenfight, 'Without the Persona of the Prince: Kings, Queens and the Idea of Monarchy in Late Medieval Europe,' *Gender and History* 19:1 (April 2007), 1–21. Also see Miriam Shadis, *Political Women in the High Middle Ages: Berenguela of Castile (1180–1246) and her Family* (London, 2002). The same collective model has been demonstrated in the aristocratic class; see Amy Livingstone, *Out of Love for my Kin: Aristocratic Family Life in the Lands of the Loire, 1000–1200* (Ithaca, NY, 2010).

9 Lucy Pick, *Her Father's Daughter: Gender, Power and Religion in the Early Spanish Kingdoms* (Ithaca, NY, 2017), 16. See also below.

10 Theresa Earenfight, 'A Lifetime of Power: Beyond Binaries of Gender,' in *Elite Women and the Exercise of Power, 1100–1400: Moving Beyond the Exceptionalism Debate* (London, 2019), 272–3.

11 Louise Olga Fradenburg, 'Introduction: Rethinking Queenship,' in *Queenship and Sovereignty*, ed. Louise Olga Fradenburg (Edinburgh, 1992), 1–3.

12 Pick, *Her Father's Daughter*, 18. Ernst H. Kantorowicz, *The King's Two Bodies: A Study in Mediaeval Political Theology*, revised edition (Princeton, NJ, 1997), 59.

13 See Chapter One: Blood, 11–33.

SOURCES

Only glimpses of Mathilda can be seen in narrative chronicle sources of the eleventh and twelfth centuries. The twelfth century, particularly, saw a dramatic upswing in the 'story sources' of narrative Latin historical writing, including monastic and clerical chronicle authors: Eadmer, Symeon of Durham, Robert of Jumièges, Robert of Torigni, Orderic Vitalis, John of Worcester, William of Malmesbury, Henry of Huntingdon, Alfred of Beverley, William of Newburgh, and Gervase of Canterbury. Other anonymous authors penned works specifically on the Norman Conquest, like the *Carmen de Hastingae Proelio*, probably written by Bishop Guy of Amiens. Yet of all these authors, only a handful mention Mathilda and typically only in passing. While it may seem surprising that she does not appear center stage in these accounts of England and Normandy, it is important to remember that narrative chronicles were modelled on the classical histories of military heroes. Men's exploits – in victory or defeat – claim the narrative. Medieval narrative writers, moreover, were almost always monks or men living in the clerical milieu. Their works were instructive, moral teleology that would allow the reader to see God's hand at work in history, rewarding the good and punishing the evil. Like the Bible, these are works that reflect the culture of their age. With the exception of the Virgin Mary, women appear irregularly in scriptural texts and almost always in supporting roles. Old Testament women who were meant to be emulated (Sarah, Esther and Ruth) and those who served as a warning (Lot's wife, Jezebel and Delilah) operated in the margins. Female judges and military heroes of the Old Testament were rare exceptions.[14] The genealogical tables of Deuteronomy, indeed, record only men and their sons. It is no wonder that medieval writers, using scriptural and classical texts to trace out their chronicles, elide women from the account unless absolutely crucial to advancing the narrative. Thus, looking for traces of Mathilda, or any woman, within these works is routinely a frustrating endeavor.

Orderic Vitalis gave Mathilda more attention than other chroniclers and, indeed, allowed her a voice.[15] There are good reasons for Orderic's familiarity with Mathilda's character and motivation. A monk of Orderic's monastic community at St Évroult, Samson, was in Mathilda's service. A trusted agent, his work for Mathilda put him in danger; Mathilda arranged his escape into the cloister.[16] Orderic claims he was wise, well-spoken and virtuous.[17] Orderic never met Mathilda himself, but he undoubtedly learned much of Mathilda's character and habits from Samson. Samson's oral testimony was a valuable

14 Examples include Judith, who beheaded Holofernes, Deborah the judge, who led an Israelite army against Sisera, and Jael, who later beheaded him.

15 See Chapter Five: Womb, 150–6.

16 See Chapter Five: Womb, 153–4.

17 *OV*, iii, 104–5.

source for Orderic and a convenient one, enclosed in the community of St Évroult with him as a brother.

Fortunately, non-narrative documentary sources for Mathilda's life are exceedingly rich. These include Domesday Book, commissioned in 1086, twenty years after her death. Traces of her remain in this legendary medieval survey, even though her properties had passed into other hands by the time it was produced or were absorbed into William's *Terra Regis*. Other crucial sources for her are legal documents and charters. She issues, signs or is evoked in 137 charters produced during her years as duchess of Normandy and queen of England. Other than her husband, no one in the Anglo-Norman realm appears in more legal documents than Mathilda.[18] She also appears in ecclesiastical records, as she passes through the clerical and monastic communities of her realm, sometimes as a patron, sometimes as a predator.[19]

Mathilda's active role in administration is reflected in a veritable mountain of documentary evidence and contrasts sharply with the English queens who came before her. Even as early as 1896, French scholars acknowledged Mathilda's participation as a defining characteristic of Norman charter production on either side of 1066. In fact, Mathilda's attestation – and its position as second only to William on a list of signators – is a defining element of a charter's veracity.[20]

Between autumn of 1081 and *c.* December 1082, Mathilda ruled England alone without William, who was in Normandy attending to conflicts in Maine.[21] During that critical juncture, her attestation is missing from charters issued in Normandy. When that separation is taken into consideration, Mathilda's charter participation percentage is even higher.[22] As noted above, Mathilda may have spent over two and a half years – in total – out of the public eye if she followed churching traditions related to childbearing.[23] Her active role in government is even more striking given those restrictions.

18 *Regesta*, 92–4.

19 Abingdon Abbey complained that Queen Mathilda seized their most beautiful items. *Chronicon of the monastery of Abingdon*, ed. J. Stevenson (2 vols., London, 1858), i, 485. See Chapter Seven: Mouth, 191–3.

20 Authentic Norman charters before and after the conquest, '…are characterized above all by the signs of validation, which are generally the subscriptions of William, Queen Mathilde, sometimes accompanied by autograph crosses, to which could be added the subscriptions of a greater or lesser number of witnesses, prelates, barons and officers'. Arthur Giry, *Manuel de Diplomatique, Diplomes et chartes* (Paris, 1894), 795. Mathilda's autograph is extant on a few documents: her signature cross is short with almost perfectly equal branches and transverse lines that cross all four ends; it can be seen in Plates 5 and 6. Musset noted 'her firm hand and very straight lines'. Lucien Musset, *Les actes de Guillaume le Conquérant et de la reine Mathilde pour les abbayes caennaises (Caen, 1967)*, 45.

21 Bates, *William*, 430–3.

22 *Regesta*, 92.

23 Approximately 1053–4 to 1068–9. Before the conquest of England, Mathilda,

MONASTICISM AND ECCLESIASTICAL REFORM

Mathilda's participation in the governance of England and Normandy included a commitment to ecclesiastical reform. The most visible of these initiatives was the primacy debate between Canterbury and York. She was the only woman – she and William were the only laity – to participate in the crucial decision that would affect English ecclesiastical politics for centuries: the primacy debate between Canterbury and York.[24] Her involvement was recorded in both versions of the Accord of Winchester: the first decided in private with only the stakeholders in attendance, the second more formal proclamation intended for distribution throughout England (see Plates 5 and 6).[25]

Mathilda founded the Abbey of Holy Trinity, Caen, in Normandy – a Benedictine community of nuns – in 1066. It was the primary recipient of her patronage and retains the most concentrated traces of Mathilda's essence. Holy Trinity's records and charters reveal her energy, drive and determination and her wholehearted embrace of the most defining characteristic of aristocratic and royal identity: the establishment of a bespoke monastic community. Her close partnership with the first abbess of Holy Trinity, Matilda of St Leger-de-Préaux, is codified in Holy Trinity's administrative records. The list of relics she gathered to enrich and promote the abbesses and nuns is revealed here, evidence of her priorities, her natal ties and perhaps even her justification of the conquest. Mathilda's last charter, a will of sorts, is preserved in the abbey's cartulary, recorded in the first person, in her own voice.

HISTORIOGRAPHY

The scholarship on medieval queenship is extensive.[26] As mentioned above, historical analysis and debate regarding the Norman conquest of England is likewise prodigious. Yet Mathilda of Flanders, who stands at the confluence of these two rich fields, has not been the subject of a rigorous scholarly biography. There have been short studies on elements of her life. Elisabeth van Houts has carefully examined Mathilda's gift of the *Mora* and the cultural

moreover, was unavailable for great stretches of time because of the restrictions around pregnancy and churching.

24 See Chapter Seven: Mouth, 199–202.

25 Plate 5, 200 and Plate 6, 201. Symeon of Durham also names Mathilda specifically as he describes how Durham was reformed by installing Benedictine monks. An appeal to the pope resulted in a papal blessing for the establishment of a community of monks at Durham. Symeon particularly notes Mathilda's involvement alongside Lanfranc. *Symeon Libellus de Exordio*, ed. David Rollason (Oxford, 2019), 226–7 and 228–9.

26 For an extensive bibliography on queenship and lordly women, see 227–48 below.

currency of the Anglo-Norman court.[27] Charlotte Cartwright has examined Mathilda's charter attestations as countess to analyze Mathilda's use of the title 'comitissa' to probe whether it might indicate something like an office for countesses.[28] George Beech has uncovered a remote reference to Mathilda in the necrology of La-Chaise-Dieu, France.[29]

These crucial smaller studies, and Mathilda's regular appearance in documentary sources, has not ensured her a place of centrality in modern memory. The purpose of this study is to redress that imbalance. It is organized in a way that best reveals Mathilda in action: through a series of thematic chapters meant to uncover her in context. *Chapter One: Blood* focuses on Mathilda's identity as a woman of royal blood and examines the parallels between Mathilda and her mother, Adela, countess of Flanders and sister to the king of France. Adela's experiences set a pattern for Mathilda's particular assumptions about her active political role as co-ruler of Normandy and later of England. This chapter also examines the Ottonian heritage Mathilda seems to have embraced as queen. *Chapter Two: Hands* examines two central physical structures that reflect Mathilda's identity: the abbey of Holy Trinity in Caen and the *Mora*, a naval vessel she commissioned for the invasion of England. Like the *Mora*, her establishment of Holy Trinity was linked explicitly to the conquest. Historians have assumed Holy Trinity was a project motivated by her penitence – a response to the lifting of the papal ban barring her marriage. Yet this impetus was replaced by the abbey's dedication in 1066. On the eve of the conquest, Mathilda's new monastic foundation stood as an offering – not of expiation – but of hope in the realization of her most daring venture. *Chapter Three: Fingers* analyzes Mathilda's collection of relics. These holy remains were her gift to Holy Trinity; they increased the prestige of her abbey and offered economic and spiritual benefits. Mathilda's participation in relic collection was also an expression of her identity. In *Chapter Four: Head*, I explore the coronation and anointing of Mathilda of Flanders on Pentecost, May 10, 1068 at Westminster. Her liturgical performance was organized around scriptural references to a lost world and the English defeat. It explicitly cast the Normans as their saviors. Immediately after her coronation, attendant members of the English nobility rebelled against their Norman overlords. The result of Mathilda's royal inauguration, I argue, was not unity but discord. In *Chapter Five: Womb*, I analyze Mathilda's strategies of motherhood. Her

27 E. van Houts, 'The Echo of the Conquest in the Latin Sources: Duchess Mathilda, her daughters and the Enigma of the Golden Child,' in *The Bayeux Tapestry: Embroidering the Facts of History*, ed. Pierre Bouet (Caen, 2004), 135–55.

28 Charlotte Cartwright, 'Before She Was Queen: Matilda of Flanders and the Use of *Comitissa* in the Norman Ducal Charters,' *HSJ* 22 (2010), 59–82.

29 George T. Beech, 'Queen Mathilda of England (1066–1083) and the Abbey of La Chaise-Dieu in the Auvergne,' in *Frühmittelalterliche Studien 27* (1993) 350–74.

relationship to two children in particular – Robert and Cecelia – reveals her character as a mother. Her support of Robert's rebellion against her husband and her creation of an ideal monastic setting for Cecelia's life are compared. *Chapter Six: Flesh* involves a close textual reading of Mathilda of Flanders' last charter, issued just before her death in 1083. Within it is her final directive to the sisters of Holy Trinity that the 'hangings from my chamber be made into a cope for a priest'.[30] Mathilda's remarkable instructions open a chapter in which I attempt to discover how Mathilda's donation of vestments interrupted male hegemony in the most rarified of ecclesiastical moments: the celebration of the Eucharist. *Chapter Seven: Mouth* reveals Mathilda handing down royal justice in Domesday Book and in charters. A remarkable innovation for queens in England, Mathilda exercised royal juridical authority based on the legal praxis of Norman manorial courts and the ideological foundation of the Ottonian imperial women for whom she was named. *Chapter Eight: Corpse* examines Mathilda's remains. Buried in the choir of Holy Trinity abbey, Mathilda's body was a visible, daily reminder of her presence and role as founder of the community. She also became the locus for disruption. Her tomb was repeatedly opened and her bodily remains scrutinized in the sixteenth, eighteenth and twentieth centuries. Her corpse was used variously as a symbol of religious corruption, absolutism or a critique of women's monastic claustration. In these cases, Mathilda's embodiment was controlled by others and her remains were vulnerable to manipulation. Somewhat miraculously, Mathilda's body remains safe beneath her tombstone in Caen even today, protected by the stone monastery she constructed.

This book is the result of a careful examination of the manuscripts produced and preserved for and about Mathilda that illuminate her life. The thematic structure of this biography, outlined above, is an attempt to bring Mathilda of Flanders to light; to reveal her queenship through action.[31] Thus, in the following chapters, I allow Mathilda's 'works to declare the probity of her life' as her memoria from Holy Trinity insists.[32]

30 Paris, Bibliothèque National Lat MS. 5650, folio 24r.

31 Simon MacLean's analysis of early Ottonian queens, like Mathilda of Saxony, likewise depend on evidence of her activity as the evidence for her is scarce. It is a fitting approach for her descendant, Mathilda of Flanders. Simon MacLean, *Ottonian Queenship* (Oxford, 2017), 21.

32 Daniel Sheerin, 'Sisters in the Literary Agon,' in *Women Writing Latin, Volume 2*, ed. Laurie Churchill, Phyllis R. Brown, Jane E. Jeffrey (New York, NY, 2002), 93–131, at 119. See Chapter Eight: Corpse, 215–16.

1

BLOOD

Mathilda of Flanders was the only daughter of a royal mother and an aristocratic father. Her potential – and the expectations for her – were rooted in her bloodline. Like every medieval aristocrat, her birth was Fortune's gift. Her connections to the most celebrated dynasties in Europe were available to be exploited, but only if she had the will and the occasion to do so. Her royal blood was celebrated and remarked upon by poets.[1] It is a central feature in the identification clauses in the charters in which she appears.[2] Chroniclers, poets and charter evidence all sing the same chorus of royal blood. This chapter reflects on the heritage that blood brought with it – practical, philosophical, dynastic – bequeathed to Mathilda from her experience as the daughter of the Flemish court in the eleventh century. Medieval Flanders has a substantial historiography and I will not attempt to distill it here. Instead, in what follows, I attempt to trace out the primary elements of Mathilda's natal context that informed her choices and expectations. These center on three chief themes: First, her mother Adela's experiences in Flanders, raised as a young woman of French royal blood in the Flemish court, who became its countess. Second, the influence of the Ottonian foremothers that Adela herself embraced. Adela commissioned her own copy of the *Epitaph of Adelheid*, that celebrated the famous empress's life and experiences. Third, Mathilda's experience of the political and social contours of her natal court. In conclusion, because the *Epitaph* provided models for Mathilda's conception of royal rule, a comparison between Mathilda and Adelheid is considered.

1 Poems and epitaphs to Mathilda were authored by the great writers of her day. Works include Godfrey of Reims 'Consilli virtus,' in *The Anglo-Latin satirical poets and epigrammatists of the twelfth century*, ed. Thomas Wright (2 vols., London, 1872), ii: 150; Fulcoius of Beauvais, 'Certe si fortis' and 'Tempore quae nostro' in *Mélanges Julien Havet; Receuil de Travaux D'Érudition dédiés a la memoire de Julien Havet, 1853–1893*, ed. M.L. Delisle (1895; repr. Geneva, 1972), 223–4 and 224–5, respectively; and the anonymous epitaph 'Egregie pulchri tegit,' *OV* iv, 44–5.

2 In the foundation charter for Holy Trinity, for example, Mathilda is styled, 'reginarum nobilissima, Baldoini incliti ac strenuissimi Flandrensium comitis filia regisque Francorum Henrici neptis clarissima. ('the queen, most noble wife, daughter of Baldwin the renowned and most vigorous count of Flanders and daughter of the French king Henry's most illustrious daughter'), *Regesta,* 292–5.

ADELA OF FRANCE

Mathilda's mother Adela was the second daughter of Constance of Arles and Robert II 'the Pious,' king of France. Adela's French royal blood was a central element of her identity, and she used her connections to the French throne – through her father and then her brother, Henry – in identifying clauses throughout her life.[3] Chroniclers openly characterized Adela's royal birth as far more celebrated than that of her young affianced, the future Baldwin V.[4] Yet Adela spent very few years in her natal court. William of Jumièges claimed that Adela was still 'in the cradle' when she was brought to live at the comital court in Flanders, well before her marriage.[5] Thus the influence of her mother and father should be contextualized by that of her mother-in-law, Ogive of Luxembourg. Adela was probably about nineteen when her marriage was consecrated in Paris early in 1028.[6] Among other properties, she received the royal 'abbatia' of St Peter's on the Somme as dower, which encompassed the lordship of its ecclesiastical territory, with its manors, its knights, and its seigneurial rights, especially over the emerging town of Corbie, and its famous abbey.[7]

Royal women like Adela were foundational to early Flemish history; Countess Judith, the eldest daughter of Charles the Bald, provided the original '*pagus Flanderiensis*' that would become the heart of the comital base around Bruges.[8] Judith eloped with Baldwin 'Iron Arm' in 863. The northern

3 In 1038, with Baldwin V for the abbey of Marchiennes, she is styled 'Adela comitissa, conjuge mea, filia regis Roberti', in *Opera Diplomatica et historica*, ed. Miraeus-Foppens (4 vols., Louvain, 1723–1748), i, 659, and 'Adela, regiae prolis comitissa' in the 1039 foundation charter for the Abbey of Phalempin in Picardy (Miraeus-Foppens, *Opera* i, 53–4). The sixteenth-century *Opera* also displays Adela's family tree with the legend 'Origo familiae Capeticae ex qua prodiit Adela' and inserts an additional genealogy of the entire Capetian royal line which reiterates Adela's place, to guide his readers. She is 'Adelaidis, seu Adela, Roberti Francorum regis filia' in Philip I's charter at Harelbeke. In an additional charter of Philip I, she is styled 'Adele comitisse, uxoris Balduini comitis Flandrie filieque regis Roberti,' M. Prou, *Recueil des actes de Phillippe Ier, roi de France* (Paris, 1908), 184. After her death, confirming her gifts to Messines, Robert the Frisian styled her 'matris meae, Adelae videlicet commitissae, Roberti regis Francorum filiae,' *Opera* i, 69.

4 William of Poitiers, *Gesta*, 32–3.

5 *GND*, ii, 52–3.

6 Christian Pfister, *Études sur le règne de Robert le Pieux, 996–1031* (Paris, 1885), 79; F.L. Ganshof, *La Flandre Sous Les Premiers Comtes* (Brussels, 1949), 36.

7 Corbie Abbey was a significant element of Adela's dowry. She would consider it hers even after the property slipped out of her hands. Nicholas N. Huyghebaert, 'Adela van Frankrijk, Gravin van Vlaanderen, Stichteres Van de Abdij Van Mesen (ca. 1017–1079)', *Ipres Kwartier*, Vol. 158: 3 (1979), 68–70.

8 Eljas Oksanen, *Flanders and the Anglo-Norman World, 1066–1216* (Cambridge, 2012), 8–9.

territories of Flanders were Judith's marriage portion after her father finally consented to her union. Thus, the very roots of the country's existence were established from the hands of a royal woman as a result of her defiance.[9] Her son, Baldwin II, married Ælfthryth the daughter of Alfred the Great of England *c.* 883 and established early ties between England and Flanders.[10] Baldwin III, *c.* 960, also married a woman with prestigious connections; Mathildis Billung, the daughter of Otto I's most trusted captain, Hermann Billung. Flemish relationships with the Ottonians were thus established for the first time. They had a son, Arnulf II, before Baldwin III died of a sudden illness. Mathildis remarried a year later to Godfrey of Verdun, leaving Arnulf behind to be raised in Flanders and eventually rule it.[11] Nevertheless, imperial ties remained. Between 974 and 977, Otto II funded St Bavo's architectural renovations, producing an abbey church in the Ottonian style.[12] The Flemish comital abbeys of St Peter's and the abbey of St Bavo in Ghent thus bore Ottonian elements in the heart of the comital family's domain, architectural styles that would influence later generations.[13]

Years later, Baldwin IV married Ogive of Luxembourg, the niece of the sainted Empress Cunigunde, the last Ottonian empress. Baldwin V was Ogive's

9 Pauline Stafford, 'Judith, Charles the Bald and England' in *Charles the Bald, Court and Kingdom*, ed. M. Gibson and J. Nelson (Oxford, 1981), 137–44. William of Poitiers included a celebration of the brilliant marriage unions the counts of Flanders enjoyed. William of Poitiers, *Gesta*, 30.

10 Ælfthryth established a new comital necropolis at Ghent in 918, when she buried Baldwin II at the monastery there. The monks at the foundation of Saint-Bertin, located in ancient city of Saint-Omer, refused Ælfthryth's request that she would one day lie next to her newly deceased husband, so she chose St Peter's Ghent, thus shifting the center of Flemish administration away from Saint-Omer. Karine Ugé, *Creating the Monastic Past in Medieval Flanders* (York, 2005), 3–4.

11 Mathildis Billung's dowry portion Ename – given to her by Otto II in celebration of her second marriage to Godfrey of Verdun – was the very Ottonian city that Baldwin V and Adela would claim almost 85 years later, in 1047, its 'palace' still intact. Dirk Callebaut, 'Ename and the Ottonian west border policy in the middle Scheldt region,' in *Exchanging Medieval Material Culture: Studies on archaeology and history presented to Frans Verhaeghe*, ed. Koen De Groote, Dries Tys and Marnix Pieters (Brussels, 2010), 217–43 at 227 and 243; An Van den Bremt and Geert Vermeiren 'Archeologisch vooronderzoek op het Sint-Pietersplein en aan de Tweekerkenstraat,' *Handelingen der Maatschappij voor Geschiedenis en Oudheidkunde te Gent* 58 (2004), 23–58, at 31–6.

12 These were begun under Abbot Odwinus (c. 981–998) and continued into the twelfth century. M.C. Laleman, 'Het stenen verleden. Een beknopt overzicht van bouwactiviteiten, bouwkundige ontwikkelin en monastieke architectuur' in *Gand & Blandinium: de Gentse abdijen van Sint-Pieters en Sint-Baafs*, ed. G. Declerqc (Ghent, 1997), 115–46.

13 Including Mathilda of Flanders herself. See Chapter Two: Hands, 35–72.

only known child, born *c.* 1012. Though not much is recorded about Ogive, her ties to the Saxon Ottonians place her squarely in the tradition of high-status Flemish countesses. Through Ogive's father, Frederic I of Luxembourg, Baldwin V could claim imperial Saxon identity, though not imperial blood directly. Baldwin V's links to the Ottonian dynasty may have been secondary but they were arguably as close as those of Conrad II, the first Salian emperor.[14]

Adela of France stepped into this tradition of powerful royal woman who condescended to become Flemish countesses. William of Jumièges noted that Adela was brought to the Flemish court by Baldwin IV and 'educated in his own house with diligent care'.[15] She received an erudite intellectual education, one suitable for a royal daughter. Arriving as a child in Flanders, Adela's upbringing was no doubt supervised by her mother-in-law.[16] Ogive would have familiarized Adela with the celebrated Ottonian women of her family, including those connected to the Flemish past.[17] While the Flemish counts had yet to write their own histories, the Ottonians most certainly had.[18] Adela's education in Flanders would no doubt have encompassed some of these readily available materials. Consequently, Adela's royal Capetian identity existed alongside one situated within the Ottonian tradition.

As a girl raised in her fiancé's court to be his bride, immersed in all things Flemish, one might assume that Adela would be compliant and agreeable. Like her royal predecessors, however, she would soon demonstrate her mettle. Adela's influence was felt almost immediately. Within just two years of their wedding, Adela and Baldwin planned and executed a rebellion against the old Count. Sometime before 1030, when Adela was in her early twenties, she and Baldwin threw Baldwin the Bearded out of Flanders. Mortifyingly for the old Count, the military coup had the full support of the majority of Flemish

14 'Perhaps in recognition of this, Ogive's uncles revolted against Henry's assumption of the imperium even after his marriage to their sister, Cunigunde. F.L. Ganshof, 'Les origines de la Flandre impériale. Contribution à l'histoire de l'ancien Brabant,' *Annales de la Société royale d'Archéologie de Bruxelles* XLVI (1942–1943), 99–173.

15 *GND*, ii, 52–3. Adela's education was Latinate.

16 Bates places Ogive's death at 1030 but contemporary sources report that at Baldwin IV's return from Normandy, he was already married to Eleanor of Normandy. David Bates, *Normandy before 1066* (New York, NY, 1982), 66–8.

17 Jean-Marie Kreins, *Histoire du Luxembourg: des origines à nos jours* (Paris, 2007), 10–20.

18 The works of Liudprand of Cremona, Theitmar of Merseburg, Regino of Prüm, Adalbert of Magdeburg, Widukind of Corvey, Odilo of Cluny and Hrotsvit of Gandersheim and the anonymous annals of Gandersheim and Essen were circulating throughout the Continent. See Laura Wangerin, 'The governance of Ottonian Germany in historiographical perspective,' *History Compass* 15:1(2017), 1–10; Kerstin Schulmeyer-Ahl, *Der Anfang vom Ende der Ottonen Konstitutionsbedingungen historiographischer Nachrichten in der Chronik Thietmars von Merseburg* (Berlin, 2009), especially 30–49 and 309–72.

courtiers. Chroniclers lay the impetus for all of this – the plot, the attack and Baldwin IV's humiliation – at Adela's feet.[19]

Modern historians have characterized young Baldwin's bid for power as a result of the youth's intoxication with his new status because he now had a royal wife.[20] The view of William of Jumièges, writing sometime in the 1050s, suggests minor but important adjustments to this interpretation.[21] According to William, there was more to the coup than simply Baldwin's new sense of entitlement. William reports, 'The young Baldwin, enjoying the noble girl's (Adela's) embraces and relying on royal support, drove his father from his own country and deprived him of the fealty of the Flemish court.'[22] William drew a direct line between Adela's royal identity and resources. In William's version of events, Adela offers to sponsor the military coup; the 'royal support' William diplomatically describes was armed. Baldwin wholeheartedly accepts both marital and martial resources from Adela; wifely affection and her parallel commitment to supply Baldwin with royal knights. In William's assessment, their coup was a joint enterprise instigated by Adela and Baldwin together.

Initially, the rebellion was wildly successful and old Baldwin IV was forced to retreat to Normandy.[23] Though contemporary chroniclers are close-lipped about its details, the revolt would have been months, perhaps even years, in the making. Adela's dowry supplied her with armed men from the 'abbatia' of St Peter's, and others, as noted above. She seemed to have planned for French royal reinforcements should the need arise. At the very least Adela had carefully calibrated her father's response and counted on approval from France. Baldwin the Bearded seems to have assumed she and Baldwin would get it; he did not seek reinforcements in Paris from his traditional overlord, but in Normandy. As he gathered troops from the Duke of Normandy, Baldwin IV also married Duke Richard's sister, Eleanor, as part of their pact of friendship. The count returned to Flanders with Countess Eleanor and a large army of Normans. The latter burned the castle at Chocques to the ground 'with everyone in it'.[24] The Flemish nobility was horrified at the Norman's brutality and, fearing they would suffer the same fate, rushed to make amends with Baldwin the elder. The support that had buoyed the young married couple evaporated quickly. Young Baldwin and Adela's insurrection was over.

19 *GND*, ii, 52–4.

20 Nicholas claims the 'royal marriage went to the youth's head'. David Nicholas, *Medieval Flanders* (London, 1992), 48; Ganshof, *Les Premiers Comtes*, 36. See also Pfister, *Études sur le règne*, 79 and 222.

21 'Cuius filius mox, amplexibus cepit frui, nobilis puella affiniaitate fretus regali, patrem a proprio solo pepulit, Flandrensibus ab eius fidelitate auulis.' *Gesta Normannorum Ducum*, ii, 52–4.

22 *GND*, ii, 52–3.

23 Nicholas, *Medieval Flanders*, 48.

24 *GND*, ii, 52–3.

When Baldwin the elder faced his son with the Norman army at his back he was able to prevail, yet the settlement he made afterwards speaks of a new sense of cooperation; younger Baldwin began to rule jointly with his father.[25] The *Gesta Normannorum Ducum* states that they exchanged the kiss of peace and 'at once restored their former affection'.[26] A record of the reconciliation of young Baldwin with his father in 1030 can be found in the annals of St Peter's Ghent. The ceremony was combined with a Peace of God ritual at which the relics of many saints were displayed and used to swear oaths.[27] The public concord allowed for a reimplementation of the Peace of God in Flanders and a new more active role in governance for young Baldwin.[28] Sometime between 1030 and 1035, Eleanor of Normandy and Baldwin IV had a daughter, Judith, enlarging the comital family.[29]

According to William of Jumièges, then, Adela was a driving force behind these events or, at the very least, a co-conspirator with Baldwin. William's account should be given significant weight; he was writing while Adela was not only alive, but still an active political force in Flanders. William dedicated his work to Adela's son-in-law, William the Conqueror. There was certainly the possibility that Adela herself might read it. William's account shows that while the rebellion did not make Adela and Baldwin permanent rulers in Flanders at this stage, its outcome was positive; the new joint rule enjoyed by young Baldwin was, in fact, the direct result of their coup. Adela's daughter Mathilda would eventually draw strategies from her mother's playbook.[30]

In 1035, Baldwin IV died; Baldwin V and Adela ruled Flanders. Adela's charter attestations and public acts increased dramatically as she came into her own as countess. Analysis of Flemish charters during this period reveals that 67% of charters issued during Baldwin's reign include her either as co-issuer

25 *GND*, ii, 53–4.

26 *GND*, ii, 54–5.

27 *Les Annales de Saint Pierre de Gand et de Saint-Amand*, ed. Philip Grierson (Brussels, 1937), 89. For Peace of God rituals in Flanders, see Geoffrey Koziol, 'Monks, Feuds and the Making of Peace in Eleventh Century Flanders', in *Historical Reflections / Réflexions Historique* Vol. 14, No. 3 (Fall 1987), 531–49. Also, Thomas Head, *The Peace of God: Social Violence and Religious Response in France Around the Year 1000* (Ithaca, NY, 1992).

28 Historians have recently theorized that the Peace of God accords occurred regularly in a six-year cycle as opposed to a permanently established state. Sam Janssen, 'A Pattern of Alternating Interests: The Peace of God in the Archdiocese of Reims in the First Half of the Eleventh Century', in *Episcopal Power and Personality in Medieval Europe, 900–1480*, ed. Peter Coss et al. (Turnhout, 2020), 203–22.

29 For a detailed analysis of Judith's life, see Mary Dockray-Miller, *The Life and Books of Judith of Flanders* (Burlington, VT, 2015).

30 See Chapter Five: Womb, 154–6.

or as attestor.[31] In comparison to later countesses, Adela's influence on comital administration is marked.[32]

Likewise, Flemish traditions and history also marked Adela, particularly their links to the Saxon Ottonians. Not long after she became countess, we see the first acknowledgement of Adela's interest in her marital Ottonian heritage, and perhaps Ogive's influence. For while the days of the Ottonian Saxon emperors had ended, and the Salians now claimed the imperial throne, Saxon ideologies and histories remained. The Saxon Ottonian dynasty committed significant resources to the production of narrative texts and annals. They supported courtiers and professional religious who wrote them: Liudprand of Cremona, Theitmar of Merseburg, Regino of Prüm, Adalbert of Magdeburg, Widukind of Corvey, Odilo of Cluny and Hrotsvit of Gandersheim.[33] Approximating the influence of these authors on later generations is difficult. It is indisputable, however, that the readership of Odilo of Cluny's *Epitaph of Adelheid* included at least one Flemish countess: Adela.

COUNTESS ADELA AND THE *EPITAPH OF ADELHEID*

Adela of Flanders commissioned her own copy of the *Epitaph of Adelheid* sometime after she became countess in 1034. The evidence for this can be found in the dedicatory statement to the work, which accorded her the title:

> The way Queen Adelheid lived in Rome,
> Odilo the abbot who witnessed it, wrote down,
> Countess Adela has ordered us to copy his work,
> that she might draw from it an example,
> to shun evil (but) rather live a good life.
> May this praiseworthy virago ever reign with the Lord,
> she who flees the wicked and desires to follow the righteous.[34]

31 Out of Baldwin's thirteen extant comital charters, Adela appears in nine. Penelope Adair, 'Ego et Uxor Mea: Countess Clemence and Her Role in the Comital Family and in Flanders', PhD dissertation (University of Santa Barbara, 1995), 65. Adair carefully analyzes the dower lands and administrative activity of the Flemish countesses. She also cites Huyghebaert, 'Les Femmes laïques dans le vie de religieuse des XIe et XIIe Siècles dans le province ecclésiastique de Reims', in *I laici nella "societas christiana" dei soceli XI e XIII, Atti della terza Settimana internazionale di studio, Mendola, 21–27, 1965* (Milan, 1968), 346–95, at 381.

32 'In contrast, Gertrude, Marguerite and Elizabeth (the next three countesses of Flanders) barely appear.' Adair, 'Ego et uxor Mea', 65.

33 For a review of Ottonian history writing in the tenth and eleventh centuries, see Schulmeyer-Ahl, *Der Anfang vom Ende der Ottonen*, especially 30–49 and 309–72.

34 'Quo more regina Adalaida Romae, Odilo quae vidit abbas, quae scripta notavit, Nobis haec Atala scribi iussit comitissa, Exemplum vita sibi quo captaret in ista,

The dedication identifies Countess Adela as the commissioner of the work and names 'Garinus' as its author.[35]

What did the *Epitaph of Adelheid* contain that drew Adela? The *Epitaph* narrates Adelheid's adventures; a royal girl of impeccable lineage. She marries Lothar, king of Italy at the age of 16 and is crowned queen.[36] Only three years later, Lothar dies, leaving Queen Adelheid a young royal widow. Duke Berengar of Italy seizes the throne and, with his wife Willa, pressures Adelheid to marry their son Hugh thus bolstering their tenuous position.[37] When she refuses, they imprison the young queen. Adelheid endures threats and harsh treatment before executing a daring escape under cover of night with the help of her priest and her maid. As the cleric dashes off to find help, Adelheid and her maid hide in swamps and ditches, with Berengar in hot pursuit. Heroic adventures occur – they brave discovery when they stumble across a fisherman; starving, they beg for a meal. He feeds them sturgeon from his catch and they share a fireside dinner together, while Adelheid carefully disguises her true identity.[38] Soon her priest returns with the welcome news that friendly forces – the troops of Bishop Adelhard of Reggio – are on their way. Adelheid and her faithful servants intersect the bishop's troops and Adelheid is safely transported to his castle in Canossa. At this juncture, Berengar besieges Adelheid and her friends but is repelled by the brave castellan, Adalbert Atto.[39] Odilo's version of her story omits Adelheid's call to Otto I for rescue, which is included in later versions like the one written by Hrotsvitha of Gandersheim. Odilo merely notes that Adelheid chose to trade a royal palace for an imperial one. Odilo inserts a poetic section – apart from the main text for emphasis – in which he claims that Adelheid brought the princes of Italy and 'obstinate Germany' under her authority together and she herself 'set' Otto I over Rome.[40]

Nolle malum, sed velle bonum deducere seclum. Regnet cum Domino semper laudanda virago, Quae pravos vitat, iustos imitarier optat.' Huyghebaert, 'Adela,' 71.

35 Garinus's identity is a mystery. Any one of the houses Adela patronized could have presented her with a willing author, perhaps especially St Bavos or St Peter's Ghent, given Otto's patronage in the tenth century. Huyghebaert's opinion was that Garinus was French but even that sliver of evidence rests on his assumption that 'Garinus isn't a Flemish name.' Huyghebaert, 'Adela', 71.

36 The following description is taken from Sean Gilsdorf's English translation and analysis of the Epitaph. Gilsdorf also analyzes the two contemporary 'Lives' of the Empress Mathilda, mother of Otto I: the 'Early' life or *Vita Antiquior*, written *c.* 973–4 and the 'Later' life, *Vita Posterior*, written *c.* 1002–3. Sean Gilsdorf, *Queenship and Sanctity: The "Lives" of Mathilda and the "Epitaph" of Adelheid* (Washington, DC, 2004), 128–43. Simon MacLean refers to the narrative as Adelheid's 'prison break'. MacLean, *Ottonian Queenship*, 99–126.

37 Gilsdorf, *Queenship and Sanctity*, 130.

38 Gilsdorf, *Queenship and Sanctity*, 131.

39 Gilsdorf, *Queenship and Sanctity*, 131.

40 Gilsdorf, *Queenship and Sanctity*, 131.

The rest of Adelheid's epitaph offers fewer dramatic escapades but provides ample illustrations of how a woman might successfully rule 'Ottonian style'. Odilo first describes Adelheid's coronation as empress in 961. Once her authority is divinely enshrined, he proceeds to recount the highlights of her reign. Adelheid hands down justice in her courts, creates and founds cities, endows monasteries.[41] She is at the inflection point of the empire, knitting together alliances, persuading warring parties to cooperate, taming the arrogance of princes. When her son Otto II disrespects her, however, she leaves in a rage, as 'apostolic precept' demanded – shaking the dust off her feet.[42] Otto II repents, approaches her with humility and begs her forgiveness: she relents. Adelheid rules Germany and Italy with generosity and charity, continuously giving alms to the poor. She is constantly moving, traveling back and forth across her realm, governing at an almost superhuman pace. She convenes church synods, supports the episcopate, lavishly underwrites religious entities of all description. After Otto II's death, Adelheid resists nobly the poor behavior of her daughter-in-law, the 'Greek queen' Theophanu, who Odilo does not stoop to name. Theophanu acts as regent for her son Otto III, but Odilo infers that Adelheid cheats Theophanu by outliving her. After the Greek queen's death, Adelheid assumes the regency for Otto III, her grandson. Odilo recounts how he himself met with Adelheid, late in her life. Finally, Adelheid dies on 16 December after committing her riches to the worthy and her soul to Christ. Miracles of healing are reported at her tomb.[43]

Sean Gilsdorf has demonstrated that Odilo's description of Adelheid's activities as a ruler is supported by ample chronicle and charter evidence. The *Epitaph* focuses on Adelheid's career and the many facets of her imperial life, lived in a fascinating and sometimes turbulent era. Her relationships with husbands and sons, by contrast, form the backdrop for her imperial accomplishments, not the core of her story.[44]

The *Epitaph*'s dramatic narrative offered a compelling illustration of how women's autonomous authority functioned and how one queen-turned-empress created opportunities for active rule.[45] Considering Adela of Flanders' own experience as a young bride, recounted above, Adelheid's daring escapades undoubtedly struck a chord in Adela. It was enough to motivate Adela to commission the work and, perhaps, to name her daughter Mathilda, just as Adelheid did. Moreover, while there is no explicit evidence, the strategies of queenship Mathilda herself adopted – which were groundbreaking for England – indicate that she read it, too.

41 Gilsdorf, *Queenship and Sanctity*, 135–6.
42 Gilsdorf, *Queenship and Sanctity*, 133.
43 Gilsdorf, *Queenship and Sanctity*, 143.
44 Gilsdorf, *Queenship and Sanctity*, 194.
45 Gilsdorf, *Queenship and Sanctity*, 128–43.

Some modern historians struggle to make sense of the *Epitaph* because Odilo neglects Adelheid's wifely and motherly aspects.[46] That commentary reveals something about the countess's preference for it; Adelheid's activities as an empress were the narrative's focus.[47] Adelheid's secular authority and accomplishments, not her relationships, were the elements Odilo celebrated.[48] Evidentially, this was precisely the sort of mirror for queens Adela wished to peer into, as did her daughter. Here they could view together, in the comfort of their own court, Adelheid's imperial authority come to life.

MATHILDA AND THE FLEMISH COURT

Mathilda of Flanders was born *c.* 1031, before her mother was countess, and not long after her parents rebelled against Count Baldwin IV, Mathilda's grandfather.[49] Mathilda was probably her parents' middle child; her older brother Baldwin VI was born *c.* 1029 and her youngest brother, Robert, called 'the Frisian' *c.* 1035, after the old Count's death.[50] The children's names, of course, were important indicators of their identity, status, legitimacy and,

46 'Adelheid was a holy woman, twice married, and provided with children. What role is given to this aspect of her existence? What judgment is made on her married and family life? Do we find in the work some of the typical motifs of medieval discourse on women? The analysis carried out so far shows that these are not themes of primary importance; however, there is no reason to neglect them.' Patrick Corbet, *Les Saints Ottoniens: Sainteté Dynastique, Sainteté Royale Et Sainteté Feminine Autour de l'An Mil* (Freiburg, 1986), 108.

47 Odilo's method is much like that of the current study. Simon MacLean also called his examination tactic 'queenship in action'. MacLean, *Ottonian Queenship*, 94.

48 Ironically, the twentieth-century French historian accuses Odilo of not being a feminist because of this approach. If the *Epitaph of Adelheid* was to be a mirror for queens, as Odilo claims, then, Corbet asked, 'How could such an eminent career, led at the head of the Empire, serve as a model for sovereigns dedicated above all to 'cura domestica?' Corbet was also mystified by Adela of Flanders' commissioning of the *Epitaph*. There is no question, he asserts, that the *Epitaph of Adelheid* was commissioned by Adela as an instructive text, yet it was clearly a failure because it did not enshrine feminine virtues. Corbet, *Les Saints Ottoniens*, 108.

49 Historians estimate Baldwin's birth *c.* 1030 and Mathilda's birth *c.* 1031–3. If this is accurate, Mathilda could have been between 18 and 21 in 1051–2 at the time of her marriage. Detlev Schwennicke, *Europäische Stammtafeln: Stammtafeln zur Geschichte der Europäischen Staaten, Neue Folge* (16 vols., Marburg, 1978–1995), Tafel 5.

50 Eleanor of Normandy seems to have left Flanders after the old Count's death, leaving her young daughter Judith behind. Adela and Baldwin raised Judith in the Flemish court; her age was such that she would have been more like a daughter than a step-sister to the comital pair. Baldwin and Adela would arrange Judith's marriage to Tostig Godwineson, third son of Earl Godwine, and eventually another claimant for the English throne. After Tostig's death, Judith would marry Welf of Bavaria. See Dockray-Miller, *Judith of Flanders*.

more particularly, fitness for rule.[51] Adela and Baldwin were deeply conventional with their sons' names: Baldwin for the heir to the comital seat and Robert, their second son, to honor Adela's royal father. The name Mathilda, however, does not appear in the Capetian line. Choosing Constance for her daughter would have been expected, especially as Adela's mother died in 1032; Adela might even have been pregnant with Mathilda during Constance's final illness. If Constance was still a controversial figure in the French court (especially for Henry, Adela's brother, who now ruled France), Adelaide or Ava – Adela's royal grandmother and great-grandmother respectively – would have been predictable choices. Yet Adela's royal blood, surprisingly, did not feature in the selection of her daughter's name. Instead, Adela and Baldwin elected to use a name with deep connections to the Ottonian past.

Mathilda was born only about seven years after the Ottonian dynasty's legitimate Saxon heirs had died out. Baldwin and Adela may have been signaling their dynastic connections to the legitimate Ottonian Saxon line at a moment when – in their view – it was open to appropriation through their choice of their daughter's name.[52] The name Mathilda had multiple Ottonian connections: Mathilda of Ringelheim was the first Ottonian queen and mother of Otto I. Empress Adelheid, of course, named her only daughter, Mathilda, the famous imperial abbess of Quedlinburg and prince.[53]

Mathilda's name was not the only benefit her parents bequeathed to her. After they came to power, her parents created a court that was the envy of its neighbors. Wealthy, urbane and regularly peopled with glamorous refugees from foreign places, eleventh-century Flanders was the trading hub of northern Europe. It had not yet reached the pinnacle of its twelfth-century economic might or population, but it was also not yet in the grip of the famine and economic collapse that same century would bring.[54] Standing at the crossroads

51 'Among the aristocrats of the Carolingian and post-Carolingian world, the naming of children was serious business.' Jean Dunbabin, 'What's in a name? Phillip, King of France', *Speculum* 68: 4 (1993), 949–68.

52 They would not be the first to name their daughter 'Mathilda' as a political maneuver. In 948, the Saxon Queen Gerberga and Louis IV of France named their daughter Mathilda to signal a significant change in court politics, as they moved into an alliance with Otto I. The name Mathilda was also a tribute to Gerberga's mother, Mathilda of Saxony, the first Ottonian queen. MacLean, *Ottonian Queenship*, 54.

53 For a detailed analysis of Mathilda's life, see Phyllis G. Jestice, *Imperial Ladies of the Ottonian Dynasty: Women and Rule in Tenth-Century Germany* (Cham, 2018); Gilsdorf, *Queenship and Sanctity*, 2; *Sarah Greer, Commemorating Power in Early Medieval Saxony: Writing and Rewriting the Past at Gandersheim and Quedlinburg* (Oxford, 2021).

54 Flanders was cash-rich in some part because laws of inheritance allowed women to alienate property regularly. 'The high degree of liquidity in the marketplace is essential for commercial pre-eminence. In this respect, more than any other, Germanic Flanders was extremely progressive, and there is strong evidence that the change to a property regime fostering easy alienability came in the mid-eleventh

of east and west, it was favorably placed not only to receive beautiful things, rich food and sumptuous fabrics, but new theologies, ideas and a steady flow of people who were – if only temporarily – on the losing side of political reshuffling. Mathilda's parents hosted high-status exiles in palatial style for visits that could stretch to years, resulting in a remarkably cosmopolitan court. Indeed, rival claimants to European thrones could be found living in elegance at any given time in Bruges. Members of Mathilda's own family, the French ruling house of Capet, and their court also crossed the border to Flanders regularly. Despite the royal blood they granted her, Mathilda's familiar French connections might have paled next to more interesting visitors from further abroad, especially from England, including Earl Godwine and his wife Gytha, their sons, Swein, Tostig and Gyrth.[55] Mathilda would not need an interpreter, as her future husband did, when she became queen of England. Her early years provided intensive language study.

The *Encomium Emmae Reginae*, written at the behest of Queen Emma of England, describes Flanders and her reception there in about 1037:

> And so, having enjoyed favorable winds, they crossed the sea and touched at a certain port not far from the town of Bruges. The latter town is inhabited by Flemish settlers, and enjoys very great fame for the number of its merchants and for its affluence in all things upon which mankind places the greatest value. Here indeed she was, as she deserved, honorably received by Baldwin, the Marquis of that same province, who is the son of a great and totally unconquered prince, and by his wife Adela [Athala], daughter of Robert, king of the French, and Queen Constance. By them, furthermore, a house in the above-named town, suitable for royal outlay, was allotted to the queen, and in addition a kind offer of entertainment was made…[56]

The *Encomium* records that Harthacnut soon joined his mother in Bruges, 'with his chosen companions' and stayed with his mother in her sumptuous accommodations.[57] The comings and goings of aristocratic visitors, received in honor and royal style, thus formed a constant in Mathilda's experience. An even more interesting pair of Norman refugees arrived in Bruges in the early months of 1041. Gilbert of Brionne was one of the guardians assigned to the child-duke William the Bastard after his father left on Crusade.[58] Gilbert was murdered

century, in a shift of marriage customs that contributed to a degree of economic equality between the sexes in Flanders exceptional for the time.' David Nicholas, 'Of Poverty and Primacy: Demand, Liquidity, and the Flemish Economic Miracle, 1050–1200', *American Historical Review* 96: 1 (1991), 17–41.

55 Emma Mason, *The House of Godwin: the History of a Dynasty* (London, 2004), especially 68–70.

56 *Encomuim Emmae Reginae*, ed. and trans. Alistair Campbell (London, 1949), 47–8.

57 *Encomium*, 49–51.

58 Gilbert of Brionne was the son of Godfrey, one of Duke Robert of Normandy's illegitimate sons. *GND*, ii, 60–1, 92–3.

by assassins when he was out riding. His two sons, Richard and Baldwin, immediately fled to the court of Flanders in fear for their lives.[59] Richard and Baldwin were sheltered in Flanders as guests in the ducal residence. Richard and Baldwin were young men with stories to tell; they were eyewitnesses to the young William's adventures and mishaps. Their information was no doubt in demand at the Flemish court. The vicissitudes of the Norman duke's minority were not only interesting gossip, but would have a direct impact on the balance of power in Francia. Mathilda's reaction to these tales of William's precarity is unknowable, but the stories would soon become very familiar to her. The two brothers spent ten years with her in Flanders and only returned to Normandy with Mathilda at her marriage to William. They would remain Mathilda's friends throughout her life.[60]

Adela and Baldwin's welcoming impartiality to aristocrats from all political persuasions was famous. It also reflected a sober reality: the Flemish comital family had to stay nimble. Squeezed between the Capetians and the Ottonians – then Salians – Flanders was always at risk of being absorbed by one or both of them. The Flemish rulers held pieces of their comital lands variously from both French kings and German emperors, and as a result, were necessarily adept at playing them off against one another. It is no accident that the counts of Flanders regularly engaged in regional warfare and changed alliances frequently.[61] The Salian emperors became the sustained target of her father's aggression as he expanded east. In Mathilda's lifetime, the borders of her home were still shifting. In 1047, the changes markedly increased the balance sheet in Flanders' favor; notably, her parents acquired Ename, a ready-made Ottonian palatial settlement on their eastern border.[62]

59 *GND*, 92–5, 110–1. See also J.C. Ward, 'Royal Service and Reward: the Clare Family and the Crown, 1066–1154,' *ANS* 11 (1989), 261–5. Like Gilbert of Brionne, Duke William's tutor, Turold, was also assassinated. William's guardian, Count Alan of Brittany, was poisoned. Osbern the Steward was murdered after a fight in the young duke's bedroom. Osbern was the father of William fitz Osbern, one of William and Mathilda's closest allies, and one of the wealthiest Domesday tenants-in-chief. *GND*, ii, 94–5.

60 Both men participated in the conquest of England. Richard fitz Gilbert would receive lands in excess of £750, and Baldwin between £200 and £400. Judith Green, *The Aristocracy of Norman England* (Cambridge, 1997), 28–30. Mathilda herself gave Baldwin, later called Baldwin of Meules, thirty acres of her land in Shalford. *DB* Essex, ii, 3b. He married Emma, a kinswoman of William's, who appears in charters for Holy Trinity, including its foundation charter.

61 David Defries, 'The Emergence of the Territorial Principality of Flanders, 750–1050,' *History Compass,* 11: 8 (2013), 619–31 at 627.

62 Defries, 'Principality of Flanders,' 626–7.

THE COMITAL HOUSEHOLD

Mathilda's early years were characterized by mobility; like most medieval rulers, the Flemish comital family was peripatetic, moving from place to place throughout the year.[63] This would provide excellent training for her eventual adult experience of cross-channel governance.[64] The cash wealth of thriving Flanders allowed Baldwin and Adela to found new cities; these were added to the circuit of the Flemish comital itinerary Mathilda would have followed.[65] Mathilda no doubt gained valuable experience watching her parents form urban centers from the ground up and establish new markets.

There is no specific record of the comital itinerary but it would have encompassed their major urban centers.[66] Some of these were established by the Romans: the seaport of Saint-Omer, the ancient hilltop city of Cassel, and Bruges – the administrative center of Flanders – where Queen Emma was lavishly welcomed, as described above.[67] The ecclesiastical center of Ghent was home to the Flemish comital necropolis and would have held a place in the comital itinerary. Its two abbeys – St Peter's and Saint Bavo's – were once both led by Einhard, Charlemagne's biographer. After 1047, the court's circuit may have ranged farther east to include Ename.

The newest Flemish towns by contrast were laid out and built when Mathilda was a child: Lille and Ypres.[68] These two were only beginning to reach their potential when Mathilda left for Normandy and their construction was doubtless rather rudimentary in its nascent state. Yet Lille, especially, afforded

63 There is no evidence that Mathilda was convent-raised, and her mother certainly was not, as noted above.

64 The complexity of taking an entire aristocratic household from one place to the next is rarely considered in modern analysis but Theresa Earenfight notes that decisions about who would go and who would stay were not just logistical but political. Theresa M. Earenfight, 'Raising Infanta Catalina De Aragón to be Catherine, Queen of England', *Anuario de Estudios Medievales* 46:1 (2016), 417–43.

65 Just as the counts before him, Baldwin V set favorable commercial protections that drew merchants from all over the medieval world. David Nicholas, *Trade, Urbanisation, and the Family: Studies in the History of Medieval Flanders* (London, 1996), 4–6. Mathilda's experience in Flanders may have guided her expansion of protections for the mercantile activity of her nuns. See Chapter Five: Womb, 161.

66 The monks of Lobbes carried their patron, Saint Ursmer, in the famous Peace of God pilgrimage throughout Flanders in 1060. Their itinerary provides some clues as to the most populous centers in Flanders, including Ghent, Bruges, Lille, Cassel. Paulo Charruadas, 'Principauté territoriale, reliques et Paix de Dieu. Le comté de Flandre et l'abbaye de Lobbes à travers les Miracula S. Ursmari in itinere per Flandriam facta (vers 1060)', *Revue du Nord* 2007/4 (no. 372), 703–28.

67 Saint-Omer was one fortification that repelled even the Vikings, but Cassel had been destroyed by them and rebuilt by Arnulf II.

68 Baldwin established the merchant center at Lille before either a castrum or a moat. Nicholas, *Trade, Urbanisation,* 152.

Mathilda early exposure to the raising of a comital city from almost nothing. The city was, like Mathilda and William's creation of Caen, purely the result of comital resolve.[69] Baldwin and Adela first established Lille with a market at its heart, then an administrative center, a castrum, and two churches, St Maurice-de-Fins and St Stephen's.[70] It may have also been an example of their appropriation of Ottonian status.[71] In a notable parallel with their daughter, Baldwin and Adela also founded a new church dedicated to St Peter, at Lille in August of 1066.[72] Like Caen, all of this would create a thriving ducal administrative center from a 'one-horse town'.

Mathilda's parents thus contributed significantly to the sacred geography of Flanders. In addition to Lille above, they established monastic centers at Aire, Harlebeke, and Ename (See Map 1). They founded Messines *c.* 1057, where Adela would choose to be buried. Adela continued the work of monastic foundation without Baldwin after his death.[73] Adela's reputation as a generous and active patron became legendary. In fact, the church canonized her: she is known as St Adela of Messines.[74] Adela's eventual beatification would have come as a surprise to the Flemish court of her early years, who witnessed her armed rebellion as a young married woman against Baldwin IV.

Warfare was a regular feature of life at the Flemish court for Mathilda, too. From the time that Mathilda was about ten years old until she left Flanders to marry, *c.* 1051–2, her father Baldwin V and the emperor Henry III were

69 Nicolas Dessaux, 'Les enjeux politiques et religieux des translations de reliques à Lille au XIe siècle,' *Revue du Nord* 102: 436 (2020), 489–509. For Caen, see Chapter Two: Hands, 39–40.

70 Baldwin may have dedicated the church to Saint Maurice as a swipe at the Salians. Saint Maurice was not well known in Flanders but was the traditional patron saint and protector of the empire. 'everything [at Lille] was established as if Baldwin V wanted to testify to his sovereignty in the very place where he had won the battle against Emperor Henry III'. Dessaux, 'Les enjeux politiques', 491–2.

71 'from this moment, the whole to which we give the name Imperial Flanders was formed'. Ganshof, *Flandre imperiale*, 134. See, with caution, Kelly DeVries, 'Count Baldwin V of Flanders: Broker of Eleventh-Century Power', in *Military Cultures and Martial Enterprises in the Middle Ages: Essays in Honour of Richard P. Abels*, ed John D. Hosler and Steven Isaac (Woodbridge, 2020), 81–98. DeVries mistakenly identifies Baldwin's mother as Eleanor of Normandy and thereby struggles to explain some of Baldwin's chief motivations for his enmity toward the Salians.

72 Baldwin would be buried at St Peter, breaking the mold of earlier counts who were interred at Ghent, granting a new significance to Lille, just as his daughter did at Caen. Dessaux, 'Les enjeux politiques et religieux', 491–2. See Chapter Eight: Corpse, 213–26.

73 Adela established a new priory at Watten with her son, Robert in 1072. 'Chronica monasterii guatinensis', MGH *SS* 14, 167. See also Steven Vanderputten, *Monastic Reform as Process: Realities and Representations in Medieval Flanders, 900–1100*, 160–3.

74 Her feast day is September 8.

at war. Mathilda's parent's enmity against the Salian dynasty – and its pope, Leo IX – was something of an organizing principle. In 1050, the aggression of Emperor Henry III increased and the southern reaches of Flanders were regularly under attack.[75] The death of Henry III in 1056 signaled the end of the conflict, a final 'victory' of attrition. Mathilda, however, was duchess of Normandy by this time, and thus viewed her parents' triumph from afar. The long-term conflict between her parents and the emperor also had a material effect on Mathilda's betrothal and marriage, as evidenced below.

In 1048, at Pentecost (May 23), King Henry of France hosted a high festal court at Senlis. The important vassals of his realm attended, doubtless with their families and retainers. Baldwin of Flanders, of course, was numbered among them. For Adela, particularly, this would have been a welcome opportunity to visit her natal family in France with her children, now growing into adulthood and of marriageable age. Duke William of Normandy was also in attendance at Senlis, fresh from his victory at Val-ès-Dunes.[76] He was enjoying the royal favor of King Henry, Mathilda's uncle, and the first fruits of coming into his own as duke after his difficult minority. Count Baldwin and Duke William signed a charter together with King Henry restoring property to Saint-Médard of Soisson.[77] Among other things, they no doubt debated their next response to the threat of the emperor.

This was the occasion when Mathilda may have first met William, and their betrothal was arranged.[78] The union was announced sometime between May 1048 and October 1049. Sometime before July in 1049, Mathilda's father Baldwin V was excommunicated by Pope Leo IX for taking up arms against the Salian Emperor Henry III. Mathilda's marriage was banned by Pope Leo in the very same year – October, 1049 – at the council at Rheims. Her response to Pope Leo IX was colored by her family's long history of aggression toward him and the pope's devotion to and kinship with the Salians.[79] These undoubtedly set the tone for Mathilda's indifference toward Leo's ban of her marriage. The Salian house was not, from the Flemish perspective, an appropriate inheritor of Ottonian glory, and its pope's authority was questionable at best.[80] After a lifetime of her family's implacable aggression toward the Salian emperors, Mathilda would surely treat the papal declaration with something

75 Ganshof, *Flandre impériale*, 124.

76 Bates, *William*, 81–90.

77 *Recueil*, ed. Fauroux, no. 114.

78 Bates, *William*, 92–3.

79 Leo was related to the Salians and had also served in Conrad II's private chapel.

80 The response of the Flemish court to papal policy contrasts significantly with the Norman response which, according to Bates, was far more engaged and eager. The rulings of the Council of Rheims in 1049 were greeted with great sobriety by William of Normandy and his prelates, who were anxious to act in accordance with them, especially the rulings on clerical behavior. Bates, *William*, 101.

like contempt. Mathilda's marriage ceremony proceeded despite Pope Leo's disapproval. In the company of her parents, she left Flanders for her wedding ceremony at Eu, *c.* 1051–2. A few days later, she entered Rouen as the duchess of Normandy, 'with greatest ceremony and honor'.[81]

THE EMPRESS AND THE QUEEN

A few parallels can be drawn between the political complexities of the Ottonian *reich* – the world of Adelheid – and Mathilda's developing Anglo-Norman realm.[82] More particularly, these similarities come into view when Otto I and Adelheid began their conquest of Italy in 962 to remove Berengar II as king. In the context of invasion, both Ottonians and Normans had to negotiate an offensive that was considered morally indefensible. To answer those charges, a significant raft of history writing was employed in both cases.[83] It resulted in a reimaging of queenship for both Adelheid and Mathilda. Both women had a royal pedigree, but that was merely a place to start.[84] The ability of each woman

81 *OV*, ii, 128–31.

82 To compare Adelheid and Matilda of Canossa, see Penelope Nash, *Empress Adelheid and Countess Matilda: Medieval Female Rulership and the Foundations of European Society* (London, 2017). Studies on Adelheid include MacLean, *Ottonian Queenship*, especially 95–126; Greer, *Early Medieval Saxony*; Megan Welton and Sarah Greer, 'Establishing Just Rule: The Diplomatic Negotiations of the Dominae Imperiales in the Ottonian Succession Crisis of 983–985', *Frühmittelalterliche Studien* 55:1 (2021), 315–42; Laura Wangerin, 'Ottonian Women, Textual Memory and Dynastic Legitimacy', in *Gender, Memory and Documentary Culture, c. 900–1300,* ed. Laura L. Gathagan and Charles Insley (Woodbridge, 2025), 145–62.

83 The resultant new historiographies that attempted to justify an invasion and craft a new ruling ideology for both Ottonians and Normans might repay comparative attention. There is wide-ranging scholarship on each of these two fields of study separately. For selected works on the Ottonians, see Hans-Herbert Räkel, 'Geschichte mit allen Registern', *Archiv für Kulturgeschichte* 64.1 (1983); Schulmeyer-Ahl, *Der Anfang vom Ende der Ottonen*; David Warner, *Ottonian Germany: The Chronicon of Thietmar of Merseburg* (Manchester, 2001); David A. Warner, 'Reading Ottonian History: The Sonderweg And Other Myths', in *Challenging the boundaries of medieval history: the legacy of Timothy Reuter,* ed. Patricia Skinner (Turnhout, 2009), 81–114. For the Normans, works include *Constructing History across the Norman Conquest: Worcester, c. 1050–c. 1150,* ed. Francesca Tinti and D.A. Woodman (York, 2022); *Writing History in the Anglo-Norman World: Manuscripts, Makers and Readers, c. 1066–c. 1250,* ed. Laura Cleaver and Andrea Worm (York, 2022); Benjamin Pohl and Elisabeth van Houts, 'History and memory', in *The Cambridge Companion to the Age of William the Conqueror*, ed. Benjamin Pohl (Cambridge, 2022), 244–71.

84 Penelope Nash demonstrated this convincingly for Adelheid, noting that despite her pedigree she formed a new model of queenship 'but not without a struggle'. Nash, *Empress Adelheid and Countess Matilda*, 140.

to initiate a new type of queenship depended on her response to the events around her. For Adelheid and Mathilda, these included significant challenges to their husband's legitimacy that they were called upon to solve by virtue of their bloodline and position. Both ruled a newly formed, extensive and relatively unstable realm with shifting borders that had come about through conquest. Both women oversaw the creation of a new 'corporate identity' in the composition of their realm. In the case of Adelheid, the conquest of Italy launched the Ottonian Empire: she and Otto received imperial inauguration in 962, initiating the Saxon Ottonian dynasty which lasted until 1024. Adelheid was no longer just a queen, but an empress. For Mathilda, the conquest of England also completely re-formed the nature of her authority and created an 'Anglo-Norman realm', which lasted until 1154. Mathilda was no longer just a duchess, but a queen. The future was uncertain for both Mathilda and Adelheid and the self-conscious dynasty building they undertook was a necessary strategy to combat the doubt of the uneasy early years and the establishment of firmer footing. Adelheid actively shaped all three Ottonian emperors' rule. Mathilda provided the sons and daughters that would ensure the Norman governance for the next generations, though she would not live to see that come to fruition. Yet both women stood at the head of a nascent dynasty that required, and resulted in, a style of female rule that broke new ground.

The experiences of Adelheid and Mathilda of Flanders, however, cannot be precisely aligned. The Ottonian offices of queen and empress were already mature in Adelheid's lifetime, set in motion by her predecessors, Mathilda of Saxony, Edith and Gerberga. While Adelheid provided a rationale for the eventual invasion of Italy and the removal of Berengar, the office of queenship had already been expanded significantly. Adelheid's centrality is a demonstration of the office at its most expansive, bearing the fruit of the earlier generations of Ottonian royal and imperial women: Mathilda of Saxony, Edith and Gerberga. By contrast, Mathilda was initiating those changes in the face of an uncertain future. Her successors would likewise benefit from the revolution she began.[85] Mathilda's context resembled that of the earlier Ottonian queens. Gerberga ruled at a time when the office of queenship was forming in response to a political redistribution within the Ottonian family. MacLean describes an inchoate time of 'provisionality' that allowed her to carve out a more active role for herself that resembles the fluid, dynamic years immediately after the conquest of England.[86]

The challenges to their husband's legitimacy present another contrast between the circumstances of the two women rulers. Adelheid, as queen of Italy, provided legitimacy for Otto I's invasion and a rationale for ruling Italy. Duke William of Normandy's illegitimacy was not a political metaphor but

[85] See Chapter Eight: Corpse, 213–26.

[86] MacLean, *Ottonian Queenship*, 18.

a physical reality. While recent historiography has played down the effect of his irregular birth, it remained an eleventh-century topic of conversation and, until his coronation in 1066, 'bastard' was a familiar appellation for him.[87] His marriage to Mathilda gave their children royal blood. Her natal kin knit him into a crucial network that allowed the conquest of England to go forward. Her family neutralized the Capetian threat that would certainly have made the invasion of England impossible. Mathilda's natal networks and her impeccable lineage, like Adelheid's, made her indispensable. William of Poitiers records William's unease at his impending coronation on Christmas Day, 1066 because he wanted Mathilda beside him.[88] William of Poiteirs characterizes this as marital affection but William's hesitation to be crowned without Mathilda also reflected his awareness, despite his recent military victory, that she was necessary to make the case for Norman rule of England. The chaos of his coronation liturgy no doubt corroborated that belief when his Norman soldiers set fire to the buildings surrounding Winchester cathedral.[89]

Political unrest and a preoccupation with legitimacy, MacLean argues, placed necessary emphasis on queenship as an office for Ottonians.[90] MacLean maintains that powerful Ottonian queens owed their status 'to the very discontinuities and uncertainties of the tenth century itself'. In fact, instability was the very reason Ottonian royal women were central to imperial authority at all levels. The 'provisionality' of Ottonian rule in its nascent period, before the 960s, provided room for, indeed required, powerful royal women who actively held authority.[91]

MacLean's argument can also be made for Mathilda of Flanders. The conquest of England had just begun after 1066, notwithstanding the military victory at Hastings. Mathilda and her new dynasty struggled to pacify their kingdom and quash rebellions and plots that necessitated careful diplomacy and, eventually, military reprisal. At least until 1070, and the 'harrying of the north', Mathilda and William were regularly scrambling to retain control of their cross-channel realm. Their shared rule was the product of necessity; newborn Norman royal authority demanded a broadening and deepening of the responsibilities and powers of queenly rule. Both Mathilda and Adelheid's charter activity bear this out. After their respective coronations – Adelheid as empress, Mathilda as queen – both appear in over a third of their husband's

87 Bates, *William*, 15–24.

88 William of Poitiers, *Gesta*, 148–9.

89 At the shout of acclamation in the rite, they mistakenly assumed that William was being attacked. *OV*, ii, 182–5. See Chapter Four: Head, 107–8.

90 MacLean holds this is true for Ottonian queens generally, not only for Adelheid. MacLean, *Ottonian Queenship*, 94.

91 MacLean, *Ottonian Queenship*, 19.

charters.[92] David Bates has noted that no one appears in more royal charters, save William, than Mathilda in the first generation of Anglo-Norman rule.[93]

MacLean's analysis of Ottonian queens revealed a significant break with Carolingian queenship. With the disintegration of the Carolingian world, the strivings of 'nouveau royal' kings placed a new emphasis on queenship as an office.[94] The majority of Ottonian queens already bore royal blood; they consented to marry down a rung on the social ladder thus buoying their husband's status. Their public exercise of authority in the realm was crucial for the establishment of a new dynasty, 'to project their families as natural wielders of royal power'.[95] This tendency can be juxtaposed with Carolingian practice, as potential royal brides hailed from regionally important aristocratic families and ascended to the imperium from the local nobility.[96] Ottonian queens, because of their prestigious birth, had a central role in dynasty building and retained active links to their natal courts and families.

The contours that McLean traces out for the early Ottonian dynasty look very much like the first years of the new Anglo-Norman realm. Like early Ottonian queens, Mathilda's power and authority can be seen against a backdrop of the insecurity surrounding the struggle to govern England. To paraphrase MacLean above, the provisionality of the Anglo-Norman dynasty made Mathilda more powerful, not less.[97] Adelheid's story may have been open at Mathilda's elbow, but Adelheid represented an apogee in royal and imperial authority for women that had been generations in the making. Mathilda's world resembled more closely that of Gerberga, unstable, dynamic and rich

92 MacLean, *Ottonian Queenship*.

93 *Regesta*, 92–6. Of the 343 charters issued or signed by William as king of England, Mathilda's participation is recorded in 103 of them. Before the conquest of England, William issued 114 ducal charters that are possibly datable from the time of their marriage in c. 1052. Mathilda signs between one half and one third of these: 38 of 114. At least 49 of William's ducal charters, however, have possible dating parameters from before their marriage. If these are excluded, her percentage of attestations to ducal charters climbs to 58%, over half. Davis et al. characterized her participation in 'over half' of William's charters. *Regesta Regum Anglo-Normannorum*, ed. H.W.C. Davis, C. Johnson, H.A. Cronne and R.H.C. Davis (4 vols., Oxford, 1913–69), i, 93–4; *Recueil*, ed. Fauroux, 284–453; *Regesta*, 93–4.

94 MacLean, *Ottonian Queenship*, 42.

95 MacLean, *Ottonian Queenship*, 42.

96 Though the parallel can be pushed too far, Edith of Wessex bears some of the characteristics of the Carolingian model. Her influence was felt regionally on traditional queens' lands and expressed mostly through pious donations and foundations.

97 'attempts to establish their families as dynasties…created an exponential level of political uncertainty which amplified rather than restricted the queen's opportunities for action. We should remember that the endurance of Ottonian power remains highly provisional at this stage…' MacLean, *Ottonian Queenship*, 94.

with possibilities.[98] The following chapters demonstrate that Mathilda's engagement in royal authority echoes an Ottonian style of rule for women.[99]

The English queens before Mathilda did have authority and influence. The dowager Queen Edith was still alive at the conquest. Her acquiescence to Norman rule provided crucial support in the early uneasy months of their reign. Queen Emma, in particular, was central to Cnut's political legitimation and provided space for robust queenly authority. Yet unlike her English predecessors, Mathilda was a conquest queen – there had never been another Norman queen of England – and could rewrite the rules of queenship. As a result, she fashioned an office that took part in every facet of Norman royal rule: diplomatic, juridical, ecclesiastical, synodal, dynastic.[100]

CONCLUSION

Mathilda's awareness of her lineage seems to have been deeply influenced by her mother. Adela's interest in Ottonian traditions offered Mathilda a model of queenship she could access after the conquest of England. Recent scholarly analysis of Ottonian queenship, and the translation of imperial texts such as the *Epitaph*, help to explain Mathilda's transformation of English female rule.[101] The circumstances of the early Ottonian queens, especially before Ottonian hegemony was established, display some similarities with Mathilda's own circumstances. These royal women provided exemplars as she faced new frontiers after the conquest. All of these early lessons were learned in her home court of Flanders.

If, as Sarah Greer maintains, 'The Ottonians were the major success story of the tenth century', then the Normans could surely claim that title for the eleventh.[102] It is especially fitting that Mathilda might pattern herself – especially her style of queenship – after the ruling women of the famous tenth-century empire. In appropriating that branch of her genealogy, Mathilda might have taken advantage of something like an 'Ottonian vacuum'. Like her parents, Mathilda may have considered imperial legitimacy as something there for the taking. The end of the old Saxon dynasty led to its replacement by a wobblier Salian authority. The Salians' rapport with the papacy, after Leo, declined and their interactions were characterized by growing antagonism. The breakdown of that relationship allowed further space for the Normans –

98 'the ever-shifting map of tenth-century politics was the absolutely essential framework in which Gerberga's career took shape'. MacLean, *Ottonian Queenship*, 94.

99 See Chapter Seven: Mouth, 185–212.

100 See especially Chapter Two: Hands, 35–72.

101 MacLean, *Ottonian Queenship*; Gilsdorf, *Queenship and Sanctity*.

102 Greer, *Early Medieval Saxony*, 7.

both in Sicily and in Mathilda's Anglo-Norman realm – to step in.[103] Mathilda's relationship with Pope Gregory was warm; his letters to her are characterized by kindness and affection.[104]

Mathilda of Flanders' formative years and early adulthood in her natal home, daughter of the comital house, with royal blood running in her veins, no doubt contributed to the confidence she displayed as an adult. She watched and learned about the prime movers of urban growth and the benefits of social movements like the Peace and Truce of God.[105] Mathilda's mother took risks; young Adela's part in the rebellion against the old Count was a bold rejection of authority. To Mathilda, it might also have indicated that sometimes taking up arms against one's family could lead to a beneficial outcome. Her encouragement of her son Robert's rebellion against his father, and her military and financial support of it, is easier to comprehend in light of her mother's experience.[106] Likewise, her parents' response to papal authority was often characterized by hostility, as Mathilda's father took up arms against the empire and its pocket pope, Leo IX. Leo himself regularly demonstrated that the disdain was mutual. Surely this context explains somewhat Mathilda's surprising equanimity as her marriage was banned by Leo, and even as the prohibition dragged on for ten years, through three more popes.[107] Mathilda reacted to the ban with a *realpolitik* that seems to have bordered on indifference.

Mathilda also had Odilo's models of Adelheid – the 'empress in action' – at hand and, as subsequent chapters will illustrate, internalized them.[108] When the opportunity presented itself, she demonstrated how well she had learned the lessons of the Ottonian women in her genealogy. As the generatrix of a dynasty, Mathilda had the rarest of opportunities – to create new traditions

[103] By 1059, the popes had consistently favored Mathilda and her Norman family. Nicholas II lifted the ban on Mathilda's marriage and allied himself with the Sicilian Normans, her kin by marriage. In 1066, Alexander II, Nicholas's successor, allowed the invasion of England to go forward. Historians now question whether Alexander granted the pallium to William before Hastings or later, after 1070, but in either case Mathilda and the Normans did not suffer papal censure for the English invasion. Dan Armstrong, 'The Norman Conquest of England, the Papacy, and the Papal Banner', *HSJ* 32 (2020), 47–72

[104] Gregory calls Mathilda 'filia karrissima', an appellation only otherwise used for Matilda of Tuscany and Beatrice of Lorraine. Both extant letters are accessible online, 'Epistolae: Medieval Women's Latin Letters' (Columbia University), https://epistolae.ctl.columbia.edu/letter/50.html and https://epistolae.ctl.columbia.edu/letter/51.html

[105] Dessaux, 'Les enjeux politiques et religieux' 490–2; Charruadas, 'Principauté territoriale, reliques et Paix de Dieu', 703–728.

[106] See Chapter Five: Womb, 105–58.

[107] Victor II (13 April 1055–28 July 1057), Stephen IX (2 August 1057–29 March 1058) and Benedict X (4 April 1058–24 January 1059). See Chapter Two: Hands, 35–72.

[108] MacLean, *Ottonian Queenship*, 17–18.

at the head of the Anglo-Norman royal house. While William's kingship followed traditional models in England, Mathilda used the Ottonian style of female rule learned at her mother's knee to adopt sovereignties that shaped a new version of English queenship.

2

HANDS

Let your hands be strong so that the temple may be built.
Zachariah 8:9

A central focus of Mathilda of Flanders' energy was her construction of a Benedictine abbey for women, Holy Trinity in Caen, dedicated in 1066. Mathilda's choice to establish her new monastic foundation in honor of the Trinity, as opposed to a saint or the Virgin Mary, was an early indicator of her spiritual preference for the Holy Spirit and, through it, apostolic authority. The mysteries of the Holy Spirit were connected in scripture to prophesy, which would be another fascination for her.[1] Historians have long argued that Holy Trinity was founded as a penance for Mathilda's marriage in the face of a papal ban.[2] Yet her creation of Holy Trinity eventually swept over the past to embrace a breathtakingly uncertain venture: the Norman invasion of England. In what follows, I consider Holy Trinity in light of the Norman conquest. Holy Trinity was Mathilda's first contribution to Norman victory. Mathilda established the monastery's connections to the military offensive from the beginning, despite the uncertainty of its success, and the conquest remained a central element of its character long after her death. The second contribution was the *Mora*, the ship she had constructed for the invasion, that carried William to England.[3] Thus, through the work of her hands, she placed herself at the heart of the Norman Conquest. To these two conquest gifts, one must add the most notable – her daughter, Cecelia. Given as an oblate on the day of Holy Trinity's dedication, Cecelia's role in the family's success was a critical one. Her career as the second abbess of Mathilda's new foundation was surely planned from the start.

After the success of the conquest, Holy Trinity became a physical expression of Mathilda's new royal dynastic identity. Physical evidence of her original construction is difficult to identify after centuries of renovation, but Mathilda's

1 See Chapter Four: Head, 119–22 and Chapter Five: Womb, 160.

2 See Chibnall, *Charters and Custumals*, xxi; Bates, *William*, 157–61.

3 See Chapter Five: Womb. See also Laura L. Gathagan, '"You conquer countless enemies even as a maiden": the Conqueror's daughter and dynastic rule at Holy Trinity, Caen', *History: The Journal of the Historical Association* 103 (2017), 840–57.

original church bore the stamp of Ottonian influences. A central argument of this book is that Mathilda consciously chose to embrace her familial connections to the Ottonians.[4] These elements appear again in her arrangements for Holy Trinity, both in its physical structure and its practice. Holy Trinity would signal Ottonian prestige through her architectural choices, like the abbeys of her Flemish homeland, both the Flemish comital necropolis of St Peter's Ghent, and her parents' new acquisition at Ename,[5] Likewise, in parallel with the famous Ottonian women's abbeys of Quedlinburg and Gandersheim, Mathilda established Holy Trinity with a royal daughter as abbess, to serve particularly as a monument to Norman dynastic rule. The abbey would become a female necropolis for the first generations of the Norman dynasty. The extant textual evidence demonstrates an essential element of that identity; the monastery's robust documentary culture. The early development of literate bureaucracy would be one of Holy Trinity's defining features. The documents the women of Holy Trinity produced were utilized to further knit the community to its conquest roots. Holy Trinity, like its imperial Ottonian counterparts, developed a literary culture as a monument and *memoria* to the royal Normans, though some of these textual monuments have left only traces. The manifestations of that identity which do survive are bureaucratic initiatives, not literary creations or deluxe Gospel books.[6] Even so, Holy Trinity, just as Gandersheim and Quedlinburg did, took on the task of creating a collective memory that was intended to set in amber a glorious moment in the history of the Norman royal dynasty, a moment that coincided with its own birth. Holy Trinity resembled imperial monasteries in many ways, but its particular identification with the Norman invasion of England would set it apart from other monastic foundations throughout western Europe. Thus, while historians have often characterized its construction as Mathilda's payment of an old debt, her approach to Holy Trinity explicitly pointed to the future.

4 See Chapter One: Blood, 11–33.

5 Van den Bremt and Vermeiren 'Archeologisch vooronderzoek op het Sint-Pietersplein en aan de Tweekerkenstraat', *Handelingen der Maatschappij voor Geschiedenis en Oudheidkunde te Gent* 58 (2004), 23–58, at 31–36.

6 For the library collection at Quedlinburg, see Helene Scheck, 'Queen Mathilda of Saxony and the Founding of Quedlinburg: Women, Memory, and Power', *Historical Reflections* 35:3 (2009), 21–36. Holy Trinity's library, like those of many women's monastic houses destroyed in the French Revolution, is almost impossible to trace. But, like the Ottonian foundations, Holy Trinity's rich collection of relics left a record. See Chapter Three: Fingers, 75–104.

HOLY TRINITY: THE CONQUEST ABBEY

> '...my most honorable wife Mathilda, daughter of Duke Baldwin of Flanders, when she saw that our affairs and our power were flowering in their greatness, she built a basilica in honor of the Holy Trinity in a place which the natives call Cadom in ancient times, which after all the ecclesiastical conveniences had been arranged, at the time of the dispensation, the pontiffs of our empire coming from the abbeys, the most holy fathers, all the clergy, the most devoutly religious people, all duly disposed, together with us on the 14 kalends of July, in the regnal year of Philip, king of France, Henry, ruling the Roman parts by imperial right, Pope Alexander, possessing the apostolic see of the most pious see, in the year from the Incarnation of the Lord 1066, the fourth indication, consecrated to the Lord Almighty. [7]

The two abbeys founded by Mathilda and William in Caen – Holy Trinity for women and St Stephen's for men – have long been considered the price they paid for the lifting of the papal prohibition of their marriage. Their marriage was banned in 1049 by Leo IX, for unspecified reasons, along with two other high-status unions: Adelaide of Aumale – William's sister – to Enguerrand II, Count of Pontheiu, and Goda/Godgifu – sister of Edward the Confessor – to Eustace II of Boulogne. Each of the three marriages threatened the political position of the Salian emperor Henry III, Leo's patron and kinsman. Pope Leo's prohibition of all three – each a decision against the interests of Normandy or its friends – raised eyebrows and was seen as openly partisan.[8] Nevertheless, two of the couples dissolved their connections; Adelaide and Enguerrand

7 '...honestissima conjunx mea Mathildis subnixa, nobilissimi ducis Flandrensium Balduini filia, cum res nostras atque potentiam sua pro magnitudine florere conspiceret, in honorem Sancte Trinitatis, concessa a me digne peticionis licentia, in loco qui Cadomum prisco ab incolis nuncupatur nomine, sanctimonialibus construxit basilicam, quam paulo post, omni commoditate exornatam ecclesiastica, spirituals constituto desponsationis tempore, convenientes imperii nostri excellentissimi pontifices, ex abbatiis sanctissimi patres, omnis clerus, summa cum devotione religious populus, omnibus rite dispositis, una nobiscum, XIIII. kalendas Juli, regnante in Francia rege feliciter Philippo, Romanis partibus imperial jure dominante Henrico, apostolice sedis cathedram religiosissimo possidente papa Alexandro, anno ab Incarnatione Domini MLXVI'. Paris, Bibliothèque Nationale de France, MS Latin 5650, folio 9r–13v at 9r (Hereafter BNF 5650). Printed in Fauroux, *Receuil*, 444; Musset, *Les actes*, 54 (no. 2). The charter date uses the Gregorian calendar, which corresponds to the modern date June 18, 1066. For the complete text of the charter, see appendix to this chapter, 73–4.

8 Pope Leo IX chose not to condemn Theobald II of Champagne, Emperor Henry's ally, when Theobald abandoned his wife in favor of another woman. Bates notes that Abbot John of Fécamp explicitly complained to Leo that his partisanship was not advancing the papal agenda of reforming lay marriage. Bates, *William*, 102. For Abbot John of Fécamp's letter: *PL* cxliii, cols. 799–800.

annulled their marriage,[9] as did Eustace and Goda: she later returned to England.[10] Mathilda and William proved immovable. Even though their marriage had not yet taken place, and the betrothal could have been dissolved, they did not change their plans. In the previous chapter, some reasons for Mathilda's refusal to back away from the union were outlined; primarily, her family's longstanding enmity against the Salians. Leo IX was their kinsman and faithful supporter and a regular adversary of Flanders. Whatever the case, her patience was no doubt tested as papal approval was slow in coming. Ten years passed until in 1059 when, probably as part of a larger recognition of Norman partnership with the papacy in Sicily, Pope Nicholas II lifted the ban on Mathilda and William's marriage.[11] The lifting of the ban is not the only tantalizing hint of cooperation between the two parallel Norman administrations; one in Normandy and one in Sicily. Four years later, in 1063, Robert Guiscard provided a permanent home for Robert of Grandmesnil, the former abbot of Saint-Évroult, who William had dubiously charged with unspecified crimes. Guiscard both served the papacy, and perhaps saved his northwestern kin embarrassment, by finding an abbacy for Robert as abbot of St Euphemia in Calabria, Guiscard's recent foundation.[12]

Did Mathilda and William cooperate with Pope Nicholas's decision to legitimize their marriage by constructing Holy Trinity and St Stephen's? It is not certain; the original proceedings of the papal council of 1049 are not extant. Orderic is the first to establish the link between papal approval and the

9 Adelaide of Aumale's annulment of this union led to her marriage to Lambert II, Count of Lens, who would die in battle at Lille in 1054, supporting Mathilda's father, Baldwin V. The union of Goda and Eustace, however, was childless and may have become undesirable for all parties, thus the ban may have given the necessary cover for a desired annulment. See Kathleen Thompson, 'Being the Ducal Sister: the role of Adelaide of Aumale', in *Normandy and its Neighbors, 900–1250. Essays in honour of David Bates*, ed. David Crouch and Kathleen Thompson (Turnhout, 2011), 43–59.

10 Godgifu's name is inscribed in a manuscript eventually given to the Cathedral at Rochester, British Library, Royal MS1 D III. Elisabeth van Houts, 'Edward and Normandy', in *Edward the Confessor; the man and the legend*, ed. Richard Mortimer (Woodbridge, 2009), 63–76 at 64.

11 For papal relations between both sets of Normans and the papacy, see Maria Vezzoni, 'Alexander II and the Normans: Borders as Instruments of Dialogue and Compromise', in *Borders and the Norman World: Frontiers and Boundaries in Medieval Europe*, ed Dan Armstrong, Áron Kecskés, Charles C. Rozier and Leonie Hicks (Woodbridge, 2023), 127–47.

12 By 1066, the families were on friendly terms again. Hugh de Grandesmil, Robert's brother, accompanied William on the invasion of England. Giuseppe Occhiato, 'Roberto de Grandmesnil, un abate "architetto" operante in Calabria nell'XI secolo', in *Calabria bizantina. Testimonianze d'arte e strutture di territorio. Atti dell'VIII e IX Incontro di Studi Bizantini, Reggio Calabria 1985–89*, ed. Soveria Mannelli (Catanzaro, 1991), 129–75. My thanks to Maria Vezzoni for this reference.

establishment of the two Caennaise monasteries by the ducal pair.[13] The section of his *Historia* that addresses the penance was composed sometime between 1123 and 1131, only a generation after Holy Trinity's official foundation ceremony. Yet there are some grounds to question Orderic's characterization. Margaret Gibson considered the evidence for the penance 'surprisingly late'; her expectation was that – if true – the motive would have been woven into the foundation charters of the two monasteries.[14] 'Even a phrase in the proemium such as "moved by conjugal affection" or a circumlocutory reference to the papacy would meet the case, but there is nothing.'[15]

Papal encouragement was not necessary, moreover, for Mathilda to embrace monastic patronage by founding an abbey; it was a fundamental expression of aristocratic piety and a marker of elite status. Her own parents provided a model. They founded three churches of canons regular – Aire, Lille and Harlebeke – and two Benedictine monastic communities, Messines in 1057 and Ename sometime after 1047. As noted in the previous chapter, Mathilda's mother Adela was also particularly involved in the founding and construction of the abbey of Watten. Indeed, the monastery's records recount her sitting with the masons and builders as they worked in the sun, a 'hands-on' patron.[16] Mathilda's opportunity to follow her mother's example also came packaged within an even more ambitious initiative; the transformation of Caen into a second capital city.

The decision to expand a relatively sleepy little town into a robust center of ducal patronage and authority changed forever the geography of Normandy's political power grid. Under Mathilda and William, Rouen, the traditional heart of ducal influence, was superseded in crucial ways by Caen to its northwest. The financial and juridical heart of Normandy – the exchequer –

13 *OV*, ii, 147–8.

14 Margaret Gibson, *Lanfranc of Bec* (Oxford, 1978), 69.

15 Furthermore, contemporary reports of Nicholas II's reversal of the marriage ban do not mention this condition. Gibson *Lanfranc of Bec*, 69. See also Elizabeth M. Hallam, 'Monasteries as "War Memorials": Battle Abbey and La Victorie', *Studies in Church History* 20 (1983), 47–57.

16 'No sooner had the woman (Adela), inspired by heaven, came to Watten and as one of the commoners, sat on a low seat with the masons and diggers, suffering under the fierce sun, she laid the foundations of the holy edifice, which is still there to this day, and departing time, she left not a small assessment for the expenses of the plasterers by the hand of Sir Odfrid our Father.' (Necdum animo satis dederat femina coelitus inspirata, imo Guatinum venit, et quasi una de minoribus, humili subsellio cum caementariis ac fossoribus operi immorata, sub divo solis patiens, sancti aedificii quod usque hodie est fundamenta jecit, et abscedens hac vice non modicum censum ad plastarum expensas per manum domni Odfridi Patris nostri dereliquit.), 'Chronico Watinense (Chronicle of Watten)', *PL*, CXLIX, 1520–1. Adela accompanied Odfride to Rome in 1077 to obtain the protection of Pope Gregory VII. Later, she laid the first stone at the construction site.

was now centered in Caen, not Rouen. Thus, while Rouen was still the place the Norman dukes were invested, and remained wealthier than Caen, the new city was the true administrative center of Normandy until the thirteenth century.[17] Like a miniature version of Constantine's shift of the Roman empire to Constantinople, the recentering of the ducal administration allowed for new construction to manifest ducal power. It was an ideal opportunity for self-fashioning. Caen would boast all the elements necessary for any thriving commercial center: a merchant quarter, a busy port, and multiple markets granted by the ducal couple. It would also feature tangible representations of governance both secular and ecclesiastical. The triangle of ducal influence would consist of the ducal castle, set above the growing city, Mathilda's abbey of Holy Trinity, slightly to the east and on a promontory at the same elevation, and St Stephen's to the southwest, in a slight depression, near the route to Bayeux. The new capital offered Mathilda a new start and the chance to cast her identity – and eventually that of her royal dynasty – in stone.[18]

From its initial days Holy Trinity's construction leapt ahead of its neighbor, St Stephen's, which only began to rise after the conquest, on the eastern side of the town. Mathilda's early activity might reasonably be even earlier; choosing the site, identifying quarries, and hiring personnel, including the first abbess of the community, Matilda of St Leger-de-Préaux.[19] The material construction of the twin abbeys diverged as well.[20] Indeed, neutron analysis of the stone used at the two houses has revealed that their building materials were from separate quarries despite their proximity to each other, only 2 kilometers apart. St Stephen's stone was quarried at La Maladrerie quarry, west of Caen.[21] By contrast, samples from four of Holy Trinity's carvings correspond to stone from the Mondeville quarry, which has been suggested by art historians as a source. However, the majority of materials sampled at Holy Trinity are not from any of the five major local quarries and indeed originate from a site that has yet to be identified.[22]

17 Lindy Grant, *Architecture and Society in Normandy 1120–1270* (New Haven, CT, 2005) 12.

18 'The development of Caen represented a massive statement of William and Matilda's standing as rulers.' Bates, *William*, 206.

19 By contrast, all major work on the foundation of St Stephen's occurred after the conquest. The first dedication was in 1077 for the choir and the altar; in 1081 the transept and the nave of St Stephen's were complete. After William's death, the west end was finished, probably *c.* 1096–1100, and the nave and transept were both vaulted by about 1125–35. Musset, *Les actes*, 14.

20 Maylis Baylé, *La Trinité de Caen; sa place dans l'histoire de l'Architecture et du Décor Romans* (Geneva, 1979), xxxxx, 7.

21 L.L. Holmes and G. Harbottle, 'In the Steps of William the Conqueror: Neutron Activation Analysis of Caen Stone', *Archaeometry* 45, 2 (2003) 199–220.

22 Holmes and Harbottle, 'Neutron Analysis of Caen Stone,' 210–20. The analysis conducted by Holmes and Harbottle surveyed five of the local quarries in Caen but

By the early summer of 1066, there was already enough building fabric to schedule the official dedication ceremony of Mathilda's abbey church. The wording of the charter indicates that there was something to dedicate. Maylis Baylé, in her landmark study of Holy Trinity, compared the wording of Holy Trinity's dedication charter that refers to a basilica that Mathilda 'built' (construixit) to St Stephen's dedication charter, which used the gerund form 'he (William) is building' (construendum).[23] By the time of Holy Trinity's dedication, there was certainly the first version of the choir, the altar, and a surrounding building, including an early western elevation.[24]

Holy Trinity's rapid construction, compared to St Stephen's, was almost certainly driven by Mathilda's choice to tie her abbey to the impending invasion of England. The six months between Edward the Confessor's death in January of 1066 and Holy Trinity's dedication in June of that year were, no doubt, a period of feverish activity on the eastern promontory overlooking the growing city of Caen. As Holy Trinity's construction grew up, its presence over the city referenced Mathilda's own authority over the new administrative control center of Caen.

Romanesque architecture is one of the most visible expressions of the Norman dynasty's newfound confidence and pretensions, but Holy Trinity's first phases pre-dated many of the later innovations connected to that movement. When Mathilda first raised Holy Trinity, it may have appeared old-fashioned. Holy Trinity's earliest style contrasted with many of the later innovations connected to it, which were introduced in the next generation. Elements of the original abbey church, Baylé affirms, were 'archaic' and even pre-Romanesque, hearkening back to an earlier time, and were crafted on Ottonian and Carolingian designs.[25] Nineteenth-century architectural authorities like Ruprich-Robert, writing of the two abbeys, confessed confusion at the differences between Holy Trinity's early construction and St Stephen's. The motivation behind their design seemed, to him, completely at odds.[26]

---

was not exhaustive. They theorize that other quarries in Caen, no longer accessible, provided the materials for Holy Trinity's construction.

23 See note 12 above. 'sanctimorialibus construxit basilicam…' BNF 5650, folio 9r–13v; Fauroux, *Receuil*, 444; Musset, *Les actes*, no. 2.

24 'In 1066, a construction already existed; apart from the fact that a dedication applies only to a building and cannot be limited to an altar, the text specifies that Mathilde had a basilica erected: the term "construxit" refers to the past.' Baylé, *La Trinité*, 13.

25 Baylé, *La Trinité*, 36.

26 'We must bring out here a fact of the greatest importance, which is that the two nearly contemporary buildings seem however to have absolutely nothing in common in terms of style: neither the same principle of art, nor, certainly, the same direction, presided over their creation. The Abbaye-aux-Dames was built, like the first buildings that we have just mentioned, according to the principle of

Holy Trinity was a traditional Latin basilica, while St Stephen's construction, after the conquest, featured significant innovation. Later, Baylé noted the same dissimilarity in design between the two churches.[27] I would argue that the disconnect that flummoxed Ruprich-Robert demonstrates Mathilda's conscious choices about what Holy Trinity's appearance was meant to evoke. She embraced an imperial identity that referenced the past and made claims for the legitimacy of her authority. Her basilica, designed on imperial lines, was a fitting choice for her new capital.

When Mathilda officially dedicated Holy Trinity, the original purpose of the abbey as expiation – if that was indeed its first function – was overwritten by the presence of the Norman fleet floating in the harbor at Dives, 25 kilometers away, as the liturgy was performed. The dedication charter was signed by the highest members of the ducal court from all over Normandy, many of whom were on hand as they gathered ships and arms for the attack.[28] The secular lords in attendance included those in the ducal inner circle: Roger of Montgomery, William fitz Osbern, Roger Montgomery, Ranulf Viscount of Bayeux, Hugh de Monforte, Richard of Beaufour. These courtiers provided foundational support for the invasion of England, including ships, troops and funding. Indeed, Mathilda herself was amongst these military suppliers.

The foundation charter reveals that the ecclesiastical luminaries from the regions surrounding Caen were in attendance as well: Archbishop Maurilius of Rouen, bishops Hugh of Lisieux, John of Avranches, Baldwin of Evreux and Bishop Odo of Bayeux, who donated land and funds to Holy Trinity himself.[29] The abbots of St Vigor, Evreux, Saint Wandrille, Mont-Saint-Michel, Fécamp, Saint-Ouen and Lonlay Abbey were all present. The charter for Holy Trinity also boasts a signature of the famous founder of Le Bec Abbey, Herluin; it was the sole document he signed outside of his

the Latin basilica, traditional in the country; one must imagine seeing it, of course, as it was on its first day, that is to say, with its matching pillars in the nave, both the nave and the aisles covered by exposed frameworks (these were replaced in the twelfth century by vaults), while that at Saint-Étienne was the result of a new idea, the importation into Normandy of a plan which was probably unknown there until then.' Victor Ruprich-Robert, *L'église Ste-Trinité (ancienne Abbaye-aux-dames) et l'église St-Étienne (ancienne Abbaye aux Hommes) à Caen* (Caen, 1864), 62.

27 '(Holy Trinity's abbey church) expressed a certain archaism of design, especially if one thinks of the novelties with a promising future presented by the almost contemporary abbey church of Saint-Étienne: this opposition between the two constructions has long been underlined, and it is not necessary to insist on this point…' Baylé, *La Trinité*, 54.

28 BNF 5650, folio 13v. The fleet would eventually move to the larger port at Valery-sur-Somme sometime before 12 August.

29 For Odo's gift, see below, 64–5.

own community.[30] David Bates characterized Holy Trinity's dedication as a 'culmination' of conquest preparations: a symbolic act of religious solemnity before the Norman fleet set sail.[31] The Benedictine community Mathilda built can also be considered a petition for divine help – an early good faith offering before the invasion. Mathilda's abbey, perhaps once expiation for her marriage, was also an appeal for divine favor in the face of an uncertain battle.

In this way links between Holy Trinity and the conquest were initially established by Mathilda and her new community. The strongest of these, of course, was the oblation of Mathilda and William's daughter, Cecelia, on that same day, recorded in the final lines of the foundation charter:

> Moreover, the aforementioned most renowned count, and his wife together with their children, on the same day offered their daughter Cecelia in name, to God, with the archbishop of Rouen being favorable, as well as the other bishops, in order that in the same place – namely, that of the divine Trinity itself – she might perpetually serve in the cloth of religion, [and] by whose service they understand that they have both their child and all other good things.[32]

Contemporary writers drew fundamental connections between Cecelia's entrance as a nun of Holy Trinity and the Norman invasion; Cecelia's oblation was a down payment on her family's victory over the English.[33] Hildebert of Lavardin, the twelfth-century poet, wrote of Cecelia 'You conquer countless enemies, even as a maiden.'[34] In the words of her contemporaries, then, Cecelia was a conquering nun.[35] Ducal, then royal, daughter, Cecelia would rule the foundation after 1103 and metamorphose from conquering nun to conquering abbess.[36]

In the earliest expression of Holy Trinity's existence, the conquest was continually evoked. The foundation charter was the first communication of Holy Trinity's purpose and identity (see appendix to this chapter, 73–4). It used

30 Jean-Hervé Foulon, 'The foundation and early history of Le Bec', in *A Companion to the Abbey of Le Bec in the Central Middle Ages, 11th–13th Centuries*, ed. Benjamin Pohl and Laura L. Gathagan (Leiden, 2019), 11–38 at 13.

31 Bates, *William*, 85.

32 BNF 5650, folio 13r; Musset, *Les actes*, 57.

33 See Chapter Five: Womb, 158–63.

34 Hildebert of Lavardin, 'Versus ad Ceciliam abbatissam Cathomi', in *Carmina Minora*, ed. Alexander Brian Scott (Berlin, 2002), 37. For a full treatment of Cecelia's abbacy, see Gathagan, 'Maiden', 840–857.

35 Musset, *Les actes*, 52–7.

36 Gathagan, 'Maiden', 854–7.

unusual scriptural themes and distinctive language to reference the specific context of its creation and its founder.[37]

> Indeed, the Apostle says, 'Certainly you are heirs of God, but also joint heirs with Christ.' For in the gospel, when the Lord foretold the future reward of those who had performed good deeds, he designated those who are striving with a worthy army to be co-heirs of the heavenly joys, saying, 'And they shall inherit eternal life'.[38]

Two passages are notably referenced here: Romans 8:17 and Matthew 19:29. Romans 8:17 reads, 'And if sons, heirs also; heirs indeed of God, and joint heirs with Christ: yet so, if we suffer with him, that we may be also glorified with him'. Matthew 19:29 expands upon the same theme, 'And every one that hath left house, or brethren, or sisters, or father, or mother, or wife, or children, or lands for my name's sake, shall receive a hundredfold, and shall inherit everlasting life.' These scriptures are highly unusual in a foundation charter. Catherine Letouzey-Réty has noted that these references look very curious – even 'awkward' – in a monastic foundation charter, but posits that the passages were consciously used.[39] Traditional invocations of salvation were replaced with pointed references to inheritance. In the context of the upcoming invasion of England, repeated references to Mathilda and William as 'heirs indeed of God, and joint heirs with Christ' were central to the document.[40]

37 BNF 5650, folio 9v; Printed in *Receuil*, ed. Fauroux, 444; Musset, *Les actes*, 54.

38 'Dicit enim apostolus "heredes quidem Dei, coheredes autem Christi". Dominus namque in evangelio, cum in bonorum actuum exhibitione (g) operatoribus future retributionis munus prediceret, eosdem digno exercitu persistentes proposito gaudiorum coheredes esse celestium designavit, dicens "et vitam eternam possidebunt."' BNF 5650, folio 9v. See appendix to this chapter for full text, 73–4.

39 'the long preamble of the charter of dedication of La Trinité is a development on the theme dear to Saint Augustine of the heirs and co-heirs of God, developed in sermon 86. This preamble is the only one produced by either of the two Caen abbeys to make explicit reference to the Gospel, to the Epistles of the Apostles, and, more broadly, to the idea of one of the Fathers of the Church justifying donations granted to the abbey, and not simply adhering to the typical idea of the expectation of eternal salvation. If the text of La Trinité is somewhat awkward, it demonstrates a real desire to mobilize this Augustinian theme.' (Translation mine). Catherine Letouzey-Réty, 'Les abbesses de la Trinité de Caen, la Reine Mathilde et l'Angleterre', *Annales de Normandie* 69: 1 (2019), 57–69; Catherine Letouzey-Réty, 'Écrit et gestion du temporel dans une grande abbaye de femmes anglo-normande: la Sainte-Trinité de Caen (XIe-XIIIe siècle)' PhD dissertation (3 volumes, Université de Paris I Panthéon-Sorbonne, 2011), i, 144.

40 'The insistence on the theme of the heirs and co-heirs of God takes on a very special meaning not only for the monastery (which receives its initial endowment of land on the occasion of this particularly grandiose dedication ceremony), but also for the duchy: it is just before the departure of William's army for Hastings, at a time

Likewise, Matthew's reference to leaving 'house, or brethren, or sisters, or father, or mother, or wife, or children, or lands for my name's sake' is open to a multivalent interpretation. It refers to the nuns of Holy Trinity who left brothers, sisters, fathers and mothers behind to serve God as a husband in their new spiritual unions. The Normans would also soon leave behind their homes and families for England. Though explicit papal approval for the invasion may have come much later, the scripture used in Holy Trinity's foundation charter may indicate an early attempt to cast the invasion in religious terms. The careful positioning of Matthew's gospel passage into the dedication allows it to touch both initiatives: the nuns' sacrifice was connected to the military venture. Later Norman apologists, like William of Poitiers, would repackage the brutal Norman invasion to make it palatable to the eleventh-century world. It was variously characterized as a fitting response to Harold Godwinson's broken oath to William, or as an effort to reform English churches. The papal pallium was granted to William by Alexander II as an endorsement of the conquest and has often been used as evidence for the latter interpretation.[41] These attempts to cast the invasion in a more flattering light were only possible after the war had been won. In Mathilda's charter for Holy Trinity, by contrast, we may see an early attempt to provide a spiritual rationale for the invasion. This would not be the last time Mathilda used scripture to cast herself and the conquest in an apostolic mold; in her coronation liturgy she pointedly modeled herself as an apostolic authority.[42]

The charter's preamble relied on carefully chosen scripture to underscore Holy Trinity's conquest identity. It also articulated it by employing the language of militarism; in founding the monastery, Mathilda and her community were striving with 'a worthy army' to be co-heirs to heavenly joys. Likewise, the charter describes each professed nun as a permanent '*supplementum*' to the holy church, a Latin word that might be translated as 'additions' or as military reinforcements, just as Livy did.[43] The nuns and abbess of Holy Trinity could consider themselves spiritual warriors, lending their prayers – strengthened by the power of their sacrifice – to the invasion.

---

when the notion of inheritance, and above all the legitimacy of this inheritance, takes on a very particular resonance.' Letouzey-Réty, 'Écrit et gestion', i, 145.

41 Dan Armstrong has convincingly argued that the pallium was probably presented at the Council of Winchester, perhaps at the crown-wearing Mathilda and William celebrated there in 1070, at Easter. This was after the 'Harrying of the North' – and the successful repression of rebellion there. Dan Armstrong, 'The Norman Conquest of England, the Papacy, and the Papal Banner', *HSJ* 32 (2021), 47–72.

42 See Chapter Four: Head, 105–33.

43 'If reinforcements were needed, he should supply them with the legions which Publius Cornelius, propraetor, was in charge of in Sicily…' '(Si supplemento opus esset, suppleret de legionibus quibus P. Cornelius pro praetore in Sicilia praeesset…'). Livy, *Ab Urbe Condita*, Book 26, ed. Robert Seymour Conway and Stephen Keymer Johnson (Oxford, 1935), 11.

The document weaves in apostolic authority and explicitly references the future; 'Faith, confirmed by the apostle's authority as well as by the promise of the Lord, is directed to that which must be undoubtedly believed.' Again, two lines further down, the preamble describes Christ foretelling the future of his faithful. These passages point to Mathilda's understanding of the mysterious and unknowable future of her and her family's greatest venture, by way of the Holy Spirit through the apostles.[44] As noted above, the invocation of apostolic authority, prophecy and the Holy Spirit seemed to have particular resonance for Mathilda and would reappear at key moments of her life. One of these would be her coronation at Pentecost in 1068.[45] Another would be her search for clarity as she struggled to bridge the rift between her firstborn son, Robert, and her husband.[46]

Holy Trinity's charter offers an early example of Mathilda's preoccupations. It did not cleave to traditional monastic rhetoric but rather utilized scripture that reflected the particular context of the invasion of England and of Mathilda's own preferences. Its targeted language forged links to the conquest. The text also reveals Mathilda's understanding of the role of fate in her life, and her desire to use prophecy to guide her. These impulses arguably had their most concrete expression in another work of her hands, the *Mora*.

THE *MORA*

Mathilda commissioned the ship that would carry William to England, which she christened the *Mora*.[47] The ship is described in the extant shiplist of the invasion (Plate 1). It famously carried a golden child on its prow with a horn to its lips. It appears in a central position on the Bayeux Tapestry, foregrounded in the depiction of the fleet.[48] Elisabeth van Houts has argued convincingly that *Mora* referenced the 'Moira' or Greek fates, the spinning and snipping

44 van Houts has theorized that Mathilda's state of mind may have made prophetic writings especially compelling to her, given the anxiety of 1066. She notes that a copy of a sibylline prophecy was preserved in a manuscript at Fécamp, a monastery that Mathilda patronized: van Houts, 'The Echo of the Conquest,' 192. See Chapter One: Blood, 11–33. See also Letouzey-Réty, 'Les abbesses de la Trinité de Caen,' 60.

45 Chapter Four: Head, 105–33. See also Laura L. Gathagan, 'Audi Israel: Apostolic authority in the coronation of Mathilda of Flanders,' *ANS* 43 (2020), 89–104.

46 Beech, 'Queen Mathilda and the Abbey of La Chaise-Dieu,' 350–74; van Houts, 'The Echo of the Conquest,' 192.

47 Oxford, Bodleian Library MS E Museo 93 folio 15v. For a detailed examination of the possible meanings of the ship's name and close analysis of it, see van Houts, 'The Echo of the Conquest,' 135–55.

48 Bayeux Tapestry, scene 38. The entire embroidery is available for viewers online: https://www.bayeuxmuseum.com/en/the-bayeux-tapestry/.

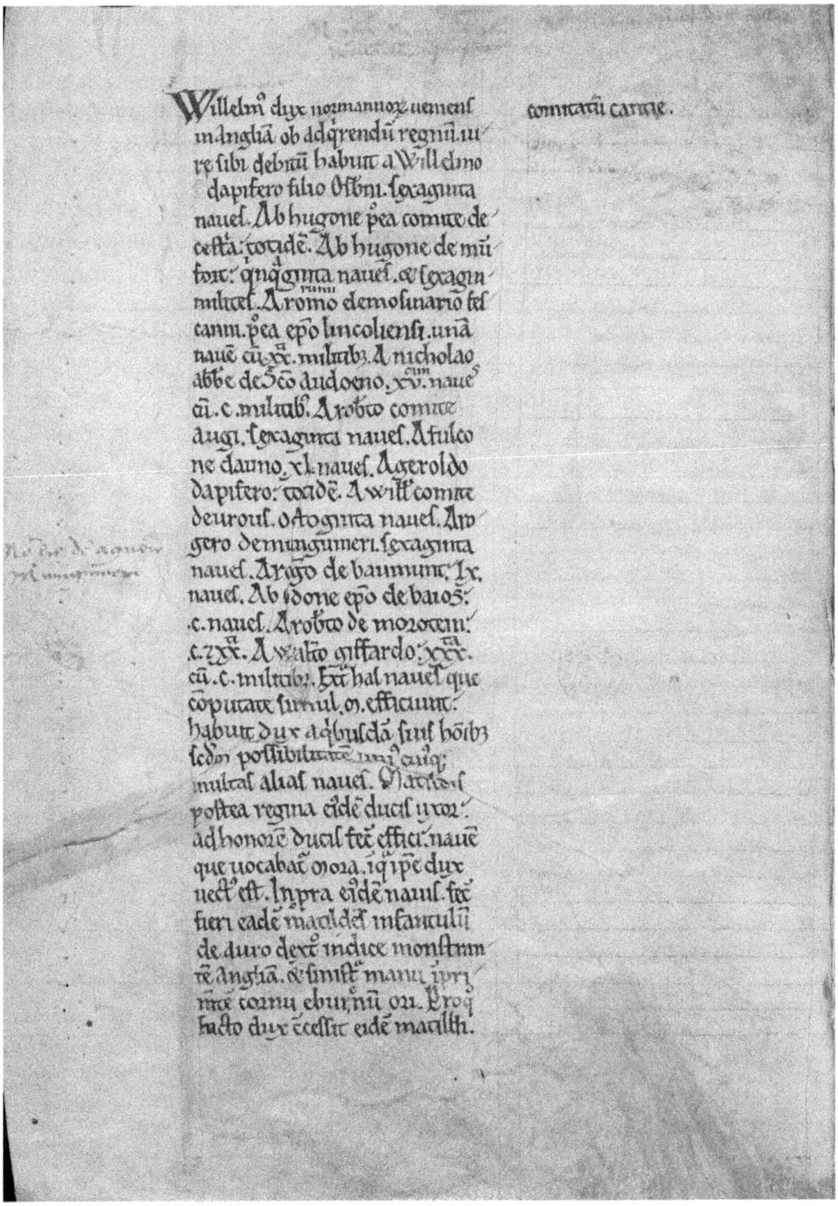

Plate 1. The Shiplist of William the Conqueror. Oxford, Bodleian Library, MS E Museo 93, folio 15v. The description of the *Mora*, and Mathilda's role in its production, begins on line 26 and continues to the end of the document.

goddesses on whose mysterious movements the success and failure of mortal events rested.[49] Mathilda's awareness of her uncertain future and the hazards that attended the invasion cannot be overstated. The scriptural themes of holy mysteries, apostolic revelation and ancient prophecy that were referenced in the foundation charter of her abbey reappear in the *Mora*. Mathilda's obligation to the shared enterprise of ducal authority was to stay behind and rule Normandy. Even so, I would posit, she created a conduit through which to appear on the beach at Pevensey, and thus lend her presence to the conflict in England.

Brigitte Bedos-Rezak has argued that in the eleventh and twelfth centuries, heraldry and other emblems of status were 'harnessed to yield meaning, a meaning that could mediate between worldly components as well as between the terrestrial and the divine…Materiality, the tangible, the concrete, and artifacts themselves entered into new relationships with the imaginary and the ideal.'[50] That is, material things enclosed within them the ideal, the spiritual, the absent. Bedos-Rezak claimed heraldry and items that reflected status especially functioned as 'extensions of a person'.[51] These were not merely symbols but material pieces of the one who sent them out into the world. Bedos-Rezak's claim, that 'people came to think about themselves and their identities increasingly through the medium of things' was directed at seals, whose figural aspect could stand in for their 'referent' as more than simply a representation, but an embodiment.[52] In this same way, therefore, Mathilda was signified on the English beach at Pevensey by the *Mora* and its golden child. Her ship's human figure, blowing a gonfanon, was strikingly unusual in eleventh-century maritime symbolism. Van Houts argues that the figurehead of the child on the *Mora*'s prow represented the unborn child Mathilda was carrying at the time of the launch. This was Mathilda's youngest daughter, Adela. If so, there could scarcely be a more intimate connection between

49 van Houts, 'The Echo of the Conquest', 152.

50 Bedos-Rezak, 'Medieval Identity,' 1503.

51 'Materiality, the tangible, the concrete, and artifacts themselves entered into new relationships with the imaginary and the ideal; so did the fleshy, corporeal, and physical with the spiritual… the semiotic realization of the actual took many new palpable forms: the transubstantiated Eucharist, natura as a locus of renewed interest, craftsmanship revalorized, ecclesia increasingly petrified, images and objects of devotion, the body as a site of inscription, the written word, heraldry and other emblems of status, signs of infamy, pilgrim signs, and those ultimate signs of identity, seals. As such technological extensions of a person came to circulate through society, people came to think about themselves and their identities increasingly through the medium of things.' Brigitte Miriam Bedos-Rezak, 'Semiotic Anthropology: The Twelfth-Century Approach' in *European Transformations: The Long Twelfth Century*, ed. Thomas F.X. Noble, and John Van Engen (Notre Dame, IN, 2012), 426–67 at 428.

52 Bedos-Rezak, 'Medieval Identity', 1490.

the warship and Mathilda's own body. Like the liturgical gifts of vestments discussed in the following chapters, Mathilda – through her gift of the *Mora* – inserted herself into an all-male space where to modern eyes she did not belong: the battlefield of the conquest.[53] She appeared there through a physical manifestation of her pregnant body and the child who would be its ultimate fruition. The Eucharistic controversy of real presence, so powerful in this period, would affect the medieval world for centuries to come. Its insistence on the participation of the bread and wine in Christ's corporeal body – not as a mere representation but as Christ's flesh and blood in reality – was a radical departure, but one that was fully embraced in Mathilda's world. Lanfranc, a prime mover of this theory, had already written his famous tract before the conquest; *De corpore et sanguine Domini* was produced *c.* 1060–3. The tract became orthodox doctrine and was regularly used in medieval florilegium. His role in the ducal court will be discussed in later chapters; he was a commanding figure there.[54] Lanfranc was prior at Bec when his abbot Herluin signed the foundation charter of Holy Trinity at its dedication. According to Orderic, Lanfranc came to Caen permanently in July of 1066, not long after the dedication. At this point, Mathilda's preparations for the invasion were in full swing.[55] Viewed against Lanfranc's doctrine regarding real presence, mediation and representation, Mathilda's *Mora* did more than simply represent her, it participated in her essence.

Like the conquest abbey she constructed, the *Mora* pulled Mathilda into the frame of the military venture to England. But her ship was more than just a remembrance, or even a symbol of her participation in the war. She was consciously channeled through this famous, visible gift. Her identity as the *Mora*'s patron was legendary; the extant shiplist of William the Conqueror, preserved at Fécamp, culminates in a lengthy description of her vessel. In the 35-line recording of the ships given to William, Mathilda's gift occupies 10 lines.[56] It monopolizes nearly one-third of the document. One is tempted to wonder if the true purpose of the Fécamp document was to celebrate her ship. Notably, the same monastery at Fécamp that preserved the shiplist also held

53 See Chapter Six: Flesh, 171–83.

54 The tradition of the *Vita Lanfranci*, that Lanfranc's opposition to Mathilda's marriage drove him into exile, has been all but debunked by recent historians. Bates first questioned the *Vita*'s account in the 1980s in *Normandy Before 1066*, 200–1 and has recently expanded his thoughts on the matter. Whatever the case, Lanfranc's approach to the marriage transformed into full-throated support by the 1060s. Bates, *William*, 108.

55 *OV*, iii, 144–7. There is some debate about Lanfranc's starting date at St Stephen's. H.E.J. Cowdrey theorized 1063 but was confounded by the absence of Lanfranc's signature on Holy Trinity's foundation charter. H.E.J. Cowdrey, *Lanfranc: Scholar, Monk, Archbishop* (Oxford, 2003), 24–5.

56 See Plate 1, 47.

a copy of the sibylline prophecy in its archive. If what van Houts theorizes is true, it is a short distance indeed between the sibylline inspiration for Mathilda's vessel and the manuscript that celebrates it in such detail.[57]

The *Mora* – first in the harbor at Dives-sur-Mer, then Valery-sur-Somme, and ultimately at Pevensey – was thus a prominent, visible reminder of Mathilda's presence. Indeed, her body and its potential were explicitly referenced, as the naval invasion commenced. According to contemporary accounts, the little golden child pointed its left hand toward England, while the right held the horn at its lips. The ship, I would argue, conflated the past and future, Normandy and England, Mathilda and William on the battlefield as the little child on its prow headed toward the English shore. The *Mora* referenced Mathilda's pregnant body and her child; it engaged the same themes of inheritance, prophecy and the conquest as the foundation charter of her monastery. The potential of Mathilda's pregnancy, embodied by oar and sails, bore William both physically and metaphorically into the unknown. Her essence, her person, her imperial blood and fecund body led the vessels of the conquest across the water and to triumph.

A NEW IDENTITY CAST IN STONE: HOLY TRINITY AFTER THE CONQUEST

In the aftermath of Norman victory, the possible became real; Mathilda's future was a mystery no more. Her new monastery was now poised to fulfill its potential as an Ottonian-style dynastic foundation. Mathilda headed a royal family that would rival, not ape, her Capetian kin. In his work on Dudo of St Quentin, Benjamin Pohl demonstrates that even before the English expedition, *translatio* and *imitatio imperii* were defining aspects of Norman ducal rule. These were explicitly displayed at Holy Trinity, even before the success of 1066. As it morphed from a monument of Mathilda's penance to that of her royal triumph, the monastic foundation's new identity concretized.[58] Drawing on Ottonian models allowed Mathilda to exchange her celebrated blood ties to Charlemagne – an extraordinary ancestor, but one who was already appropriated – for another set of illustrious connections.[59] Mathilda's genealogy was widely acknowledged to combine both royal 'stems'; Orderic described her as '…a kinswoman of Philip, the king of France, she sprang from the stock of the kings of Gaul and emperors of Germany and was renowned equally

57 van Houts, 'The Echo of the Conquest', 135–55.

58 Pohl, *Dudo of St Quentin*, 128.

59 The 'upstart' Salian kings, whose nascent dynasty was a frequent adversary of Mathilda's Flemish family, were considered by them as unworthy and illegitimate successors to Ottonian imperial glory. Her own blood ties to the Ottonians were, in fact, just as direct. See Chapter One: Blood, 11–33.

for nobility of blood and character'.[60] England had longstanding ties to the Ottonian world, moreover, that conveniently furthered Mathilda's adoption of a new identity.[61] Her establishment of Holy Trinity provides further suggestive evidence for this dynastic focus. In analyzing the endowments of Ottonian queens, Simon MacLean noted that 'they had a programmatic character and should be interpreted as conscious acts of dynasty-building: the grants were not passively reflective of how queenship worked – they were demonstrative acts which actively constructed it'.[62] Likewise, Mathilda's continued construction of Holy Trinity post-conquest was a constitutive element of her Ottonian-style of queenship.

There is no textual evidence for how the abbey's construction proceeded after the conquest so, as Baylé has noted, we are left to reconstruct its possible shape through archeological evidence.[63] Stylistic associations in architecture are challenging even when churches are relatively untouched; attempting to pin down their interpretation at a single time and place is difficult.[64] In the case of Holy Trinity, multiple building campaigns, as early as the twelfth century, have obscured much of the eleventh-century fabric of the original church. Nevertheless, some of Mathilda's abbey church can be uncovered. The details of her early design point again to an imperial sensibility that evoked the past. Instead of embracing innovation, Holy Trinity was consciously archaic and embraced Ottonian forms.[65]

60 *OV*, ii, 224.

61 Simon MacLean, 'Monastic reform and Royal Ideology in tenth-century England: Æthelfryth and Edgar in Continental Perspective', in *England and the Continent in the Tenth Century: Studies in Honour of Wilhelm Levison (1876–1947)*, ed. David Rollason and Hannah Williams (Turnhout, 2010), 255–74; Dan Ioan Mureşan 'Ego Wilhelmus victoriosus Anglorum basileus: Les circonstances de la synthèse impériale anglo-normande', *Annales de Normandie* 69:1 (2019), 107–64; Laura Wangerin, 'Holy relics, authority, and legitimacy in Ottonian Germany and Anglo-Saxon England', *HSJ* 27 (2016), 15–38; David A. Warner, 'Comparative approaches to Anglo-Saxon and Ottonian coronations', in *England and the Continent in the Tenth Century: Studies in Honour of Wilhelm Levison (1876–1947)*, ed. David Rollason and Hannah Williams (Turnhout, 2010), 275–92.

62 MacLean, *Ottonian Queenship*, 41.

63 Baylé, *La Trinité*, 18.

64 Leonie Hicks, 'Magnificent Entrances and Undignified Exits: Chronicling the Symbolism of Castle Space in Normandy', *JMH* 35:1 (2009), 52–69. For a broader study of monastic space, see Leonie V. Hicks, *Religious Life in Normandy, 1050–1300: Space, Gender and Social Pressure* (Woodbridge, 2007).

65 'Understood in this way, the architecture of La Trinité showed greater rigor in the scansion of space, an alliance of simplicity and harmony that the embellishments of the twelfth century distorted. In this way, it is linked to the essential criteria of the large structural churches of the north of France and of the Ottonian domain.' Maylis Baylé, 'La Trinité de Caen,' *Congrès archéologique de France* 132 (1978), 22–58, at 54.

Mathilda's church was a cruciform abbey, with an east-facing apse and a western massif facade flanked by two towers. These elements were standard-issue Anglo-Norman ducal style in church architecture and can be found in earlier versions at abbeys like Jumièges (*c.* 1030) and Countances (*c.* 1030).[66] Yet, while Holy Trinity followed these most basic outlines, some architectural anomalies can be dated convincingly to the first dedication of the abbey or shortly thereafter. While some of these physical characteristics drew direct imperial connections, as noted above, other structural elements responded to the same foundational, and radical, Lanfrancian Eucharistic liturgical philosophy that informed Mathilda's choices elsewhere.[67] Three specific physical characteristics are worthy of note; a tribune gallery at the original western end of the church, the construction of choir towers to frame its eastern apse, and a sequestered choir – completely inaccessible to the laity – elongated and partitioned off from the nave. These fundamental features of Mathilda's eleventh-century abbey, some no longer extant or visible, allow us to imagine a very different church than the present-day Abbaye-aux-Dames.

Holy Trinity's original westwork looked very different than its current west end, punctuated as it is now by three grand entrances (Plate 2). Maylis Baylé has shown that Holy Trinity initially had two side entrances on the western end, not a central entrance in the middle of the westwork.[68] Importantly, the western end featured a tribune gallery, now destroyed. Holy Trinity's original stair tower on the southwest corner is still visible today and it once led into the now-lost tribune gallery overlooking the nave.[69] Tribune galleries were an important statement of power with roots in imperial Rome.[70]

The tribune in the ancient world allowed for the metaphorical movement of the emperor between heaven and earth mirroring the theory that imperial rulers partook in both natures, divine and human. This philosophy of the ruler as 'persona mixta' is a direct antecedent, historians have long argued, for medieval anointing at coronations.[71] This liturgical rite accords to the anointed a share in divine power, if only through the office itself. Tribunes were a feature of Carolingian and Ottonian imperial church structures. There is some evidence that Norman rulers, too, were eager to make use of them

66 Jos Stover, 'Beschouwingen bij een "bouwschool": voretlijke elementen aan elfdeeeuwse kerken in Normandie' in *Bouwen en duiden: studies over architectuur en iconologie* (Canaletto, 1994), 53–77.

67 See below, 55–6 and Chapter Six: Flesh, 171–83.

68 Maylis Baylé, 'Les relations entre massif de façade et vaisseau de nefen Normandie avant 1080', *Cahiers de civilization médiévale*, 34: no. 135–6 (Juillet-décembre 1991): 225–35 at 232; Baylé, *La Trinité*, 21–22; Baylé, 'La Trinité de Caen', 35.

69 Baylé, 'La Trinité de Caen', 22–58 at 36.

70 Stover, 'Beschouwingen bij een "bouwschool"', 62.

71 See Chapter Four: Head, 115–44. Kantorowicz, *King's Two Bodies*. See also H.E.J. Cowdrey, 'The Anglo-Norman Laudes Regiae', *Viator* 12 (1981), 37–78.

Plate 2. Abbey of Holy Trinity, Caen. Westwork. The west end of the abbey is not its original. It was renovated after Mathilda's death by Abbess Cecelia, her daughter.

Plate 3. Abbey of Holy Trinity, Caen. The eastern stair towers are just visible on the exterior of the apse.

even before the conquest. Jos Stover has noted that eleventh-century abbey churches for men founded by the Norman dukes had galleries, including Jumièges and Mont-Saint-Michel. Using Baylé's evidence, Stover conceded that Holy Trinity should be added to the list of ducal foundations that utilized an imperial-style gallery. Mathilda's abbey church is the only Norman, or Anglo-Norman, example of a women's monastery with a tribune gallery on the west end.[72]

Mathilda's imperial signaling continued with the choir. It was built with two eastern stair towers, still just visible today, flanking the opening to the eastern apse (Plate 3). Because of their position, framing the opening to the choir, they are often called 'choir towers'. These are rarely found in eleventh-century construction. There are only two examples in Normandy: Holy Trinity and the later construction of Cerisy-la-Forêet.[73] Choir towers were what Stover called a 'regal' abbatial feature, that is, a characteristic of only those churches with particular connections to the ruling house.[74] While every Norman church had a transept crossing tower, early choir towers were only a feature of royal Norman abbeys.[75] Holy Trinity's example of this feature – the first in Normandy – would become *de rigeur* in the twelfth century. In the thirteenth century, moreover, after the conquest of Normandy by Philip II Augustus, choir towers were installed at St Stephen's in Caen and the cathedrals of Bayeux, Coutances and Lisieux. According to Stover, these later examples were directly related to Holy Trinity's earlier use as an expression of royal status.[76] Installed after the conquest's success, the choir towers can be seen as manifesting Mathilda's pre-conquest ambitions.

Immediately after the conquest, during Mathilda's lifetime, two adjustments were made to parts of the abbey church that had already been standing at the dedication in 1066: the choir was lengthened and the footprint of the abbey enlarged.[77] The choir was always inaccessible to the nave – there were no side entrances to it – and this was not changed. Holy Trinity's original

72 After the construction of Holy Trinity, moreover, Cerisy-la-Forêt (*c.* 1070–1100) and St Stephen's also adopted tribune galleries. Stover, 'Beschouwingen bij een "bouwschool"', 68–72.

73 The abbey of Cerisy-la- Forêt was a ducal abbey, foundationally influenced by the style and structure of Holy Trinity, especially its twelfth-century capitals. Baylé, *La Trinité*, 146–7.

74 Stover, 'Beschouwingen bij een "bouwschool"', 68–9.

75 'all royal churches that have retained their original choir section are equipped with choir towers, while we never find them in churches of a lower order, just like the gallery and the double tower façade'. Stover, 'Beschouwingen bij een "bouwschool"', 68.

76 Stover, 'Beschouwingen bij een "bouwschool"', 69.

77 'The original plan included a shorter choir, undoubtedly corresponding to the part of the building which was the subject of the dedication of 1066: indeed everything suggests this idea.' Baylé, *La Trinité*, 40.

choir, and this elongated second version, were both partitioned off from the main area of the nave by solid walls. Mathilda, once again, chose not to follow the newest fashion in architecture. The most prestigious eleventh-century royal abbeys in France at this time introduced an ambulatory choir. This new French innovation had radiating chapels that could accommodate the flow of the laity around the back of the choir. By contrast, the arrangement of Holy Trinity's choir followed an old 'Roman' style, like its western tribune gallery, and conformed to Ottonian structures.[78]

Holy Trinity's choir – elongated but cut off from the nave – may also reflect the contemporary impact of one influential theologian: Lanfranc. Valerie Chaix speculated that the abbeys in Lanfranc's particular orbit, built during the years of his involvement in Norman court life, embraced a rigorous style of monastic observance.[79] Lanfranc famously eschewed liturgical processions,[80] for instance, and suppressed any unnecessary movement in the space where the Eucharist was celebrated.[81] Chaix concurred with earlier opinions that the partitioned choir was a Roman imperial style. But she saw the revisitation of it as a signal of Lanfranc's philosophical embrace of Gregorian reform. Moreover, Lanfranc's approach to Eucharistic piety, especially his insistence on the actual physically present body of Christ as the host, encouraged the celebration of the mass away from the flow of lay traffic. It is this last element of Lanfranc's influence that accords closely with the choir's construction at Holy Trinity. Later chapters will show that Lanfranc's eucharistic philosophy had a profound influence on Mathilda's court.[82]

The women at Holy Trinity were not claustrated and regularly moved through the city. The leadership of the monastery, including its first and second abbesses, were active players in Caen's administrative authority, judicial process and civic life. As demonstrated above, their separation from lay affairs, such as the Norman Conquest, was inconceivable. Their corporate identity and purpose were closely knit to secular, indeed military, concerns. Yet their Eucharistic observance, through the construction of an elongated choir, inaccessible to the laity, accorded with the philosophical demands of a liturgy that celebrated Christ's real presence. The partitioned choir was a structural characteristic that reflected the monastery's embrace of Lanfranc's

78 Louis Grodecki, *L' Architecture Ottonienne*, 23.

79 Valerie Chaix, 'Les choeurs cloisonnés du monde anglo-normand dans la seconde moitié du XIe siècle', in *Ars aura gemmisque: prior mélanges en hommage a Jean-Pierre Caillet* (Turnhout, 2013), 241–9.

80 Benjamin Pohl, 'Processions, Power, and Public Display: Ecclesiastical Rivalry and Ritual in Ducal Normandy', *Journal of Medieval Monastic Studies* 6 (2017): 1–49.

81 Christophe Lazowski, 'La "mise en scène" d'une théologie eucharistique: la procession anglo-normande des Rameaux', in *Liturgie, pensée théologique et mentalités religieuses au haut Moyen Âge: Le témoignage des sources liturgiques* (Munster, 2016), 127–60.

82 See Chapter Six: Flesh, 171–83.

liturgical radicalism which, by the time of Holy Trinity's construction, was widely accepted.[83] Stover noted that Norman abbeys and churches with partitioned choirs – St Stephen's would also construct such a choir – were all exempt from lay interference. Holy Trinity, free from such obligations, fits the profile.

Both nineteenth-century architectural historians like Ruprich-Robert and modern ones like Stover save their highest praise for St Stephen's and its technological advances. But both indicated, if only in passing, that Holy Trinity's construction drew unique imperial connections. Of the architectural 'regal elements' outlined above, all were a part of Holy Trinity's original early construction. Some of these features, like the tribune gallery, were dismantled to make way for the innovations of the centuries that followed, and are now hidden or destroyed, yet architectural historians have exposed the evidence remaining in Holy Trinity's fabric. They include a double-towered western massif with side entrances, a tribune gallery accessed by stair towers, choir towers flanking the eastern apse, and an elongated, sequestered choir. Stover maintained that only one other extant eleventh-century example includes all of the features at Holy Trinity: the Ottonian women's foundation of Gernrode Abbey in Germany, commonly called St Cyriakus.[84]

OTTONIAN ANTECEDENTS

Founded by the Margrave Gero *c.* 959 in the East Saxon March, Gernrode Abbey, or St Cyriakus, was a house of canonesses with important imperial connections.[85] Early in Gernrode's history, it was placed under imperial protection by Otto I. The first abbess of Gernrode was Hathui, the niece of Empress Matilda of Saxony, Otto's mother. The abbey was intended as a burial place and memorial site for Gero and his two sons, who both pre-deceased him. Gernrode Abbey had numerous links to other imperial Ottonian women's foundations. Gernrode was part of a 'prayer confraternity' of imperial women's houses that included Quedlinburg, Gandersheim, and Essen.[86] Abbess Adelaide of Quedlinburg

83 See Chapter Six: Flesh, 171–83.

84 Stover, 'Beschouwingen bij een "bouwschool"', 62.

85 Gero had obtained the relics of Saint Cyriakus on pilgrimage and donated them to the abbey; it was rededicated to the saint and retains that name today.

86 There may be some evidence of manuscript exchange between the communities as well; a tenth-century 'Hathuui' appears on a manuscript of Jerome's letters from Quedlinburg. Helene Scheck, 'Queen Mathilda of Saxony and the Founding of Quedlinburg: Women, Memory, and Power', *Historical Reflections* 35:3 (2009), 21–36 at 28. See also *A Companion to the Abbey of Quedlinburg in the Middle Ages*, ed. Karen Blough (Leiden, 2022), 51. Gretsch argues that commentaries and psalters on loan from German houses, like Gernrode, influenced the tenth century ecclesiastical reform instituted by Athelstan and his court. Gretsch assumed, without evidence, that a male cleric was the author of the Psalm commentary:

became Gernrode's second abbess. Gernrode had the same exalted status as other imperial abbeys led by Ottonian royal women: all four abbesses had imperial status as 'princes' with attendant imperial rights.[87] Gernrode was still considered a key member of the imperial abbatial quartet until the thirteenth century. Thus, in the 1050s, as Mathilda conceived the plans for her church, Gernrode was a prestigious Ottonian house with an imperial pedigree that might have provided a suitable model for Holy Trinity.

Gernrode's construction gives some clues to how Mathilda's early version of Holy Trinity might have looked before its later renovations, though Gernrode experienced 'modernizations' of its own that obscure some parallels.[88] Gernrode's tribune remains intact as does its western 'massif' end with side entrances (Plate 4).[89] Ottonian galleries did not provide architectural support; they were liturgical, ceremonial features found only in women's abbey churches.[90] At Holy Trinity, Mathilda's original tribune followed this Ottonian practice.[91] Gernrode is considered to have significantly influenced later German Romanesque architecture but is not generally studied as an antecedent for structures in Normandy. Indeed, Holy Trinity is the only church that seems to have assumed so many of its features. Mathilda referenced a unique set of Ottonian buildings in her construction of Holy Trinity: imperial women's houses.

There is no positive evidence that Mathilda was familiar with Gernrode Abbey; however, her family did have ties to Gero. Gero and Herman Billung, Mathilda's great-great-grandfather, were brothers-in-arms in support of Otto I, and were both granted margravates by Otto along the Baltic Sea. Herman proved to be a valuable ally; he offered military support to Otto especially in

---

'perhaps one of the canons who acted as priests and spiritual advisers to the canonesses'. Given the high level of literacy in imperial circles, this assumption is not supportable. Mechthild Gretsch, *The intellectual foundations of the English Benedictine reform* (Cambridge, 1994), 432–6 at 435.

87 Hans K. Schulze and Günter W. Vorbrodt, *Das Stift Gernrode* (Böhlau, 1965), 89–90.

88 Gernrode's current rounded apse to the west is not original. The rounded western end mirrors Gernrode's eastern circular apse creating a very traditional Ottonian, 'double-apse' plan – as can be seen at Hildesheim – but it was installed in the twelfth century.

89 The change necessitated a shift in axis, making Gernrode something of an architectural curiosity. A crypt was also added later – it is mentioned in a source from 1149.

90 Grodecki, *Ottonienne*, 136.

91 By contrast, Norman tribune galleries installed in the eleventh century – at Jumièges, for instance – were constructed as stabilizing elements for support. Grodecki, *Ottonienne*, 136.

Plate 4. Abbey of Gernrode (St Cyrakios), Saxony-Anhalt, Germany. Westwork. Gernrode's west end likely resembles the original west entrance of abbey of Holy Trinity, Caen.

troublesome Saxony, the heart of the Ottonian dynasty.[92] Herman's reward for this support included a close relationship with the emperor which extended to his daughter, Mathildis; indeed, her marriage gift from Otto himself included the town of Ename which she expanded in an architectural style that honored their Ottonian patron.[93]

As mentioned in the previous chapter, Mathilda did have significant exposure to Ottonian styles of sacred architecture in her own home of Flanders. Between 974 and 977, Otto II restored part of the monastery's possessions in East Francia. He was also a benefactor of their architectural renovations, begun under Abbot Odwinus (*c.* 981–98) that continued into the twelfth century. These produced an abbey church in the Ottonian style though, over the course of time, St Bavo's appearance changed, melding architectural influences from other regions.[94] St Peter's and the abbey of St Bavo in Ghent both bore Ottonian elements with which Mathilda would have been very familiar. In addition to these Ottonian examples, in 1049 Mathilda's family also obtained Ename; a palatial Ottonian outpost at their eastern border.

After the Salians claimed the imperial dignity, Baldwin V regularly clashed with the emperors and, after a particularly hard-won conflict, the cost of reparations paid to Baldwin V and Adela was the town and castle of Ename which had been held by his own great grandmother, Mathildis, many years earlier.[95] When Baldwin V and Adela claimed Ename, it was considered 'a showpiece of Ottonian steadfastness'.[96] The church of St Lawrence, especially with its blind arches, and western choir with side entrances, was a monument to Ottonian style. Mathildis and her family had consciously chosen to evoke their imperial patron with the style of their church.[97] Adela and Baldwin acquired Ename in 1047 and quickly made it their own. By 1063 they had founded a new Benedictine community there.[98]

Stylistic links are regularly used, in the realm of architectural history, to indicate connections between structures but those hypotheses can only be suggestive. Even so, there is little doubt that Mathilda, and her parents,

92 'He entrusted Herman Billung with the margraviate along the Baltic Sea and Gero with the other one, known as Nordmark…' Callebaut, 'Ename', 227.

93 Callebaut, 'Ename', 239.

94 M.C. Laleman, 'Het stenen verleden. Een beknopt overzicht van bouwactiviteiten, bouwkundige ontwikkeling en monastieke architectuur' in *Gand & Blandinium: de Gentse abdijen van Sint-Pieters en Sint-Baafs*, ed. G. Declerqc (1997), 115–46.

95 See Chapter One: Blood, 13.

96 Callebaut, 'Ename', 242.

97 Callebaut, 'Ename', 239.

98 Adela and Baldwin built a new abbey for them, over the remains of an ancient Roman gate across the road. St Lawrence remained the comital church in Ename. Callebaut, 'Ename', 242.

were familiar with Ottonian architecture. In 1047, years before Mathilda left for Normandy, Ename was in her family's gift. Perhaps the origins of the Ottonian settlement, her grandmother's dower, made Ename an especially fitting residence.[99]

The imperial abbeys of Quedlinburg, Essen, Gandersheim and Gernrode were vital to Ottonian identity but when the Salian emperors took their place, the centrality of these imperial foundations was lost. The legitimizing function of the 'prayer confraternity' of Gandersheim, Quedlinburg, Essen and Gernrode was dissolved and the Salian emperors turned their backs on the Saxon foundations. Instead, the Salian dynasty established its own site of dynastic celebration at the center of their rule: Speyer.[100]

These events played out and, indeed, were woven into the fabric of Mathilda's family and life experience. The Salian emperors' abandonment of the Saxon abbeys – with all of their storied imperial *memoria* and legitimizing function – meant that these elements of imperial identity were 'up for grabs'. Mathilda and her family could appropriate Saxon imperial identity, especially that which was expressed through royal women's religious houses. I argue that Mathilda's construction of Holy Trinity in the Ottonian mold was a conscious attempt to lay hold of that tradition and usurp it.[101]

In the next chapter, we will see how Holy Trinity's relic collection also mirrored that of imperial Ottonian houses. The holy pieces of saints' bodies held at the imperial women's houses did not generally perform miracles.[102] Likewise, in its 700-year history, there are no accounts of healing or visions within its walls performed by the abbesses and nuns at Holy Trinity. Despite its important collection of relics, no extant narrative claims miracles for them.[103] I would argue, however, that Holy Trinity's foundation miracle was

99 It may have even inspired Adela to commission her *Epitaph of Adelheid*, the precise date of which remains unknown.

100 In fact, the Saxon abbeys harbored rebellious aristocrats who defied the Salians. Blough, *Abbey of Quedlinburg*, 24–5.

101 Holy Trinity's primary responsibility was much like the Ottonian houses, 'to preserve the memory of its patrons, to advocate for their souls in the spiritual realm, and to further royal interests in the material world by cultivating the image of royal or imperial piety'. Scheck, 'Queen Mathilda of Saxony', 22.

102 Quedlinburg's foundress, Mathilda of Saxony, was credited with miracles; her acts of sanctity were modest and highlighted her care for the poor, and her ability to see the future on her deathbed, and revealed her skills at soothing a doe who had swallowed consecrated wine. Gilsdorf 'Queenship and Sanctity,' 82.

103 There is evidence for an early chronicle history of Holy Trinity as late as 1525. It is mentioned by Gervaise de la Rue who claimed it was organized as an annal. 'The abbess in these documents sometimes quoted the early the chronicle of her abbey…they wrote of the memorable facts which occurred in the year, on different (parchment) rolls of great length, certainly written within the abbey of

adopted immediately after its dedication: the Norman Conquest. The extant documents created by the community in the twelfth century and beyond regularly evoke the 'miracle story' of its birth; the victorious Norman invasion of England. The collective memory fashioned by the women of Holy Trinity, of which it was both a central player and a constitutive agent, was intended to inform the social practice of the Anglo-Norman realm. Consequently, the women within Holy Trinity maintained their connection to the most famous invasion of the eleventh century by means of the documents they commissioned, created and preserved.

Manuscript production at Holy Trinity served, from the founding of the community, to establish the special place of the abbey in the Anglo-Norman realm. Charter production and preservation formed the bedrock on which the community of women stood. In the early twelfth century, the community undertook some of the most famous, and precocious, bureaucratic instruments of their day.[104] These significant bureaucratic initiatives, however, were the work of the next generation of Norman royal women. The documents produced during Mathilda's life time, from 1059 to 1083, form the center of the following analysis of Holy Trinity. And thus, we turn to the administrative activity of the community in its earliest years.

LITERACY AND DOMINATION: THE QUEEN AND THE ABBESS

Holy Trinity's foundation charter was only the first textual production of Abbess Matilda and Queen Mathilda as they used documentary practice to push forward their agenda. In 1080, another pancarte was issued on behalf of the abbey which indicated Holy Trinity's rapid growth.[105] The pancarte recorded considerable increases in rents, tithes and land holdings; the fourteen years between the two charters saw a flood of new donations. England's queen now

Holy Trinity itself. Abbess Isabella of Bourbon appended the entries of these rolls to the chronicle of St Trinity, in the memoirs of a trial she pursued in 1525 against the inhabitants of St Giles.' Gervaise de la Rue, *Essais sur le ville de Caen, Volume II* (Caen, 1820), 28–9. See Chapter Three: Fingers, 75–104, for a discussion of the relic collection Mathilda gathered for Holy Trinity.

104 Catherine Letouzey-Réty examines the surveys in connection to the other twelfth-century products of Holy Trinity's scriptorium, including the mortuary *rotulus* of Abbess Matilda, created by Abbess Cecelia and the nuns, *c.* 1113, to mark the death of their first shepherd. Catherine Letouzey-Réty, 'Memory and Documentary Culture at Holy Trinity Abbey, Caen in the eleventh–twelfth centuries', in *Gender, Memory and Documentary Culture, c.900–1300*, ed. Laura L. Gathagan and Charles Insley (Woodbridge, 2025), 254–70.

105 BNF 5650, folio 34v–36v. Printed in Musset, *Les actes* (no. 11), 92–5; *Regesta* (no. 59), 271–86.

found herself with an entire kingdom's wealth in her hands – it was inevitable that Holy Trinity would see a significant increase in income. The pancarte exists in two versions; the original, shorter version was begun in 1080 and contains only that date. The longer second version contains more details about the properties and contains additional grants; it also uses 1080 as its initial date, but a completion date of 1082. Both versions reveal Mathilda's active deal-making at work, especially in her use of countergifts.[106] She bartered and exchanged manors and rights for Holy Trinity, encouraging numerous donors to support her new abbey by tempting them with countergifts. Countergifts were cash payments made to persuade a donor, to oil the machinery of a transaction. This was one of Mathilda's characteristic maneuvers. Emily Zack Tabuteau was struck by how often Mathilda used countergifts to move her business along smoothly. 'No other person engaged in the same practice, nor did any other church benefit from it, with anything like the same frequency…'[107] Tabuteau has noted that countergifts were sometimes used to manipulate the consent of a reluctant benefactor, or to give the public impression, recorded in a charter, that a recalcitrant consenter had capitulated. In the 1082 version of the pancarte, Mathilda explicitly recorded a countergift at least fifteen times.[108]

Queen Mathilda bought land, mills, churches, vineyards, sheaves of tithe, and the services of peasants; she paid off reluctant landlords and fief holders, paid grants in exchange for donations, and redeemed lands and the services owed from lands, all so that her foundation would prosper. She coerced, made deals and exchanges, applied pressure, and provided ready money, no doubt from her English kingdom, to allow for the growth and fiscal health of her abbey. Her donations to Holy Trinity in cash and lands, exclusive of English estates, add up to millions of dollars in modern monetary valuation.[109]

Lucien Musset has suggested that the exchanges Mathilda undertook made collecting rents more convenient for the abbess.[110] That may have motivated some of the adjustments, but the queen and the abbess were happy to accept certain far-flung holdings that appealed to them. The islands of Jersey and Guernsey, for instance, seemed to have been worth an annual trip to collect rents and tithes. Ouistreham and Quettehou further up the coast of Normandy were a day's journey away but offered salt pans, fishing rights and

106 Emily Zack Tabuteau, *Transfers of Property in Eleventh-Century Normandy Law* (Chapel Hill, NC, 1988), 115–17.

107 Tabuteau, *Transfers of Property*, 28.

108 In almost every case, the countergift is specifically mentioned as the motive for the donation or consent. Tabuteau, *Transfers of Property*, 115–17.

109 Lucien Musset, 'La Reine Mathilde et la fondation de la Trinité de Caen (Abbayes-aux-Dames)', *Mémoires de l'Académie des Sciences, Arts et Belles-Lettres de Caen* (1984), 191–210 at 200.

110 Musset, 'La Reine', 201.

commercial monopolies that would support the nuns for hundreds of years. Rents and tithes from English properties were added to Holy Trinity's balance sheet, making travel to its shores a new, and permanent, feature of the abbess's obligations and privileges.

It was one of Mathilda's exchanges that would result in a legal dispute between Holy Trinity and St Stephen's abbeys, the first time the women had the need, and the opportunity, to prove their mettle against an opponent. It would certainly not be the last time the women of Holy Trinity engaged in a dispute to protect their interests. The case demonstrates the occasional tension between the two monastic communities as both sought to expand across the city as it grew. More importantly for the current study, it also provides evidence for Mathilda's response when the jurisdiction of her foundation was threatened, and for the lengths to which she would go to protect her abbey's interests. As she and her husband faced off across the bargaining table, she showed characteristic resolve. Mathilda may have even used her own terminal illness to win the day.

Sometime before 1080, Queen Mathilda exchanged land in Fresne-Camillie with her brother-in-law Bishop Odo of Bayeux on behalf of Holy Trinity. The property in Fresne-Camillie was originally given to her by Adelaide Hadlup, a nun at the abbey. In exchange, Mathilda gained from Odo two churches just outside of Caen closer to her monastery; St Étienne-le-Vieux and St Martin.[111] She donated these churches with their tithes – and the rights of jurisdiction over them – to Holy Trinity. Probably no more than two years later, Gilbert, the third abbot of St Stephen's, began construction of a new church. It was dedicated to St Nicholas and would eventually be called 'St Nicholas-in-the-Fields' as it was in the suburbs of Caen, outside the city walls. The site was meant to serve the suburban community to the west, not far from the monks' monastic precinct. The site of the new construction, however, was located on the very property Odo had exchanged with Mathilda merely two years before, which now belonged to Holy Trinity. Only after construction had already begun did the monks realize, no doubt with some discomfiture, that the abbess of Holy Trinity would have spiritual authority over their newly constructed suburban church of St Nicholas. While evidence from absence is not proof, there is no record of Queen Mathilda, or Abbess Matilda, calling a halt to the monks' project as it hummed along. Indeed, it proceeded to completion, on an estate that both women knew very well was Holy Trinity's.

Mathilda's donation was well attested; the pancarte included signatures from all the local bishops and secular lords in the region, though the Abbot Gilbert of St Stephen's was not among them. There is no doubt that the property remained in the hands of the abbess and nuns throughout the monks' construction of

[111] *Regesta* (no. 59), 271–2, 279.

their new church.[112] Thus, the monks had invested in the building project – planned the site, consulted builders, acquired materials and quarried stone – all unaware that the property was not theirs to use. Abbess Matilda, certainly cognizant of her rights from the beginning, waited to press Holy Trinity's claims. She only demanded that her jurisdiction over St Nicholas be acknowledged after the church was built and, evidently, after Queen Mathilda had returned to Caen from England to defend her community.

At this point in the chronology, one feels compelled to ask a few questions. First, if Mathilda's exchange with Odo, and subsequent donation, was so well attested why was Abbot Gilbert unaware of it? The answer may lie in the timing of Gilbert's abbatial election. In 1079 William Bona Anima, the second abbot of St Stephen's, left the brothers at Caen and was made archbishop of Rouen. Father Gilbert stepped into the leadership of St Stephen's the same year. In this transition moment, perhaps some information about lands and tenants could have been mislaid or forgotten. While the first record of Mathilda's exchange with Odo is 1080, the actual arrangement of the trade – which resulted in the abbess's prerogatives over St Étienne-le-Vieux and St Martin – might easily have been arranged at least a year earlier. Perhaps this was just as Gilbert assumed his new role. Adjusting for the time necessary to reach the agreement of all parties, one could push the negotiation back a year before it was committed to vellum. Certainly, the final version of the agreement seems to have been signed at least two years after the gift was made. This chronology is only suggestive, of course. The exchange is recorded in both the 1080 and 1082 versions of the pancarte but not in the original foundation charter of 1066, the only *terminus a quo* date for the exchange.

Some indication exists that Abbot Gilbert was less well versed in buying and selling real estate than his predecessor, William Bona Anima.[113] A record of the purchases of the first three abbots was produced between 1080 and 1083, and recounts for Mathilda and William all the purchases made by Lanfranc, William Bona Anima and Gilbert. Abbot William is credited with over 37

112 'Dedit etiam hec eadem Adelaidis: Fraxinivillam et Maisnile Urselli, quas ego Mathildis regina excambivi ecclesie sancte Marie Baiocensi per Odonem ecclesie eiusdem antistitem, concessu domini mei regis, pro ecclesiis cum decimis sanct Stephani et Sancti Martini Cadomi, sicut Anschitillus filius Urf eas tenuerat, et pro ecclesia sancti Georgii de castro Cadomi (Adelaide also gave Fresne-Camilly and Mesnil-Oury which I, Queen Mathilda, exchanged for the cathedral church of St Mary, by means of Odo Bishop of Bayeux, by the concession of my lord, with the tithes of the churches of St Étienne-le-Vieux and St Martin, Caen, as they were held by Anschitil son of Urf, and for the church of St George in the castle of Caen).' *Regesta*, 279.

113 David Spear concluded that fewer properties were available as Caen developed, but that Gilbert might also have been unwilling or ill equipped to make purchases in the same way. David S. Spear, 'William Bona Anima, abbot of St Stephen's of Caen, 1070–1079', *HSJ* 1 (1989), 51–60.

purchases of property for the abbey, while Abbot Gilbert made only nine.[114] While Abbot William clearly had a talent for real estate development, Spear has shown that Gilbert may not have relished this component of his abbatial responsibilities.[115] Thus there might have been, in addition to the confusion regarding land and tenants during the transition, a lack of experience or aptitude on the part of the abbot.

As for Abbess Matilda, Queen Mathilda's itinerary seems to have affected her timing. Queen Mathilda's last act in Normandy was a charter signed at Bonneville-sur-Touques dated July 14, 1080.[116] Mathilda spent Christmas 1080 in Gloucester and remained in England for the entirety of the next two years, 1080–1082, and into early 1083. Her juridical activity and charter attestations place her variously in Salisbury (February 1081), Winchester (May 1081), throughout the West Midlands (autumn 1081), at Ely (late 1081), and somewhere in the south of England, most likely Hampshire and Wiltshire (late 1082, early 1083). William and their sons – Robert, William Rufus and Henry – accompanied their father as they managed the renewed threat of Fulk Rechin's attacks on Maine. Her absence on important charters in Normandy, signed by the entire ducal/royal family, provide further evidence that Mathilda remained in England alone. By July 1083, she was back in Caen. It was at this moment the legal proceedings begin regarding the nuns' jurisdiction over the monks' new church, St Nicholas-in-the-Fields. Thus, Abbess Matilda did not act until her queen had stepped foot on Norman soil.

Once Mathilda returned, the monks and abbot realized their difficulty. One can only imagine their reaction. Did the community at St Stephen's cast about for a solution themselves? Either Gilbert and the monks were unable to suggest something suitable or they felt out of their depth. Whatever the case, the monks were unable to convince the queen and the abbess to release their claim to the property now underneath the monk's new church. They turned to their own founder, Duke William, now king of England, for assistance. The monks' miscalculation would cost him considerably. Facing William as an adversary might have convinced Abbess Matilda to yield had she not been supported by Queen Mathilda. The abbess chose not to press her claim before her queen and founder returned from her long stay in England. But with Mathilda at hand, the women refused to concede to their duke/king

114 Musset, *Les actes*, 103–11.

115 Spear, 'William Bona Anima', 52. Serlo of Bayeux, a canon and poet living in Caen, wrote scathingly satirical verse criticizing Abbot Gilbert. According to Serlo, Gilbert gorged himself while the monks fasted, was more like a juggler and a buffoon than an abbot and giggled excessively. Celestine Hippeau, *L'abbaye de Saint-Étienne de Caen* (Caen, 1855), 31–2; Elisabeth van Houts, 'The Fate of Priests' Sons in Normandy with special reference to Serlo of Bayeux', *HSJ* 25 (2013), 57–105.

116 *Regesta* (no. 175), 577–84.

without gaining something valuable in return. To satisfy the community of Holy Trinity, and the queen at their back, William had to make significant concessions.

Three different charters were produced as a result of William's negotiations with Holy Trinity in the summer of 1083. All three are extant in the original. They were first analyzed by Lucien Musset and then examined by David Bates as both historians attempted to untangle the relationship between the documents.[117] The manuscripts reveal the chronology of the legal challenge and its resolution. Within these three parchments, moreover, a careful reading may allow for something else to emerge: the character of Mathilda of Flanders, the woman at the heart of the dispute.

The first charter was drawn up by the monks at St Stephen's and dated July 18, 1083.[118] It describes William's first attempts to mediate between the two parties and outlined new rights for Holy Trinity. Preserved by the monks, it has neither signa nor seal and does not appear to have arrangements for either. The document claims that William, in order to bring about an agreement, did two things for the nuns. First, he allowed them to take control of a large portion of his land, namely the suburbs of Calix and Caen, just outside the city walls to the southeast of the city. This property was close to their parochial church of St Giles and to the center of their administrative base. The abbess and nuns were allowed to take over the buildings and houses already there with the exception of three houses William owned on the bank of the Orne. He also specified that he would retain his river rights in the area.[119] The other additional constraint on the women's new expansion was that they could not pursue business for profit with William's merchants in that section of town.[120] This suburban property would, in effect, repay Holy Trinity for the houses that the monks would now hold in the suburbs of the west and on which St Nicholas-in-the-Fields was constructed. In exchange, the nuns would allow

117 Musset, *Les actes*, 113–19 (no. 17 and 17 bis), *Regesta* (no. 64), 298–300.

118 This document was preserved at St Stephen's. Caen, Archives de Calvados, H1830, no. 4.

119 'from the road in front of the home of young Godfrey, by the divide taken through the wall into Fulcold's garden, up to the 44 perches appointed, all the way to a stone that is there and from that stone, across towards the church, continued to the right pass by the barn, and also from Godfrey's home, divided through to the Saxon's house down to the water'. *Regesta*, 300.

120 Version II reads 'But I retain the last three houses situated on the water in my lordship, and also the whole shore and all the water next to the burg itself, and none of my burghers should be received [by the nuns] in the burg itself, or if staying in a house in Caen for a fee.' ('Retineo autem tres ultimas domos super aquam sitas in domino meo, rivagium quoque totum et totam aquam iuxta ipsum burgum et ut in ipso burgo nullus meus recipiatur burgensis vel in Cadomo in domo per mercedem manens.') The last phrase, 'vel in Cadomo in domo per mercedam manens' ('or staying in a house in Caen for a fee') is inserted in the monks' final version (Version III) but does not appear in Version II.

St Stephen's to have control of all the new houses built in the precinct of St Nicholas church. Holy Trinity would concentrate on a new expansion in the west and southwest portions of the city, while the monks would continue to expand toward Bayeux in the northeast. William gave up his own land outside the walls of Caen and allowed the abbess and nuns rights to it.

More was needed, however, before William could convince the women to let go. Despite the exchange of property and tenants closer to their abbey, the nuns clearly wanted to maintain some influence in their former holding. So, while the women of Holy Trinity allowed the monks to hold all the *new* houses on their former property, they negotiated to keep the tithes and jurisdiction of those parishioners who currently lived there; those inhabitants remained Holy Trinity's tenants. Even more, after those tenants died and their property passed into new hands, the abbess and nuns would retain rights over those properties in perpetuity.[121] All of these terms were laid out in the first unsigned, unsealed charter, which both Musset and Bates designate 'Version I'.[122] As noted above, the document has no arrangement for sealing and no autograph signa, but listed as 'testes' are Bishop Gilbert of Bayeux, Bishop Michael of Avranches, Bishop Gilbert of Lisieux, Abbot Baldwin of Bury St Edmunds, Robert of Mortain, Robert of Bellême, Osbern Giffard, Hugh de Port, 'and many others'.[123]

The second version of the agreement, also dated 18 July 1083, was preserved in the archive of Holy Trinity. The original charter is still extant but is now held privately.[124] It has autograph signa, including: Mathilda, William, Robert Curthose, William Rufus, Robert of Mortain, Gilbert bishop of Bayeux, Gilbert bishop of Lisieux, Baldwin abbot of Bury St Edmunds (and William's physician), Baldwin bishop of Bayeux, Samson, Robert of Bellême, Alan of Brittany, Bishop Michael of Avranches, Richard de Cours, Hugh de Port, William of Tornebu.[125] It varies in important ways from the first version the monks drafted for their use; it includes two critical new concessions that considerably undercut the monks' position in their new property. The second agreement allows the abbess and nuns of Holy Trinity to maintain their jurisdiction over the two original churches in their gift, that is, St Étienne-le-Vieux and St Martin, along with the income and tithes of both. The monks now retained only the jurisdiction over the newly built St Nicholas church, but lost all rights and privileges over the other two churches in the area permanently.

121 Five tenants are named specifically as exceptions to this agreement. Perhaps those five either moved in after the construction started or served St Stephen's in a particular way.

122 Musset, *Les actes*, Version I, 113–14; *Regesta*, Version I, 299–300.

123 'et alii plures…' *Regesta*, 300.

124 A photograph of the original is reproduced in Musset's 1963 published version of the acts of Holy Trinity; Musset, *Les actes*, Plate VI.

125 This may be the same Samson who was the head of Mathilda's spy network. See Chapter Five: Womb, 145–67.

The monks did retain rights to the cemetery of St Étienne-le-Vieux, but all the other tithes and jurisdictional privileges are regained by the nuns. Musset and Bates refer to this document as 'Version II'.[126]

The other notable innovation in this second version of the agreement is a list of names and occupations of 67 original parishioners over whom the nuns would retain rights.[127] The tenants who would remain under the nuns' control in Version I are now explicitly identified by name in Version II. These tenants were settled in the contested area before the monks built the church and would remain under the jurisdiction of the nuns. A list of the names of these 67 was drawn up and also replicated in St Stephen's archive with identifying descriptors, such as the parishioner's occupation or relations. These provide a snapshot of the nuns' tenants and, more broadly, of life in Caen in the eleventh century.[128] The properties held by the 67 tenants stayed within Holy Trinity's jurisdiction in perpetuity. Even after the death of these tenants, the chain of title would lead back to the abbesses and nuns into the future forever. These are significant changes from the original unsigned draft and represent important concessions won by the women of Holy Trinity.

An original of the third version exists in the records of St Stephen's and is almost identical to the nuns' version. It outlines the same agreement but the signa are different. It bears William's autograph cross, and two other lines of autograph signa, with non-autograph crosses; but neither Mathilda's cross nor signa is included. This has led both Musset and Bates to conclude that Mathilda was dead by the time this final agreement was drawn up. The *terminus ad quem* for this original version of the charter, then, is the date of Mathilda's death: November 2, 1083. Unlike the first iteration of the agreement with William, by the time the third version was drafted, the women of Holy Trinity had regained authority over the two original churches, as well as the new property in the southeast. The monks were also compelled to make a record of Holy Trinity's tenants in the property, naming and recording the 67 parishioners over whom the abbess still retained jurisdiction indefinitely.

The timing of the legal battle outlined above reveals two pieces of evidence that relate to Queen Mathilda. First, the legal claim was presented only after the monks had already begun to build the church of St Nicholas-in-the-Fields. The language of the charter makes it clear that the new church's spiritual jurisdiction was in the abbess's hands through Queen Mathilda's

126 Musset, *Les actes*, 118–19, *Regesta*, 300–1. (Version II in both Musset and *Regesta*),

127 Musset, *Les actes*, 7 bis, 119.

128 The tenants include clerics, students, farmers, carters, cobblers, drapers, parchment makers, fullers, seamstresses, artisans who worked in horn, pelterers, tailors, ploughman, and cheesemakers. The document also provides evidence for Caen's place in the ongoing dispute about clerical celibacy; one tenant, Godfred, was a priest who lived with his grandson. 'Ansorum nepotis Berengarii presbiteri', Musset, *Les actes*, 119.

financial arrangements in 1080. But the claim over the jurisdiction was undertaken only after the church had been built, when Mathilda returned to Caen from England. Second, St Stephen's new suburban complex was just under 2 kilometers away from Holy Trinity – about a 20-minute walk. It is inconceivable that Abbess Matilda was unaware of the monks' construction. That the building works were situated within a neighborhood where 67 tenants owed rent and service to the abbey of Holy Trinity makes the situation unambiguous. There is simply no possibility that Abbess Matilda would be unconscious of the construction on St Nicholas-in-the-Fields taking place on Holy Trinity's property. But the abbess took no action. Only on Mathilda's return from England was the parley set in motion.

Second, if one accepts the dating of Musset and Bates, the final negotiation of the transaction related to the new St Stephen's church was underway while Queen Mathilda was dying. Mathilda was alive when William was pushed to make his initial compromises with her community. The first detailed, signed record of the settlement, Version II, bore her signature cross. Yet by the time the second version of the accord had been drafted for the archives, Version III, she was dead.

Did Mathilda use her terminal illness as a lever to advance the claims of Holy Trinity? If she indeed had a sense of her life reaching its end, she may have pressed to have the negotiations settled. Clearly the women of Holy Trinity waited until Mathilda's return, as the monks invested significantly in their building project, before initiating their legal claim. The case had a superior chance of turning out in Holy Trinity's favor once the monks had committed financial resources, labor and time to its construction. Abbot Gilbert was more likely to pay a higher cost to get out from underneath Holy Trinity's control once the church was set on its foundation. As the case against the monks was initiated only when Mathilda returned to Caen, one is tempted to assume that she herself began the proceedings. William's acquiescence, moreover, may have been further encouraged as Mathilda, his wife, was dying. Mathilda spent two years in England, 1081–1083, before sailing home to Normandy. Once home, only a few months elapsed until Mathilda's death, and the negotiations over St Nicholas-in-the-Fields spanned that period. The abbey was the focus of her attention and care, the home of her daughter, her favorite beneficiary, and would be her final resting place. Did Queen Mathilda use her love for Holy Trinity, and the devotion of her husband, to expand Holy Trinity's rights? Queen Mathilda's political acumen and her ability to wring concessions from William are indisputable.[129] His final, more generous,

[129] Laura L. Gathagan, '"Mother of heroes, most beautiful of mothers": Mathilda of Flanders and royal motherhood in the eleventh century', in *Virtuous or Villainess? The Image of the Royal Mother from the Early Medieval to the Early Modern Era*, ed. Ellie Woodacre and Carrie Fleiner (London, 2016), 37–63. See also Chapter Five: Womb, 150–2.

settlement to the abbey coincided with her final illness. This hypothesis can only be suggestive – we have no first-hand evidence for Mathilda's thoughts in her final days – but there is an indication that Holy Trinity, her burial place, was at the forefront of her mind as she lay dying.

Her last document, produced at just this time, granted her crown and scepter, her horses' accoutrements and her golden bed hangings to Holy Trinity.[130] This text is analyzed more closely in Chapter Seven, but here it provides evidence that Mathilda gave Holy Trinity the most elemental material reflections of her personhood: her royal rule, her endless hours on horseback, and an imperial golden cloth from her private apartments. If Mathilda did indeed utilize her final days as a lever to force William's hand, it would be in service of the place she built specifically to hold her in death. Her third conquest gift, her daughter Cecelia, was Holy Trinity's future abbess – in 1083, already gathering up the reigns of its leadership – and the ideal custodian of her mother's memory.[131] Thus, Holy Trinity had a singular claim to Mathilda's affection.

Whether or not Mathilda used her last illness to force her husband's hand there is no question that the timing is revealing. Queen Mathilda may not have heard from the abbess that the construction of St Nicholas-in-the-Fields was underway, but Abbess Matilda herself could not have avoided it. On the queen's return from her last extended visit to England, moreover, the wheels of justice began to move and the settlement ramped up quickly. Just under four months elapsed between William's first written attempt at a settlement and Mathilda's death. In support of her monastery, there seems to have been no gift too great. Mathilda appeared willing to use even her dying body to further Holy Trinity's interests. Given this evidence, the epitaph quoted above, engraved on Mathilda's tomb, assumes a new, more profound implication: '… in death she adorned with her bones the chapel that she had embellished with her love while alive'.[132]

CONCLUSION

Lisa Reilly has argued that Norman identity and legitimacy were established through a 'visual vocabulary' of cultural and architectural construction that paralleled the written, often mythic, histories the Normans created for themselves'.[133] While Reilly focuses on St Stephen's to make her claim, Holy Trinity enshrined both of these impulses. Its physical placement high above

130 *Regesta* (no. 63), 296.

131 By 1088, only five years later, Cecelia was already producing charters and agreements without Abbess Matilda's assistance. Gathagan, 'Maiden', 854–7.

132 Sheerin, 'Sisters in the Literary Agon', 119.

133 Lisa Reilly, *The Invention of Norman Visual Culture: Art, Politics, and Dynastic Ambition* (Cambridge, 2020), 57.

Caen referenced Norman identity in the strongest possible terms. Its design and architectural features advertised its imperial status through a conscious archaism. It thus made claims for a new dynastic identity, crafted in the famous Caen limestone, but appropriated from Ottonian forms. It stands as evidence of Mathilda's startling achievement. Whatever the past required in terms of the papal prohibition of her marriage, Mathilda's new construction met and exceeded it.

For many women and men, a papal charge of consanguinity was a significant threat to their status and it often spelled the end of marital alliances. Mathilda lived, and thrived, with that uncertainty hanging in the air for ten years. Her position as duchess of Normandy, despite her royal blood, could have been precarious; her children's legitimacy was threatened and thus her dynastic ambitions. But Mathilda refashioned her penance into a statement of dynastic triumph. Moreover, when given the opportunity to link her newfound abbey to the invasion of England, she did not hesitate. She translated the imposition of a penance into a monument to the conquest of England, an enterprise that risked everything. Holy Trinity rose above Caen as the physical embodiment of her Norman victory – over the papacy, over the English, over fate – a victory that was uniquely Mathilda's own.

The tumult of later periods did not spare Holy Trinity, and its appearance changed dramatically over time. Yet, throughout its history, the abbey maintained its militaristic character and connections. The antiquarian Dawson Turner, writing in the nineteenth century, noted 'The abbey bore the two-fold character of nunnery and fortress. Strangely inconsistent as this union may appear, the fact is undoubted.'[134] Of course, the 'two-fold character' that so surprised Turner was perfectly consistent with Holy Trinity's nature as Mathilda envisioned it. Woven into the militarism of the Norman Conquest, the community of women celebrated Holy Trinity's links to Norman victory until its dissolution in 1830, just as their founder intended.

[134] Dawson Turner, *Account of a tour in Normandy: undertaken chiefly for the purpose of investigating the architectural antiquities of the duchy* (2 vols., London, 1820), ii, 183.

APPENDIX

FOUNDATION CHARTER OF HOLY TRINITY, DATED JUNE 18, 1066

Paris, Bibliothèque Nationale de France, MS Lat 5650, Folio 9v; Printed in *Recueil*, ed. Fauroux, no. 231; Musset, *Les Actes*, no. 2

By the divine clemency of the eternal father, I, William, the leader of the Normans, to the true of the most blessed of mother church wherever they are distributed, faithfully to be known to all who believe in Christ, grant them not to be deprived of the inheritance of blessedness, but to exist as worthy co-heirs of God, who are placed in the midst of this unstable life, those things which they seem to possess by hereditary right, in the places consecrated to God, in the necessary continuous prayers of those vacant there, fulfilling their duty to charity, arrange to share them by hereditary emancipation. Faith, confirmed by the apostle's authority as well as by the promise of the Lord, is directed to that which must be undoubtedly believed. For the Apostle says, 'Indeed you are heirs of God, but joint heirs with Christ.' For in the gospel, when the Lord foretold the future reward of those who had performed good deeds, he designated those who persevered with a worthy army to be co-heirs of the heavenly joys, saying, 'And they shall inherit eternal life.' Therefore, we shall not consider those who write down their father Christ as heir to their earthly labors to be deprived of the eternal inheritance of the celestial kingdom.

Now then, strengthened as she was by this hope of so great a reward, my most honorable wife Mathilda, daughter of Duke Baldwin of Flanders, when she saw that our affairs and our power were flowering in their greatness, she built a basilica in honor of the Holy Trinity in a place which the natives call Cadom in ancient times, which after all the ecclesiastical conveniences had been arranged, at the time of the dispensation, the pontiffs of our empire coming from the abbeys, the most holy fathers, all the clergy, the most devoutly religious people, all duly disposed, together with us on the 14 kalends of July, in the regnal year of Philip, king of France, Henry, ruling the Roman parts by imperial right, Pope Alexander, possessing the apostolic see of the most pious see, in the year from the Incarnation of the Lord 1066, the fourth indication, consecrated to the Lord Almighty.

Having thus solemnly celebrated the spiritual unions (of the nuns), having advocated with the aforesaid fathers, the primates of our land, and with the consent of all our children and friends, we have allowed them to be possessed forever as a reinforcement to the holy church, for the redemption of souls; that is, on the condition that if someone were reckless by daring to steal from us the benefits granted to venerable mother church indeed, by persisting in the community of the orthodox, he incurs the wrath of the Almighty, becoming a perpetual anathema.

Latin Text:

Divina Patris eterni disponente clementia, ego Normannorum dux Guillermus, veris beatissime matris ecclesie quocumque diffusis cultoribus, fideliter in Christo credentibus cunctis notum esse percupimus, celesti eos non privari mansure beatitudinis hereditate, sed dignos Dei coheredes existere, qui in hujus instabilis vite discursu positi, ea que tanquam hereditario jure possidere videntur, Deo consecratis locis in necessaria continuis ibidem vacantium precibus, suum caritati adimplentes officium, mancipatione hereditaria communicare disponunt. Ad quod indubitanter credendum apostoli auctoritate necnon promissione dominica fidelium confirmata dirigitur fides. Dicit enim apostolus "heredes quidem Dei, coheredes autem Christi". Dominus namque in evangelio, cum in bonorum actuum exhibitione operatoribus future retributionis munus prediceret, eosdem digno exercitu persistentes proposito gaudiorum coheredes esse celestium designavit, dicens "et vitam eternam possidebunt", non igitur illos celestis regni hereditate perpetua privatum iri putemus, qui patrem suum Christum in terrenis laboribus heredem prescripserunt.

Ea ergo tante repromissionis spe, honestissima conjunx mea Mathildis subnixa, nobilissimi ducis Flandrensium Balduini filia, cum res nostras atque potentiam sua pro magnitudine florere conspiceret, in honorem Sancte Trinitatis, concessa a me digne peticionis licentia, in loco qui Cadomum prisco ab incolis nuncupatur nomine, sanctimonialibus construxit basilicam. Quam paulo post, omni commoditate exornatam ecclesiastica, spiritualis constituto desponsationis tempore, convenientes imperii nostri excellentissimi pontifices, ex abbatiis sanctissimi patres, omnis clerus, summa cum devotione religiosus populus, omnibus rite dispositis, una nobiscum, XIIII. Kalendas Julii, regnante in Francia rege feliciter Philippo, Romanis partibus imperiali jure dominante Henrico, apostolice sedis cathedram religiosissimo possidente papa Alexandro, anno ab Incarnatione Domini millesimo.LXVI quarta indicione, omnipotenti consecraverunt Domino.

Nuptiis ergo solenniter celebratis spiritualibus, advocatis cum patribus predictis terre nostre primatibus, firmissima prolis nostre tam filiorum quam amicorum omnium concessione, hec de nostris in supplementum sancte ecclesie, pro redemptione animarum in perpetuum possidenda permisimus, ea videlicet conditione ut si quis temerario ausu, venerande matri ecclesie concessa a nobis beneficia surripere temptaverit, persistendo orthodoxorum communitate careat, iram omnipotentis Domini anathema factus perpetuam incurrat.

3

FINGERS

Rise, o saints, from your dwellings, sanctify the place, bless the people…

Romano-Germanic Pontifical Rite, XL, 131.

…the Lord, my rock, trains my hands for war, and my fingers for battle.

Psalm 144:1

The physical city of Caen rose up rapidly in the middle of the eleventh century as Mathilda and William constructed its primary elements. These included the ducal castle, the abbey of Holy Trinity and, lastly, St Stephen's Abbey. The merchant community of Caen grew alongside it, encouraged by the ducal presence and the navigable waterways of the Orne and the Odon which fed Caen. The previous chapter provides evidence for the expansion of a bustling city with neighborhoods of tenants and workers developing in the boroughs of the abbess, the abbot, and those dependent directly on the ducal couple. As the contours of Caen emerged in the physical world, Mathilda was also building a parallel city; spiritual, ephemeral, liturgical. This spiritual city was governed by the presence of holy bodies: saints whose remains shaped the religious observance of Caen as it developed. Caen's liturgical city was organized around temporal observance of feast days. The assemblage of holy bodies also shifted the spiritual center of Normandy towards Caen.

The saints Mathilda collected and had placed – or translated – into her monastery at Holy Trinity can be imagined as a parallel liturgical construction to the stone abbey she commissioned and oversaw. This chapter discusses the holy fingers, bones and other sacred objects Mathilda procured to be translated into her community. The word 'translation' can be imagined here in two related ways. The first sense of the word is the movement of holy bodies and the liturgical celebration of holy remains, collected by Mathilda, into the treasury at Holy Trinity. The second meaning of the word 'translation' refers to the sense in which Mathilda transmitted various messages through the relics she chose to collect. The group of relics she composed communicated her priorities to the inhabitants of Caen, to the duchy of Normandy, and to the wider world. A close reading of these sacred remains reveals that her collection was carefully curated, not chosen randomly. Thus, I will also argue that her relic choices can be analyzed to demonstrate her preoccupation with her Flemish and royal identities. Just as royal and ducal rulers did before her, the saintly remains she gathered were expected to do the work of legitimizing her abbey, her rule and perhaps even the invasion of England.

The conception of a sacred city described by holy bodies, that paralleled the physical city of Caen, is neither fanciful nor merely a philosophical exercise. The ritual created for the dedication and consecration of a church explicitly describes the invisible liturgical construction that stood inside the physical city. There were numerous regional variations to the consecration rite of a church, and the development of the liturgy over time variously increased its pomp and then slimmed it down again. Louis Hamilton has shown that particular elements remained central to its performance. These included the notion of 'an ideal sacred city within the earthly city'.[1] The central element of church dedication was the deposit of relics inside it.[2] Holy relics were at the heart of church dedication liturgies, like Holy Trinity's dedication examined in the preceding chapter.[3]

Unlike Augustine's 'City of God' that stood as a contrast to the cities built by humankind, Mathilda's construction of the two worlds was intertwined. These two elements – physical/spatial and spiritual/liturgical – cannot be separated. They would not have been separated, I contend, in the mind of the woman who planned and oversaw their construction. Mathilda's assembly of her collection of saints' bodies and the construction of the church which housed them were both forms of veneration. This is likewise true for the physical landscape of the abbey church and the parallel development of its spiritual landscape through the acquisition of relics. Dominique Iogna-Prat has argued that the medieval conceptions of a saint's *locus* or *loculus* came to designate 'place' in ever-widening circles: the relics of a saint, and the shrine that contained them, and the structure that sheltered them.[4] The abbey of Holy Trinity of Caen was thus a vast stone reliquary.[5] The physical presence of saints' bodies within the abbey church made it sacred; it was also inescapably connected to their temporal

1 Louis I. Hamilton, *A Sacred City: Consecrating Churches and Reforming Society in Eleventh-Century Italy* (Manchester, 2010), 16.

2 Dominique Iogna-Prat, 'Le lieu de culte dans l'Occident médiéval entre sainteté et sacralité (IXe-XIIIe siècles)', *Revue d'Histoire des Religions* 4 (2005), 463–80, at 470.

3 'While variance was considerable, the sine qua non of the consecration was the anointing of the altar and the deposition of relics within it.' Hamilton, *A Sacred City*, 22.

4 'in the West in the early Middle Ages, we gradually moved from the holiness of persons (the saints) to the sacredness of the place of worship which little by little was conceived as a true persona' ('…dans l'Occident du haut Moyen Âge, l'on passe progressivement de la sainteté des personnes (les saints) à la sacralité du lieu de culte peu à peu conçu comme une véritable persona.'). Iogna-Prat, 'Le lieu de culte', 469.

5 Iogna-Prat, 'Le lieu de culte', 469.

celebration. Expressed through the calendar of feast days, the saints shaped annual religious observance in the city of Caen, saints introduced by Mathilda's choices. Her army of holy women and men recentered the liturgical landscape of Normandy to include the new spiritual center of Caen. The translation of these saints and their residence in the city affected religious observance for the citizens of Caen hundreds of years into the future.

THE RELIC LIST

> We have these relics. A piece of the True Cross of Christ three pieces, and his manger, and a piece of the cloth that he was swathed in and of the sponge, and the ointment, one piece, and of the sepulcher, two pieces. Of the hair of the most blessed Mary, mother of God, and her clothing, two pieces. Of the bones of the prophets Isaiah and of Samuel, one piece. Of the hair and beard of St Peter the apostle, and of his cross and cloak and tunic, and the belt he had around him in the sea. Of St Andrew the apostle. Of the blood of St Stephen and a stone with which he was stoned. A hair of St Denis, and St Rusticus and St Eleutherius. Of the dust and bones of St Vincent and St Demetrios, St Savianus, and St Potentius. The blood of St George in an ampula. A finger of St Nicholas of Myra and his oil. The beard and clothing of St Martin. Of the beard of St Germanus. A finger of St Eligius of Noyon, and bones of St Florent and St Gaudentius. A tooth of St Arnulf. Three pieces of the hair of Mary Magdalene. The finger of St Cecelia, the virgin. Of the hair of St Margaret, and the hair of St Agatha and some of their bones. The hair of St Julian. Of the bones and hair of St Aurea. The hair of St Geneviève. The oil of St Catherine and St Demetrius. The body of one of the Innocents, and the body of St Giles, and many more martyrs, and part of the rod of Aaron.[6]

6 'De his sanctis reliquias habemus. De ligno Domini in III locis et de presepio ipsius et de pannis quibus involutus fuit, et de spongia et unguento in uno loco et de sepulcro in duobos locis. De capillis sanctissime Marie genitricis Dei et de vestimento ipsius in duobus locis. De ossibus prophetarum Ysaie et Samuelis in uno loco. De capillis et barba sancti Petri apostoli et de cruce ipsius et casula et tunica qua succinxit se in mare. De sancto Andrea apostolo. De sanguine sancti Stephani et de lapide unde lapidatus fuit. De capillis sancti Dionisii et de sanctis Rustico et Eleutherio. De pulvere et ossibus sancti Vincentii et Demetrii, Saviani atque Potentiani. De sanguine sancti Georgii in una ampula. De digito sancti Nicholai et de oleo ipsius. De barba et vestimento sancti Martini. De barba sancti Germani episcopi. De sancto Eligio digitum unum et de ossibus sanctorum Florentii et Gaudentii. De sancto Arnulfo dentem unum. De capillis sancte Marie Magdalene in tribus locis. De digito sancte Cecelia virginis. De capillis sancte Agathe et de capillis sancte Margarite et de ossibus ejus. De capillis sancte Juliane. De ossibus et capillis sancte Auree. De capillis sancte Genovefe. De oleo sancte Katerine et de sancto Demetrio. Corpus unius Innocentis et corpus sancti Egydii et plurimorum martirum et de virga Aaron.' BNF 5650, 25v–26r.

The relic inventory of Holy Trinity is recorded in its twelfth-century cartulary, BNF 5650. The cartulary contains two extensive land surveys, and a collection of charters, grants, notices and legal documents that outline the abbey's rights and holdings.[7] The relic list is bound next to a catalogue of valuable personal objects Mathilda granted to the abbey on her death, including her scepter and crown.[8] Though the inventory of relics was recorded in the twelfth century, Musset argued that it was produced by the end of the eleventh century, connected to the earliest of Holy Trinity's documents.[9] The relic list does not name Mathilda specifically as its donor; however, its placement in the cartulary near her other donations argues for her as its collector. Musset also argued convincingly that the items listed were gathered by Mathilda herself. No other patron would have the wealth and the reach to compile such a collection.[10]

Other important questions about the collection remain unanswerable. The first is the timing of the treasury – when were these items obtained? Holy Trinity was dedicated before the conquest and relics were a necessary part of church dedication, as argued above. Thus, Mathilda would have gathered some of these sacred items for the pre-conquest dedication as she and the Normans faced the uncertain future of their military venture. Some of these relics, however, may have been added after the success of the conquest. Secondly, the tantalizing phrase at the end of the list 'and many more martyrs' signals that the description is incomplete and consequently the inventory should be treated with care. It may not be a comprehensive reflection of Mathilda's choices for her abbey though it certainly enshrines the treasures deemed most worthy of recording.

The inventory is generally organized in the sequence common to martyrologies.[11] Relics related to Christ open the list, then those of the Virgin, the apostles and other biblical characters, then martyrs, next 'confessors', that is, bishops and evangelists who 'confessed' Christ through evangelism, combating heresy or otherwise defending the faith. Closing out the inventory

7 Printed editions of the cartulary are described in two important works: *Charters and Custumals of the Abbey of Holy Trinity Caen*, ed. Marjorie Chibnall (Oxford, 1982), and *Charters and Custumals of the Abbey of Holy Trinity Caen, Part 2 The French Estates*, ed. John Walmsley (Oxford, 1994).

8 BNF 5650, folio 26r-27v. For an analysis of Mathilda's last gifts, see Chapter Six: Flesh, 171–83.

9 Musset, *Les actes*, 18.

10 Ibid.

11 The organization of Holy Trinity's list is similar to other earlier examples of relic inventories, including the tenth-century Exeter collection of Athelstan, and the later relic list of Abingdon Abbey in the twelfth century. Michael Swanton, *Anglo-Saxon Prose* (London, 1975), 14–19.

are holy virgins, both male and female.[12] Mathilda's collection contains some foundational relics that have comparators in many relic collections and seem to be essential. Remains of Christ's birth and passion were the 'headliners' of most relic treasuries and were almost mandatory: the cross, the manger, the sponge, ointment, wine and pieces of Christ's tomb.[13] The holy accoutrements of Mary were also regularly included, usually her hair, her veil, or her gown. Mathilda's collection contained these regularly featured relics.

A few other holy objects Mathilda obtained might seem predictable. She acquired relics of St Stephen, perhaps as a nod to William's foundation – the twin brother of Holy Trinity – across the city in Caen.[14] William shared his relics of the protomartyr with the abbey of Plessis-Grimoult, so it is reasonable to imagine he might have done the same for Mathilda.[15] Likewise, St Nicholas and St Martin had international reputations as 'healing' saints by the eleventh century and no proper relic collection would be without them. If Mathilda had any pretensions to building an assortment of holy bodies that would inspire esteem, St Nicholas and St Martin would be necessary anchor pieces. St Nicholas especially had a wide following, celebrated in Byzantium, Italy, France and England.[16] The development of Nicholas's cult was also supported by the Ottonian dynasty which ensured the wide dissemination of his cult.[17] Abbot Isembert from La-Trinité-du-Mont in Fécamp was credited with bringing relics of St Nicholas to Normandy.[18] Shortly before Mathilda's arrival new offices for Nicholas and Catherine had been produced at Rouen

12 Many relic inventories of this period follow this organization but there are exceptions. St Peter's church in Bath seems to follow no organization at all. *Two Chartularies of the Priory of S. Peter at Bath*, ed. W. Hunt (London, 1893), lxxv–lxxvi.

13 Both Exeter's donation from Athelstan and Abingdon Abbey's list contain these objects. Swanton, *Anglo-Saxon Prose;* see also *Chronicon Monasterii de Abingdon*, ed. J. Stevenson (2 vols., London, 1858), ii, 155–8.

14 Even without that connection, relics of St Stephen appear in almost every collection in Normandy. Musset, *Les actes*, 16.

15 'A canon of Plessis, relying on a "printed writing" of the monks of Caen which seems lost, explains that King William "shared these precious relics between the abbey of Saint Étienne of Caen and that of Plessis-Grimoult…mainly he shared this beautiful vial full of blood of Saint-Étienne the martyr, he had a second one made covered in silver which he filled with this precious blood and gave it to Sanson, the first prior of Plessis-Grimoult."' Musset, *Les actes*, 19.

16 C.W. Jones, 'The Norman Cult of Sts. Catherine and Nicholas, Saec.XI', in *Hommages à André Boutemy*, ed. G. Cambier (Brussels, 1976), 216–30, at 222–3.

17 Jones, 'Cult of Sts. Catherine and Nicholas', 223.

18 The collection of Saint-Ouen in Rouen also recorded relics of the saint in its inventory. Véronique Gazeau and Jacques Le Maho, 'Les origines du culte de saint Nicolas en Normandie', in *Alleorigini dell'Europa: il culto di San Nicola tra Oriente e Occidentel*, ed. Gerardo Cioffari and Angela Laghezza (Bari, 2010), 153–60.

to accompany their relics. The presence of these relics in her collection is not at all surprising. Both saints were also accredited with effluvia that healed. St Catherine is paired with St Demetrius at the end of the relic list. Because of this position, we can tentatively identify this saint as Demetrius of Thessaloniki, because his relics also exuded myrrh, as opposed to Demetrios, bishop of Alexandria, who is placed with the 'confessors' further up on the list.

There are other saints whose connections to Mathilda are not as obvious but whose remains were readily available in Normandy. Relics of St Mary Magdalene were held at Fécamp, as were the remains of St Margaret and St Agatha. Relics of the Innocents could be found at all three abbeys that collected holy bodies in the diocese of Rouen: Saint-Wandrille, Saint-Ouen and La-Trinité-du-Mont, Fécamp.[19] The church of Sainte-Madeleine-de-Bayeux had relics of St George and Mary Magdalene.[20] Pieces of the True Cross were available in France while Mathilda was building her collection.[21]

Further down the list, St Cecelia appears: a necessary part of the collection in honor of Mathilda's daughter. The relics of St Giles were also requisite as he was the patron of the eponymous parish church, which was founded as an adjunct to Holy Trinity and located immediately outside its gates. Once past these carefully chosen essentials, Mathilda's gathering of relics begins to look unusual for a few reasons.[22] Mathilda procured two Old Testament saints for Holy Trinity that are not readily found in other medieval collections: the relics of Isaiah and Samuel. Their placement on the list is also remarkable because they appear immediately after Mary, and before the apostles.[23] Isaiah and Samuel were prophets connected to regime change and dislocation; both have associations that might have made them particularly attractive to a duchess pursuing conquest. Isaiah was renowned for his role in encouraging the king of Judah, Hezekiah, to make war against Israel's enemies. Isaiah's many warlike speeches are unexpected for Old Testament prophets, who generally concern themselves with sin. At least one passage in Isaiah described the disinheriting of Israel's enemies;

19 Lucile Trân-Duc, 'Le culte des saints en Normandie (IXe-XIIe siècle): Enjeux de pouvoir dans les établissements bénédictins du diocèse de Rouen', PhD dissertation (2 vols., Université de Caen, 2015), i, 178–9. See also Trân-Duc, ii, Appendix 22 for Saint-Ouen and Appendix 23 for Saint-Wandrille.

20 Lucien Musset, 'Autour des origines de Saint-Étienne de Fontenay', *Bulletin de la société des antiquaires de Normandie* 56 (1963), 668.

21 A. Frolow, *La relique de la Vrai Croix* (Paris, 1966), 26–8 and 272. Countess Adeliza of Burgundy, William's aunt, donated a piece of the True Cross to Saint-Martin-de-Sees sometime between 1083 and 1089, perhaps in a related act. Lucien Musset, 'L'Exode des reliques du diocèse de Sées au temps des invasions normandes,' *Bulletin Société historique et archéologique de l'Orne* 88 (1970), 3–22.

22 Musset describes the collection as 'universal' and 'ecumenical'. Musset, *Les actes*, 18.

23 Musset, *Les actes*, 16.

> Enlarge the place of your tent, stretch your tent curtains wide, do not hold back; lengthen your cords, strengthen your stakes. For you will spread out to the right and to the left; your descendants will dispossess nations, and settle in their desolate cities. [24]

Isaiah was even more renowned in medieval theology for his prophecies about the coming of Christ. Isaiah was the prophet most often quoted in the New Testament, and medieval exegetes believed he had received special revelation from God about the Incarnation that set him apart from other Old Testament prophets. More than any Old Testament figure, Isaiah foretold the revolution that was the Messiah.[25]

Samuel likewise had a special place in medieval theology. His origin story was monastic; it began at the temple, where he had been made an oblate by his mother Hannah. She was barren, but promised to commit her son to God's service if she were to become pregnant. Hannah kept her word when she gave birth to a son.[26] As a child in the temple, Samuel served the famous prophet of Israel, Eli. In a well-known Bible story, Samuel heard God's voice calling out to him in the still of the night, but mistook it three times for the voice of Eli. After the third occurrence, Eli counselled Samuel to answer the voice should it call him again, and ask God's will of it. Samuel's story was often used as a shorthand for the call to the monastic life but there is more to Samuel's narrative. After God gains Samuel's attention, the message He speaks is portentous.

> Then the Lord said to Samuel: 'Behold, I will do something in Israel at which both ears of everyone who hears it will tingle. In that day I will perform against Eli all that I have spoken concerning his house, from beginning to end. For I have told him that I will judge his house forever for the iniquity which he knows, because his sons made themselves vile, and he did not restrain them. And therefore, I have sworn to the house of Eli that the iniquity of Eli's house shall not be atoned for by sacrifice or offering forever.[27]

The biblical passage is explicit that Eli would be disinherited because of his failure to be faithful to God's commands to curb his sons – and no reparation is possible. Eli's house will be wiped out because of their 'iniquity'. Eli's

24 Isaiah 54:2.

25 Medieval theologians insisted Isaiah's prophecies be historically contextualized; Isaiah's prophecies foretold details of the physical life of Christ, not merely underlying an ahistorical interpretation. In their approach to Isaiah, Israel was figured as Christianity and medieval believers filled the role of the people of Judah. Elisabeth Mégier, 'Christian Historical Fulfilments of Old Testament Prophecies in Latin Commentaries on the Book of Isaiah (ca. 400 to ca. 1150)', *The Journal of Medieval Latin* 17 (2007): 87–100.

26 Samuel 1:1–28.

27 Samuel 3:11–13.

inability to control the immorality of his sons is linked to Israel's loss of the Ark of the Covenant to the Assyrians in the next passage. When Eli hears of the ark's capture, he dies, falling backward and breaking his neck.[28]

In biblical tradition, moreover, Samuel is especially notable as a critic of Saul, Israel's famous king. Samuel prophesied that Saul's rule would see no dynastic succession – his sons would never reign after him. Samuel anoints and crowns David as the king of Israel in secret and hides him when an enraged Saul seeks to murder him. David's anointing takes place in the city of Bethlehem, a precursor to Christ's birth. Thus, Samuel is a disruptor of dynasties: Eli's prophetic genealogy and Saul's royal one both end as God designates other, more worthy inheritors.

Mathilda may have chosen Old Testament prophets whose legends had resonance for her conquest abbey and for her own rule over England. The Old Testament, of course, is replete with examples of God's judgement falling on the heads of those wielding illegitimate authority; Israel's behavior often resulted in the threat of lost inheritance or the loss of their special status as God's people. The presence of Isaiah and Samuel in the relic list, however, connects to scriptural passages in Baruch 9, the scripture featured at Mathilda's anointing and coronation in 1068.[29] They engaged the same themes. Mathilda's coronation liturgy used the Baruch passage to link Israel's loss to England's defeat at the hands of the Normans. The same leitmotifs appear in her relic collection, through Isaiah and Samuel. Isaiah promotes the expansion of the kingdom and the occupation of its abandoned cities. He was also the primary prophetic voice for the ultimate 'regime change': from the Old Testament to the New Testament – from the Old Law to the New Law. In Samuel, the scripture illustrates the disruption of an inheritance as a punishment for illegitimate behavior. This occurs in two dimensions: Samuel replaces Eli as prophet and disinherits his sons and Samuel crowns a new king, David, who supplants Saul and ends his royal dynasty. The bilateral loss of an inheritance is central in Samuel's story. Medieval writers – including Bede and Stephen of Ripon – engaged the Samuel and Eli / Saul and David paradigm when they wanted to illustrate a worthy figure who supplanted a past leader ruined by corruption.[30]

The inclusion in Holy Trinity's relic collection of these two Old Testament figures is deeply idiosyncratic. Though the evidence cannot be considered exhaustive, relics of Isaiah and Samuel do not appear in extant contemporary collections in England and Normandy.[31] Not all relic collections have left

28 Samuel 4:1–18.

29 See Chapter Four: Head, 120–3.

30 Conor O'Brien, 'Moses, Aaron, and the Abbacy of Wearmoth-Jarrow in 716', in *All Roads Lead to Rome: The Creation, Context and Transmission of the Codex Amiatinus*, ed. Jane Hawkes and Meg Boulton (Turnhout, 2019), 105–14, at 108.

31 For comparison, see relic lists for Exeter, Abingdon and Durham. Swanton, Anglo-Saxon Prose, 14–19; Hunt, *Priory of S. Peter at Bath*, lxxv–lxxvi; *Chronicon*

textual evidence of their inventories, but it can be said with certainty that neither prophet was a regular associate of relic treasuries. By selecting these Old Testament prophets of regime change, Mathilda seems to have argued for the legitimacy of her Norman conquest and rule. Both Isaiah and Samuel were prophets that might have been particularly attractive to a duchess pursuing conquest – and to a queen celebrating it.

The last Old Testament figure, the prophet and high priest Aaron, is referenced at the end of the inventory, a position that could be a place of special importance. The rod of Aaron is the last-named relic listed. Aaron was Moses' older brother who acted as his mouthpiece as they led the nation of Israel out of Egypt. His rod was a representation of priestly authority. In a moment of debate between the twelve tribes of Israel, each tribe offered a rod and laid them in a row. God miraculously caused Aaron's rod to bloom and produce almonds. This was the sign that Aaron's tribe alone – the tribe of Levi – would raise up priests for Israel. The priests of Aaron's lineage were responsible for teaching the divine laws to the Israelites and judging the clean from the unclean. In Rabbinic literature, the rod of Aaron was made of sapphire, which was the stone traditionally used for bishop's rings in the Middle Ages. Indeed, a bishop's sapphire ring was found on Mathilda of Flanders' finger when she was exhumed.[32] Aaron's rod may have been another indicator of priestly, apostolic authority that Mathilda would claim in her coronation liturgy.[33]

The apostles that Mathilda chose to honor – Peter and Andrew – are also worthy of examination.[34] The first two apostles called by Christ, both brothers were originally fishermen. Mathilda's Petrine relics refer to a biblical scene involving Peter after Christ's death and resurrection. Christ appears on the shore as Peter and the disciples are in a boat, trying unsuccessfully to catch fish.[35] Calling from the shore, Jesus advises them to try the other side of the boat, and their nets fill to bursting. Peter then recognizes Christ, shrugs on his tunic and belts it, then throws himself into the water to cross to shore. Once he reaches the sand, he throws himself at Christ's feet. The rest of the disciples follow in the boat, unsure if this is indeed

Monasterii de Abingdon, ii, 155–8; *Historiae Dunelmensis Scriptores tres: Gaufridus de Coldingham, Robertus de Graystanes, Etc Willielmus de Chambre*, ed. J. Raine (London, 1839), appendix cccxxvi–cccxxix. Extant relic lists for England can also be found online: https://locasanctorum.neocities.org/reliclists For an exhaustive survey of relics in Rouen, see Trân-Duc, 'Le culte des saints en Normandie', i, 172–222.

32 See Chapter Eight: Corpse, 216–18.

33 See Chapter Four: Head, 105–33.

34 Sometime before 1066, Mathilda's parents, Baldwin V and Adela of Blois, procured relics of St Peter's chains. It is tempting to connect these events.

35 John 21:4–12, especially verse 7.

Christ. Eventually they all come ashore, but are afraid to ask Jesus' identity, as he cooks them breakfast.[36] Peter's impulsive, even reckless, dash into the water proves to be a virtuous act of faith. He arrives in Christ's presence before any of the other disciples, unafraid of the hazards of the sea.

The scene has often been called the 'Restoration of Peter'. In the passage, Christ commands Peter three times to feed his sheep, the reversal of Peter's denial of Christ in John 18. The exchange officially begins Peter's leadership of the church. An irrational idea, that Christ is alive, powers Peter's risky venture into the waves. The result is the fulfillment of Peter's destiny – to lead Christ's church on earth.

Once again Mathilda has chosen a set of sacred objects that could reference the conquest. Other relic collections in Normandy contain Peter's beard and even his cross, but these last two relics together that Peter wore 'in the sea' from this Biblical tale are not found.[37] Mathilda's particular Petrine relics may have had a specific purpose and message that linked to her rule of England. Like Peter's hazardous journey through the sea, the invasion may have seemed rash and even imprudent, but fulfilled Mathilda's destiny in England.

Turning to the remainders of her collection, the great majority of the sacred bodies Mathilda chose referenced the Frankish royal house. For instance, Mathilda acquired relics of three linked saints with special meaning for the Carolingian royal house: St Denis, St Rusticus and St Eleutherius. The *Gesta Dagoberti* (*c.* 830) recounts the legend of how the royal church at St Denis was founded.[38] Before he came to the throne, a young Dagobert I took refuge in a ruined chapel where the remains of martyrs – Rusticus and Eleutherius – had been hidden. The saints appeared to him and demanded that he make their burial place a worthy shrine. In exchange, they promised their help. After he was crowned, Dagobert kept his part of the bargain; their sarcophagi were uncovered and Dagobert built the church of Saint-Denis over them.[39] Historians have remarked on the legend as an early alliance between royal power and martyred saints.[40] Mathilda acquired relics of the saints written into the ninth-century legend: St Denis, St Rusticus and St Eleutherius. Mathilda's choice of this coherent grouping speaks to significant planning and conscious choices. Her acquisition is also mimetic: Mathilda is Dagobert, elevating the same Carolingian saints, thus transmitting her own royal identity. The meticulousness of Mathilda's choices also shows evidence that she was familiar with the narratives celebrating her royal past.

36 John 21:12.

37 Trân-Duc, 'Le culte des saints en Normandie', ii, 23–31.

38 Edina Bozóky, 'Hagiography, Relics and Secular Politics in Western Europe, 6th–13th Centuries' in *Hagiography and the History of Latin Christendom, 500–1500*, ed. Edina Bozóky (Turnhout, 2019), 272–96, and 273–4.

39 *Gesta Dagoberti*, § 2–4 and 7–10, ed. B. Krusch, *MGH* SRM, 2 (Hanover, 1888), 396–425 at 401–4.

40 Trân-Duc, 'Le culte des saints en Normandie' i, 13.

Mathilda's collection included St Germanus of Auxerre, a Frankish saint who sailed to England to combat the Pelagian heresy. He also led the Britons to a military victory.[41] According to legend, he commanded the native Britons in an armed clash against Pictish raiders. St Germanus also either discovered, or promoted very early, the cult of St Alban (literally 'the man from Albion', the ancient name for Britain) in England. St Germanus commissioned the earliest written version of Alban's *vita* after his visit to Britain and may have promoted his cult in Auxerre.[42] St Germanus's mission to Britain, his victorious military leadership there, and his championing – even invention – of an important British saint make him an ideal part of Mathilda's collection.

Her Carolingian saints also included St Arnulf of Metz, who was considered the earliest-known Carolingian ancestor of Charlemagne.[43] St Florent was celebrated by Louis the Pious who built a church to house the saint's remains; Louis had translated them from Strasbourg. Closer to Normandy, the saint was celebrated at an abbey Mathilda herself patronized – Saint-Florent de Saumur in Maine-Loire – a monastic house founded in the ninth century to honor the saint.[44] Mathilda confirmed a number of grants in favor of Saint-Florent.[45] Moreover, Abbot Sigon of Saint-Florent wrote Mathilda directly sometime before 1066 to ask for her help in returning Saint-Florent's property in the Cotentin.[46] As part of his plea, Abbot Sigon claims special consideration from Mathilda because St Florent had healed 'a certain prince's daughter'.[47]

41 Ian Wood, 'Germanus, Alban and Auxerre', *Bulletin du centre d'études médiévales d'Auxerre* 13 (2009), 123–9. See also Nicholas J. Higham, 'Constantinus, Germanus and fifth-century Britain', *EME* 22:2 (2014), 113–37.

42 Wood, 'Germanus, Alban and Auxerre', 128–9.

43 Paul the Deacon recorded the relationship in his *Liber de episcopis Mettensibus* (*c.* 784). Constance Brittain Bouchard, 'The Carolingian Creation of a Model of Patrilineage', in *Paradigms and Methods in Early Medieval Studies*, ed. C. Chazelle and F. Lifshitz (New York, NY, 2007), 135–51 at 141.

44 Jean Huynes and Paul Marchegay, 'Translation des reliques de saint Florent, de Roye à Saumur', *Bibliothèque de l'école des chartes* 3 (1842), 475–98.

45 *Regesta* (nos. 266, 267, 268, 269), 797–812.

46 'Chartes normandes de l'abbaye de Saint-Florent près Saumur de 710 à 1200 environ', ed. Paul Marchegay, *Mémoires de la Société des Antiquaires de Normandie*, 3rd series, 10 (1880), 633–711 at 666–7.

47 'Venerable lady, in the village of Constantine, which is subject to your lordship and your husband's dominion, by the grace of the savior Christ the speedy and mighty benefactor, our predecessors possessed a great part of their livelihood. Now we read on this date, in the life of the great confessor Christ Florentius, intercessor for God, of the health obtained for the daughter of a certain prince.' (Veneranda domina, in pago Constantino, qui quoniam tuo domino et sponso tue etiam ditioni, salvatoris Christi tocius potentie largitoris gratia, subditus est, precessores nostri magnam partem victus sui possederunt. Datam autem hanc legimus, in vita magni ad Deum intercessoris confessoris Christi Florentii, pro impetrata sanitate cujusdam principis filie.) Marchegay, 'Chartes normandes', 667.

This element of the letter has puzzled historians but the miracle Abbot Sigon referenced is probably legendary; St Florent was famous for the miraculous cure of Merovingian King Dagobert I's daughter.[48] By inserting a reminder of the legend, Abbot Sigon highlighted Mathilda's debt to St Florent while adding a flattering reference to Mathilda's prestigious bloodline. It is possible that Mathilda's relics of St Florent might have come through this channel, perhaps even in recognition of her help.[49] Evidence from an abbey charter reveals that Mathilda donated a golden chalice to Saumur.[50] The chalice could have acted as a countergift for the relic of the saint; countergifts were a strategy Mathilda used repeatedly.[51]

Further intimate connections can be seen woven throughout the list. The martyrology-inspired order of the inventory disguises some of these but deeper examination reveals the linkages between many of the saintly 'groupings' in Mathilda's assemblage. St Eligius calls St Aurea to be the abbess of his new convent in Paris; St Germanus of Auxerre picks out St Geneviève as a young girl in a crowd, and tells her she will be a great saint. St Savianus and St Potentius, martyrs who together evangelized Sens, created a diocese that was later merged with Auxerre; they are celebrated, with St Germanus, in the specific liturgical calendar of that region.[52] St Florent healed the daughter of Dagobert I, the king who rescued St Rusticus and St Eleutherius and built St Denis over them.[53]

Despite the throng of saints enshrined in her collection, Mathilda's relic inventory reveals some surprising omissions. She did not evince a keen interest in Norman saints. Historians have often argued that they would have been

48 Jean Martindale, 'Monasteries and castles: the priories of St-Florent de Saumur in England after 1066', in *England in the eleventh century: proceedings of the 1990 Harlaxton symposium,* ed. Carola Hicks (Stamford, 1992), 135–56 at 141, n. 15.

49 While Abbot Sigon promised to feed one poor person a year in her honor and pray for her on her death anniversary, Mathilda may have requested something a bit more tangible instead. 'Chartes normandes', 667.

50 In 1093, William, Abbot of Saint Florent, exchanged it for the priory of Chantocé. 'The golden chalice that Mathilda, the Queen of England had given them' paid for the priory and all its goods and dependencies – even without its golden paten, which Abbot William seems to have kept. Paul Marchegay, 'Chartes Angevines des onzième et douzième siècles', *Bibliothèque de l'École Des Chartes* 36 (1875), 381–441 at 413.

51 See Chapter Two: Hands, 35–72 and Chapter Five: Womb, 145–67.

52 In the third century, Savianus and Potentius preached in Ferrières in Gâtinais, then in the suburbs of Sens. Savianus became the first bishop of Sens and was martyred with an axe. Potentius succeeded him as bishop. They are both celebrated on October 19 in the liturgical calendar specific to the diocese of Sens and Auxerre.

53 'The oldest center of Catherine cult in the west, Saint-Trinite-du-Mont in Rouen, *c.* 1030, became renowned. There, Catherine relics began to display their miracle-working power during the rule of the first abbot, the German Isambert (d. 1054).' Jones, 'Cult of Sts. Catherine and Nicholas', 216–30.

difficult to obtain; the ninth-century Viking raids wreaked havoc on monastic communities and nearly eradicated the remains of saints in Normandy.[54] Yet, some relics of Normandy's regionally specific saints were available – in particular, St Wandrille and St Ouen.[55] St Ouen of Rouen might have been an especially fitting relic choice for Mathilda. In 1045, Queen Emma claimed to have brought relics of St Ouen to England with her after her stay in Normandy and deposited them in Canterbury Cathedral.[56] The population at Rouen disputed her claim – and indeed St Ouen's relics were used for relic rituals in the 1040s. Peace of God ceremonies were initiated in 1047 for William as a young duke. They were held outside of Caen when it was just a small village and featured the relics of Saint Ouen.[57] In addition to these saints, St Romain in Rouen and St Aubert at Mont-Saint-Michel never left Normandy, even under Viking attack, so would have been available to the duchess-then-queen.[58] Other relics of Norman saints, or at least those with Norman connections, had returned to Normandy by the eleventh century. Some of these 'refugees' could even be found in Flanders.[59] A group of relics preserved by the pre-Norman monastery in Fontenelle – before it was refounded as 'Saint-Wandrille' – was acquired by Count Arnulf I of Flanders in 944. An inventory of them was

54 Musset characterized Holy Trinity as having to 'settle' for relics that were not Norman and bemoaned their recourse to make do with objects of saints with more generic appeal. Lucien Musset, 'Les translations de reliques en Normandie (Ixe–XIIe siècles)', in *Les Saints dans la Normandie Médiévale*, ed. Pierre Bouet and François Neveux (Caen, 2000), 97–108. Felice Lifshitz countered that assumption and argued that monastic authors overstated the effect of the Vikings to obscure relic thefts they themselves committed. Felice Lifshitz, 'The migration of Neustrian relics in the Viking Age: the myth of voluntary exodus, the reality of coercion and theft', *EME* 4:2 (1995), 175–92.

55 The relics for Saint Wandrille were brought to Bruges to escape the Norse violence. After the Viking threat had subsided, moreover, Abbot Mainard, originally from Ghent, refounded the community at Saint Wandrille and reinstalled the relics. See Elisabeth M.C. van Houts, 'Historiography and Hagiography at Sant-Wandrille: the "Inventio et Miracula Sancti Vulfranni,"' *ANS* 12 (1989), 233–51.

56 Dom A. Wilmart, 'Les reliques de saint Ouen à Cantorbéry', *Analecta Bollandiana* LI (1933), 285–92; Lucien Musset, 'Les contacts entre l'Église normande et l'Église d'Angleterre de 911 à 1066', *Les Mutations socioculturelles au tournant des XIe-XIIe siècles* (Paris, 1984), 67–84, especially at 73 and 83.

57 Dominique Barthélemy, 'Le concile de paix tenu à Caen (1035/1042),' *Annales de Normandie* 71 (2021/1), 37–53.

58 The monks at Mont-Saint-Michel were the recipient of Mathilda's largesse and said prayers for the queen specifically. Jacques Hourlier, 'Les Sources Écrites de l'Historie Montiose Anterieure à 966', *Millénaire Monastique du Mont Saint-Michel 2: Vie montoise et rayonnement intellectuel*, ed. Raymond Foreville (Paris, 1967), 121–32.

59 Musset discovered that numerous saints' bodies from Normandy, especially the ducal capital in Rouen, eventually settled in the vicinity of Flanders. Musset, 'Les translations de reliques', 6.

composed at Saint Peter's in Ghent by the *custos* of the abbey, between 945 and 953 and then updated after 1073.[60] It shows the remains of at least three regional Norman saints in the eleventh-century document: St Wandrille, St Ansbert and St Vulfran. Yet Mathilda procured none of these. Mathilda did have a relic of St Catherine, however, whose cult was celebrated very early in Rouen.[61] St Catherine was an Alexandrian saint famous for her intellect. Her legend featured her confounding groups of scholars in the ancient world – who then converted – before her martyrdom. Saint-Trinité-du-Mont in Rouen was the oldest center of St Catherine's cult in the west, *c.* 1030. Her relics were so central to the abbey's identity that by 1120–1140 it was commonly known as 'Ste. Catherine à la Trinité au Mont'.[62] Though she was an Alexandrian saint, St Catherine's relics had become famous in Normandy for exuding holy oil. Her relics in Mathilda's collection seem to be the only acknowledgement of Normandy's saintly traditions.

Another extraordinary factor in Mathilda's collection is the entire absence of English saints. After 1066, they would certainly have been available to her.[63] In fact, Mathilda's cousin, Judith of Flanders – raised with her at the Flemish court – secured relics of English St Oswald. Judith was the widow of Tostig Godwinson, Harold's brother. After Tostig's death, Judith brought relics of St Oswald out of England with her. After her second marriage to Welf of Bavaria, Judith initiated Oswald's cult in Bavaria and Switzerland.[64] There she and Welf became important patrons of the monastery at Weingarten, where she deposited her relics of St Oswald.[65]

If Countess Judith was able to export St Oswald, how much more available would English relics have been to its queen? Mathilda ruled England for over seventeen years. Moreover, she ruled England alone for nearly three years, during which time she regularly adjudicated disputes and handed down royal justice.[66] Proof of innocence was often accompanied by the ordeal and swearing on holy relics. Give her juridical activity one would imagine relics of English saints would have been quite obtainable. Did Mathilda's response

60 It was then inserted in *the Sermo de adventu sanctorum Wandregesili, Ansbert et Vulframni in Blandinium*, written at this same monastery, between 945 and 950.

61 'Catherine's relics began to display their miracle-working power during the rule of the first abbot, the German Isambert (d. 1054).' Jones, 'Cult of Sts. Catherine and Nicholas', 221.

62 Jones, 'Cult of Sts. Catherine and Nicholas', 222.

63 St George was celebrated as an 'English' saint only after the fourteenth century. Before this date, he was celebrated primarily in the East (in Cappadocia) and in Germany. Musset, 'L'Exode des reliques', 3–22.

64 Her relations with the local monastic house of Weingarten produced gifts of land and the famous 'Judith Gospels', beautiful Gospel books that contain her portrait. Dockray-Miller, *Judith of Flanders*, 73–90.

65 Rev. E.P. Baker, 'St Oswald and his Church at Zug', *Archaelogia* 93 (1949), 105–6.

66 See Chapter Seven: Mouth, 185–212.

to English saints mirror the initial resistance to them demonstrated by Lanfranc? Historians now maintain that Lanfranc supported veneration of English saints after he was familiarized with them and have debunked the idea that Normans were suspicious of the saints' cults they found established in England.[67] Indeed, William promised the abbey of Fécamp that he would return the churches in England, including the church at Steyning, that Harold Godwinson had taken from them. William fulfilled this promise, and as a result, the relics of St Cuthman, a local saint, were translated to Fécamp. His *vita* was written there, no doubt to commemorate the *repositio*, and his feast day was duly celebrated.[68] Mathilda's reaction is unknowable but she did not choose to include English saints in the collection she donated to her monastery. Her neglect of them must remain a mystery.

Mathilda's relic collecting, when closely investigated, seems to have several strands: high status relics of Christ and Mary that elevated her collection, and healing saints that drove pilgrimage. Most numerous were the sacred remains that recalled Mathilda's descent from the royal line as far back as the Merovingians: Sts Denis, Rusticus and Eleutherius signaled the earliest Frankish legitimation of royal rule by relics; St Savianus and St Potentius together evangelized Sens; St Germanus evangelized Auxerre and was sent to combat the Pelagian heresy in Britain; St Arnulf brought Christianity to Le Mans; St Geneviève, of course, was the patron saint of Paris. Arguably the most fascinating element of Mathilda's collection was those unusual saints that spoke to the particular context of Holy Trinity, perhaps especially the conquest of England: Isaiah, Samuel and even Germanus, the Gaulish saint who led the Britons to military victory. The rod of Aaron, placed at the end of the relic inventory, referenced the divine prerogative of spiritual leadership of a people. A relic of the rod of Aaron was also recorded at Battle Abbey, a corporeal link between the origination of the conquest at Holy Trinity and its conclusion at Battle.[69]

RELICS AND LEGITIMACY

Using holy relics as a means of political currency was a venerable custom; the practice was centuries old by the time Mathilda gathered her army of

67 Cowdrey, *Lanfranc*, 175–85; Susan J. Ridyard, '*Condigna Veneratio*: Post-Conquest Attitudes to the Saints of the Anglo-Saxons', *ANS* 9 (1987), 179–206; Simon Yarrow, *Saints and Their Communities: Miracle Stories in Twelfth-Century England* (Oxford, 2006), 6.

68 Roger Pearse, 'Life of Saint Cuthman (BHL 2035)', translation available Open Source, https://archive.org/details/cuthman-life-bhl-2035/page/12/mode/2up

69 Carter, 'The Relics of Battle Abbey: A Fifteenth-Century Inventory at the Huntington Library, San Marino,' *The Journal of Medieval Monastic Studies* 8 (2019), 309–43.

saints in the eleventh century.[70] To play an active role in the uncovering, translating and veneration of saints was to associate yourself with them and their authority. Hagiographical sources and narrative annals are replete with exemplars of relics playing a central political function and these works, more than any other genre, were copied and disseminated throughout the Middle Ages.[71] Edina Bozóky, in her survey of these sources, found numerous examples of political rulers and their use of relics to support their authority.[72] She noted that the Ottonian writer Widukind of Corvey, *c.* 925, was the first to draw a clear line between the possession of relics and the power of a dynasty. Widukind recounts how the Franks lost the relics of St Vit to the Ottonians, and how Frankish power faltered as a result. 'Since that time, [... the affairs of the Franks began to decline, those of the Saxons, on the other hand, became more flourishing day by day'.[73] Mathilda's Frankish ancestors also provided successful models of obtaining and harnessing the prestige of saints to legitimate their rule. As noted above, Mathilda highlighted her relationship to these famous rulers by selecting relics that explicitly referenced them to her eleventh-century audience. I have argued that Mathilda constructed Holy Trinity to impress her identity upon Caen and underscore her fitness to wield authority.[74] The relics she collected served many purposes, but they were undoubtedly harnessed in service to these initiatives.

The Merovingian royal family tied their authority to particular saints by building royal churches on their tombs.[75] Clovis constructed a basilica dedicated to the Holy Apostles over the tomb of St Geneviève in Paris; it was completed by his wife Clothilde. Queen Clothilde then built a church at Auxerre on the tomb of its bishop, St Germanus. Frankish royalty also carried out important translations that helped knit them to the saint's holy identity; King Childebert brought back a relic of St Vincent from Saragossa and had built a church for the remains in Paris. It is no coincidence that Mathilda chose relics of each of these saints for her collection.

70 The formative work on medieval relics is Patrick J. Geary, *Furta Sacra: Thefts of Relics in the Central Middle Ages* (rev. edition, Princeton NJ, 1978).

71 Samantha Kahn Herrick, 'Introduction', in *Hagiography and the History of Latin Christendom, 500–1500*, ed. Samantha Kahn Herrick (Leiden, 2019), 1–10.

72 'beyond the celebration of holiness in the ecclesial liturgical framework, certain cults become bearers of ideological, even political messages'. Edina Bozóky, 'Introduction', in *Hagiographie, idéologie et pouvoir au Moyen Âge. L'écriture de la sainteté, instrument politique*, ed. Edina Bozóky (Turnhout, 2012), 5. See also Bozóky, 'Hagiography, Relics and Secular Politics', 273–5.

73 'Res Francorum coeperunt minui, Saxonum vero crescere, donec dilatatae ip ...'. Bozóky quotes from Widukind De Corvey, *Rerum Gestarum Saxonicarum Libri Tres*, I, XXXIV, MGH *SS* III, 432.

74 See Chapter Two: Hands, 35–72.

75 Bozóky, 'Hagiography, Relics and Secular Politics', 273–5.

According to contemporary hagiographic narrative, Charlemagne brought relics out of Constantinople as a reward for 'liberating' Jerusalem. These included the Crown of Thorns, the Holy Shroud, and other high-status holy items that he housed at Aachen. His successor, Charles the Bald, donated some of them to Saint-Denis, but the Holy Shroud was given to Compiègne.[76] Two centuries later, Mathilda herself donated a new gorgeous reliquary for the Holy Shroud 'from Charlemagne' at Compiègne. She joined her first cousin, King Philip I of France, to translate the Holy Shroud anew in 1080. The two descendants of Charlemagne together conducted the translation liturgy. Years later, Philip recorded the event in the charter for Compiègne and made special note of Mathilda's part in the ritual.[77] Thus, Mathilda's links to the Carolingian past were made evident through relic translation. The ceremony in Compiègne featured the very relics brought out of the east by Charlemagne himself.[78] Philip seems to have remembered this important day, years after Mathilda's death, with great affection.[79] No other member of Mathilda's family or Philip's is mentioned in this act which may suggest that, to the two of them, this translation was a particularly meaningful, personal, undertaking.

Mathilda's Capetian relatives legitimized their royal power through relics and, indeed, their dynasty was founded on them. Hugh Capet's recovery of two saints – St Valery and St Riquier – has been considered 'the most significant example of the legitimization of royal power' through relics.[80] The

76 Bozóky, 'Hagiography, Relics and Secular Politics', 227.

77 *Recueil des actes de Philippe Ier, Roi de France*, ed. M. Prou (Paris, 1908), 319. Simon of Crépy, Mathilda's kinsman turned holy hermit, also attended. H.E.J. Cowdrey, 'Count Simon of Crépy's monastic conversion', in *Papauté, monachisme et théories politiques. Volume I: Le pouvoir et l'institution ecclésiale* (Lyon, 1994), 253–66.

78 'At the instigation of God's divine mercy and with prayerful supplication of the brothers of the Church of Corneille and, especially, at the most frequent demand of the most Christian Mathilda, the queen of the English, it seemed good to us that the relics of the Lord and Savior, which the Emperor Charles, a most Christian man, and magnificent ruler of the entire world had with utmost devotion preserved, that the aforesaid queen of the English put in a venerable vessel, formed from an ivory, ornamented wondrously with gold, gems, and precious stones, be translated to the church at Compiègne and placed there.' Like her cousin Philip, Mathilda could trace her ancestry directly to Charlemagne. The charter describing the translation parallels Charlemagne with Mathilda, calling her 'xpistianissime Mathildis' and Charlemagne 'Karolus, vir xpistianissimus'. Prou, *Recueil*, 319.

79 The translation of the shroud is referenced in a 1092 charter in which Philip, in memory of the event, decrees that the feast of the translation will be celebrated on the fourth Sunday of Lent, and gives to the brothers and treasurer of the Saint-Corneille church in Compiègne the rights and justice of a market for three days for 'our ancestors and successors, for the salvation of my soul and of Emperor Charles, and the good of her (Mathilda's) soul'. Prou, *Recueil*, 318–21.

80 Bozóky, 'Hagiography, Relics and Secular Politics', 283–4.

protagonists of the event were Mathilda's relations on both sides. Arnulf I of Flanders invaded Pontieu in 930 and stole great collections of relics from their monastic guardians, as mentioned above. These included the relics of St Valery and St Riquier. Arnulf transported his treasure to Flanders, gifting churches and monasteries with them, an expression of his status as a Christian authority. The saints had allowed Arnulf to obtain them and this was a clear sign of their favor and of God's.[81] Both St Valery and St Riquier were installed at the abbey of Saint Bertin in Ghent. In 981, St Valery appeared to Hugh Capet and asked him to rescue them from Flanders and bring them home. As a reward, the saint promised Hugh would become king of France and that his successors would govern for seven generations.[82] Bozóky illustrates how this prophecy was 'interpreted as a signal of the divine will to legitimise the seizure of royal power by Hugh Capet'.[83] The relic translation of the two saints, and its accompanying legend, endorsed Hugh as the appropriate heir to the throne even though Charles, Duke of Lower Lorraine, was the next Carolingian in the dynastic line. Hugh's translation of the relics created an opportunity for Pope Stephen IV to anoint and crown him. The relic contest between Hugh Capet and Arnulf I illustrates how ducal and comital families used relics to undergird their authority; the practice was not reserved for royal dynasties.

Flemish relic veneration arguably found its fullest expression in the Peace of God movement. Driven by ecclesiastical concern for the violence of internal warfare, the power of relics was at its center. Flanders was an early adopter of the Peace of God movement and relics featured prominently in its assemblies. Mathilda's parents, Baldwin and Adela, promoted the wandering peregrinations of the monks of Lobbes, as they carried their patron, Saint Ursmer, through Flanders.[84] Adela gave permission for the monks to be admitted into her castle at Furnes and arranged to have her castellan's son – who was blind – presented to the saint's relics for healing.[85] The Peace of God assemblies were conspicuously supported by the comital pair, not least because the

81 Geary, *Furta Sacra*, 33. See also Nicole Herrmann-Mascard, *Les Reliques des saints: Formation coutumiere d'un droit* (Paris, 1975), 364–402.

82 Richard Landes, 'L'accession des Capétiens: une reconsidération selon les sources aquitaines', in *Religion et culture autour de l'an Mil. Royaume capétien et Lotharingie. Actes du Colloque Hugues Capet, 987–1987*, ed. Dominique Iogna-Prat (Paris, 1990), 151–66.

83 Bozóky, 'Hagiography, Relics and Secular Politics', 284. The characterization of Hugh's seizure of the throne has been questioned. See Yves Sassier, *Hugues Capet: Naissance d'une dynastie* (Paris, 2018).

84 Michel Belliart, 'Les Miracles de saint Adalhard de Corbie en Flandre (vers 1075)', *Revue du Nord* 102: 436 (2020), 641–52; Paulo Charruadas, 'Principauté territoriale, reliques et Paix de Dieu. Le comté de Flandre et l'abbaye de Lobbes à travers les Miracula S. Ursmari in itinere per Flandriam facta (vers 1060)'. *Revue du Nord* 372: 4 (2007), 703–28 at 750.

85 Charruadas, 'Principauté territoriale,' 725.

movement reinforced their judicial authority. The monks at Lobbes explicitly linked the Peace of God to comital justice.[86] Mathilda's Flemish family thus had a significant interest in the power of relics that unambiguously promoted comital prerogatives.

Mathilda's parents were avid relic collectors. Baldwin V obtained a relic of the Holy Blood and supplied his step-sister, Judith of Flanders, with a portion of it which she gave to Weingarten.[87] Mathilda's mother attempted a relic theft herself, though it was ultimately unsuccessful. She lured the monks of Corbie to her castle in Lille as they progressed with their saintly founder, Adalard. The monastic foundation had been part of Adela's dowry; she argued that Adalard was a relative of hers.[88] Adela also claimed that Adalard deserved to be venerated in a larger, more ornate church than he was accorded at Corbie. In an attempt to keep Adalard's body, she locked the monks and their saint into her fortress overnight and even barred the city gates of Lille. When the monks miraculously escaped in the night, they took only Adalard's bones wrapped in cloth and, in haste, left behind their silver reliquary. Once Adela realized her gambit had failed, she graciously returned the reliquary to them sending it along behind as they fled.[89] Adela's covetousness of the relics of Corbie's founder did not result in the saint's choosing to remain. Her generous response highlights the understanding of the saint's authority in the medieval world; Adalard simply did not want to stay.

A saint's selection of a permanent resting place conferred her/his most valuable endorsement. The legitimizing power of saints was often bound to their choice of resting place. A saint's movements, whether on procession or on the run, were thus driven by their guardians' desire to protect them until they found a safe haven. This is certainly true in Mathilda's marital home of Normandy. The legend of Normandy's formation under Rollo also positioned

86 This may seem surprising as Lobbes was an abbey under the control of the bishop of Liège, an ally of the imperial power, thus an enemy of Baldwin V. But the cessation of hostilities at the death of Emperor Henry III led to the diplomatic agreement between Flanders and Empress Agnes of Poitou, the regent of Emperor Henry IV. This allowed for a space of neutrality. Charruadas, 'Principauté territoriale', 750.

87 The relic of the Holy Blood is still celebrated in Ghent today.

88 Technically speaking, this is true. Adalard, the first abbot of Corbie, was a cousin of Charlemagne. Adela's father was the Capetian king, Robert II. Robert II was named for his great-great grandfather, Robert I, who married Beatrice of Vermandois, a direct descendant of Charlemagne. The Capetian dynasty a cadet branch of the Carolingian dynasty and thus Adela was 'related' to Adalard. Henri Peltier, 'Saint Adalard, Abbe de Corbie: son rôle politique et administrative' in *Corbie Abbaye Royale* (Lille, 1963), 61–94.

89 Recounted in Huyghebaert 'Les Femmes Laiques,' 374. The details are recorded in the *Liber secundus miraculorum S. Adalardi*, M.G.H. SS., XV, 862–5.

relics and their legitimizing function at its center. Before Rollo came to power, *c.* 911, relic collections were threatened by Viking incursions in the ninth and tenth centuries. The holy bodies in religious houses were displaced or removed by the monastic personnel who carried them to safety outside the duchy.[90] Somewhat ironically, Rollo's leadership of the region was legitimized when he brought St Ouen, Normandy's most famous saint, back home. Relics of the saint had been hidden abroad to protect him from men like Rollo. The translation of St Ouen, once again at rest in Rouen, cemented Rollo's position as the leader of his people and conferred legitimacy on his authority.[91] Relic veneration and collecting continued to be a central marker of Norman ducal leadership through Richard I and Richard II.[92] In 1035, Duke Robert, William's father, brought the finger of St Stephen from Jerusalem to Normandy, and gave it to the abbey of Saint-Étienne at Fontenay.[93] St Stephen's entire arm was housed at Besançon with an ampule of his blood.[94] More Norman evidence of the foundational role of relics in supporting secular rule can be found in William's minority. The Peace assemblies noted above were organized by the ecclesiastical authorities who supported William in his early embattled years.[95] The peace councils, dated *c.* 1035–1042, were arranged when he was probably no more than seven or eight years old.[96] They utilized saintly bodies, specifically the relics of St Ouen, 'the regional saint par excellence'.[97]

After William's victory at Val-ès-Dunes, moreover, the same relics of St Ouen and St Catherine – both 'long associated with princely power' – were

90 Musset, 'Les translations de reliques,' passim; Trân-Duc, 'Le culte des saints en Normandie', i, 209, 220, 442. In contrast to this view, see Felice Lifshitz, 'The Migration of Neustrian Relics in the Viking Age: the Myth of Voluntary Exodus, the Reality of Coerced the Reality of Coercion and Theft', *EME* 4 (1995), 175–92.

91 Bozóky, 'Hagiography, Relics and Secular Politics', 284.

92 For Richard I, see P. Lauer, 'Les translations des reliques de saint Ouen', *Bulletin philologique et historique du Comité des travaux historiques et scientifiques* (Paris, 1921), 119–36, at 128–9.

93 Musset, 'Saint-Étienne de Fontenay', 18–19.

94 The traditional liturgy of the abbey set the date of the relic reception at October 8. Hippeau, *L'abbaye de Saint-Étienne*, 459 and 466.

95 Barthélemy, 'Le concile de paix', 37–53.

96 Barthélemy, 'Le concile de paix', 42–3.

97 The *Miracula sancti Audoeni* describes the assembly on *sub Cadomensi territorio*, on the right bank of the Orne, not far from the church of Sainte-Paix. Trân-Duc, 'Le culte des saints en Normandie', i, 423. The vita of St Catherine also recounts the gatherings; Albert Poncelet, 'Sanctae Catharine virginis et martyrs translatio et miracula rotomagensia saec. XI', *Analecta Bollandiana* 22 (1903), 423–38, at 426–31.

once again aired for the Truce of God assembly southeast of Caen.[98] The Truce of God gathering was the ultimate expression of William's legitimacy and authority; it harnessed the saints' presence and lent their imprimatur to William's final definitive grasp of his birthright.

William chose to dedicate his monastery in Caen to St Stephen, in the tradition of his own father who had procured the proto-martyr's remains. William's relics clearly articulated an awareness of the established saints of the ducal house. Yet, his donations to St Stephen's look rather modest in comparison to Mathilda's collection for Holy Trinity. The men's monastery held a tuft of the saint's white hair with a scrap of his scalp, enclosed in a crystal reliquary, and a stone used in his martyrdom. By contrast, William's deathbed bequest to Battle Abbey contained hundreds of saints in valuable reliquaries.[99] William founded Battle Abbey in 1070, purportedly over the grave of Harold Godwinson, as propitiation for the blood shed during the invasion. Its fifteenth-century relic list is still extant.[100] A significant number of Battle's holy remains were English, and may have been from the royal treasury.[101] In the twelfth century, Wace recounted that Mathilda's husband set up tents and dined over the corpses of the English after Hastings had fallen to him. Perhaps this was a dramatic set piece – rich with biblical allusions – spun out for a Norman audience.[102] Nevertheless, it reads like a mimesis of Battle Abbey built on the noble English dead. Cast as expiation, Battle still dragooned English saints, possibly from the royal treasury, into its relic collection. The abbey was invested with its own army of saints – many of them English – to support the Norman invasion and conquest.

A NEW LITURGICAL CITY

Just as the construction of the ducal castle of Caen created a second capital city, the spiritual presence of Mathilda's treasury of saintly relics created a new axis of sacrality. The assemblage of saints added spiritual bulk to Caen and the liturgical landscape of Normandy was altered as a result. The recentering of Norman spiritual and liturgical life toward Caen was an oscillation caused by the presence – the spiritual weight – of holy bodies Mathilda ensconced in the

98 'Il s'agit de reliques rouennaises, en l'occurrence celles de sainte Catherine et surtout du corps de saint Ouen, associé de longue date au pouvoir princier.' Trân-Duc, 'Le culte des saints en Normandie', i, 453.

99 *The Chronicle of Battle Abbey*, ed. and trans. Eleanor Searle (Oxford, 1980), 91.

100 Carter, 'The Relics of Battle Abbey', 309–43.

101 Far more than St Stephen's, Caen, Battle Abbey's relic inventory resembles Holy Trinity's in terms of its scope. As might be expected, unlike Mathilda's collection, it has a significant number of English saints. Carter, 'The Relics of Battle Abbey', 327–40.

102 Wace, *The History of the Norman People: Wace's Roman de Rou*, trans. Glyn S. Burgess (Woodbridge, 2004), 191–2.

city. Caen's social and religious space was transformed by the presence of these saints, first – and perhaps most visibly – by their initial translation into the abbey church of Holy Trinity. The resultant liturgical ripples, however, were permanent as they transformed the calendar of Caen's religious observance and eventually drew visitors to its shrines.[103]

As mentioned above, the establishment of a holy body in a new location was always dependent on the will of the main actor in the translation: the saint. Her or his willingness to be placed in a new home was in itself miraculous. It was also public. Martina Caroli demonstrated the distinction between obtaining saintly relics – often a hidden, even secretive transaction – and the laying of the saint in her/his final resting place.[104] Their relocation into a space, often purpose-built for their remains, required something that can better be described as *repositio*, 'a gesture which needed to be public because it publicly affirmed the harmonious sympathy between earth and heaven, and thus required an appropriate liturgy, a public legitimacy, and a strong visibility'.[105]

The *translatio* or *repositio* of holy relics were moments of intense hierarchy; the first authority was the saint, whose body part or element would lie in state inside a reliquary. The second layer of authority was the patron who obtained the relic. The agent of the translation was the bishop who performed the liturgy itself. Finally, the inhabitants of the city, for whom the liturgy was performed, were also the beneficiaries of the translation. Their city had now acquired the prestige of a saintly body, and her/his protection. The introduction of a new feast day, and perhaps eventually a new shrine or cult center, was a valuable addition to their pride in their rising city center and even their quality of life. Alms, and gifts of food and drink, were typical feast day benefits. With Mathilda's relic collection, the people of Caen gained a robust calendar of such events that would have benefitted ordinary citizens of the city and required expenditures from the institutions that supported the charity; abbeys, churches and the ducal coffers. The ducal house was committed to providing alms on feast days and holidays. The outline of the liturgical city was traced by celebration and its economic effects.[106]

The relic collections of an abbey thus affected Caen's economic life. They molded both the devotional culture of their cities and their financial rhythms.[107] Just as the modern calendar gives rhythm to the seasons – New

[103] See Chapter Three: Fingers, 75–104.

[104] Martina Caroli, 'A woman's body for the empire's salvation: the translatio of Queen Bathild's body and the crisis of the year 833' in *Relics, Identity, and Memory in Medieval Europe*, ed. Marika Rasanen, Gritje Harnnann, and Earl Jeffrey Richards (Turnhout, 2016), 91–113.

[105] Caroli, 'A woman's body for the empire's salvation', 103.

[106] Geary, *Furta Sacra*, 73.

[107] '…it is clear that the possession by a great abbey of certain relics affected its kalendar and its liturgical year. Since the great feasts of an abbey were those of its

Year's, Easter, Christmas – Mathilda's choices imposed a particular flow to the year. An abbey's fair, for instance, was central to its fiscal health and was usually granted on the founder's feast day. Sometime after Mathilda was crowned queen, she and William granted a fair to Holy Trinity on the eighth day after Pentecost.[108] This was the day after 'Trinity Sunday' in the liturgical schedule, which aligned with the abbey's Trinitarian identity. The fair would also have been the last celebratory feature of the season of Pentecost. Pentecost season opened with Pentecost Sunday, the day of Mathilda's royal anointing as queen of England at Winchester in 1068.[109] The charter instituting Holy Trinity's fair styled Mathilda 'the most noble of queens, the daughter of Baldwin, the famous and most vigorous count of Flanders, and the illustrious niece of Henry of the Franks'; one of the most laudatory clauses of all her charters. The unusually detailed recitation of Mathilda's queenly prestige and illustrious heritage might argue for the charter's production soon after her coronation. In any case, the day chosen for the fair underscored both Holy Trinity's identity and the moment of Mathilda's triumphal anointing; the ultimate acknowledgement of her legitimacy.

The celebration of Pentecost, through the establishment of the abbey's fair, was only one economic and liturgical focal point in Caen's calendar. The saints Mathilda obtained resulted in feast days sprinkled throughout the year, in all seasons except Lent. Every month outside of the Lenten season had at least two saints' feast days, with concentrations in July (Sts Aaron, Arnulf, Margaret, Mary Magdalene, Germanus), and October (Elutherius, Aurea, Dimitrius of Alexandria, Savinianus and Potentius, Gaudentius and Dimitrius of Thessolonika). Holy Trinity's dedication day was June 18, another day of celebration. These seasonal feasts gave a rhythm to Caen's fiscal and spiritual life.

---

district and possessions, they affected economic life by determining the dates of fairs and markets. Since a new altar requires a relic, an abbey's collection of relics affected tbc dedications of its subject churches and chapels: and the cults which they represented gave a particular bent to local devotion. Finally, a relic collection represents a conspicuous consumption of wealth, and, since shrines were often melted and pawned, of investment, thus reshape the sacred landscape of a place.' Denis Bethell, 'The making of a twelfth-century relic collection', in *Popular Belief and Practice,* ed. C.J. Cuming and Derek Baker (Cambridge, MA, 1972), 61–72, at 63.

108 The charter dates from sometime after Mathilda's coronation, as she is described as 'regina'. The opening clause in its entirety reads: 'William, the most excellent king of the English and leader of the Normans, the son of Count Robert, and his wife the most noble of the queens, the daughter of Baldwin, the famous and most vigorous count of Flanders, and the illustrious niece of Henry of the Franks, named Mathilde' ('...Gwillelmus Anglorum rex excellentissimus ac Normannorum dux, Roberti comitis filius, coniunxque sua reginarum nobilissima, Baldoini incliti ac strenuissimmi Flandrensium comitis filia regisque Francorum Henri neptis clarissima Mathildis nuncupate.'), *Regesta* (no. 62), 292–5.

109 See Chapter Four: Head, 105–33.

The famous translation of St Nicholas in 1087 demonstrates how a saint's body could reinvigorate a city, on many levels: economically, politically and liturgically.[110] When the citizens of Bari in Italy stole the body of St Nicholas from Myra and transported him to their city, the arrival of his relics was a civic triumph. It was intended to help solve Bari's failing fortunes. In the competition for shipping success, Venice had been a clear winner. Bari's acquisition of St Nicholas answered that economic dominance with a religious and cultural win. The financial benefits of pilgrimage traffic were just as rewarding as mercantile activity for Bari.[111] Moments of political and economic need could be met by a saint's presence.

The concentration of relics in Caen also had a political effect on the city as it became a center of ducal and royal power. Bozóky has shown how nascent dynasties, especially those whose legitimacy might be considered questionable, built churches in new political centers and gathered relics within them. Her hagiographic accounts center on the eighth century but they have resonance with Mathilda's activity.[112] Bozóky's examples include Prince Arechis II of Benevento (*c.* 758–87) who styled himself as heir to the Lombards and built a new 'Sacred Palace' at Benevento and the church of Sancta Sophia, for the 'salvation of his people'.[113] He gathered relics from four different southern Italian towns and translated them to the high altar. In a similar effort, Alfonso, King of Asturias (*c.* 788–842), built a new capital at Oviedo. He had the body of St Eulalia transferred to the palatine chapel alongside a large ark-shaped reliquary full of relics. This 'Arca Sancta' contained dozens of holy items: relics from Christ's passion, from Mary and Old Testament saints, jostled inside with local Spanish holy men and women.[114]

These examples of royal dynasties are not completely analogous to the eleventh-century Normans but there are some parallels. Mathilda and William created a second center of ducal power in Normandy, and Mathilda invested it with the spiritual capital necessary to promote and protect Caen. She also harnessed the relics' saintly prestige and reflected glory to crown her endeavors. As she gathered relics from all over the medieval world, she – like Arechis and Alfonso – drew these saints' parts together to create a wholly greater 'sum'; a new holy citizenry for her newfound abbey within a city center created by ducal will. Her assembly also shifted the political center of Normandy to Caen.

110 Marjorie M. Chibnall, 'The translation of the relics of St Nicholas and Norman historical tradition', in *Piety, Power and History in Medieval England and Normandy*, ed. Marjorie Chibnall (Farnham, 2000), 33–41.

111 Geary, *Furta Sacra*, 73.

112 Bozóky, 'Hagiography, Relics and Secular Politics', 275.

113 Bozóky, 'Hagiography, Relics and Secular Politics', 276.

114 Ibid.

DEDICATION

The dedication of Holy Trinity in 1066 provides an instructive example of the integration of Mathilda's collection of relics in their liturgical setting in the midst of the city of Caen. More elaborate dedication rites for churches developed beginning in the tenth century, in parallel with the Peace of God movement.[115] Both assemblies constructed ideologies of the inviolate organized around holy bodies. Consequently, Holy Trinity's dedication brings together multiple contextual strands of Mathilda's veneration and use of relics. As we have seen in the previous chapter, Holy Trinity had a crucial role to play in the conquest, and its dedication liturgy was an acknowledgement of this, attended by the great and the good throughout Normandy especially those preparing for the invasion. The dedication was also an opportunity to reinforce the civic identity of the new city.

Louis Hamilton has demonstrated that through the liturgy of dedication, the lay populace was encouraged to imagine themselves as part of a new community built up around the abbey church.[116] On this important occasion, Mathilda's saints were essential; relics were a normative feature of church dedications from as early as the fourth century. Each relic would have required an altar of some kind, a tradition codified by papal dictate from the eighth century.[117] While there were significant regional variations in church dedications in the eleventh century across Europe, Hamilton analyzed the core elements of the consecration of churches in the eleventh century and found some liturgical commonalities.[118] These features undoubtedly would have appeared in Holy Trinity's church dedication and demonstrate that, even if Holy Trinity's rite was at the modest end of the spectrum, its dedication would have been notable to the inhabitants of the city.[119] An overnight vigil of the relics in tents outside the church would precede the ceremony. The next morning, they would be carried on a bier toward Holy Trinity in a solemn procession led by Maurilius, the archbishop of Rouen, Mathilda and William, the other attending bishops, the abbess, the clergy, the nuns, the aristocratic laity and the populace of Caen. The archbishop would have knocked on the

115 Thomas Head and Richard Landes, *The Peace of God: Social Violence and Religious Response in France around the Year 1000* (Ithaca, NY, 1992), 3–9.

116 Hamilton, A Sacred City, 56–79.

117 The establishment of altars for the holy dead was related to but separate from the much more elaborate rite of the consecration of the abbey church. 'Council of Nicaea II (787)' in *Decrees of the Ecumenical Councils, Volume One*, ed. Norman P. Tanner (Georgetown, DC, 2016),144–5. The remains of more than one saint, however, might be included together at one altar or even in the same reliquary.

118 Hamilton has laid out comparative tables of dedication liturgies, including the most widely copied, the Romano-Germanic Pontifical Rite (PRG), for analysis. Hamilton, *Sacred City*, 27–50 (Tables 1–3).

119 Hamilton, *Sacred City*, 13–15 and 27–50.

door of Holy Trinity three times, reciting psalms, and then processed around the exterior of Holy Trinity three times, with the entire assembly following.[120] The archbishop would knock on the door of Holy Trinity's church again and entered the church alone as the rest of the faithful waited outside, singing. He would bless the liturgical vestments, instruments and trace out blessings inside the church. All the while, the relics and the crowd would wait outside, singing. Finally, Archbishop Maurilius anointed the altar seven times with holy chrism, and the relics processed in. At the end of the procession, the archbishop addressed the assembly on the peace of the church, and demanded oaths of support from the 'lord and constructor' of Holy Trinity. Holy unction was performed on the relics and they were placed inside the altar. The entire church would be then be illuminated with candles. Lastly, the Eucharist would be performed for the first time inside Holy Trinity's abbey church.

Throughout the procession, the antiphons sung by the clergy and the people identified Holy Trinity with the New Jerusalem, the holy city of God. The archbishop sang out 'Walk, o saints of God, enter into the city of the Lord, indeed a new church is built for you, where the people ought to adore the majesty of the Lord.' The inhabitants of Caen were encouraged to imagine themselves in the New Jerusalem as they processed around Holy Trinity's walls, singing the *Kyrie eleison*. The clergy responded, singing 'The streets of Jerusalem will rejoice and all its districts sing songs of joy'.[121] The two cities – physical and liturgical – became intertwined through the text sung by the clergy and the movement of the crowds. In Hamilton's words, 'The two groups became linked and the two cities fruitfully confused.'[122] Holy Trinity's architectural footprint would continue to expand after the conquest but its liturgical construction was thus complete.

On June 18, 1066, Caen's laity – both common and aristocratic – might have been particularly receptive to suggestions of community and unity around the new abbey of Holy Trinity and their duchess. In the face of the upcoming military invasion, Mathilda and the Normans were on the precipice of either great triumph or costly failure. Like a prayer chain of a modern-day church, people of all classes throughout Normandy might have come together to offer support. These inhabitants of Normandy had a role to play in providing a successful launch for the military forces on their way to England. Citizens of Normandy, both modest and exalted, had much to gain from the success of this venture and were knit together to form a web of reinforcement. Had the conquest been a failure, doubtless some of the aristocracy – those who waged war against him in 1047 – would have relished their chances against a

[120] The circuits around the church varied; at least two and usually three. Hamilton, *Sacred City*, 15.

[121] Hamilton, *Sacred City*, 18.

[122] Hamilton, *Sacred City*, 19.

vulnerable Duke, limping home chastened. Yet even they stood to be enriched and privileged from a Norman victory over England just as did the everyday citizens of Normandy.

Mathilda was not the only relic collector using her networks to support the invasion. The abbeys in Rouen were amassing relic collections of their own over the course of the late eleventh century as they repaired the losses of the past.[123] Abbot Nicolas of Saint-Ouen in Rouen (*c.* 1040–1090) was particularly active, and gathered a significant treasury of relics at precisely the same time Mathilda was gathering her saintly army.[124] Even though Caen was supplanting Rouen as the center of the Exchequer and other important administrative functions, the abbot was less a rival, more a collaborator in the Norman effort. Evidence provided by the shiplist of the Norman Conquest reveals that Abbot Nicolas provided 15 ships and 100 knights to the Norman invasion force (Plate 1).[125]

Abbot Nicolas's gift to support the invasion and the dedication of Holy Trinity's abbey church allow us to think more broadly about the gathering of resources throughout Normandy for the military project of 1066. One imagines institutions throughout the duchy proffering whatever support they could: men, arms, gold, relics, prayers. Seen from this angle, Abbot Nicholas's relic collecting was another offering to promote the invasion of England. Perhaps Nicolas, too, gathered up saints not just to heighten the prestige of Saint-Ouen but in aid of the Norman endeavor against England. According to contemporary sources this is precisely what came to pass. After the success of the conquest, Normandy was enriched enormously. William of Poitiers singles out Norman churches and monasteries especially as beneficiaries of ducal

123 'Through these various processes, the Norman Church succeeded, certainly by the middle of the eleventh century, in restoring its "hagiographic capital" (if we can use that expression). Certainly, it was not, from the spiritual point of view, its principal claim to glory, but it is one of its most curious and perfect successes, due to the constant support of the ducal dynasty.' ('Par ces procédés divers, l'Église normande parvint, en général vers le milieu du XIe siècle, à reconstituer son « capital hagiographique » (que l'on nous passe l'expression). Certes ce ne fut pas, du point de vue spirituel, son principal titre de gloire, mais c'est l'une de ses plus curieuses et parfaites réussites, due à l'appui constant de la dynastie ducale.'). Musset, 'Les translations de reliques', 8.

124 Abbot Nicolas was the son of Richard III, who was duke of Normandy for only a year before his death, and thus Nicolas was William's cousin. The Ricardian party was generally hostile to William's rule early in his life but Nicolas was supportive. Before his installation as abbot, Nicolas was a monk at Fécamp. Véronique Gazeau, *Normannia monastica (Xe-XIIe siècle): Princes normands et abbés bénédictins et Prosopographie des abbés bénédictins* (2 vols., Caen, 2007), ii, 403.

125 See Plate 1, 47. See also Elisabeth van Houts, 'The Ship List of William the Conqueror', *ANS* 10 (1987), 176–9.

largesse on William's triumphant return in March 1067.[126] After the conquest, Abbot Nicolas revived the cult of St Vulgan, an English evangelist whose body lay in Lens. He wrote the *vita* of St Vulgan which is preserved in the twelfth-century 'Black Book' of the abbey.[127]

The conflict traced out between the two abbeys in Chapter Two illustrated the value of the people of Caen as dependents, who provided rents and services.[128] Yet, they were more than merely this; they were parishioners. They were the flock, the faithful. Spiritual guidance of and intercessory prayer for them was one of the defining features of monastic life. The liturgical experience of Caen's population was organized by the nuns and monks of the city who maintained the remembrance of the saints placed into their care, including their feasts. Holy Trinity's relic treasury provided thirty-six different saints who ostensibly required thirty-six feast days to be inserted into the city calendar of Caen's observance. This way, the city of Caen became a physical manifestation of Mathilda and William's authority in the ways historians like Leonie Hicks have taught us to recognize: liturgical, spatial, seigneurial.[129] The sacred city that grew up around Caen had a liturgical topography that paralleled the city's corporeal shape. It also linked Caen to a world of believers: in Alexandria, in Thessalonica, in the Holy Land – the world of Isaiah and Samuel.

CONCLUSION

The foremost challenge of Mathilda's and William's administration – the pursuit of royal rule in England – illustrates how enmeshed relics were with their political lives.[130] Harold Godwinson's oath not to seek the crown of England was sworn publicly on relics in front of the Norman court. Broken in 1066, it rendered his occupation of the English throne unlawful. Mathilda's gathering of saintly protectors and supporters, discussed here, was one strategy in legitimizing the launching of the conquest through their presence at Holy Trinity's dedication – an event that has been widely understood as preparation for the invasion of England.[131] When the invasion force was delayed at St Valery-sur-Somme, William himself processed with St Valery's relics down to the port.[132] The weather lifted and St Valery was credited with the miracle – the very saint

126 'He (William) rewarded this dutiful affection immediately with treasures of many kinds, giving vestments, gold bullion and other magnificent gifts to the altars and servants of Christ.' William of Poitiers, *Gesta*, 176–7.

127 Trân-Duc, 'Le culte des saints en Normandie', i, 226.

128 See Chapter Two: Hands, 68–9.

129 Hicks, *Religious Life in Normandy*, passim.

130 Carter, 'Relics of Battle Abbey', 313–14.

131 The abbey's dedication charter was woven through with scripture that pointedly referenced the conquest. See Chapter Two: Hands, 43–6.

132 William of Poitiers, *Gesta*, 111.

responsible for Hugh Capet's legitimacy so central to Mathilda's past. On the battlefield at Hastings, moreover, William fought for England wearing around his neck the same relics Harold had disregarded.[133] At each turn, Mathilda and William embraced the presence of relics and employed their power to authenticate the English enterprise. Furthermore, Mathilda conducted the relic translation of the Holy Shroud, mentioned above, at a moment when civil war threatened her family.[134] As she worked toward the reconciliation of her husband and son, relics were at the center of her efforts.[135]

Biblical exegesis and interpretation are not hard sciences. Like so many elements touching Mathilda's life, the analysis of the relics she chose and utilized above must be considered suggestive without hard evidence of her internal thoughts. It is evident, however, that in constructing her ephemeral city through relic observance she mirrored the intentionality she demonstrated in other areas. Through the construction of her abbey church, her coronation liturgy, her embrace of an Ottonian-style queenship, her pious donations of religious vestments, Mathilda's choices indicate a remarkably unified self-fashioning. It focused on the Norman Conquest and her embodiment of its victory, grounded in her prestigious genealogy of powerful ruling women. Her relic collection once again indicated these preoccupations, this time in an area over which she had substantial control. She sought out and obtained a large collection of holy 'ornaments' for Holy Trinity that would add prestige to her foundation and attract the faithful. Her selection of Isaiah and Samuel, unusual Old Testament saints, may have referenced the conquest of England and expressed an understanding of her own destiny. High-status healing saints like St Nicholas and St Martin accorded prestige to her collection and referenced both her royal and her imperial genealogy. Eastern and Roman saints may have spoken to an imperial sensibility Mathilda demonstrated elsewhere.[136] More than any other type of relic, Mathilda's choices of royal Frankish saints – 'deep cuts' of Dagobert and Charlemagne – were a declaration of her membership in the glorious Frankish dynasty of the past.

Just as an ornate reliquary was intimately connected with and sometimes a mimetic device for the holy remains within it, one can imagine the crypt under Holy Trinity, where the relics were housed, as a reliquary itself. Even further,

133 *Gesta Guillelmi*, 124–5.

134 At a battle waged at Gerberoy in January 1079, Robert unhorsed his father and, not recognizing him, nearly killed him on the battlefield. William M. Aird, *Robert Curthose, Duke of Normandy, c. 1050–1134* (Woodbridge, 2008), 86–90.

135 She may have provided the jeweled reliquary as expiation. See Chapter Five: Womb, 151–8.

136 Interestingly, the emperors of Germany also made claims to some of the relics Mathilda chose, including St Denis. Edina Bozóky, 'Les reliques, le prince et le bien public', in *Le Prince, Son Peuple et Le Bien Commun: De l'Antiquité tardive à la fin du Moyen Âge*, ed. Joëlle Quaghebeur, Hervé Oudart and Jean-Michel Picard (Rennes, 2013), 203–15.

Mathilda may have conceived of the entire city of Caen as a reliquary on a larger scale. Like Russian nesting dolls, each enclosed the relic: the reliquary, the crypt, the abbey church of Holy Trinity, the city of Caen, the duchy of Normandy, the kingdom, the wider world of believers. Mathilda's own body would lie within Holy Trinity, thus becoming a sort of relic, too, a reality she doubtless planned for from the beginning of the abbey's construction.

Unlike some of the older monastic houses in Normandy traditionally supported by the ducal family, Mathilda's community of Holy Trinity had no founding saint.[137] Consequently, her relic choices were unburdened by the necessity of acquiring a specific holy body. Instead, she invested Holy Trinity with relics that evoked the Frankish royal past and made the argument for her new abbey as the inheritor of a holy regal genealogy. Like her ancestors, the army of saints she obtained also lent their authority to her new enterprise. Her collection, I would argue, was both an act of veneration and of self-expression. She amassed her collection for the good of Holy Trinity but her choices revealed her preoccupations: dynasty, legitimacy and conquest.

137 Trân-Duc analyzes the anxiety about reclaiming the lost bodies of their founding saints betrayed by Saint-Ouen and Saint-Wandrille. Trân-Duc, 'Le culte des saints', i, 222–6.

4

HEAD

This day set a crown of pure gold upon her head, so enrich her royal heart with thine abundant grace, and crown her with all princely virtues through the King Eternal Jesus Christ our Lord.

'Deus tuorum Corona fidelium' prayer

The night of May 10, 1068 was a scene of great solemnity in Westminster Abbey. Candles pierced the darkness throughout the nave, gleaming as the vigil of Pentecost unfolded. Of all the nights in the church calendar, this one – save perhaps the night before Easter – was the most sacred. In the morning, a triumphal mass would commemorate the coming of the Holy Spirit upon the apostles in the Upper Room in the form of a mighty wind, in tongues of flame. In this miraculous moment, according to scripture, the apostles spoke in many languages – a sign that the Spirit of God inhabited them. This was a fundamental mystery of the church year. The next morning the church would be filled with music; Pentecost mass featured special chants and songs dedicated to the Holy Spirit and the beginnings of Christ's church on earth. Pentecost Sunday at Westminster 1068, moreover, would see another beginning. Mathilda of Flanders' coronation and anointing in this church would transform her through sacred ritual into a persona mixta – a 'mixed person'; part human, part divine.[1] The mass of Pentecost would enfold a different, parallel mystery that transmuted a woman into Christ's representative on earth. Something more, then, was playing out on that late Saturday night in May, before the gathered crowd of English and Normans, standing together in the dark. The expectation of the central event – the crowning of a new Norman queen – charged the atmosphere in the shadowed church. Mathilda stood as the central figure as the sacred readings for the Pentecost Vigil were recited in the gloom. The Norman conquerors were probably thrilled with their new queen, every inch an unparalleled royal presence. The English in the crowd also looked over their new royal mistress, so different from Edith, the dowager English queen. Edith's blood had been aristocratic,

1 For the function of anointing in creating a medieval 'persona mixta' and its theoretical underpinnings, the germinal study remains Ernst Kantorowicz, *The Kings Two Bodies: A Study in Medieval Political Theology* (Princeton, NJ, 1957).

but Mathilda's was imperial – a heady convergence of Carolingian and Ottonian bloodlines. Edith had been vulnerable, at one time even banished, suspected of adultery. Mathilda's presence was crucial to Norman rule; she was indispensable. Where Edith was childless, Mathilda was fecund. And she was visibly pregnant – on that very night as she awaited her royal inauguration – with yet another Norman soon-to-be royal child.

Through this rite, Mathilda was, like kings, 'hallowed' and made quasi-divine.[2] She was a queen crowned by God.[3] Obedience to her was now the duty of every English citizen and her judgements had gained the force of law.[4] Her royal inauguration included innovative triumphalist elements confected solely for her.[5] It also was the first time the ritual was performed for a queen of England who was noticeably pregnant. Mathilda's last child, the future Henry I, was born – at the latest – in early September 1068, four months after she became a divinely ordained ruler.[6] Henry may have been born even earlier; the Winchester Annals claim that Henry was born 'not too many days' after Mathilda's liturgy.[7] On Pentecost in 1068, Mathilda

2 *ASC*, 1068, Worcester Version (D), 'This Easter came the king to Winchester; and Easter was then on the tenth before the calends of April. Soon after this came the Lady Matilda hither to this land; and Archbishop Eldred hallowed her to queen at Westminster on Whit Sunday'.

3 Her rite identifies her as 'Mathylide serenessima a Deo coronate regina'. See appendix to this chapter, 134–43.

4 See George Garnett's discussion of the changes in penance for soldiers before and after William was crowned king. George Garnett, 'Coronation and Propaganda: Some Implications of the Norman Claim to the Throne of England in 1066: The Alexander Prize Essay,' *Transactions of the Royal Historical Society*, 36 (1986), 91–116 at 94–7.

5 Until recently, historians generally used the term 'coronation' for this rite, which inherently preferenced the crowning element of the ritual. But crowns were worn repeatedly; it was anointing that truly was at the heart of the royal claim to quasi-divinity. Dale contends that royal inauguration is a more accurate term for the collection of rites that made up the liturgy: anointing, presentation of the ring, coronation, acclamation, the Mass, the presentation. We can add the laudes regiae to this collection of rituals for Mathilda's inaugural rite that served to elevate and position her to rule. Johanna Dale, *Inauguration and Liturgical Kingship in the Long Twelfth Century: Male and Female Accession Rituals in England, France and the Empire* (York, 2019), 28.

6 Warren Hollister and Amanda Frost, *Henry I* (New Haven, CT, 2003), 30–1. Mathilda's itinerary in 1067 and William's presence in Normandy both argue for, at the latest, early to mid-September.

7 '1068: Matilda is consecrated this year in London by Ealdred, archbishop of York and not too many days later her son, Henry, was brought into the light' ('MLXVIII: Hoc anno Matildis consecrata est apud Londoniam ab Aldredo Eboracensi archiepiscopo, et post non multos dies Henricum filium suum in lucem protulit.'). *Annales monasterii de Wintona, Winchester Annals*, ed. H.R. Luard, Rolls Series 36

embodied the success of Norman rule, highlighted by the contours of her pregnant body.[8]

William was anointed and crowned on Christmas Day, 1066, at Westminster. Contemporary sources claim it was hastily thrown together amidst the grumblings and misgivings of at least some of the Norman nobility.[9] William himself, according to William of Poitiers, was deeply unsure about the timing of the coronation. He puts these words in William's mouth: 'It is still turbulent; some rebel. I prefer the kingdom to be quieted rather than the desired crown. Further, if God allowed me the honor, I wish my wife to be crowned with me.'[10] William's desire to have Mathilda consecrated next to him is a reasonable justification for delay, according to contemporary narratives. His anxiety, and the way chroniclers reflect it in eleventh-century sources, fits well with what we know from previous chapters. Mathilda's royal bloodline, stretching back to Charlemagne and Otto I, had helped to bolster his position since their marriage. In the end, however, William was persuaded to go forward with his inauguration that Christmas. William wagered that his royal ritual, and the claims it made for his legitimacy, 'would ultimately triumph'.[11] The gamble did not pay off.

The narrative reports of the event show William's coronation as a scene of violence and pandemonium; his soldiers set part of London on fire.[12] Orderic claims William's troops were unfamiliar with an English inauguration rite. As his consecration was taking place, an acclamation to William was shouted out –

(London, 1865), 27. The thirteenth-century annalist was writing many years after the events, but perhaps the memory of Henry's impending birth at Mathilda's royal rite is evidence that it was notable.

8 Mathilda of Flanders would be classified today as 'grand multiparous', that is, she had more than seven children. Women who experience grand multiparity show signs of pregnancy much more quickly and dramatically than primiparous women. This is because the effect of grand multiparity is reduced muscle function of the pelvic floor. Mathilda's pregnancy at five months would have shown more dramatically than primiparous women.

9 David C. Douglas, *William the Conqueror* (Berkeley, CA, 1964), 248. William of Poitiers, *Historie de Guillaume la Conquérant*, ed. Raymonde Foreville (Paris, 1952), 215–16.

10 '...res adhuc turbidas esse: rebellare nonnullos; se potius regni quietem quam coronam cupere. Praeterea, si Deus ipsi hunc concedit honorem, secum velle conjugem suam coronari.' William of Poitiers editorializes, 'Sanctam esse intellexerant; sancteque diligebat conjugii pignus ('Sacred was this understanding; sacred and loving the marriage pledge.'). William of Poitiers, *Gesta*, 216–18.

11 'One must suppose, then, that to perform a ritual with an end in mind was to gamble that one's desired interpretation would ultimately triumph.' Philippe Buc, *The Dangers of Ritual: Between Early Medieval Texts and Social Scientific Theory* (Princeton, NJ, 2001), 8.

12 *OV*, ii, 182–5.

in at least two languages – by the attending crowd within the cathedral. The acclamation was part of the liturgy. But the soldiers, attuned to the possibility of trouble from a barely pacified city, assumed William was being attacked within the church. The garbled shout of acclamation sounded perhaps more like a mass roar. Convinced William was in danger they took action. They set diversionary fires to the surrounding buildings in London, causing panic and mayhem.

The attending crowd, the audience for William's liturgy, rushed out of the church to see what was happening. William was left standing alone, 'trembling from head to foot', as Normans and English poured out of the church.[13] As the rite continued without an audience, he was anointed and crowned. His archbishops – Ealdred and Stigand – were the only participants to remain and witness what should have been the high point of his victory. The rite was not an auspicious beginning to Norman rule. If nothing else, the heightened anxiety of ritual moments is demonstrated by his soldiers' behavior. They were convinced that his inauguration was a likely moment for William to suffer an attack; they expected trouble.

By contrast, a pregnant queen was generally considered 'the guarantor of the realm's survival and integrity and so of peace and concord'.[14] For the English in the crowd, victims of Norman conquest, subjugated and dislocated, Mathilda's pregnant body surely provoked a very different response. Elizabeth L'Estrange has shown that, for images of pregnancy and maternalism, the viewers' cultural context dictates their own 'sensitivities'.[15] One's sensitivities when confronted with Mathilda's pregnancy, on that weekend in May 1068, had everything to do with whether one was a victor or a victim in 1066. For the victorious Normans in attendance, who supported and participated in the conquest, Mathilda may have referenced the nascent promise of Norman governance: burgeoning life, a new beginning, the expanding riches of their new realm. Certainly her pregnancy called to mind the emerging Norman royal dynasty. Mathilda had already produced healthy heirs for the duchy and the throne, with children to spare. Thus her royal inauguration was a celebration of dynastic success, untinged with apprehension. The Norman archbishops, bishops and their supporters, especially those who helped to craft her inauguration liturgy, would have been gratified to see their handiwork come to life through the performance. Perhaps even some English churchmen, invested in the possibility of reform, might have been cautiously optimistic about the

13 *OV*, ii, 184–5.

14 Janet L. Nelson, 'Royal Inaugurations', in *Politics and Ritual in Early Medieval Europe* (Ronceverte, 1986), 293–308 at 304.

15 In her analysis of medieval maternal art, L'Estrange recognized that different audiences had various sets of 'cultural equipment' they would have brought to seeing and understanding maternal images. This internal context allowed for various levels of 'sensitivity' to those images. Elizabeth L'Estrange, *Holy Motherhood: Gender, Dynasty and Visual Culture in the Later Middle Ages* (Manchester, 2008), 250.

chances of a new upsurge in lay support. Mathilda had already founded a monastery in Caen and embraced monastic largesse as something that defined her. New monastic and clerical donations could be seen on the horizon. Two royal bilingual diplomas – written in Latin and Old English – had already been produced for signatures later that day to celebrate Mathilda's queenship. A generous donation of properties and liberties was made to the church of St Martin-le-Grand in London.[16] The second diploma granted thirty acres in Barnwell to Giso, bishop of Wells, who had been Edward the Confessor's chaplain.[17] The estate in Barnwell was lost to Giso as a result of Harold Godwinson's predation. A false king in Norman eyes, Godwinson's rapacious behavior provided a convenient moment to contrast him with the new queen's generosity. Royal largesse on a grand scale – at least to the church – was thus linked to Mathilda's liturgy. It may have given Mathilda's inauguration a hopeful glow for those churchmen willing to be optimistic. The reception of this visual must have been vastly different, however, for the remnants of the English nobility. Mathilda's crowned authority signified oppression and coercion. Her liturgy may even have lit the fuse of English rebellion.

The diplomas help locate the English attendees, at least the high-status ones, of Mathilda's inauguration. They read like a 'who's who' of the English aristocracy. The archbishops of York and Canterbury, and the bishops of every occupied see in England were present.[18] Norman nobleman, like Odo of Bayeux, William fitz Osbern, Robert of Mortain, Roger of Montgomery, and Robert of Eu rubbed shoulders with the remaining English nobles: Earl Edwin of Mercia, Earl Morcar of Northumbria, Earl Waltheof of Northampton and their followers and retainers.[19]

The English present in Westminster Abbey had experienced the unthinkable two years earlier at Hastings: the loss of their kingdom, their language and their way of life. They were still reeling from the death on the battlefield of their brothers, husbands and sons. Over the last two years, Norman dominance had

16 *Regesta*, 594–601.

17 *Regesta*, 863–5.

18 These included Stigand of Canterbury (whose signature comes before Ealdred of York, despite Stigand's deposition), Ealdred of York, William bishop of London, Odo bishop of Bayeux, Hugh bishop of Lisieux, Gosfrid bishop of Coutances, Herman bishop of Sherborne, Leofric bishop of Exeter, Giso bishop of Wells, Eadwin bishop of Westminster, Wulfwold of Chertsey, Baldwin abbot of Bury St Edmunds, Ælgesin abbot of Bath, Turstin abbot of Glastonbury, Brand abbot of Peterborough, Ælfwin abbot of Ramsey, Ælgwi abbot of Evesham and Sihtric abbot of Tavistock.

19 Richard fitz Gilbert, William Malet, and Arfast the Chancellor also signed. The 'King's chaplain', Michael signs next and then a list of seven chaplains probably from Mathilda's staff: Gilbert, Osbern, William, Thomas, Bernard, Walter and Robert. Cardinal John, the papal legate, and Cardinal Peter, also chancellor, were added later. *Regesta*, 599.

slowly encroached on English holdings and rights. Norman French had become the language of the elite, replacing native Old English. The daily grind of dislocation was their new reality; their survival depended on their ability to accept it and adjust. But hopes for an uprising or a rebellion that would right the English world, currently turned upside down, still lived. The teenaged Edgar Ætheling, the last surviving member of the royal house of Wessex, had submitted to William in 1066, despite his patrimony. His presence at the Norman court provided a reminder for the English that all might not yet be lost.[20] The expectation of yet another Norman royal heir, discernible in Mathilda's shape, however, made the continuation of Norman predation palpable.

The long history of queen's coronations is an important factor in analyzing the liturgy Mathilda and her ministers crafted for her in 1068.[21] By the time she ascended to the throne, queen's coronation ordos had been developing for centuries. Indeed, some of the earliest surviving records of this kind are for queens, not kings. Queen's coronations became central to establishing royal power in the Carolingian period. Carolingian churchmen like Hincmar, Archbishop of Rheims (*c.* 806–882), worked on multiple fronts to establish monogamous, indissoluble marriage in Carolingian society. As the foremost woman of the realm, the queen could act as a model for her kingdom. Royal marriage

20 Edgar Ætheling was the grandson of Edmund Ironside and his claim to the English throne was better than Harold Godwineson's. Edgar was elected by the English council, the witan, in London before the conquest but not crowned. After Hastings, Edgar's supporters stepped back. Edgar submitted to the Normans and his election was set aside.

21 The historiography of queen's coronation ordos is significant and stretches back to the nineteenth century. More recent foundational studies include Janet L. Nelson, 'The Rites of the Conqueror', *ANS* 4 (1981), 117–32; Janet L. Nelson, 'Ritual and Reality in Early Medieval Ordines', in *Politics and Ritual in Early Medieval Europe* (London 1986), 329–39; Gunther Wolf, 'Königinnen-Krönungen des frühen Mittelalters bis zum Beginn des Investiturstreits,' *Zeitschrift der Savigny-Stiftung für Rechtsgeschichte* 107:76 (1990), 62–88; Richard A. Jackson, *Ordines coronationis Franciae: texts and ordines for the coronation of Frankish and French kings and queens in the Middle Ages* (Philadelphia, PA, 1995); Elizabeth McCartney, 'Ceremonies and privileges of office: queenship in late medieval France', in *Power of the Weak: Studies on Medieval Women*, ed. Jennifer Carpenter and Sally-Beth Maclean (Urbana, IL, 1995), 178–219; Julie A. Smith, 'The Earliest Queen-making Rites,' *Church History* 66 (1997), 18–35; George Garnett, 'The Third Recension of the English Coronation *ordo*: the Manuscripts', *HSJ* 11 (1998), 43–71; Janet L. Nelson, 'Early medieval rites of queen-making and the shaping of medieval queenship', in *Rulers and Ruling Families in Early Medieval Europe: Alfred, Charles the Bald, and Others*, ed. Janet L. Nelson (Farnham, 1999), 301–15; George Garnett, *Conquered England: Kingship, Succession, and Tenure, 1066–1166* (Oxford, 2007); Bruno Dumézil, 'Les attributs du pouvoir et la compétition pour le pouvoir: armes et titulatures au VIe siècle', in *Genre et compétition dans les sociétés occidentales du haut Moyen Âge (Ive–XIe siècle)*, ed. Sylvie Joye and Régine Le Jan (Turnhout, 2018) 79–91; Dale, *Inauguration*.

became an important mirror of the perfect Christian union, so the dissolution of royal marriages was to be avoided at all costs. As a result, the consecration of the queen began to mutate from a simple marriage blessing to a rite that had sacrality at its core. Her link to royal rule was no longer her relationship to the king. It was her consecration – her new sacred, inviolate status – that made her queen. Her new identity as a 'persona mixta' was her armor should her royal husband wish to dissolve their union.[22] Thus those high church officials like Archbishop Hincmar, who were involved in the structure and practice of royal inauguration, gave new focus to queenly rites. His motives for their development were inextricably tied to larger socio-political concerns. In Hincmar's case, the desire to promote indissoluble, monogamous marriage and avoid royal divorce led to a new status for Carolingian queens. Hincmar's ninth-century efforts soon provided the pattern for queens throughout medieval Europe and the nature of queenship changed forever.

At the same time in England, the concept of 'spiritual queenship' developed in the tenth century, a direct parallel with spiritual kingship enjoyed by early English kings.[23] The English coronation ordo for a queen helped to establish her as sharing in the rule of the kingdom and responsibility for its religious health.[24] Early English churchmen and writers typologically linked earthly queens to the Church, dressed in finery as they awaited their bridegroom, who was Christ. Ælfric's *On the Dedication of the Church* makes this parallel as he describes 'the spiritual queen, God's church adorned with the precious ornament and manifold color of good habits and virtues'.[25] Cynewulf's 'Elena' – the legend of Helen, Emperor Constantine's mother – draws connections between the earthly queen and the queen of heaven, Mary.[26] Depictions of the crowned Virgin Mary as the Queen of Heaven, moreover, were introduced to England in the tenth century at the same time as ruler portraits linking the queen to the Virgin Mary appeared.[27] It is worth remembering that England

22 The development of a queen's position must be seen in the context of Hincmar's involvement in the marital convulsions of Lothar II. Lothar's inability to annul his union to Theutberga, after crowning her as queen, was a triumph of Hincmar's legal strategies. The result seems to have been a keen understanding on the part of the elite Carolingian 'clerical consecrators' that queenly inauguration made a queen, not merely her marriage to a king. For further discussion of Lothar's marital troubles and Hincmar's role, see Stuart Airlie, 'Private Bodies And The Body Politic in the Divorce Case Of Lothar II', *Past & Present* 161:1 (Nov 1998), 3–38.

23 Catherine E. Karkov, *The Ruler Portraits of Anglo-Saxon England* (Woodbridge, 2004), esp. 84–118.

24 Stacy Klein, *Ruling Women: Queenship and gender in Anglo-Saxon Literature* (Notre Dame, IN, 2006), 64–5.

25 *Aelfric's Catholic Homilies, Second Series, Text*, ed. Malcolm Godden (London, 1979), 340, lines 175–6.

26 Klein, *Ruling Women*, 65–6.

27 Stafford, *Queen Emma and Queen Edith*, 163, 166–9, 172–4.

was converted through its queens, a narrative made famous by Bede but also supported by the evidence of papal letters and reintroduced by Ælfric.

It would be inaccurate to argue that these traditions of queenly pre-eminence had an exact correlation to the experience of the women who ruled England. Neither Edith nor Emma, who reigned immediately before Mathilda, were able to parlay the ideology surrounding English queenship into inviolability. Each woman was vulnerable at various times during her reign. Edith was exiled and nearly repudiated; she only returned to court when her family's fortunes began to rise again. As the widow of Æthelred, Queen Emma was also politically at risk, especially after Cnut's invasion of England.[28] After her marriage, she played a central role in Cnut's bid for legitimacy and was active in administration during his lifetime. On his death, her preference for younger son Harthacnut over her older son, the future King Edward the Confessor, eventually resulted in her obviation from the royal court. English queens were not impervious despite their position as outlined in the ordo. But they could draw strength and influence from their theoretical responsibility for the spiritual well-being of their kingdom. They traditionally were held to reflect, variously, the splendor of the Church on earth and of the Queen of Heaven, Mary.

Mathilda's predecessors made the most of these connections. For example, Edith chose to be anointed and crowned on the Feast of the Purification of the Virgin.[29] As for Emma, historians consider her connections to the Virgin as impetus for the famous 'Quinity' illumination produced sometime between 1012 and 1020 at the New Minster. In this image, Mary is featured as a member of a lively discussion between God the Father and God the Son. The Holy Spirit is represented by a dove nestled into Mary's crown.[30] The Trinity, plus Mary as the Queen of Heaven, coined the title of the portrait, the 'Quinity', a beautiful remnant of the early English world. Mathilda could have used these Marian metaphors for her own version of the inauguration ritual but she did not. She chose to craft her rite on imperial Ottonian models, using innovative elements that would set her royal inauguration apart from her English predecessors. In fact, the Virgin Mary would not be playing a formative role in Mathilda's royal inauguration, despite the possible opportunity presented by her visible pregnancy.

There are three extant versions of English ordos that include queens' royal inauguration rites recorded in the tenth and eleventh centuries. Of these three recensions, or versions, many copies survive in manuscripts both in England

28 Stafford, *Queen Emma and Queen Edith*, 224.

29 Stafford, *Queen Emma and Queen Edith*, 176, note 71.

30 Ernst Kantorowicz 'The Quinity of Winchester', *The Art Bulletin* 29: 2 (June, 1947), 73–85. More recently, see Judith A. Kidd, 'The Quinity Reconsidered', *Studies in Iconography* 7/8 (1981), 21–31; Pauline Stafford, 'Emma: The Powers of the Queen', in *Queens and Queenship in Medieval Europe*, ed. Anne Duggan (Woodbridge, 1997), 13–14.

and on the continent. In fact, there is significant debate about the relationship between them that is not our focus here.[31] Each of them featured an expanding role for the queen but none of them are identified with a specific woman. Between the years 1002 and 1068, three English queens were crowned and anointed using one of these ordos or a liturgy patterned on them. The context of each was idiosyncratic; Emma was crowned queen upon her marriage to her first husband, Æthelred, in 1002. After his death, Emma was reconsecrated queen of England (but not anointed again) on her marriage to her second husband, Cnut, the Danish invader in 1017. Cnut was crowned King of England next to her within the same rite. Queen Edith was crowned and married in a combined rite to Edward the Confessor on January 23, 1045. Mathilda of Flanders was crowned in 1068 without the need of a nuptial rite attached to her liturgy. It is unclear how William participated in her liturgy as he was already anointed. He no doubt wore his crown at her inauguration but there is no evidence for how he was placed in the actual rite. Thus the context for each of these queen's rites had very little overlap. Of all three, Mathilda's liturgy is the only one untethered from a marriage rite. This decoupling is important. Joanna Dale has shown that when a queen was inaugurated separately, after the king had already been anointed, 'his role was liturgically subordinate to that of his queen'.[32]

Other examples of queens being crowned separately from marriage rites can be seen in Germany. Amalie Foßel has introduced imperial examples of royal women being crowned in the months before their marriage to their fiancé-kings.[33] Indeed Hincmar, in the ninth century, ensured that sacral queenship did not rest on a woman's marriage to a king. Her status was independent of his – a concept our contemporary notions of queenship have yet to fully absorb. Nevertheless, Mathilda's royal inauguration ordo, separated from a marriage ceremony and from William's consecration, might have been built on Emma's, Edith's or neither.

Indeed, none of the ordos analyzed by historians make room for the queen to receive a scepter and we know that Mathilda did.[34] The only ordo

31 Janet Nelson argues for the Third Recension for both William and Mathilda's inaugurations. Nelson, 'Rites of the Conqueror', 117–32. George Garnett favors the Second English Ordo for William and Mathilda. Garnett, 'Third Recension', 43–71.

32 Dale, *Inauguration*, 114.

33 Amalie Fößel, *Die Königin im mitteralterlichen Reich: Herrschaftsausübung, Herrschaftsrechte, Handlungsspielräume* (Stuttgart, 2000), 24–7. Dale has noted, 'This practice of consecrating a queen before her marriage to a king stands the conventional understanding of queenship on its head. We are accustomed to thinking of a queen as a queen due to her marital relationship to a king. Our evidence from the Empire, however, suggests that in order to marry king, it was preferable first to be a queen.' Dale, *Inauguration*, 115.

34 She willed her scepter to the Abbey of Holy Trinity in her last charter. See Chapter Six: Flesh, 171.

that explicitly allows for a queen's scepter is the 'Ratold ordo' first written for Ratold, the abbot of Corbie.[35] This monastery, as we have previously discussed, was an important part of Mathilda's mother, Adela's, dowry.[36] The Ratold ordo was used in French coronations in the twelfth century, and was considered a continental version of the Second English Ordo. It is tempting to assign this ordo to Mathilda but we simply have no way of knowing. Historians who study these ordines, like Nelson, Garnett, Jackson, Dale and others have repeatedly made the point that inauguration ordos borrowed from each other and were interrelated in ways that simply do not allow for viewing them as specific to one event.[37]

While the exact ordo has not been identified, the ordos we have contain interesting language. Most historians agree that the Second English Ordo contains the most radical changes to the queen's section of the rite. Until recently, conventional wisdom held that the coronation of William the Conqueror survived as this ordo, whose section on queenly coronation was quite innovative. The ordo stated that the English people are to rejoice that they are governed by the ability and virtue of the queen, whom God had placed above them; she, whom God wished to participate in the royal power.[38] Like the king, she was anointed with sacred unguent oil, with equal dignity and honor. These new phrases, it has been conventionally held, reflect the increased status of queens. But if the king's section of this rite might have been used for William, the connected queen's ordo certainly was not used for Mathilda. The rite specifies that the queen is the 'Glory of the Anglo-Saxons', hardly fitting for the first conquest queen of England.[39] These changes in the rite can be reasonably connected to Emma of Normandy's ordo for her second coronation in 1017, as Pauline Stafford has argued.[40] They highlighted the

[35] Dale, *Inauguration*, 88.

[36] See Chapter One: Blood, 11–33.

[37] Dale, *Inauguration*, 44; Nelson, 'Ritual and Reality', 333; Jackson, *Ordines Coronationes*, I, 34; Shane Bobrycki, 'The Royal Consecration Ordines of the Pontifical of Sens from a New Perspective', *Bulletin du centre d'études médiévales d'Auxerre* 13 (2009), 131–42.

[38] 'laetetur gens Anglica domini imperio regenda et reginae virtutis prudentia gubernanda'; 'qui regalis imperii te voluit esse participem'; 'Quique eam sua miseratione reginam constituit in populo.' John Wickham Legg, *Three Coronation Orders* (London, 1900), 61–3.

[39] Stafford, *Queen Emma and Queen Edith*, 174–5. Judith Abbot has noted that important phrases were added to the anthems and benediction of the queen's rite in this iteration: 'the queen governs with virtue and wisdom' (regine uirtutis prudential gubernanda) 'the queen is a sharer of royal power' (qui regalis imperii te uoluit esse participatem). Judith Abbot, 'Political Strategy in the Coronation of Queen Matilda', paper presented at the 1990 Meeting of the Haskins Society Conference, abstract published in *The Anglo-Norman Anonymous* 9 (1991), 5.

[40] Stafford, *Queen Emma and Queen Edith*, 174–5.

queen's role as a sharer in royal power. Emma, of course, had already been crowned queen of England with Æthelred, so a further consecration – as Cnut was crowned – would have been the underlying motive for significant changes to the rite. Emma served as a crucial bridge between the Anglo-Saxon royal house, which she represented, and the new Danish conqueror through their union. She epitomized the 'Glory of the Anglo-Saxons' as Danish and English cultures were knit together.

Janet L. Nelson argued that the 'Third English Ordo' was William's coronation rite.[41] Found in the Pontifical of Magdalen College, the structure of this rite lines up with Orderic Vitalis' report of the violent interruption of William's coronation by his own soldiers. This liturgy also has a queen's rite attached, which compares the queen to Esther; 'a partner in royal power'.[42] In the blessing of the crown, the manuscript indicates the feminine pronouns inscribed above the masculine ones, perhaps a clue that the ordo was used for a queen's coronation that occurred apart from a king's, which would fit Mathilda's particular circumstance.[43]

Thus, the textual evidence for Mathilda's inauguration rite is fragmented. Contemporary narratives are of little use, as they give only the barest outlines of the event. But there is extant manuscript evidence to piece together, apart from the ordos, and as we examine those elements of the inauguration of which we can be sure the shape of Matilda's consecration begins to emerge. Analysis of her ceremony leads to startling revelations. Her liturgy instituted for the first time on English soil dramatic changes in both the physical accoutrements of queenly inauguration and the office itself. One of these innovations would remain an integral part of English coronations: the acclamation known to the Normans as the *Christus vincit*, and to modern historians as the *laudes regiae*. Beside the laudes, there are two additional pieces of her inauguration we know were performed: the scripture passages used for the Pentecost mass linked to her anointing, Acts 2:1–11 and Baruch 3. Before we address each of these in turn, it is instructive to consult the liturgical calendar, just as Mathilda did.

The opportunity to freely choose the day of a royal inauguration was rare; the death of a royal predecessor or anxiety about succession meant most inauguration rites were scheduled within significant time constraints. Thus William's

41 Nelson, *Politics and Ritual*, 344.

42 'Benedictionis suae dominus omnipotens ancille suae uidelicet regine nostrae conferat largitatem. qui regalis imperii te uoluit esse participem et in sue uoluntatis desiderio eam semper faciat perseuerabilem. Amen.' Wickham Legg, *Three Coronation Orders*, 63.

43 In her examination of Edith/Matilda, Lois Huneycutt concurred with Nelson's analysis. Huneycutt, *Matilda of Scotland*, 3–35, 51.

inauguration planning was somewhat rushed, according to the contemporary sources, in order to crown him on Christmas Day 1066, only about two months after Hastings. Mathilda, however, had the luxury of time.[44] In the two years that passed between William's rite and Mathilda's there was ample opportunity to plan. The result included careful maintenance of important traditions: Mathilda was crowned at Westminster, the hallowed ground of English coronations for years. She was also crowned by Ealdred, archbishop of York, who performed William's ceremony. Lanfranc would later argue for (and win) the rights of the archbishops of Canterbury to crown the rulers of England. But in both 1066 and 1068, the Archbishop of Canterbury was Stigand, who was under papal censure and would eventually be deposed.[45]

Dale has shown the personnel of an inauguration was crucial but equally so was its date; the day chosen for a royal inauguration was a central concern. 'Church feasts were not just days with a festal character on which important royal acts took place, they were bearers of specific content that was made visible in the liturgy and enveloped the event with the feast's meaning.'[46] The church calendar could be exploited to underscore and deepen the meaning of a royal rite. The mass that followed the inauguration contained scripture readings and prayers that would be familiar to the attendant crowd. The resonance of a saint's feast day or high holy day was an opportunity not to be missed. Mathilda's choice of Pentecost, or Whitsunday, for her royal inauguration, was an auspicious one.[47] Second only to Easter in importance in the church calendar, it ensured that the liturgy would take place on a Sunday – the favored day for liturgical performance. The feast of Pentecost also had a vigil attached, just as Easter did in the liturgical calendar. So Mathilda's inauguration day expanded into a two-day festal event that was compulsory for visiting courtiers and dignitaries. Leading up to Pentecost Sunday, the English tradition required seven days of special hymns.[48] The eucharistic

44 *William of Poitiers, Gesta*, 148–9. *OV* ii, 182–5.

45 Taking a chance on Stigand for Mathilda's inauguration was inconceivable. In fact, Norman arguments for Harold Godwinson's illegitimate rule involved Stigand's disqualification as an agent of Harold's divine consecration. Harold's royal inauguration was stained by its censured archbishop and furthered the Normans' argument that Harold's rule was unlawful.

46 Dale, *Inaguration*, 143. Edith/Mathilda of Scotland, Mathilda of Flanders' daughter-in-law, was crowned on November 11, 1100 at Westminster. Her choice of the feast day of St Martin, or Martinmas, an important observance in Scotland was certainly a conscious one. This reference to her royal Scottish background also highlighted her heritage as the granddaughter of Edmund Ironside.

47 Certain days held meaning across kingdoms and empires. Pentecost was one such day. Both Philip I of France and Henry III of England also chose to be consecrated and crowned on Pentecost. Dale, *Inauguration*, 143.

48 Ælfric, 'On the Day of Pentecost' in *The Homilies of the Anglo-Saxon Church*, ed. Benjamin Thorpe (London, 1844), 311.

elements of the mass, of course, were the central portion of the service, but other celebratory sections were also included for Pentecost. These probably would have featured the 'sequences', or special elongated prayer structures that were sung on special holy days. The sequences were authored by the ninth-century monk of St Gall, Notker. By the eleventh century, Notker's sequences were widely copied and in use all over Europe.[49] The sequences for Pentecost were especially elaborate and in some places the celebrating priest would hold a white dove in his hands for the first few phrases and release it as soon as he took his first breath.[50] At Canterbury, in the twelfth century, a dedicated 'Pentecost hole' in the ceiling of the cathedral nave was created to facilitate the release of doves, or the lowering of other visual elements to celebrate the Holy Spirit's descent.

But the resonance of Pentecost for Mathilda's inauguration went deeper than heightened drama and an extended calendar of events. The mass for the feast of Pentecost commemorates the reception of the Holy Spirit by Christ's disciples. According to Scripture, as Christ's followers gathered in a second-floor room to celebrate the Jewish observance of the holiday, tongues of flame anointed their heads. This was the Holy Spirit, believed to be the representative of the Trinity that abided within believers, guiding their thoughts and actions into alignment with Christ's perfection. As the Holy Spirit descended, the disciples miraculously spoke in all the dialects of the Jewish people present, and could be understood by everyone assembled. The passage used for the Pentecost mass was Acts 2:6–11:

> When the day of Pentecost came, they were all together in one place. Suddenly a sound like the blowing of a violent wind came from heaven and filled the whole house where they were sitting. They saw what seemed to be tongues of fire that separated and came to rest on each of them. All of them were filled with the Holy Spirit and began to speak in other tongues as the Spirit enabled them. Now there were staying in Jerusalem God-fearing Jews from every nation under heaven. When they heard this sound, a crowd came together in bewilderment, because each one heard their own language being spoken. Utterly amazed, they asked: 'Aren't all these who are

49 One manuscript of Notker's sequences, London, British Library, Add MS 19768, was created in Mainz around 967–72 and contains an acclamation hymn (folio 58v) that explicitly names Adelheid, wife of Otto I. As mentioned previously, Mathilda's mother commissioned her own copy of the 'Epitaph of Adelheid'. BL Add MS 19768 contains two parts and the second half of this volume contains English characters which suggest, tantalizingly, that it could have been in English hands at the time of Mathilda's inauguration. Laura Wangerin, *Kingship and Justice in the Ottonian Empire* (Ann Arbor, MI, 2019), 148. Henry Parkes, *The Making of Liturgy in the Ottonian Church: Books, Music and Ritual in Mainz, 950–1050* (Cambridge, 2015), 33–81.

50 This practice continues to this day in some Roman Catholic churches.

> speaking Galileans? Then how is it that each of us hears them in our native language? Parthians, Medes and Elamites; residents of Mesopotamia, Judea and Cappadocia, Pontus and Asia, Phrygia and Pamphylia, Egypt and the parts of Libya near Cyrene; visitors from Rome (both Jews and converts to Judaism); Cretans and Arabs – we hear them declaring the wonders of God in our own tongues!'[51]

The tongues of fire anointing the disciples' heads in Scripture were a direct parallel to Mathilda's anointing, which would have happened just before the mass commenced. It was a short step indeed to move from Mathilda, anointed by God as his queenly representative on earth, to the anointing by the Holy Spirit of all English Christians, subject to her. 'The unity of the Holy Spirit' was a key element in the prayers for the day. In this context, that unity seemed to reference obedience to her rule.

There was a rich early English exegetical tradition about Pentecost already in place when Mathilda stepped onto English soil. An important part of that tradition – coming down from Gregory the Great through English intellectual giants like Bede to Ælfric – linked Pentecost with the Old Testament passage on the Tower of Babel. The scriptural passage these early churchmen used is found in Genesis 11:1–9.

> Now the whole earth had one language and one speech. And it came to pass, as they journeyed from the east, that they found a plain in the land of Shinar, and they dwelt there. Then they said to one another, 'Come, let us make bricks and bake them thoroughly.' They had brick for stone, and they had asphalt for mortar. And they said, 'Come, let us build ourselves a city, and a tower whose top is in the heavens; let us make a name for ourselves, lest we be scattered abroad over the face of the whole earth.' But the Lord came down to see the city and the tower which the sons of men had built. And the Lord said, 'Indeed the people are one and they all have one language, and this is what they begin to do; now nothing that they propose to do will be withheld from them. Come, let Us go down and there confuse their language, that they may not understand one another's speech.' So the Lord scattered them abroad from there over the face of all the earth, and they ceased building the city. Therefore its name is called Babel, because there the Lord confused the language of all the earth; and from there the Lord scattered them abroad over the face of all the earth.

For the early English exegetes, both Pentecost and the Tower of Babel were stories about linguistic variety but they were used in opposition to each other.[52] The arrogance of the Old Testament Jews building a tower to reach the heavens resulted in the confusion of many tongues – God's judgement on

51 Acts 2:1–11 (Douay-Rheims Bible).

52 Kees Dekker, 'Pentecost and Linguistic Self-Consciousness in Anglo-Saxon

their conceit. This ancient sin was answered by the New Testament miracle of Pentecost, in which the Holy Spirit allowed the Jews to once again experience the unity of one language. Gregory the Great drew connections between the Pentecost miracle and the forming of the apostolic church. The immediate after-effect of the Pentecost miracle, in the Acts passage, was the baptism of three thousand converts and the beginnings of a cohesive body of the faithful. The three thousand were the foundation of Christendom; the new world Church.[53] Historians, moreover, have seen the original mission to convert the 'Angles' by Pope Gregory in the early seventh century as a direct result of Pentecost.[54] Bede's commentary on Genesis, in the eighth century, made this link. For Bede, the two stories were the focus of an allegorical lesson – an almost Augustinian contrast – between an earthly (sinful) city of Babel built with the bricks of ignorance and the (holy) City of God, built from Christ's own body. Bede's obsession with the linguistic elements of the miracle surfaced as he debated between miracles of 'hearing' and 'speaking' at Pentecost.[55] Bede wrote a hymn to the Holy Day of Pentecost in which all the churches of the world sing in one language, celebrating God's glory.[56] Bede was widely read in the Anglo-Norman court. Bede's *Historia* was brought in, opened, and used as evidence in the primacy debate between Canterbury and York; a church council over which Mathilda herself presided.[57] Ælfric 'Grammarian', writing in the late tenth century, took up the thread in his exegesis of Pentecost; the apostle's miracle of languages as the restoration of unity lost at the Tower of Babel. He insisted that the apostles had been able to speak in all languages of the world, including those, like Old English, that would occur in the future. For Ælfric, the original pre-Babel language was Hebrew, and Old English had its roots in this ancient Judaic tongue.[58]

Mathilda and her ministers knew the Pentecost miracle of languages would have deep resonance with the gathered crowd and they could build on it. The Norman French and English tongues became, in this reading, united by the Holy Spirit. While the two peoples may have been foreign to each other, they both communicated with the godhead through the Holy Ghost's guidance. The Genesis Tower of Babel passage used in conjunction with Acts created a

---

England: Bede and Aelfric', *The Journal of English and Germanic Philology* 104:3 (July, 2005), 345–72 at 349.

53 Dekker, 'Pentecost', 351.

54 Robert Stanton, *The Culture of Translation in Anglo-Saxon England* (Cambridge, 2002), 65–6.

55 Dekker, 'Pentecost', 354.

56 Bede, *Liber hymnorum, rhythmi, variae preces*, ed. J. Fraipont, CCSL 122 (Turnhout, 1955), 424–5: 'Cunctis per orbem ut gentibus / Lingua canentes propria, / Iesu, tuam potentiam / Laudesque dicerent tuas'. Cited in Dekker, 'Pentecost', 354, n 37.

57 See Chapter Seven: Mouth, 199–202.

58 Dekker, 'Pentecost', 360.

layered message. First, the original unity of God's people, disrupted by their own ambition. Then, like so many medieval links between the Old and New Testament, Christ's coming – and the Holy Spirit's anointing – healed that ancient rupture. The unification of a people whose sin of ambition, under the old law had led God to separate them was now accomplished through the new law of Christ. They once spoke as one people but their arrogance had led God to scatter them. Now, however, under Christ, they were reconnected. Their reformation under the Holy Spirit made an old wrong right again – and fulfilled their original destiny as a unified people.

For the assembly listening to the mass, the past and present would be easily concertinaed together. The ancient Jews were conflated with the English. This was another familiar link that Mathilda and her liturgists could exploit; the English as God's new chosen people and England as the 'new Jerusalem'. The parallels between them were used in Bede, Wulfstan and Ælfric. Each of these English theological titans had likened the English to the Jewish people. The English used the Old Testament as a 'veiled way of talking about their own situation' especially in terms of warfare, royal rule and politics.[59] Tracing out the theological sinews linking the English with the Jews in the Old Testament also left space for the Normans to adopt the role of the apostles – uniting a people divided by their own godlessness. The metaphor needed little calibration to cast the newly formed polity of the Anglo-Normans, imposed on the English people, as the unity prefigured by the apostles in the New Testament. It was a theme the English would have recognized. Their resistance to the new Anglo-Norman order could be parlayed into a stiff-necked arrogance featured in Old Testament Babel. The imposition of unity upon them could have apostolic significance. As Gregory the Great used Pentecost as the prime mover to his missionary activity to the 'Angles', so the Normans could cast themselves into the role of missionaries to the heathen, fallen English church. The papal pallium eventually granted to William, in fact, asserted as much. Pope Alexander laid the reform of English churches at the door of the new Norman administration.[60] The final act of Pentecost, the conversion of three thousand and the formation of a new church also needed very little tailoring to fit the Norman narrative of reform. The English were the Jews of Babel. The Normans were their apostolic unifiers with freshly anointed pregnant Mathilda at their head.

[59] Malcolm Godden, 'Biblical Literature: The Old Testament', in *The Cambridge Companion to Old English Literature*, ed. Malcolm Godden and Michael Lapidge (Cambridge, 1991), 225.

[60] The timing of the papal pallium and its significance are re-examined in Dan Armstrong, 'The Norman Conquest of England, the Papacy, and the Papal Banner', *HSJ* 32, 47–72.

In this context of heightened awareness, the tattered remains of the English aristocracy heard the reading *Audi Israel* that fell from the priests' lips, Baruch 3:9–38.

> Hear, O Israel, the commandments of life; give ear, that thou mayest learn wisdom, how happened it, O Israel. That thou art in thy enemy's hand, thou art grown old in a strange country, thou art defiled with the dead: thou art counted with them that go down into hell. Thou hast forsaken the fountain of wisdom: for if thou had walked in the way of God, thou had surely dwelt in peace forever. Learn where is wisdom, where is strength, where is understanding: that thou mayest know also where is length of days and life, where is the light of the eyes, and peace. Who hath found out her place? And who hath gone in to her treasures? Where are the princes of the nations, and they that rule over the beasts, that are upon the earth? That take their pastime with the birds of the air, that hoard up silver and gold, wherein men trust, and there is no end of their getting? Who work in silver and are solicitous, and their works are unsearchable. They are cut off, and are gone down to hell, and others are risen up in their place. Young men have seen the light, and dwelt upon the earth: but the way of knowledge they have not known, nor have they understood the paths thereof, neither have their children received it, it is far from their face. It hath not been heard in the land of Canaan, neither hath it been seen in Theman. The children of Agar also, that search after the wisdom that is of the earth, the merchants of Merrha, and of Theman, and the tellers of fables, and searchers of prudence and understanding: but the way of wisdom they have not known, neither have they remembered her paths. O Israel, how great is the house of God, and how vast is the place of his possession. It is great, and has no end: it is high and immense. There were the giants, those renowned men, that were from the beginning, of great stature, expert in war. The Lord chose not them, neither did they find the way of knowledge: therefore did they perish. And because they had not wisdom, they perished through their folly. Who hath gone up into heaven, and taken her, and brought her down from the clouds? Who hath passed over the sea, and found her, and brought her preferably to chosen gold? There is none that is able to know her ways, nor that can search out her paths. But he that knows all things, knows her, and has found her out with his understanding: he that prepared the earth for ever more, and filled it with cattle and four-footed beasts: he that sends forth light, and it goes and has called it, and it obeyed him with trembling. And the stars have given light in their watches, and rejoiced: they were called, and they said: Here we are. And with cheerfulness they have shined forth to him that made them. This is our God, and there shall no other be accounted of in comparison to him. He found out all the way of knowledge, and gave it to

> Jacob, his servant, and to Israel, his beloved. Afterwards he was seen upon earth, and conversed with men.[61]

Here are references to a lost kingdom, a lost aristocracy who 'perished through their own folly'. A culture of artistic refinement and wealth, talented in working silver and gold. Princes who 'took their pastimes' with falcons are now cut off and 'others are risen in their place'.[62] There are story tellers who wove fables in the air. Famous warriors of ancient heritage and renown, 'expert in war' have been passed over by God. Baruch 3 even references a gold-bearer who passes over the sea to find 'her': Israel, God's chosen. Parallels to the lost Anglo-Saxon world, even from the distance of almost a thousand years, are striking.

Baruch 3:9 was an apocryphal ancient scripture that may seem an odd choice for the Pentecost Vigil in the Middle Ages. The feast of Passover in the Jewish tradition at the time of the apostles, however, centered around the fragmentation of Babel lived out across the ancient world – the Jewish Diaspora. Thus the medieval reading for the vigil of Pentecost remained distinctly elegiac in character.[63] In 1068, it was also open to an interpretation that could not be lost on its Norman and English hearers. The Pentecost Vigil mass of 1068 would have been attended by the entire court who were at Westminster for Mathilda's royal inauguration in the morning: their presence at her liturgical performance was not optional. Thus, the English aristocracy, their supporters and churchmen would have heard the special liturgy for the night. Even if some members of the crowd were not Latin literate, the bishops and archbishops were a scripturally attuned audience, well positioned to perceive it. By the morning of Mathilda's rite, none of the attendees would have to guess at the scripture and its meaning to appreciate its resonance with the plight of the gathered English. The reading for the mass at Pentecost continued to be utilized in services long after the Normans ruled England, in fact, up until the Reformation. But while Mathilda and her liturgists were not the originators of the vigil mass, the use of Pentecost as the day of her inauguration was laden with meaning. The pointed references to a lost culture – the diaspora of a fallen people – struck at the heart of the English loss. The participation of those English nobles still surviving under the new Norman

61 *Missale ad usum insignis et praeclarae ecclesiae Sarum*, Labore ac studio Francisci Henrici Dickinson (Princeton, NJ, 1891), 420–2; Douay-Rheims Bibles, Baruch 3: 9–38, 470–3. Available online: https://gutenberg.org/cache/epub/1581/pg1581-images.html

62 For pre-conquest English aristocratic pursuits see Ann Williams, *The World Before Domesday: The English Aristocracy, 900–1066* (London, 2011), 123–38.

63 *The Leofric Missal*, I: *Introduction, Collation Table, and Index*, ed. Paul Hayward; II: *Text*, ed. Nicholas Orchard (Woodbridge, 2002), ii, 196. The last additions to the missal were made by Bishop Leofric of Exeter between 1050 and 1072.

regime was compulsory that night. As the prophetic scripture readings were recited over them, it is easy to imagine their sorrow, resentment, even rage.

There is no evidence for which specific mass book was used for Mathilda's Pentecost mass but *all* extant possibilities – the Missal of Robert of Jumièges, the Leofric Missal, the '*de officialis*' of John of Avranches and the Sarum Missal – contain the readings quoted here.[64] The review of the possible mass books for her service also uncovers a startling pattern; of the four possibilities listed above, three have close links to Mathilda herself. Bishop Leofric was present at her inauguration and signed the bilingual royal diploma that celebrated it. John of Avranches was archbishop of Rouen during Mathilda's reign and was one of the most able lieutenants in her government; he also accepted her daughter Cecelia's final vows as a nun.[65] The Sarum Missal was crafted sometime in the late eleventh century, ostensibly by the Norman Archbishop Osmund of Salisbury, who came to England during the Conquest. Osmund was made Chancellor of London before being chosen as bishop of Salisbury, or Sarum, and was famous for his compositions of musical chant. He became the tutor of Henry I, the very child Mathilda carried inside her as the crown was placed on her head. Only the Missal of Robert of Jumièges was compiled before Mathilda's birth, in the early tenth century. Even this important source, however, was famously held in the library at Jumièges, a Benedictine abbey under her protection as duchess, and to which she was a benefactor.[66] The sinews that bind Mathilda to the authors of the missals, at the very least, ensure that she was aware of the readings for Pentecost and endorsed their use in her liturgy. In what was probably the most important sacred rite of her life, she chose to echo two related claims: the vigil mass recalled without question the lost cause of the English world. The Sunday Pentecost mass the next morning presented what she saw as the appropriate answer to their suffering – the unity of Pentecost under her rule. From a lost culture, 'gone down into hell', the English could be revived by the Normans and experience the unity of the Holy Spirit. Under Norman leadership, figured as apostolic in the readings of the Sunday mass, the two cultures could be rejoined. Babel reversed: a lost unity restored by God's divine plan. The apostolic actors were the Normans led by a pregnant Mathilda, heavy with a royal son within her.

64 *The Missal of Robert Jumièges*, ed. H.A. Wilson (Woodbridge, 1994 reprint) 116; Orchard, *Leofric Missal*, ii, 197, Jean d'Avranches, *Liber de officiis ecclesiasticis*, ed. D. Johannis (Rouen, 1679), 74; *Missal ad Sarum*, cols. 420–2. The Leofric Missal also contains the Baruch 3 reading for Pentecost, but places it on the Sunday of the feast day, not the Saturday night vigil.

65 See Chapter Five: Womb, 145–67.

66 Mathilda was invoked in at least two charters that favored Jumièges: one major pancarte documenting all the rights and gifts to the abbey written in 1079, and one describing the sale of land in 1080 in which the curious case of Oringa and her stolen child is heard. *Regesta*, 530–1 and 535–47 respectively.

An additional burden would be laid upon the assembly that day; the ritual acquiescence demanded by the performance of the laudes regiae. The laudes regiae was an important innovation in the history of rulership rituals. This distinct element of imperial and royal acclamation has been the subject of historical analysis from the early nineteenth century until the present day.[67] Historically, the laudes was simply an acclamation chant, sung or spoken by a crowd of supporters, celebrating a new ruler; it was a Roman classical rite, not a liturgical or spiritual ritual at all. But gradually, this tradition was sacralized and became a divine office. The medieval, sacred version of the laudes was modelled on a formal collective prayer called the 'litany of the saints', which was performed at the Easter Vigil and other special times in the church calendar. The litany included a long exhaustive list of saints who were asked to provide mercy to the faithful on earth. The laudes was also a sort of catalog of intercessors, but its purpose and feeling was quite distinct from the litany. Laudes acclamations included a much shorter, more targeted list of intercessory saints, chosen to suit their earthly counterparts by virtue of their heavenly status. Thus what was once simply a celebratory 'call and response' to a new Roman champion became a religious ritual with the weight of the whole heavenly population; the divine Trinity, the saints and the angels. In addition, the laudes' classical roots were clear as it celebrated earthly rule, instead of asking for mercy from the heavens. It had a triumphalist feeling, applauding the ruling class, one by one. As a result, the laudes acclamation was a sort of a liturgical mongrel; a classical Roman pagan institution – celebrating human victory – bred with a religious litany of saints. Unlike the litany, the saints were not invoked to help with salvation of the sinful but were charged to support earthly domination of emperor and empress, queen and king.

It was during the Carolingian period that the liturgical nature of imperial acclamations truly took root. When the Frankish emperor was acclaimed in sacred language, a key feature of his acclamation was a three-part chanted refrain of '*Christus vincit, Christus regnat, Christus imperat*': Christ conquers, Christ reigns, Christ commands. This chant came to be identified as the 'Christus vincit' or laudes. At the end of the eighth century, this section of the liturgy was sometimes used alone as an 'adventus' or entrance ritual separate from a royal inauguration ceremony. But Carolingian and Ottonian imperial practice especially maintained the laudes as a part of imperial coronations.[68] Though the acclamation had a long history, it enjoyed a new popularity in the eleventh century in the courts of the German emperors and royal courts in France.

[67] Ernst Kantorowicz, *Laudes Regiae: A Study in Liturgical Acclamations and Mediaeval Ruler Worship* (Berkeley, CA, 1946). Kantorowicz's work remains the formative study for this ritual element. See also H.E.J. Cowdrey, 'The Anglo-Norman Laudes Regiae', 59.

[68] Wangerin, *Ottonian Empire*, 134–50; Cowdrey, 'Laudes Regiae', 47.

What truly distinguished the laudes regiae, however, was not its long and illustrious history. They were the sole rites in which a victorious, kingly Christ was celebrated and joined to victorious rulers on earth, especially to support and endorse them. The laudes was also deeply hierarchical; heavenly authorities were called upon in the order that was meant to reflect their importance. The order likewise corresponded to the relative status of earthly people paired with each heavenly intercessor. Reading them in sequence can be an interesting study in how authority was conceived through the Middle Ages but, as Johanna Dale has observed, the composition of the laudes tended to be altered to fit its particular setting.[69] The saints set into the laudes were easy to adjust with each performance. Just as royal inaugurations ever since Hincmar changed to address contemporary concerns, the laudes reflected the power dynamics of the moment. Royal and imperial acclamations continued to change to respond to contemporary circumstances. In fact, tracing the changes in the laudes, especially if we examine them together, allows us to uncover something significant with regard to Mathilda's rite.

The appendix to this chapter shows five examples of medieval laudes regiae. Version A is an early Frankish laudes of the ninth century from Cologne.[70] The three-part chant (*Christus vincit, Christus regnat, Christus imperat*) is only sung twice. The refrain favored in the liturgy is the simple *Christus vincit* chant standing alone. The intercessory saints are presented immediately after their earthly counterparts; the pope was paired with Christ as *Salvator mundi* or 'Savior of the world' and the emperor with the Virgin Mary. As the laudes developed further, the saintly host came to present more precisely one's status in accordance with the temporal hierarchy. Version B, for instance, is an eleventh-century French laudes text that survives from Nevers. It illustrates that while the intercessor of the pope remains Christ as *Salvator mundi*, 'Savior of the world', the king is now aided by Christ as *Redemptor mundi* or 'Redeemer of the world'. Cowdrey noted that these two positions, at least to some degree, achieved complementary status in the hierarchy through the use of Christ into different roles, though the pope always retained the first and highest place in the order.[71] Proceeding downward on the earthly scale, the queen appeared next, usually aided by female martyr saints such as Perpetua and Felicitas. Skipping forward a bit chronologically, Version C is a Norman laudes from the late eleventh century, showing the typical position of queens in the liturgy and their accompanying intercessors. After her, the clergy was mentioned and celebrated, sometimes followed by the army. Though the laudes were originally connected to a litany of as many as twelve or thirteen

69 Dale, *Inauguration*, 66.

70 See 134–44. The appendices show the laudes in chronological order.

71 Cowdrey, 'Laudes Regiae', 44.

saints for each earthly ruler, or class of people, by the eleventh century the list of intercessors was pared down to three or four saints.

In viewing the laudes together, it becomes clear that the Anglo-Norman acclamations were innovative in a number of ways as opposed to early Frankish versions. The positioning of the acclamation at the end of the coronation, instead of earlier within the mass where it had traditionally belonged, was one Norman novelty. Pulling the laudes down and placing it at the end of the liturgy served to highlight it. Version D shows a laudes sung for William separate from a royal inauguration, often called the 'Fécamp Laudes'. This laudes was probably used first at his celebratory entry into Rouen after the conquest, then later at the Easter crown-wearing at Fécamp, the ducal house monastery in 1067, a year before Mathilda's rite. The laudes for William used on this occasion was careful to acclaim the French king first, only then mentioning William in his proper secondary place. These were not royal laudes, as they were performed for William in France, but ducal versions of the rite. Another Norman characteristic was the increased repetition of the tricolon chant, *Christus vincit, Christus regnat, Christus imperat*, that undoubtedly heightened its dramatic rhythm and effect. This rite was performed; chanted and sung. Reading the litany on the page today dampens the impact of the repetition, but it would have been very affecting in oral performance. The spoken/sung word heightened the drama and built tension. Elements of William's laudes demonstrate that it was a transitional form of the laudes in some respects. It still retains a long 'Kyrie' section at the end of the laudes itself. The phrase 'Kyrie eleison' or 'Christ have mercy' was a holdover from when the laudes was being crafted from the old litany of the saints. According to liturgical music specialists, the Kyrie section fits uncomfortably in the assertive, triumphant rite that was the laudes. Indeed, the 'Kyrie' was eventually dropped from the laudes altogether. Here one can see Mathilda's laudes forging a new path; William's ducal laudes retains the old-fashioned Kyrie section, as does Philip I's laudes of 1059–1060, shown in Version B. Scholars of medieval liturgy have remarked on the incompatibility of the triumphant spirit of the laudes when harnessed to the submissive feeling of the litany of the saints. In fact, the style and motive of these two rites were diametrically opposed. Mathilda's laudes finally dispensed with the Kyrie once and for all, which allowed the laudes 'independence and artistic unity'.[72]

Mathilda possibly heard and experienced the crucial elements of her coronation before planning her rite. Her first cousin, Philip I of France, was also crowned on Pentecost, nine years earlier in 1059. Her attendance at his ritual would not be surprising, though we cannot be sure. Her relationship with Philip was close; her mother, Adela, was Philip's aunt and her father, Baldwin of Flanders, would be Philip's guardian – along with Anne of Kiev, Philip's

[72] Manfred Bukofzer, 'The Music of the Laudes' in *Laudes Regiae: A Study in Liturgical Acclamations and Mediaeval Ruler Worship*, ed. Ernst Kantorowicz (Berkeley, CA, 1946), 188–222 at 211.

mother – when he came to the throne of France as a young boy.[73] Mathilda and Philip acted together sometime after his coronation when they oversaw the relic translation of the Holy Shroud at Saint-Corneille-de-Compiègne.[74] No other member of Mathilda's family or Philip's are mentioned in this act which may suggest that, to the two of them, this translation was a particularly meaningful, personal, undertaking. Their mutual endeavor argues for Mathilda's familiarity with Philip and perhaps a shared liturgical sensibility. Version 4B shows Philip's laudes when he was crowned next to his father, in the Capetian fashion. While there are certainly similarities to Mathilda's, notably the queen does not merit inclusion in Philip's laudes at all.

Given the use of the laudes, its long history and its liturgical significance, it is perhaps not surprising that Mathilda of Flanders' royal inauguration should provide an ideal opportunity for its use. Her updated laudes had never before been heard in an English coronation ceremony.[75] Its inclusion guaranteed that Mathilda's rite would be distinct from any other. Matilda's liturgy utilized a novelty that was sophisticatedly continental, originating in the court of Charlemagne and found in the imperial courts of Germany. The use of the laudes from these models was fitting as she bore a bloodline that stretched back to both of these powerful dynasties.[76] Her claim to this formidable dual heritage, it bears remembering, was one that William could not make.

Version E shows the laudes used for Matilda's liturgy in 1068. At first glance, it is reminiscent of William's ducal laudes originating at Fécamp. The intercessory saints, however, are markedly different. The first change occurs in the intercessory triad for the pope; instead of Christ alone, all three members of the Trinity are invoked. Moving down the hierarchy, one might be tempted to assume that, likewise, William would also merit a somewhat inflated intercessory grouping. Yet he retains the traditional archangels used in the Fécamp laudes in Version D. His group of intercessors did not change as his identity moved from duke to king. He kept the same three as before: the Virgin Mary, and the archangels Raphael and Michael. This laudes was clearly not meant to highlight him. But as one looks to Mathilda's intercessors something remarkable appears. The queen has four intercessors. Unlike the traditional saints such as Perpetua and Felicitas, moreover, they are all apostles and they are all male. No attempt has been made to relate her to virgin females – not

73 For Philip's minority, see Emily Joan Ward, 'Anne of Kiev (*c.* 1024–*c.* 1075) and a reassessment of maternal power in the minority kingship of Philip I of France' *Historical Research* 89: 245 (August 2016), 435–53.

74 See Chapter Three: Fingers, 75–104.

75 'So far as England is concerned…there is no conclusive evidence that a form of laudes regiae was used there before the Norman Conquest; nor is it demonstrable that formal crown-wearings comparable to those of the Norman kings were held, at which they might have been chanted.' Cowdrey, 'Laudes Regiae', 51.

76 See Chapter One: Blood, 11–33.

even the Virgin Mary is mentioned in relation to Mathilda. Instead, the masculine, virile heroes of the early church: John, Peter, Paul and Andrew, are matched to her. This surprising group of apostolic intercessors would never again be paired with a queen. The text of this unique rite insists on placing in her hands the authority of the apostles.

The laudes was imported from Carolingian and imperial traditions.[77] Mathilda's heritage as a descendant of Charlemagne and Otto I put her squarely in the position to understand and encourage the innovative power of the laudes. An important parallel can be found in a manuscript, the Evangelia Ottonis, produced for Otto III in the late tenth century. The 'Frontispiece to Matthew' depicts all four evangelists whose halos and gilded frames echo those of Otto's portrait in the initial page. Laura Wangerin has drawn connections between these stylistic elements and Otto III's claims for apostolic authority. Mathilda's laudes knits similar apostolic ties through liturgy.[78]

In another new twist, Mathilda's laudes also required audience participation and it is here that we see a new liturgical formula constructed as Mathilda pushed the edge of the laudes further. Instead of the cantors singing the lines that responded to each request to aid Mathilda, the entire audience was required to chant. Kantorowicz described the laudes as having a constitutive character; as the solemn assent of the bishops and archbishops was given concerning the legitimacy of the crowned and the power of the crown itself.[79] But the high churchmen of the new Norman leadership also led the crowd of attendees as they chanted in support of Mathilda as queen. After each of her saints was named – John, Peter, Paul and Andrew – the crowd was compelled to answer 'Tu illam adiuva': 'Help her.' The Latin of this phrase has been described as 'aggressive'.[80] The laudes did not request help so much as require it. In fact, 'Adiuva!' was the cry of Byzantine soldiers in the eighth century as they charged the enemy.[81] The actual music of the laudes has been described by Manfred Bukofzer as having a 'military exuberance that leaves no place for submission'.[82] As mentioned above, unlike the litany of the saints which begged for mercy, the laudes 'acquires almost the strength of a command'.[83] Along with the cantors leading the service, Mathilda's subjects demanded aid for her from the heavenly host. The attending crowd thus morphed into intercessors, too, exacting apostolic sponsorship on her behalf. The *Christus vincit, Christus regnant, Christus imperat* refrain was then to be repeated and spoken by all in attendance – not just the clergy who had

77 Cowdrey 'Laudes Regiae', 39–78.

78 Wangerin, *Ottonian Empire*, 125.

79 Kantorowicz, *Laudes Regiae*, 65.

80 Bukofzer, 'Music', 193.

81 Bukofzer, 'Music', 193 note 18.

82 Bukofzer, 'Music', 193.

83 Ibid.

fabricated Mathilda's liturgy. Everyone present was expected to chant in response explicitly agreeing to and supporting Mathilda's governance. The celebrant who led the call and response was to perform it 'alta voce': loudly, vigorously, robustly.[84] This was not a prayerful performance, with head bowed, muffled in the cowl of a monk's habit. This rite was meant to be clamorous.

Kantorowicz noted that Mathilda's laudes was not used beyond this period, and seems to have disappeared without influencing any other rite, which underscores the highly original and propagandist nature of the laudes regiae of 1068.[85] The next available example is a laudes regiae appearing in Christ Church Canterbury F, probably a festal form of the laudes. Historians have generally placed it in the reign of William Rufus because the order of the acclamation ran from pope to king, to bishop and clergy, and only then named the queen followed by the army. It almost necessarily post-dates 1079, as in that year Lanfranc finally ruled that St Alphege, who appears as his intercessor, could be considered a saint. After Pentecost 1068, Mathilda's laudes was allowed to fall out of use.

The powerful position Mathilda occupied in the laudes of 1068 reflected her role as an active ruler and her importance as the female head of the new Norman royal house. Combining as they did a grand solemn sacred tradition with an illustrative, liturgical roll call of the elite in the medieval world, they could not have failed to appeal to the new conquering class, especially to Mathilda. A sacred ritual of great weight, the nature and character of the laudes made it a useful tool for propaganda in much the same way Mathilda's royal inauguration itself was an opportunity for displaying power and cementing her authority. Mathilda's laudes, moreover, demanded an audience response. Not content with passive acceptance, Mathilda's rite pressed the audience to give active voice, confirming her authority over them.

This expectation of participation is one of the elements of liturgy that specialists agree is most fraught with tension. Ritual requires assent even if it is implicit. Everyone must cooperate; to sit where directed, stand when one is asked to do so, and respond correctly at the proper time. The pressure to conform to ritual behavior has been examined and discussed by scholars like Philippe Buc and Geoffrey Koziol.[86] Liturgies can be disrupted, manipulated by one's enemies, their intent perverted. To enact a liturgical production was to take an enormous risk.[87] This could not have been far from the minds of Mathilda and the Normans as they constructed her liturgy, considering the unfortunate circumstances of William's royal inauguration in 1066.

84 Bukofzer, 'Music', 198.

85 See also Cowdrey, 'Laudes Regiae', 60–1.

86 Buc, *The Dangers of Ritual*; Geoffrey Koziol, *Begging Pardon and Favor: Ritual and Political Order in Early Medieval France* (Ithaca, NY, 1992).

87 Buc, *The Dangers of Ritual*, 8.

Liturgy is not static. Moments of high tension and drama can encourage disruption instead of compliance. Those who construct and perform liturgies have an interest in claiming that tradition undergirds their position, reified in ritual display. But the audience, the attendant crowd, is not merely a passive body. Medieval sources provide many instances when members of the audience refused to abide by the script. Moments of heightened tension offered the perfect foil for the airing of grievances or demands for justice.[88] The marginalized and the obviated turned the tables on the powerful and acted outside their prescribed roles as acquiescent audience members. Louis Hamilton has shown evidence that eleventh-century crowds, just like the Norman soldiers in 1066, actually expected dramatic disruptions.[89] Miracles were often anticipated by those attending moments of liturgical performance. The performance of ritual, far from being a moment of stasis, was an opportunity for subversion.[90] William's inaugural rite carried an important lesson for the Normans. If rituals were indeed dangerous, one can imagine that royal inaugurations were veritable lightning rods. Anointing a ruler was not a neutral act; it codified immense political power and quasi-divinity for its recipient. Inaugurations could act as a possible 'day of reckoning for the disenfranchised'.[91] In Mathilda's case, just as in William's, there was a subjugated losing side, the residual members of which were present at her ceremony. The potential for the receiving audience to interrupt and subvert the intended function of the ritual was great. Thus, William's bungled coronation rite is an important contextual factor as we examine Mathilda's royal inauguration. It was crucial that the rite impress the legitimacy of her power upon the gathered crowd. Through the celebration of Mathilda's inauguration, the pre-eminent moment of Norman power could be re-enacted and Christmas Day 1066 could be overwritten.

Like all liturgical performance, the reception of Matilda's coronation was unpredictable. The relative strength and efficacy of competing responses, conformity versus disruption, was a pivot point for Mathilda and the churchmen who helped to plan her ritual. There was no way to assure its outcome. Would there be another outburst as there was at William's 'shabby' rite?[92] Would she also be left alone, attended only by Ealdred of York and his ministers, as the assembly rushed out of the church? The outer limits of ritual pressure are always a mystery.

This may be why all the available physical accessories of royal rule were pressed into service to ensure the success of Mathilda's rite: crown, sceptre,

[88] William's funeral provides an example. Ascelin, who claimed he had never been compensated for William's burial plot, had to be paid off on the spot. *OV*, iv, 106–9, 112–15.

[89] Hamilton, *Sacred City*, especially 56–88.

[90] Shane Bobrycki, 'The flailing women of Dijon: Crowds in Ninth-Century Europe', *Past & Present* 240:1 (April 2018), 3–46.

[91] Buc, *Dangers of Ritual*, 8.

[92] Bates, *William*, 257.

even an episcopal sapphire set in gold, just as tradition dictated for bishops.[93] Royal consecration was actually modeled on the consecration of a bishop. Both followed some of the same formulae but there were important differences, most notably the laying on of hands, which bishops did not receive. Thus, the queen by virtue of the laying on of hands and anointing, or unction, stood above mere earthly power, operating within the prerogatives of a sacred office. In all the ordos available for this period, the laying on of hands is an integral part of the queen's inauguration. Mathilda's sacred office, then, was manifest in all the available rites and physical accoutrements of office within the inauguration liturgy.

CONCLUSION

The divine support and material trappings of Mathilda's rite apparently did little to quell the resentment of its English observers. The analogy of Babel on the heels of the inflammatory scripture used for the Pentecost Vigil mass, the night before Mathilda's rite, may have been the spark that lit the rebellion of the last vestige of the English aristocracy. In fact, mere weeks after her elaborate rite, uprisings ignited into flame across the Normans' new kingdom. According to the *Anglo-Saxon Chronicle*, Edgar Ætheling, with his mother and sisters, left Westminster after the ceremony and went directly to Scotland to gather troops for a revolt.[94] At the same time, Earl Edwin of Mercia and Earl Morcar of Northumbria also chose this moment to rebel.[95] Orderic describes the revolt of Morcar and Edwin but seems unaware of Ætheling's movements or at least does not mention him. The *Anglo-Saxon Chronicle* describes Edgar Ætheling's rebellion but is silent about Edwin and Morcar. The timing of these two military actions, made concurrently but by two disparate factions, requires an explanation.

Until the summer of 1068, these English lords and their supporters had kept their heads above water and successfully integrated into the Norman court. Historians agree that a respite occurred between William's victory at Hastings and the rebellions of the English nobility in the summer of 1068.[96] The period between December 1066 and Mathilda's royal rite in 1068 was surprisingly tranquil in England. Some historians characterize the beginning

93 It was retrieved by the last abbess of Holy Trinity, Marie Aimée de Pontecoulet, and given to her father, the bailiff of Caen. Sir John Ayloff, 'The Body of the King of Edward I', *Archeologica* 3 (1770), 391. My thanks to Judith Abbott for alerting me to this source. Legg, *English Coronations*, xlvii–xlix; Schramm, *Coronation*, 84. For later examples, see also J. Wickham Legg, 'The Queen's Coronation Ring', *Archaeological Journal* 54 (1897), 1–9.

94 *ASC*, cited in the annal year 1068.

95 Bates, *William*, 295.

96 Bates, *William*, 260; Ann Williams, *The English and the Norman Conquest* (Woodbridge, 1995), 23.

of Norman rule by an 'early mildness' as some allowance was made for their new, sometimes fractious, subjects.[97] David Bates has taken issue with this and noted that William's style of rule over their new subjects was brutal and onerous from the start.[98] Nevertheless, both sides agree that after May 1068, something important shifted for the English nobility. Whatever cooperation might have been expected before Mathilda's anointing and coronation, whatever hopes for English and Norman amity, they were torn apart within weeks of her ceremony. The 'honeymoon period' came to a sudden halt in the summer of 1068. David Bates has pointed to a number of factors that could have exacerbated tensions. The harsh realities of taxation implemented after William was crowned in December of the previous year added to their growing anger. It was becoming increasingly clear, Bates argues, that Norman royal practice enriched Mathilda and William's supporters at the expense of the English nobility.[99] But the coincidence of the rebellions of Edwin and Morcar, who both attended the Pentecost weekend in 1068, may be explained further by the contents of Mathilda's liturgical performance.

Did Mathilda's pomp and ceremony, designed to legitimate her claim as queen, result in the rebellions that crackled through her kingdom? Edwin and Morcar had maintained their earldoms after the invasion and had traveled to Normandy with William after his coronation in 1066. Likewise, until Mathilda's royal inauguration, Ætheling had cooperated with the new Norman administration. The uprisings of 1068–1069 came hard on the heels of Mathilda's royal inauguration. The unusual pageantry of her rite, its surgical use of scriptural discourse aimed at the English nobility, her claims to the crown of England *Deo gratia*, even her pregnancy; any of these prods alone might have enraged the attendant English. All of them together surely did. Mathilda's heavily pregnant body added another layer of complexity to the symbolism of her liturgical rite. In the context of 1068, Mathilda's visible fertility brought succor to only one side of the English/Norman divide. It complicated an already multivalent ceremony designed with care to underscore the helplessness of the English, Mathilda's legitimacy, and the inevitability of Norman rule. The Saturday night vigil message of English hopelessness led to the Sunday morning message of concord. Great pains were taken to connect the Pentecost Sunday message of unity in the Gospels with eleventh-century Anglo-Norman attempts at hegemony. But this was harmony on Norman terms. Despite a nod to Pentecost unity, the overwhelming communication of Mathilda's rite was not amity with the English but dominance over them. The two-day festal affair of her liturgy evoked the English diaspora and seemed to revel in it.

Edwin and Morcar, joined by the Welsh king Bleddyn ap Cynfyn, staged military operations against the Normans from the Welsh border. In the north,

97 Williams, *English and the Norman Conquest*, 23.

98 Bates, *William*, 260.

99 Bates, *William*, 295–7.

Edgar Ætheling agitated against them with the backing of King Malcolm of Scotland. These were the first English rebellions that the new king and queen faced but further revolts were coming. The massive rebellion of 1070–1, that featured the invasion of Svein of Norway, was arguably already in the planning stages as William marched to quell the initial backlash against Norman rule. The rebels were pardoned in each case. They sued for peace, made oaths of loyalty, and were allowed to maintain their properties. But the revolts resulted in a new wave of Norman castle building in England at these sensitive sites on the borders with Wales and in the north at York. The revolts touched off by Mathilda's inauguration resulted in further domination of the landscape in these trouble spots. In turn, Norman castles strained existing racial tensions between the English and their new overlords.[100] In the next round of revolts, the English would not be forgiven so easily.

The Pentecost message of unity, it seems, had its limits. The carefully wrought liturgical claims of a pregnant queen and the innovative rituals designed to show her mastery could not counterbalance unrest. In fact, they exacerbated it. What was left of the English aristocracy watched Mathilda receive the crown of England, as the shape of her body revealed the certainty of the future: yet another heir of Normandy.

It is tempting to view Mathilda's royal inauguration at Westminster as the culmination of her new royal status. The *Anglo-Saxon Chronicle* gives us evidence that after Mathilda was consecrated as queen, the royal pair wore their crowns three times a year: Easter at Winchester, Pentecost at Westminster and Christmas at Gloucester. Mathilda's royal inauguration set the pattern for one of those events. The annual re-enactment of her liturgy particularly underscored her powerful position in the realm. Mathilda's reign initiated a new focus on an Ottonian style of crown-wearing in keeping with a specific liturgical calendar.[101] Crown-wearing on Pentecost at Westminster became a tradition later English rulers would follow.[102] The year of her arrival to England, Mathilda celebrated Easter with William at Winchester, and that site was concretized as the traditional Easter royal court. Likewise, with the advent of Mathilda's royal inauguration, Pentecost would ever after be held at Westminster. Just as Mathilda's coronation set the pattern of royal crown-wearings in motion, it signaled the beginning of Mathilda's conquest of England, not its apex.

100 Bates, *William*, 295.

101 Martin Biddle, 'Seasonal Festivals and Residence: Winchester, Westminster and Gloucester in the Tenth to Twelfth Centuries', *ANS* 8 (1985), 51–72.

102 English kings did have festal crown-wearings, but only with the advent of the Normans were these linked tightly to the three major feasts; Easter, Pentecost and Christmas. The schedule for English festal crown-wearings was scattered and informal. English Easter courts, for instance, were sometimes held at the great royal centers, such as Winchester and London but with little consistency. Biddle, 'Seasonal Festivals', 51–72.

APPENDIX

MEDIEVAL LAUDES REGIAE IN CHRONOLOGICAL ORDER

Laudes A: Cologne MS 138, folio (44r-v), ninth century

Exaudi Christe	Domino nostro a Deo decreto summon pontifici et universali pape vita.
Salvatore mundi	Tu illum adiuva
Exaudi Christe	Domino Nostro N. augusto et a Deo coronato magno et pacifico imperatori vita et victoria
Sancta Maria	Tu illum adiuva
Exaudi Christe	Eius precellentissimis filiis regibus vita.
Sancte Petre	Tu Illos adiuva
Exaudi Christe	Exercitui Romanorum et Francorum vita et victoria.
Sancte Theodore	Tu illos adiuva

Christus vincit, Christus regnat, Christus imperat

Rex regnum	Christus vincit, Christus regnat, Christus imperat
Rex noster	Christus vincit.
Spes nostra	Christus vincit.
Gloria nostra	Christus vincit.
Misericordia nostra	Christus vincit.
Auxilium nostrum	Christus vincit.
Fortitudo nostra	Christus vincit.
Liberatio nostra	Christus vincit.
Arma nostra invictissima	Christus vincit.
Murus noster inexpugnabilis	Christus vincit.
Defensio et exaltitio nostra	Christus vincit.
Lux, via et vita nostra	Christus vincit.

Ipsi soli imperium, gloria et potestas per immortalia secula seculorum.	Amen.
Ipsi soli virtus, fortitudo et victoria per omnia secula seculorum.	Amen.
Ipsi soli honor, laus et jubilatio per infinita secula seculorum.	Amen.

Reprinted from Ernst. H. Kantorowicz, *Laudes Regiae* (Berkeley, 1946), 105–6.

Laudes B: A Nevers laudes regiae of 1059–1060

Paris, Bibliothèque municipal MS lat. 9949, fols. 36v–37, late eleventh century

Christus vincit, Christus regnat, Christus imperat (tribus vicibus)

Exaudi Christe	Summo pontifici et universali pape vita
Salvatore mundi	tu illum adiuva
Sancte Petre	tu illum adiuva
Sancte Paule	tu illum adiuva
Sancte Andrea	tu illum adiuva
Exaudi Christe	Hugoni pontifici nostro salus et vita
Sancte Cyrice	tu illum adiuva
Sancte Nazari	tu illum adiuva
Sancte Genesii	tu illum adiuva
Sancte Simphoriane	tu illum adiuva
Exaudi Christe	Henrico regi Filippo regi serenissimo a Deo coronato magno et pacifico vita et victoria
Redemptor mundi	tu illum adiuva
Sancte Maria	tu illum adiuva
Sancte Michael	tu illum adiuva
Sancte Gabriel	tu illum adiuva
Sancte Raphael	tu illum adiuva
Exaudi Christe	Omnibus iudicibus et cuncto exercitui Christianorum vita et victoria
Sancte Dionisii	tu illos adiuva

Sancte Martine	tu illos adiuva
Sancte Remigi	tu illos adiuva

Christus vincit, Christus regnat, Christus imperat

Lux via et vita nostra	Christus vincit
Rex regum et Deus deorum	Christus vincit
Gloria et iubilacio nostra	Christus vincit
Misericordia et redempcio nostra	Christus vincit
Spes semper et fiducia nostra	Christus vincit
Auxilium et refugium nostrum	Christus vincit
Fortitudo et iusticia nostra	Christus vincit
Prudencia et temperancia nostra	Christus vincit
Liberacio et redempcio nostra	Christus vincit
Arma noster invictissima	Christus vincit
Murus nostra inexpugnabilis	Christus vincit
Victoria nostra	Christus vincit
Defensio et exaltacio nostra	Christus vincit

Ipsi soli honor imperium gloria et potestas per immortalia secula seculorum Amen.

Christus vincit, Christus regnat, Christus imperat.

Christe audi nos		Kyrrieleyson
Christe leyson		Kyrrieleyson
Te pastorem		Deus elegit
Ista sede		Te conservet
Annos vite		Deus multiplicet
Feliciter	Feliciter	Feliciter

Tempora bona habeas
Tempora bona habeas
Tempora bona habeas
Multos annos Amen

Reprinted from H.E.J. Cowdrey, 'The Anglo-Norman Laudes Regiae', *Viator* 12 (1981), 39–78.

Laudes C: The Fécamp laudes regiae

Rouen, Bibliotheque municipal MS 489 (A. 254), folio 71

Cantores Christus vincit, Christus regnat, Christus imperat
Chorus Christus vincit, Christus regnat, Christus imperat

Cantores Exaudi Christe	***Chorus***	Exaudi Christe
Chorus Illi summo pontifici et universali pape vita	***Chorus***	Exaudi Christe
Cantores Sancte Petre	***Chorus***	tu illum adiuva
Cantores Sancte Paule	***Chorus***	tu illum adiuva
Cantores Sancte Iohannes	***Chorus***	tu illum adiuva

Cantores Christus vincit, Christus regnat, Christus imperat
Chorus Christus vincit, Christus regnat, Christus imperat

Cantores Exaudi Christe	***Chorus***	Exaudi Christe
Cantores Illi Francorum regi in Christi pace vita et victoria	***Chorus***	Exaudi Christe
Cantores Sancte Michael	***Chorus***	tu illum adiuva
Cantores Sancte Gabriel	***Chorus***	tu illum adiuva
Cantores Sancte Raphael	***Chorus***	tu illum adiuva

Cantores Christus vincit, Christus regnat, Christus imperat
Chorus Christus vincit, Christus regnat, Christus imperat

Cantores Exaudi Christe	***Chorus***	Exaudi Christe
Cantores Guillelmo Normannorum duci salus et pax continua		
Cantores Sancte Maurici	***Chorus***	tu illum adiuva
Cantores Sancte Sebastiane	***Chorus***	tu illum adiuva
Cantores Sancte Adriane	***Chorus***	tu illum adiuva

Cantores Christus vincit, Christus regnat, Christus imperat
Chorus Christus vincit, Christus regnat, Christus imperat

Cantores Exaudi Christe	***Chorus***	Exaudi Christe
Cantores Omnibus pontificali honore sublimatis salitaris vite gloria	***Chorus***	Exaudi Christe

Cantores Sancte Ambrosi	***Chorus***	tu illos adiuva
Cantores Sancte Martine	***Chorus***	tu illos adiuva
Cantores Sancte Benedicte	***Chorus***	tu illos adiuva

Cantores Christus vincit, Christus regnat, Christus imperat
Chorus Christus vincit, Christus regnat, Christus imperat

Cantores Omnibus Christiane legis principibus ac iudicibus Salus eterna	***Chorus***	Exaudi Christe
Cantores Sancte Gregori	***Chorus***	tu illos adiuva
Cantores Sancte Tiburci	***Chorus***	tu illos adiuva
Cantores Sancte Frodmunde	***Chorus***	tu illos adiuva

Cantores Christus vincit, Christus regnat, Christus imperat
Chorus Christus vincit, Christus regnat, Christus imperat

Cantores Rex regum et dominus dominorum	***Chorus***	Christus vincit
Cantores Gloria et spes nostra	***Chorus***	Christus vincit
Cantores Misericordia et auxilium nostrum	***Chorus***	Christus vincit
Cantores Fortitudo et victoria nostra	***Chorus***	Christus vincit
Cantores Arma nostra invictissima	***Chorus***	Christus vincit
Cantores Lux via et vita nostra	***Chorus***	Christus vincit

Cantores	Ipsi soli regnum et imperium per immortalia secula seculorum Amen.
Chorus	Christus vincit, Christus regnat, Christus imperat.
Cantores	Ipsi soli laus et gloria per omnia secula seculorum
Chorus	Christus vincit, Christus regnat, Christus imperat.

Cantores Christe audi nos	***Chorus***	Christe audi nos
Cantores Kyrrieleyson	***Chorus***	Kyrrieleyson
Cantores Christe eleyson	***Chorus***	Christe eleyson
Cantores Kyrrieleyson	***Chorus***	Kyrrieleyson
Cantores Feliciter	***Chorus***	Feliciter

Cantores Tempora bona maneant	***Chorus***	Redempti sanguine Christi
Cantores Feliciter	***Chorus***	Feliciter
Cantores Regnum Christi veniat	***Chorus***	Deo gratias *Amen.*

Reprinted from H.E.J. Cowdrey. 'Anglo-Norman Laudes Regiae', *Viator* 12 (1981), 39–78.

Laudes D: The Anglo-Norman laudes of 1068 of Mathilda of Flanders

London, BL MS Cotton Vitellius E. XII, folio 160v, late eleventh century

Christus vincit, Christus regnat, Christus imperat

Exaudi Christe	Alexandro summo pontifici et universal pape vita
Pater de celis Deus	tu illum adiuva
Fili redemptor mundi Deus	tu illum adiuva
Spiritus Sancte Deus	tu illum adiuva

Christus vincit, Christus regnat, Christus imperat

Exaudi Christe	Wilhelmo serenissimo a Deo coronato magno et pacifico regi vita et victoria
Sancte Maria	tu illum adiuva
Sancte Michael	tu illum adiuva
Sancte Raphael	tu illum adiuva

Christus vincit, Christus regnat, Christus imperat

Exaudi Christe	Mathylde serenissime a Deo coronate regine salus et vita
Sancte Iohannes	tu illam adiuva
Sancte Petre	tu illam adiuva
Sancte Paule	tu illam adiuva
Sancte Andrea	tu illam adiuva

Christus vincit, Christus regnat, Christus imperat

Exaudi Christe	Aldrado Eboracensi archiepiscopo et omni clero sibi comisso salus et vita
Sancte Stephane	tu illum adiuva
Sancte Laurenti	tu illum adiuva
Sancte Vincenti	tu illum adiuva

Christus vincit, Christus regnat, Christus imperat

Exaudi Christe	Omnibus episcopis et abbatibus et cunctis congregationibus illis commissis salus et vita
Sancte Martine	tu illos adiuva
Sancte Benedicte	tu illos adiuva
Sancte Gregori	tu illos adiuva
Sancte Nicholae	tu illos adiuva

Christus vincit, Christus regnat, Christus imperat

Exaudi Christe	Omnibus princibus Anglorum et cuncto exercitui Christianorum vita et victoria
Sancte Maria Magdalena	tu illos adiuva
Sancte Perpetua	tu illos adiuva
Sancte Agatha	tu illos adiuva
Sancte Lucia	tu illos adiuva

Christus vincit, Christus regnat, Christus imperat

Redemptio et liberatio nostra	Christus vincit
Victoria nostra	Christus vincit
Misericordia nostrum	Christus vincit
Prudentia et iustitia nostra	Christus vincit
Fortitudo et temperantia nostra	Christus vincit
Auxilium nostra	Christus vincit
Defensio nostra	Christus vincit
Letitia et gloriatio nostra	Christus vincit

Vita et salus nostra	Christus vincit

Ipsi soli honor ( ) per infinita secula seculorum.	Amen.
Ipsi soli decus potestas et imperium per infinita secula seculorum.	Amen.
Ipsi soli gloria laus et iubilatio per infinita secula seculorum	Amen.

Reprinted from H.E.J. Cowdrey, 'The Anglo-Norman Laudes Regiae', *Viator* 12 (1981), 70–1.

Laudes E: The Canterbury laudes regiae

Durham, University Library, Cosin V. V. 6, fols. 19v–21, late eleventh century

Christus vincit, Christus regnat, Christus imperat *Hoc ter*

Et chorus respondeat

Cantores Exaudi Christe	***Chorus***	Summo pontifici et universali pape vita
Cantores Salvatore mundi	***Chorus***	tu illum adiuva
Cantores Sancte Petre	***Chorus***	tu illum adiuva
Cantores Sancte Clemens	***Chorus***	tu illum adiuva
Cantores Sancte Sixte	***Chorus***	tu illum adiuva

Cantores Christus vincit, Christus regnat, Christus imperat

Chorus idem

Cantores Exaudi Christe	***Chorus***	N. regi Anglorum a Deo coronato salus et victoria
Cantores Redemptor mundi	***Chorus***	tu illum adiuva
Cantores Sancte Eadmunde	***Chorus***	tu illum adiuva
Cantores Sancte Erminigelde	***Chorus***	tu illum adiuva
Cantores Sancte Osuualde	***Chorus***	tu illum adiuva

Cantores Christus vincit, Christus regnat, Christus imperat

Chorus idem

Cantores Exaudi Christe	***Chorus*** N. archiepiscopum et omnem clerum sibi commisum Deus conservat
Cantores Salvatore mundi	***Chorus*** tu illum adiuva
Cantores Sancte Augustine	***Chorus*** tu illum adiuva
Cantores Sancte Dunstane	***Chorus*** tu illum adiuva
Cantores Sancte Ælphege	***Chorus*** tu illum adiuva

Cantores Christus vincit, Christus regnat, Christus imperat

Chorus idem

Cantores Exaudi Christe	***Chorus*** N. regine Anglorum salus et vita
Cantores Redemptor mundi	***Chorus*** tu illam adiuva
Cantores Sancta Maria	***Chorus*** tu illam adiuva
Cantores Sancta Felicitas	***Chorus*** tu illam adiuva
Cantores Sancte Perpetua	***Chorus*** tu illam adiuva

Cantores Christus vincit, Christus regnat, Christus imperat

Chorus idem

Cantores Exaudi Christe	***Chorus*** Omnibus principibus et cuncto exercitui Anglorum salus et victoria
Cantores Salvatore mundi	***Chorus*** tu illos adiuva
Cantores Sancte Maurici	***Chorus*** tu illos adiuva
Cantores Sancte Georgi	***Chorus*** tu illos adiuva
Cantores Sancte Sebastiane	***Chorus*** tu illos adiuva

Cantores Christus vincit, Christus regnat, Christus imperat

Chorus idem

Cantores Rex regnum	***Chorus*** Christus vincit
Cantores Rex noster	***Chorus*** Christus regnat
Cantores Gloria nostra	***Chorus*** Christus imperat
Cantores Auxilium nostrum	***Chorus*** Christus vincit

Cantores	Fortitudo nostra	***Chorus***	Christus regnat
Cantores	Liberatio et redemptio nostra	***Chorus***	Christus imperat
Cantores	Victoria nostra invictissima	***Chorus***	Christus vincit
Cantores	Murus noster inexpugnabilis	***Chorus***	Christus regnat
Cantores	Defensio et exultatio nostra	***Chorus***	Christus imperat

Cantores Ipsi soli laus et iubilatio et benediction per infinita seculum seculorum Amen.

Chorus Christus vincit, Christus regnat, Christus imperat.

Cantores Ipsi soli laus et iubilatio et benediction per infinita seculum seculorum Amen.

Chorus Christus vincit, Christus regnat, Christus imperat.

Chorus Ipsi soli honor et claritas et sapientia per infinita secula seculorum Amen.

Chorus Christus vincit, Christus regnat, Christus imperat.

Reprinted from H.E.J. Cowdrey, 'The Anglo-Norman Laudes Regiae', *Viator* 12 (1981), 72–3.

5

WOMB

Unlike the queens who ruled England after her, Mathilda left behind a tombstone that utterly ignores her children.[1] The text of her epitaph celebrates her royal genealogy and her activities as ruler – especially the construction of Holy Trinity – while the maternal element of her identity is completely marginalized. It is revealing that this contemporary representation of Mathilda does not communicate that she had any offspring at all.

> The lofty structure of this splendid tomb hides great Mathilda, sprung from royal stem; child of a Flemish duke; her mother was Adela, daughter of a king of France, sister of Henry, Robert's royal son. Married to William, most illustrious king, she gave this site and raised this noble house, with many lands and many goods endowed, given by her, or by her toil procured; comforter of the needy, duty's friend; Her wealth enriched the poor, left her in need. At daybreak on November's second day, she won her share of everlasting joy.[2]

While the omission indicates that other identifying features took precedence, Mathilda gave birth to nine children, which had a significant effect on her life and rule.[3] Mathilda successfully delivered five daughters and four sons all

1 The epitaph of Queen Matilda II of Scotland reads: 'Here lies Matilda II, the good queen of the English, formerly the wife of King Henry I, mother of the Empress Matilda, and daughter of the Lord Malcolm the former king of the Scotts and his consort, Saint Margaret. She died on the first day of May in the year of grace 1118, and if we wished to speak of her goodness and probity of her character, a day would not be sufficient. May her spirit be greatly soothed. Amen.' Huneycutt, *Matilda of Scotland*, 148. For the Empress Matilda, the famous lines 'Great by birth, greater by marriage, greatest in her offspring: here lies Matilda, the daughter, wife, and mother of Henry' have been used repeatedly by modern scholars to describe her. Recent scholarship, however, offers a different perspective. See Mariah Cooper, 'A Female King or a Good Wife and a Great Mother? Seals, Coins, and the Epitaphic Legacy of the Empress Matilda', *HSJ* 32 (2020), 149–62.

2 *OV*, iv, 44–46.

3 Minor portions of this chapter are drawn from my previously published work with the kind permission of Palgrave MacMillan, '"Mother of heroes, most beautiful of

between 1053 and 1069. Their birth order is not completely certain but Mathilda bore Robert 'Curthose', Richard, William 'Rufus', Adelheid, Cecelia, Mathilda, Constance, Adela and Henry.[4] Conflicting records leave historians with a puzzle over the possible existence of another daughter, Agatha.[5] With or without daughter Agatha, contemporary childbearing expectations of Duchess-Queen Mathilda were clearly met and exceeded. Scholars have turned their attention toward many of Mathilda's offspring. Robert Curthose, William Rufus, Cecelia, Adela and Henry have all been the subject of sustained historical interest.[6] This chapter, however, attempts to uncover Mathilda's generative *modus operandi* – and how her rulership and her maternal strategies informed each other. Her children's careers are all deserving of historical study but for my purposes, two of her children provide evidence of Mathilda specifically in her role as genetrix: Robert and Cecelia. In what follows, evidence for Mathilda's approach to motherhood is examined through two roughly contemporary sources: Orderic Vitalis' *Historia* and the 'Jephthah' poem, penned by Fulcoius of Beauvais.

The theme of this book is Mathilda's embodiment of conquest: the legitimacy she provided through her bloodline; her monastic construction and acquisition of holy remains in its service, and her coronation which concretized it. More than any other chapter, however, Mathilda's body is central here. Precisely how her multiple pregnancies shaped her sense of self is unknowable but one clue

---

mothers": Mathilda of Flanders and royal motherhood in the eleventh century', in *Virtuous or Villainess? The Image of the Royal Mother from the Early Medieval to the Early Modern Era*, ed. Carey Fleiner and Elena Woodacre (New York, NY, 2016), 37–63; see also Gathagan, 'Maiden', 840–57.

4 'He took as his wife the highly born Mathilda, daughter of Baldwin, count of Flanders, and niece of Henry king of France through his sister. The marriage was blessed with sons and daughters: Robert, Richard, William, and Henry; Adelheid, Constance, Cecelia and Adela.' *OV*, ii, 104–105. Orderic lists Mathilda's children again in the next book of his *Historia*: 'She (Mathilda) was a kinswoman of Phillip, the king of France, she sprang from the stock of the kings of Gaul and emperors of Germany and was renowned equally for nobility of blood and character. She bore her distinguished husband the offspring he desired, both sons and daughters: Robert and Richard, William Rufus and Henry, Agatha and Constance, Adelheid, Adela and Cecelia.' *OV*, ii, 224–5.

5 See below, 148.

6 Selected works include Aird, *Robert Curthose*; Frank Barlow, *William Rufus* 2nd edition (New Haven, CT, 2000); Warren Hollister and Amanda Frost, *Henry I* (New Haven, CT, 2003); van Houts, 'The Echo of the Conquest in the Latin Sources: the Duchess Mathilda, her Daughters and the Enigma of the Golden Child', in *The Bayeux Tapestry: Embroidering the Facts of History*, ed. Pierre Bouet (Caen, 2004), 135–55; Kimberly LoPrete, *Adela of Blois, Countess and Lord, c. 1067–1137* (Dublin, 2007); Amy Livingstone, 'Pious women in a "den of scorpions": the piety and patronage of the eleventh-century countesses of Brittany', *Historical Reflections / Réflexions historiques* 43:1 (2017), 45–61; Gathagan, 'Maiden'.

might be found in her construction of the *Mora*, the ship Mathilda commissioned for the conquest, featured in Chapter Two.[7] Mathilda's craft was a gift to William as he sailed to conquer England and it bore a golden child on its prow. This extraordinary personification allows us to imagine her self-identification with her own pregnant, childbearing body. Her physicality was put in service to conquest and to the success of her dynastic initiatives.

Mathilda's dynastic position was deeply affected by her successful childbearing. It allowed for an almost puritanical embrace of indissoluble monogamy in the context of serial marriages and outright polygyny that typified the rest of the northern Europe.[8] There were no illegitimate children, no second marriages; the conventionality of Mathilda and William's nuclear family was unique across the ruling dynasties of Christendom. When the papacy finally embraced Mathilda's marriage after ten years of prohibition, she and William were celebrated as an example of the perfect pious marriage.[9] Mathilda's ability to produce healthy children, while no doubt a source of personal satisfaction and relief, also significantly enhanced her political position. Her maternity established her centrality as the lynchpin of the Norman ruling house. Moreover, it was a foundational element of Norman success at home and abroad.

It is not hyperbolic to claim that Mathilda's reproductive success was fundamental to the achievements of the Anglo-Norman dynasty. Mathilda's notable fecundity gave the Normans reason to hope for stability in the duchy after the turbulence of William's minority. Mathilda's fertility had the same effect abroad in England; the initial victory of 1066 may have been provisional but the Norman dynasty was ready-made. By the time of the invasion, Mathilda had already given birth to seven of her nine children. She was pregnant when the *Mora* sailed for Hastings and pregnant when she was crowned queen of England.[10] Hers was not the desperate and poignant position of her immediate predecessor on the English throne, Edith Godwinson, whose barren state robbed her of the influence an heir might have accorded her at court. Queen Edith provided a foil against which Queen Mathilda shone: the conquering and generative Norman queen.

7 Chapter Two: Hands, 35–74.

8 Laura L. Gathagan, 'Family and Kinship', in *The Cambridge Companion to the Age of William the Conqueror*, ed. Benjamin Pohl (Cambridge, 2022), 143–62.

9 Papal letters between Gregory VII and Mathilda were effusive. He calls her 'beloved daughter' ('filia dilecta') and 'dearest daughter' ('filia karissima'). Gregory only used these addresses for two other people: his stalwart prince, Matilda of Canossa, and her mother Beatrice. MGH, *Epistolae Selectae, Das Register Gregors VII*, ed. Erich Caspar (Berlin, 1920–23), ep.1.71, pp.102–3, dated April 1074 and ep.7.26, p. 507, dated May 1080, respectively.

10 See Chapter Four: Head, 105–33.

Mathilda gave birth to her firstborn, Robert, *c.* 1053–4.[11] Her last child, Henry, was born in early September 1068, about four months after her royal inauguration and anointing.[12] After Henry, Mathilda's childbearing years came to an end.[13] This calculation illustrates that Mathilda's identity, for great stretches of her adult life, was a ruling woman in a pregnant body. Apart from the physical repercussions of her multiparity, Mathilda's offspring shaped her dynastic strategies. These were not monolithic; Mathilda seems to have delicately calibrated her response to her individual children. The evidence for her approach is the contested nature of the 'maternal Mathilda' found in eleventh-century sources.

The inconsistency of eleventh-century accounts is illustrated in the evidence for daughter Agatha, noted above. Agatha is not named in the contemporary work of William of Jumièges. She does appear in Orderic's *Historia* but only in one of the two accounts he compiled within it. Orderic may have conflated Agatha with daughter Mathilda, whom all eleventh-century narratives erase even though there is firm evidence for her landholding in Domesday Book.[14] The inaccuracy about the number and identity of Mathilda's children does more than simply frustrate historians. It raises a rich set of questions about Mathilda's role as mother. Like Orderic's confused catalog, Mathilda's maternal character is blurred. Chroniclers' and poets' perception of Mathilda as mother was as tangled as their identification of her children. Two particular sources reveal the tug of war about Mathilda's maternal identity: her speech found in the fifth book of Orderic's *Historia* and Fulcoius of Beauvais' poetic interpretation of the Old Testament story of Jephthah.[15] Each of these addresses Mathilda's relationship to a particular child. Orderic's text provides evidence

11 Aird, *Robert Curthose*, 20.

12 '1068: Matilda is consecrated this year in London by Aldred archbishop of York and not too many days later her son, Henry, was brought into the light' ('MLXVIII: Hoc anno Matildis consecrata est apud Londoniam ab Aldredo Eboracensi archiepiscopo, et post non multos dies Henricum filium suum in lucem protulit.'). *Annales monasterii de Wintona, Winchester Annals*, ed. H.R. Luard (London, 1865), 27. Mathilda's itinerary in 1067 and William's presence in Normandy both argue for, at the latest, early to mid-September. Hollister, *Henry I*, 30–1.

13 The consequence of this terminus point is that it further compresses Mathilda's active childbearing. In the fifteen years between Robert's birth and Henry's, she was pregnant or recovering from pregnancy – 'unchurched' – for eleven of them (and three months).

14 She appears in the survey for Hampshire, where 'Geoffrey, the chamberlain of the king's daughter, Mathilda, held land (from King William) for his service to her.' *Domesday-book; seu, Liber censualis Willelmi Primi regis Angliae*, ed. John Morris (Chichester, 1985) *DB* Hampshire, 1: 49b.

15 *OV*, iii, 104 and Marvin L. Colker, 'Fulcoius of Beauvais: Poet and Propogandist,' in *Latin Culture in the Eleventh Century* (2 vols., Turnhout, 2002), i, 144–57.

for Mathilda's bond to her firstborn son, Robert – the heir to Normandy – and her response to his rebellion against William in 1077. Fulcoius' poem was written to celebrate Cecelia's final vows as she was dedicated to Mathilda's monastic foundation at Holy Trinity as an adult in 1075. Orderic's Mathilda is forceful, fierce and uncompromising, while Fulcoius' Mathilda is pitiable. The purpose of this chapter is to make sense of these vastly different depictions found in contemporary sources. They reveal a tension surrounding Mathilda as a mother and offer different interpretations of her maternal character as it related respectively to Robert and Cecelia.

Orderic Vitalis himself drew comparisons between Robert and Cecelia. Orderic begins his fifth book, after some time away from his history, with Cecelia's ceremony of final vows at Easter in 1075.[16] Orderic's previous fourth book, moreover, concluded with Robert Curthose's rebellion against his father and his subsequent exile. Orderic describes Robert and his aristocratic companions as ruthless troublemakers; they despoiled Normandy and created instability all through the region. Here Orderic ends his fourth book, 'And now, numbed by the winter cold, I turn to other pursuits; and, weary with toil, resolve to end my present book here.'[17] Readers are encouraged to imagine the rebellion of Robert against his father as the winter of Normandy.

After his respite, Orderic takes up his history again in the 'warmth of spring'; he opens his fifth book with the celebratory scene of Cecelia's dedication at Easter in 1075.[18] Orderic bookends these volumes of his history with Mathilda's two children. He compares them implicitly; Robert represents the bitter cruel winter of Normandy and Cecelia the exultant rebirth of the duchy in spring. Her dedication on Easter was couched in terms of the resurrection of Christ. Yet by embracing this dramatic structure – ending Book Four with Robert and beginning Book Five with Cecelia – Orderic had to make a hash of his chronology. In truth, Cecelia's dedication in 1075 predates Robert's rebellious military actions and his exile in late 1077 or early 1078.[19] Orderic's literary contrast of Mathilda's two children so appealed to him that he employed it despite the disruption of his narrative. His willingness to do so speaks to his perception of their centrality to the fate of the Norman dynasty. Mathilda's maternal response to these two children, similarly, will be the focus of this chapter.

16 He tells his reader that 1075 was the year of his birth, so he thought it fitting to begin his fifth book with an accounting of that year. *OV*, iii, 8.

17 *OV*, ii, 361–2.

18 *OV*, iii, 8–11.

19 Aird, *Robert Curthose*, 78–86.

MOTHER OF ROBERT

Robert Curthose was born shortly after Mathilda's marriage to William, *c.* 1051–1052.[20] As the eldest son and heir to the duchy, Robert's birth and early life commanded care and attention. While there is little direct evidence of Robert's early life, it is probable that he spent much of his time in the company of his parents as they directed public policy. It is indicative of his position as heir that sometime in 1054, the one-year-old Robert, perhaps with Mathilda or William guiding his tiny hand, made the mark of a cross on the bottom of a piece of vellum next to the words '*Signum Robertis juvenis comitis*'.[21] Robert's first charter, signed alongside his mother and father, confirmed to the abbey of Saint-Wandrille the donation of a freehold estate called Gilcourt, which was originally given a few years earlier by William, the count of Arques. The written charter confirmed the previous work of William and Mathilda, before Robert's birth. One is tempted, in light of his later difficulties, to see a premonition in this act. Ascribing his support as a small child to something arranged by his parents, Robert's 'affirmation' was a simulation concocted for public view.

Robert would regularly sign charters with his mother and father as he matured, as did William Rufus, Richard, Cecelia, and Henry to a lesser degree. And while charter evidence offers little in the way of Mathilda's daily maternal activities and attitudes, it does suggest that Robert was with her at important moments in her career.[22] Further, it demonstrates that Mathilda involved her son in the administrative life of the duchy. Exposure to the workings of ducal administration would have been the focus of Mathilda's educational duties as a mother, and perhaps the premier learning environment she herself provided for Robert. She could demonstrate first-hand the daily responsibilities it necessitated. She was doubtless involved in choosing tutors for her children.[23] Robert's staff of *magisters* and teachers is known to us because of their inclusion in his charters as a young man. Raherius, 'consularius infantis'

20 For a full examination of the life of Robert Curthose, see Aird, *Robert Curthose.*

21 Fauroux dates this charter to 1051, but more recent analysis has placed it to 1054 based on Isembert's abbacy at Saint-Wandrille. *Recueil*, ed. Fauroux, no. 228, 437–8, but see Jean-Claude Richard, 'Les "miracula" composés en Normandie aux XIe et XIIe siècles' (PhD dissertation, L'École des Charters, 1975), 185; Christine Walsh, *The Cult of St Katherine of Alexandria in Early Medieval Europe* (Farnham, 2007), 80.

22 Aird, *Robert Curthose*, 34–40.

23 C.C. Swinton Bland, *The Autobiography of Guibert, Abbot of Nogent-sous-Coucy* (London, 1925), Book I, chapter 4. Michael Clanchy, 'Did Mothers Teach Their Children to Read?' in *Motherhood, Religion, and Society in Medieval Europe, 400–1400*, ed. Conrad Leyser and Lesley Smith (Farnham, 2001), 129–53. On the education of children throughout the Middle Ages, see Shulamith Shahar, *Childhood in the Middle Ages* (London, 1990), especially 209–24.

and Tetboldus, 'gramaticus' both appear in the same document.[24] Ilger or Hilgerius, 'pedagogus', witnessed legal texts with Robert well into his late teens.[25] Ironically, efforts to provide appropriate guidance and training for his future may have contributed to Robert's later rebellion. The presence of these handlers eventually chaffed Robert as he attempted to leave behind his minority and move into his own as a ruler.[26] The charter confirming the rights of the abbey of Marmoutier, for instance, includes precise language about Robert's status as an adult; 'Robert, his son confirmed it because he was already at the age of majority and could authorize it immediately.'[27] Even so, his tutor was still present at his side and signed it with him.[28]

Robert's impatience for genuine authority and an authentic role in governance reflected the expectations and frustrations of an eldest son in the eleventh century; no longer a youth, but not quite an independent lord.[29] Medieval lords repaid their supporters' loyalty by largesse. Keeping their knights well supplied and, indeed, enriching them was the lords' responsibility. Scholars have interpreted Robert's break with his father as colored by his sense of dishonor in the public world of the Anglo-Norman court.[30]

It is against this background that Robert's expectations – and those of his mother – should be considered. After the invasion of England, William's military activities kept him from Normandy, and provided the ideal opportunity for Robert to finally take control of the duchy. Robert was, in fact, formally invested with Normandy in the winter of 1067, as his father prepared to return to England.[31] Robert stayed in Normandy at Mathilda's side in William's absence but the government of Normandy was held in her capable hands. Though Robert signed charters with his mother, it was clear from the outset that Mathilda would be standing at the head of the justiciarship of Normandy.[32] When Mathilda herself traveled to England in 1068 for her coronation, however, Robert was in Normandy ruling on his own – her bilingual coronation diploma, issued in favor of St Martin-le-Grand and signed at Winchester, bore her son Richard's signature but not Robert's.[33]

24 *Cartulaire de l'abbaye de la Saint Trinité du Mont de Rouen*, ed. A. Deville (Rouen, 1840) no. 60.

25 Aird, *Robert Curthose*, 37–8.

26 Numerous eleventh-century chroniclers comment on this, including William of Jumièges, *GND*, ii, 194–5 and *OV*, iii, 98–9.

27 Roberti, filii sui faceret confirmari, quia scilicet majoris jam ille etatis ad prebendum spontaneum auctoramentum idoneus esset.' *Recueil*, ed. Fauroux, no. 228, 437–8.

28 *Recueil*, ed. Fauroux, no. 228, 438.

29 Aird, 'Frustrated Masculinity', 43.

30 Aird, *Robert Curthose*, 73–6.

31 William of Jumièges, *Gesta* ii, 178–9.

32 David Bates, 'The Origins of Justiciarship', *ANS* 4 (1981), 1–12.

33 *Regesta* (no. 181), 594–601.

Yet while Robert was officially duke of Normandy, he was not allowed resources or funds to maintain his own household or reward his followers.[34] William maintained control of his son, and the duchy, by withholding the financial means necessary for his autonomy.[35] Robert's resentment at his father's refusal to loosen his grip on Normandy resulted at last in an enduring rift that would have a permanent effect on the Anglo-Norman realm.[36]

Robert Curthose rebelled against his father late in 1077 or early 1078, revealing a fissure in a dynasty that seemed otherwise unstoppable. Robert's disaffection pulled in its wake the younger sons of the post-conquest generation who were his colleagues and men-at-arms. They both encouraged him and followed his lead as he fled Normandy and sought support with Mathilda's family first in Flanders and then France.[37] For Mathilda, it was a seminal moment that reveals to us her active role as a mother and the response of her contemporaries to her. When forced to choose sides, Mathilda chose her son against her husband. Orderic's account exposes his ambivalence about her choice:

> Queen Mathilda, feeling a mother's affection for her son, often used to send him large sums of silver and gold and other valuables without the king's knowledge. On getting word of it, he ordered her, in a passion, never to do such a thing again. When she recklessly renewed her offense, the king exclaimed in anger, 'How very true here and now is the maxim of a certain sage, "A faithless wife brings ruin to the state". After this, who in the world shall ever find a trustworthy helpmate? The wife of my bosom, whom I love as my own soul, whom I have set over my whole kingdom and entrusted with all authority and riches, this wife, I say, supports the enemies who plot against my life, enriches them with my money, zealously arms and succors and strengthens them to my grave peril.' Whereat she replied, 'O my lord, do not wonder that I love my firstborn child with tender affection. By the power of the Most High, if my son Robert were dead and buried seven feet deep in the earth, hid from the eyes of the living, and I could bring him back to life with my own blood, I would shed my life-blood for him and suffer more anguish for his sake than, weak woman that I am, I dare to promise. How do you imagine that I can find joy in possessing great wealth if I allow my son to be burdened by dire poverty? May I never be guilty of such hardness of heart; all your power gives you no right to demand this of me.'[38]

Orderic's description shows William enraged and Mathilda unrepentant. Orderic has William berate her as unfaithful, but empowers Mathilda to fire back at him from the high ground of a mother's moral obligation to her child.

34 *OV*, iii, 100–1.

35 Aird, *Robert Curthose*, 73–5.

36 *OV*, iii, 100–1.

37 Aird, *Robert Curthose*, 86.

38 *OV*, iii, 104.

While Orderic uses the topos of a 'weak woman' he then gives her a will of iron. Orderic sets the competing demands of wife and mother in opposition within the family drama of the Anglo-Norman dynasty and it is unmistakable from his tone that motherhood has prevailed. While Orderic was not an eyewitness to William and Mathilda's confrontation, he had an excellent source for the contours of the confrontation, and takes pains to reveal it in the passage immediately following the confrontation:

> On hearing this, the stern duke grew pale with anger and, bursting with rage, he commanded one of the queen's messengers named Samson, a Breton, to be arrested and blinded. However, when Samson got wind through friends of the queen of the king's wrath, he speedily took refuge in the monastery of Saint-Évroul. There at the queen's plea, he was received by the Abbot Mainer, and prudently adopted the monastic way of life to save both body and soul. He was shrewd and eloquent and chaste; and he lived for twenty-six years under the monastic rule.[39]

Saint-Évroul was Orderic's home from the age of seven, when he became a child oblate there. His daily contact with Samson, both as a young man and later as an author, informed his *Historia*.

Samson's first-hand experiences of Mathilda's household provided intimate glimpses of the activities of the ducal family. Samson's 'eloquence' was a crucial characteristic, not just for Orderic's use while writing the *Historia*, but for his role as a covert operative for the queen. Medieval messengers carried letters, but for sensitive and confidential information they memorized and recited the wishes, instructions and directives of the sender.[40] This was common practice as letters could be misplaced or intercepted. For instance, in Pope Gregory's letter to Mathilda in 1080, he closes his letter with the phrase, 'your servant Hubert, who we both trust, will tell you the rest'.[41] William's attempted attack reveals Samson's importance in Mathilda's underground network.[42] It also

39 *OV*, iii, 104–5. William of Malmesbury notes that Mathilda used funds from 'royal estates' which could well have been her own. William of Malmesbury, *Gesta Regum Anglorum: The history of the English kings, Volume 1*, ed. and trans. R.A.B. Mynors, R.M. Thompson and M. Winterbottom (Oxford, 1998), 500–3.

40 Giles Constable, *The Letters of Peter the Venerable* (2 vols., Cambridge, MA, 1967) ii, 25–8.

41 'Cetera, que dimisimus, per Hubertum filium nostrum et fidelem communem mandamus.' MGH, *Epp, Das Register Gregors VII*, ed. Erich Caspar (Berlin, 1920–3), 507 dated May 1080. Translated online at *Epistolae: Medieval Women's Latin Letters* http://epistolae.ccnmtl.columbia.edu/

42 Mathilda's later generosity to Saint-Évroul was doubtless in part because of their role in providing shelter and safety for Samson. Mathilda paid 100 Rouen pounds for a stone refectory at the abbey so 'that all the monks could eat together'. Near the end of her life, she paid a visit to the abbey to pray, and donated a chasuble 'decorated

demonstrates that Mathilda herself was untouchable. William sought an outlet for his anger by revenge against Mathilda's knights, not Mathilda herself. Orderic is clear that this scene was occasioned by a second offense; Mathilda's support of Robert had already been discovered. Whatever warning or threat had been made at the initial uncovering of Mathilda's web of secrets, she had refused to heed. She repeatedly defies William and denies his right to govern her behavior.

Mathilda's network of agents and arms suppliers had not been disbanded after its initial detection. William was unable to disrupt or neutralize her web of contacts. Her trusted accomplices would have been implicated in her treason. Their loyalty to her, even in the face of exposure to the king's notorious temper, was profound. Mathilda's financial support of her son in exile brings forward fascinating evidence for the shape and scope of Mathilda's maternal activities on his behalf and highlights important elements of her role as a medieval mother. She maintained an underground system of some sort that allowed funds and arms to be funneled from her estates to Robert. Evidence of her military personnel is sparse – only Samson has left any evidence – but Mathilda's staff of chamberlains and confessors are traceable. She employed at least five chamberlains in England: Humphrey, Reginald, Gerard, Aubrey and John.[43] There seems to have been a separate staff in Normandy comprised of at least William Le Flamand and Fulchold – both designated *camerariius regine* on Norman *acta* – and Stephen, who served Mathilda before she was queen.[44] Her English agents regularly funneled taxes and funds to Normandy for her use. Mathilda also employed her own messengers like Hubert, mentioned above.

During the period of Robert's exile, from the end of 1077 or beginning of 1078, Mathilda was chiefly in Normandy. Her location would have made it easier to oversee the transport of money and valuables to Robert. In the first part of Robert's exile, he found refuge with Duke Robert 'the Frisian', Mathilda's younger brother. Robert had usurped the throne of Flanders from

with gold and pearls' and left a mark of gold on the altar for the monks. She gave this in exchange for prayers both for herself and for her daughter Constance. Orderic claims she had promised to do more, but that her death prevented it. The timing of this gift was after Constance's marriage to Alan of Brittany. The pair had no children; Mathilda's singling out of her daughter with this gift may have been connected to prayers for conception. *OV*, ii, 148–50 and also at iii, 240–1.

43 Gerard held Kemerton in Gloucestershire, John held land at Twyning and Fairford in Gloucestershire. *DB* Gloucestershire 19, 2; *DB* Gloucestershire 1, 50. Aubrey, the 'queen's chamberlain' was probably Aubrey de Vere, who held Carswell, Benham and Curridge in Berkshire from Mathilda. *DB* Berkshire, 63.

44 The two groups of financial agents do not appear together on documents which may indicate that one set of chamberlains handled her continental wealth, its collection and distribution, while the second group fulfilled the same function in England. Musset, *Les actes*, 136–40. For Stephen, see *Recueil*, ed. Fauroux, 445.

his nephew, Arnulf III, still a minor, on the death of his older brother Baldwin VI. Mathilda had sent troops to wage war against her brother Robert, and indeed a key ducal advisor and friend, William fitz Osbern, led the expedition.[45] Mathilda's mother, Adela of Flanders, also supported Arnulf's claim, and both royal women provided money and troops to support him. Adela and Mathilda, Arnulf's grandmother and aunt, fulfilled their roles as noble medieval matrons through military support. Acting in concert, they also joined Arnulf's mother, Richilde of Hainaut, in seeking the support of Philip of France.[46] At the Battle of Cassel in 1072, Arnulf III was killed, as was William fitz Osbern, allowing Robert the Frisian to rule Flanders. Orderic claimed that Mathilda was terribly distraught by these losses, though she was eventually reconciled with her brother.[47]

Mathilda's support of her firstborn's rebellion against his father presents a different type of ideal mother than modern readers might expect. It reveals that her understanding of a mother's duty was, if not primarily martial, then substantially so. Chapter One provided evidence that Mathilda's parents may have been the model for her approach to her son Robert.[48] Adela influenced Mathilda's father Baldwin, still a young heir and not yet reigning as Baldwin V, into armed rebellion against his father Baldwin IV, soon after they were married. Though the attempt eventually failed, Baldwin's relationship with his father improved markedly afterward and he was recognized as an adult.[49] Mathilda's parents instigated a successful military coup that woke his father to awareness of his son's maturity. Could Mathilda have been drawing connections from her own father's experience to her son's? Her sympathy for his position might lead one to that conclusion. Whatever the case, the complex network of power and militarism that led from mother to daughter then mother to son in Mathilda's family illustrates the nature of aristocratic motherhood in the eleventh century. Mathilda's own experience of mother as military patron and financier may look more warlike than maternal but these roles were interconnected. The other actors in the Flemish civil war were also

45 Mathilda's ties to William fitz Osbern were of long standing. Mathilda's first charter as duchess was signed in confirmation of fitz Osbern's monastic foundation at Notre-Dame-sur-Lyre. He remained in Normandy during the Conquest as part of her governing coalition. See C.P. Lewis, 'The early earls of Norman England', *ANS* 13 (1991), 207–23; David C. Douglas, 'The Ancestors of William fitz Osbern', *EHR* 59 (1944), 62–79.

46 See Chapter One: Blood, 11–33.

47 *OV*, ii, 284–5. Orderic claims that the relations between Normandy and Flanders were strained from this time forward, not only because of the death of Mathilda's nephew, but because of William fitz Osbern's death.

48 See Chapter One: Blood, 11–33.

49 *GND*, ii, 52–4. See also Pfister, *Études sur le règne*, 222. See Chapter One: Blood, 11–33.

mothers and grandmothers – Richilde and Adela – who supplied military support for their son and grandson.

Robert's rebellious behavior had no positive result. William neither awoke to Robert's competence nor introduced an arrangement of shared governance as Mathilda might have hoped. In January 1079, William's exasperation with his son resulted in pitched battle. William besieged Robert at Gerberoy, where he occupied the castle, in the winter of 1079.[50] On the battlefield outside the fortress Robert and his father met in combat, though unknowingly. Robert unhorsed his father. He was prevented from killing him only when William cried out, and Robert, recognizing his father's voice, immediately relented. Robert allowed his wounded father to remount his horse and watched as he rode away, still bleeding. According to John of Worcester, William ended the siege and returned to Rouen humiliated.[51] Robert stayed in exile while William attempted to recover. Mathilda then turned her energies anew to constructing a reconciliation.

Mathilda was instrumental in arranging the truce between William and Robert, enlisting the help of friends and churchmen to accomplish it. Simon of Crépy, a kinsman of Mathilda's and a great favorite of William's, was raised as a young man in their court. A powerful lay lord, Simon left behind his position and entered the monastic life.[52] He was pulled out of contemplation and peace to lend his weight to Mathilda's arguments for reconciliation. He joined Mathilda and Philip I in the weeks before Easter, as they translated a Carolingian relic of the Holy Shroud at Compiègne.[53] The ritual may have been an acknowledgement of the political perilousness of Mathilda's family.[54] Like her Carolingian ancestors, Mathilda may have sought heavenly support to dispel the clouds on her dynastic horizon.[55] Simon's presence at the translation

50 Aird, *Robert Curthose*, 86–7.

51 *The Chronicle of John of Worcester*, ed. and trans. P. McGurk (Oxford, 1998), iii, 32–3.

52 Cowdrey, 'Count Simon', 253–66.

53 See Chapter Three: Fingers, 91.

54 Mathilda commissioned an ornate jeweled reliquary for the Shroud, but that does not seem to have been a gesture of expiation. Simon's *vita* records her tearful pleas for Simon's help in bringing her family together, but there is no indication that Mathilda felt personally responsible for widening the rift between her son and husband. Milo Crispin 'Vita beati Simonis comitis Crespeiensis auctore synchrono', *PL* CLVI, 1211–24 at 1220–2.

55 Martina Caroli demonstrated Louis the Pious's attempt to use St Baldthild's holy body as a bulwark against his son's impending rebellion. Martina Caroli, 'A woman's body for the empire's salvation: the translatio of Queen Bathild's body and the crisis of the year 833' in *Relics, Identity, and Memory in Medieval Europe*, ed. Marika Rasanen, Gritje Harnnann, and Earl Jeffrey Richards (Turnhout, 2016), 91–113, esp. 106.

liturgy at Compiègne in March, immediately before the reconciliation at the Easter court, argues for a link between the two events. Mathilda may have had recourse to the relic's political benefits to defuse her family's rebellion; the Holy Shroud, a relic of Christ himself, acquired by Charlemagne, might rescue the Norman dynasty from disaster.[56]

Pope Gregory, as mentioned above, wrote letters to Mathilda, Robert and William to assist in repairing the breach. Gregory's letters are responses to lost communications from Mathilda. It is possible that she requested his help and pressed him to write in support of reconciliation. William's promised reform of English churches, the lure that obtained papal support for the conquest, would be hampered by Robert's rebellion. From Gregory's perspective, William's uncontested authority was necessary to enact sweeping ecclesiastical reform in England. And yet the pope addresses Mathilda as his 'dearest daughter', a term he uses very sparingly, even after she has acted to undermine William.[57] Though it is impossible to ascertain whether Gregory was aware of the details of Mathilda's military support for Robert, he may have subtly indicated his knowledge of her position in his letter after the reconciliation. He praises her love for God and for her neighbor and suggests that 'With these and similar weapons arm *your husband*, [emphasis mine] when God gives you the opportunity, and do not cease to do so.'[58] In 1080, Robert's exile was ended, and he returned home. His reconciliation with his father would only hold until its architect, Mathilda, died in 1083. After her death, Orderic tells us, Robert left the Norman court. He only returned after the death of his father in 1087 to take his place as duke of Normandy.

Despite Orderic's ambivalence about Mathilda's position as treasonous wife, he portrays her maternal activities favorably. He allows her morality as a mother to take precedence over William's demands as a husband. In fact, though William's '*ira*' at her behavior is justified, his attempt at revenge, when bent toward Samson, reduces William to impotence. Samson escapes by the queen's arrangements and, at her request to the Abbot of Saint-Évroult, is saved 'body and soul'.[59] Mathilda's maternal care for Samson echoes her assistance to Robert. Once again, Orderic tells us, Mathilda's contacts and networks are put to good use. Samson is blameless, 'shrewd, eloquent and chaste'; by acting as his champion, Mathilda's salvific qualities are demonstrated. Orderic vilifies Robert

56 Caroli, 'A woman's body for the empire's salvation', 92.

57 Gregory addressed her as *filia karissima*. Gregory used this appellation for only two other people; Mathilda of Tuscany and Beatrice of Lorraine. H.E.J. Cowdrey, *The Register of Pope Gregory VII: An English Translation* (Oxford, 2002).

58 'His armis et aimilibus virum tuum armare, cum Deus tibi oportunitatem dederit, ne desistas.' MGH, *EPP* 7. 26, 507; Cowdrey, *Register of Pope Gregory*, 357 and 462–3.

59 *OV*, iii, 104–5

as an 'Absalom' in his *Historia*, but Mathilda shares no blame in his rebellious and perfidious character.[60] She redeems her son and Samson, supports them both materially and martially, sees to their safety and activates her extensive system of ecclesiastical and lay 'clients' on their behalf. For Robert, Mathilda as mother is a lioness: active, martial, authoritative and fearless.

MOTHER OF CECELIA

Like Robert, Cecelia was born before the conquest, one of Mathilda's older children. Cecelia also grew up in the comital court surrounded by tutors. But here her resemblance to her brother ends. Robert's tutors had nothing like the peerless intellectual pedigree of Cecelia's educators. Contemporary sources identify Cecelia's teacher as Arnoul of Chocques. Born in Flanders, Arnoul was one of the great literary minds of his day, famous for his eloquence and oratory.[61] Arnoul himself was educated under intellectual giants including Lanfranc and William Bona Anima.[62]

Cecelia was chosen for a very different destiny than Robert, but hers was no less crucial to the dynastic objectives of her family. As discussed previously, as military preparations were underway to ensure the success of the Norman invasion, Cecelia's parents vowed to dedicate her to God as an oblate.[63] Her oblation to Holy Trinity was recorded in the foundation charter of the monastery, the apex of Mathilda's support for her abbey, appearing as the finale in the account of Mathilda's gifts and countergifts.[64] Though her parents' vows to dedicate her as an oblate occurred in 1066, Cecelia's own acceptance of monastic life as an adult came later in 1075.[65] The liturgical celebration of her profession was no less symbolic than the dedication of Holy Trinity eleven years earlier. Then the conquest was a cause for hope and, no doubt, deep misgiving. Cecelia's oblation was one dynastic tactic Mathilda pursued in her support of the invasion; Cecelia's own acceptance of monastic life was her contribution to victory over the English.[66]

60 *OV*, iii, 98–9.

61 Raymonde Foreville, 'L'École de Caen au XIe siècle et les origines Normandes de l'Université d'Oxford,' in *Etudes médiévales offertes à M. le Doyen Augustin Fliche* (Paris, 1952), 89; Elisabeth M.C. van Houts, 'Latin Poetry and the Anglo-Norman court, 1066–1135: the "Carmen de Hastingae proelio,"' *JMH* 15:1 (1989), 39–62; André Boutmey, 'Trois oeuvres inédites de Godefroid of Reims', *Revue de moyen âge latin* 3 (1947), 343.

62 *The Deeds of God through the Franks: a translation of Guibert de Nogent's Gesta Dei per Francos*, ed. and trans. Robert Levine (Woodbridge, 1997), 136.

63 See Chapter Two: Hands, 35.

64 See Chapter Two: Hands, 43.

65 *Recueil*, ed. Fauroux, 442–6.

66 See Chapter Two: Hands, 35.

The Easter festal court of 1075 was an opportunity to revisit Cecelia's sacrifice, this time in the context of Norman victory. Easter was the highest holy day of the liturgical year and the most well-attended of the celebrations in Normandy. The setting of Cecelia's rite – at Fécamp – was also deeply meaningful. Before the establishment of Caen, Fécamp was the ducal necropolis.[67] William's triumphant adventus after the conquest was held at Easter in Fécamp.[68] Eight years later, when Cecelia took the veil from Archbishop John of Rouen, in the presence of her family and all the great women and men of Normandy, echoes of Norman triumph reverberated.[69] Cecelia's dedication made a deep impression on the duchy as evidenced by Orderic's literary choices illustrated above. This was the occasion for the presentation and performance of Fulcoius of Beauvais' poetic interpretation of the Old Testament Jephthah story.[70]

Fulcoius, a secular cleric and poet, reinterpreted the Biblical story of Jephthah that was based on an Israelite military hero found in Judges 11:29–40. The key element of the biblical narrative describes Jephthah making a capricious vow to God as he faces an enemy army of Ammonites; he promises to sacrifice as a burnt offering whatever first comes out of his door on his return. [71] Jephthah is successful in battle and his homecoming is joyous. But his victory dissolves into tragedy, as his only daughter is the first living thing to come out of his house to greet him.[72]

Fulcoius refashioned the Jephthah tale for his eleventh-century Norman audience and his choice was brilliantly fitting (see appendix to this chapter, 168–70). Cecelia embodied the virgin as sacrifice to her father's battle victory. The success of the invasion of England had changed the course of the Norman dynasty's future; Cecelia's sacrifice for her family's triumph had a direct impact on the Norman achievement. Furthermore, Fulcoius could draw upon the fortuitous shared root of the heroines' names: Selia and Cecelia.[73] The Old Testament story revealed that Jephthah was also illegitimate. Like William, Jephthah was the product of an irregular union.

67 Both Duke Richard I of and Richard II of Normandy were born at Fécamp and William's father, Duke Robert, was buried there.

68 *OV*, ii, 196–9.

69 *OV*, iii, 8–11.

70 Elisabeth van Houts, *The Normans in Europe* (Manchester, 2000), 132; L.J. Engels, *Dichters Over Willem De Veroveraar; Het Carmine de Hastingae prelio* (Groningen, 1967), 6–7.

71 Judges 11: 29–40

72 Judges 11: 34–35.

73 According to Alexiou and Dronke's commentary on the *Liber Antiquitatum Biblicarum*, there are over twenty extant manuscripts of the text. While none of this evidence points directly to Fulcoius' use of the pseudo-Philo, it is a distinct possibility. Howard Jacobsen, *A Commentary on Pseudo-Philo's Liber Antiquitatum Biblicarum: With Latin Text and English Translation* (Leiden, 1996).

Despite the notable parallels that made Jephthah's story a fitting theme, Fulcoius made significant adjustments to the story in order to fit it into the Norman context. The most notable of these was the inclusion of Mathilda into the Jephthah story. The original Biblical version made no mention of a mother. But Fulcoius inserts references to Mathilda into his design in two innovative ways. In the opening lines, Fulcoius draws attention to her by the verse, 'At this time a queen lived; from the south she came'. This obscure reference to a queen does not name Mathilda herself, but Fulcoius' reference to a queen early in the work places Mathilda, at least referentially, into the poem at the start.[74] More explicit references to Mathilda occur in the lines at the end of the poem. Jephthah's daughter closes it with the words, 'I am the only daughter of my father and my wholly wretched mother, I came out first; I entered the vow that he vowed. Let him not consider anything of me, but let him pay the debt.' References to Mathilda thus act as a frame for the poem; she is invoked at its beginning and at its end. In the original Biblical tale there is no mention of a mother at all; she is invisible and voiceless. Fulcoius finds ways to insert a mother, and a queen, into his rewrite for Cecelia's dedication at the Easter court of 1075. It seems Fulcoius needed to find a way to make Mathilda present in his piece. That he does so speaks to her crucial role in the oblation of her daughter. Mathilda's presence at the festal court would necessitate an acknowledgement of her part in Cecelia's oblation.

In 1075, Cecelia was only a nun, but the rhetoric of her investment ceremony was a clear signal to the gathered crowd. Her father's vows were now her own; by the assumption of his obligations, she also assumed some of his authority. Her elite education in grammar and dialectic, the cooperation of her family in her oblation, the very structure of Holy Trinity itself – referencing Ottonian forms – all spoke to an assumption from the beginning that she would ascend to the abbacy at Holy Trinity. Cecelia's life was designed to be a career of active abbatial administration and lordship. Even more, as a princess/abbess in the Ottonian mold, promotion of the new royal Norman dynasty and its remembrance was now her occupation – her part to play. The royal abbatial responsibilities she would eventually shoulder formed the subtext of the ceremony.

For Cecelia, as for her mother Mathilda, liturgical performance was also deployed and translated into active rule. In Cecelia's case, the performance of the Jephthah poem at Easter in 1075 was echoed by her ascension to abbatial authority as she took her place to rule Holy Trinity for the 'vow her father vowed'. Like Mathilda's royal inauguration, Cecelia's formal acceptance of

[74] Fulcoius, 'Epistolae', 245. Elisabeth van Houts has suggested that Fulcoius inserted this section to underscore the magical properties of divination; Sheba was often linked to Sibyl, the prophetess, in the eleventh century. Mathilda's recourse to a hermit visionary at least once in her life offers evidence that she may have been a devotee: van Houts, 'The Echo of the Conquest', 148.

the veil was a dramatic liturgical scene backlit by the appropriation of an Old Testament story of male militarism. As seen in Chapter Four, Mathilda's laudes inserted male apostles as her intercessors, not traditional virgin female saints. Both ceremonies featured female appropriations of masculine scriptural authority: Mathilda borrowed the mantle of the apostles and Cecelia the story of a militaristic Old Testament leader. They were overt assertions of female agency, reinforced by the invocation of biblical authority and concretized through ritual.[75]

Yet Fulcoius' representation of Mathilda as desolate and somewhat powerless, heartbroken at the loss of her daughter, jars with both Orderic's characterization of her and with what we know of Mathilda's life. In light of Fulcoius' portrayal, the sacrifice of Cecelia to the monastic world demands close analysis. Mathilda's foundation of Holy Trinity has been examined in Chapter Two; provision for Cecelia was one element of its purpose. Mathilda's intent is revealed in her arrangements for Holy Trinity's financial health; they are astonishingly detailed. A charter issued by Mathilda for Holy Trinity in 1082 adjusted and refined some of the abbey's original gifts and is a study in micro-management.[76] Mathilda assigned income streams to the express needs of Holy Trinity by name. For the lighting of the nun's dormitory, the tithe of the toll of Ecouché; for lighting the infirmary, forty shillings from four tenants in Les Moutiers; for the nuns' food, a significant portfolio of investments: the tithe of coins and the whales from Saint-Étienne at Bavent and on the Diveta, two ploughlands, ten acres of meadow, one and a half mills, the tithe of the malt and bread of the abbey of Caen, and seven manors throughout Caen.[77] The sacristy received all the offerings made at the altar, gold and deluxe fabrics granted to the abbey, and the income of the churches in Falaise, except for the corn. For wood, and for the needs of the nuns' chambers, the income from three English estates was to be used: Felsted in Essex, Tarrant in Dorset, and Penbury in Gloucestershire.[78] Previous chapters have already demonstrated Mathilda's persistent recourse to countergifts to persuade and coerce donors.[79] Moreover, unlike many Norman nobles who, enriched after the conquest, founded abbeys on English soil, Mathilda never founded another monastic

75 Laura L. Gathagan, 'The Trappings of Power: the Coronation of Mathilda of Flanders', *HSJ* 13 (1999), 21–39 at 28–30; Chapter Four: Head, 115–44.

76 Musset, *Les actes* (no. 8), 77–90.

77 The manors are Ouistreham, Barge, Chaffour, Foulbec, Escanneville, Capriquet, and Sallen. Musset, *Les actes* (no. 8), 81.

78 'Other donors to other churches occasionally indulged in the same practice, but the frequency with which Mathilda used it is unparalleled. If the difference is real, if Holy Trinity was not merely less reticent than other abbeys, it probably stemmed from Mathilda's desire to create a large endowment for her new nunnery as quickly as possible.' Emily Zack Tabuteau, *Transfers of Property in Eleventh-Century Norman Law* (Chapel Hill, NC, 1988), 115–17.

79 See Chapter Two: Hands, 63.

house. Instead, she funneled all the new wealth available to her into Holy Trinity. It was, without question, the richest female house in Normandy by the time of her death. Cecelia's succession to the abbacy of Holy Trinity can be seen as the furtherance of her mother's vision. Holy Trinity was to be a dynastic center in the imperial German style. Thus, Cecelia's ascension to the abbatial seat – an abbess-princess in the Ottonian mold – would fulfill her dynastic destiny. Though Cecelia was raised to the abbacy in 1113, years after Mathilda's death, Cecelia's ascension mirrored the Ottonian precedents Mathilda embraced for her foundation.[80] Mathilda's strategy from Holy Trinity's dedication was to set Cecelia at its head. As the new Norman female necropolis, Holy Trinity was the recipient of enormous resources, the focus of Mathilda's time, energy and wealth, and the beneficiary of all her powers of persuasion and management. In creating Holy Trinity, Mathilda also created an ideal setting for her daughter: a woman of letters and ambition. It is in this context that one must view Cecelia's new home.

As abbess, Cecelia pursued her own agenda of administrative, financial and architectural changes after the death of her mother in 1083.[81] She arranged for and initiated a survey of all the lands and holdings of Holy Trinity, a process that would have involved significant resources, both human and financial, to arrange and carry out inquests in England and Normandy.[82] Cecelia also embarked on an architectural program that would result in some of the most remarkable Romanesque innovations of the time: a complete revamping of the abbey's interior, including barrel vaulting, false sexpartite ribs and soaring ceilings.[83] After her mother's death, Cecelia stamped the abbey with her own identity and shaped it into her image. The evidence of Cecelia's own life suggests that, in fact, Holy Trinity was Mathilda's gift to her daughter rather than the reverse.[84]

Life in the cloister had its benefits for medieval women, not the least of which was the opportunity for education and a life of the mind.[85] I would posit that in Cecelia's case, a career at Holy Trinity offered far more than just protection from the fatalities of childbirth or the demands of a family. The monastic nest her mother so assiduously feathered for her may have been the perfect setting for a life of wealth, influence and, most of all, autonomy.

80 See Chapter Two: Hands, 51–6.

81 Gathagan, 'Maiden', 847–9.

82 Gathagan, 'Maiden', 854–6.

83 Baylé, *La Trinité*, 59–71.

84 Cecelia's commanding intellect ensured her active role in the aristocratic literary cultural of the eleventh and twelfth centuries. She patronized at least two poets, Baudri of Bourgeil and Hildebert of Le Mans.

85 Holy Trinity was not claustrated. Movement of the abbess, and even the nuns, in and around the city of Caen was expected. Gervase de la Rue, *Essais historiques sur la ville de Caen et son arrondissement, Tome 2* (Caen, 1820), 19–20.

Moreover, Mathilda's burial at Holy Trinity allowed her presence in Cecelia's life even after her death. 'So', as Holy Trinity's mortuary roll declared, 'that in death she might adorn with her bones the chapel that she had embellished with her love while alive.'[86] Mathilda's dynastic imperatives also served Cecelia's future. Her contribution to the conquest included her daughter but Mathilda's creation of Holy Trinity – wealthy, beautiful, the locus of Cecelia's autonomy – ensured that she could, in the language of the charter, retain 'both their child and all other good things'.[87]

How do we interpret Fulcoius' image of Mathilda as a desolate mother, grieving the loss of her daughter in light of this evidence? And indeed, how can we square such a representation with Orderic's picture of a vigorous, martial mother defiant in the face of her husband? Fulcoius' rewriting of the Jephthah story allowed Mathilda a role as mother that the original biblical passage never permitted. Fulcoius evoked a queen, moreover, whose presence is outside the tale itself and adds nothing to the trajectory of the narrative. One can only assume that Mathilda's role in Cecelia's future was so central Fulcoius could not afford to ignore it. Portraying Mathilda as a grieving mother, even if it employed significant artistic license, allowed the poet to draw attention to her. If William, as Jephthah, is 'pitiable' and 'rent his clothes as he remembers his promise' then Mathilda, as Selia's mother, must also grieve. If the sacrifice of the father lent him heroic status, despite the rashness of his vow, how much more heroic the mother, whose suffering was blameless? Jephthah's daughter 'badly makes a fool of her father' but her mother is irreproachable. Fulcoius used his Jephthah poem to emphasize Mathilda's piety and the morality of her sacrifice, notwithstanding the adjustments he had to make to cut out a space for her in the narrative. Likewise, he adjusted reality by ignoring the benefits to both women of this arrangement and casting it, as writers before him had, as a kind of death for Cecelia. In fact, Fulcoius' portrayal of Mathilda as a mother was modified and altered almost out of recognition. The wretched passive mother, helpless at her daughter's sacrifice, and powerless against her husband's oath, was a fiction crafted to suit Fulcoius' composition. Inserting a mother and a queen into his creation seems to have been imperative. Once done, granting her piety and the moral high ground was relatively effortless, but casting Mathilda, the military financier, into the Jephthah story would have been glaringly out of place. The militaristic mother who supported Robert through arms and money against her own husband, the resourceful, relentless patron who – through countergifts – pressed her nobles and subjects to donate land to her monastic house, the administrator who arranged that

86 Daniel Sheerin, 'Sisters in the Literary Agon', in *Women Writing Latin, Volume 2*, ed. Laurie Churchill, Phyllis R. Brown, Jane E. Jeffrey (New York, NY, 2002), 93–131, at 119.

87 BNF 5650, folio 13r; Musset, *Les actes*, 57.

the tithe of whales from William's seaside abbeys support her nun's dinner fare was not the appropriate mother for Fulcoius' Jephthah story. Orderic and Fulcoius thus present a contested depiction of her.

The Easter court of 1075 was perhaps the last time the royal family celebrated together without the tension that would later develop between William, Mathilda and Robert. By 1077, Robert had broken with his father and left Normandy, supported by his mother's resources. After the disaster at Gerberoy in 1079, however, the Norman royal family met once again at Fécamp at Easter. The festal court of Easter 1080 was the setting for Robert and William's reconciliation, noted above, which took place against the same dynastic scrim as so many other moments of high ritual for the ducal/royal family: William's adventus in 1067; Cecelia's dedication in 1075; William and Robert's reconciliation in 1080. Mathilda was the prime mover of their peace.

For the next two years, William and Robert attempted to work together. Robert was dispatched with his father's blessing to Scotland and performed very successfully. He re-established peace in Scotland and even stood as a godfather to Malcolm of Scotland's daughter, Edith. His mother Mathilda was with him. A twelfth-century account places Queen Mathilda as Edith's godmother; Edith supposedly grabbed at Mathilda's veil, a sign that she would also one day be queen.[88] While the legend has roots in other *vitae*, it is probable that Mathilda was present. She spent nearly all of 1080–82 ruling England while William was in Normandy. Robert stayed in England until the winter of 1080–1 at which time he returned home – without his mother – to address the threatening situation in Maine by his father's side. As they campaigned together, Robert appeared regularly in charters with his father. Yet, Mathilda's death on November 2, 1083 reopened the deep fissure between the two men. Their relationship dissolved without Mathilda's mediating presence. Robert Curthose once again decamped from Normandy in January 1084, just two months after Mathilda's death in November.[89] He would not see his father alive again.

ROYAL DAUGHTERS

The textual evidence for Mathilda's relationship with Cecelia and Robert dictated the parameters of this chapter. Her other children, particularly her daughters, deserve but have not received sustained scholarly attention. There are some notable exceptions.[90] Adela of Blois, in particular, has enjoyed a thorough examination made possible by the prodigious documentation

[88] *Letters and Charters of Gilbert Foliot*, ed. A. Morey and C.N.L. Brooke (Cambridge, 1967), 60–6.

[89] Aird, *Robert Curthose*, 95.

[90] van Houts, 'The Echo of the Conquest', 135–54; Gathagan, 'Maiden'; LoPrete, *Adela*.

that survived her.[91] Adela's life, more than all of Mathilda's other daughters, resembles her mother's active rule; like Mathilda, Adela's son would also rule England. Her sons Stephen and Henry, raised at her brother King Henry's court in England, would disrupt the royal Norman bloodline through their illicit seizure of the English throne. Very much in her mother's mold, Countess Adela of Blois would hand down comital justice, engage in military ventures and rule alone. Her authority over Blois was so established that the death of her husband Stephen, while on Crusade, seems to have created little more than a ripple in the county. Even after she retired to monastic life, she actively worked to reconcile Anselm and her brother Henry, hosting diplomatic events to persuade them to mend fences.

Constance also pursued a secular life of public administration but left behind only a few pieces of evidence.[92] She married Count Alan Fergand of Brittany in a ceremony at Caen.[93] She adjudicated disputes in her own court.[94] Constance was an active monastic donor. She patronized traditional recipients of comital largesse but also made more idiosyncratic choices; she favored Ste Croix of Quimperlé, a foundation that seems to have appealed to her personally. She was only countess for four years before her death in 1090. Constance was buried in Redon Abbey where the dukes of Brittany rested for generations.

Adelheid was probably the eldest daughter and was chosen early to support Norman political initiatives. She was intended for various partners in succession including Herbert, Count of Maine before 1062, Harold Godwinson before 1066, and an unnamed king of Galicia.[95] The *vita* of Simon of Crépy claims other candidates requested Adelheid's hand – King Alphonse of Spain and Robert Guiscard – both were considered inappropriate by her parents.[96] None of these marriage negotiations came to fruition. Adelheid eventually

91 LoPrete's thorough examination of Adela is the foundational work on Mathilda's youngest daughter and includes a complete list of her charters and the legal cases she decided. LoPrete, *Adela*, 439–534.

92 Livingstone uncovered references to Constance in *Hubert Guillotel: Actes des ducs de Bretagne (944–1148)*, ed. Philippe Charon, Philippe Guigon, Cyprien Henry, Michael Jones, Katharine Keats-Rohan and Jean-Claude Meuret (Rennes, 2014), 386–8 and *Cartulaire de l'abbaye Sainte-Croix de Quimperlé*, ed. Léon Maitre and Paul de Berthou, 2nd, ed. (Rennes, 1902), 268–9. Livingstone, 'Scorpions', 55–7.

93 *OV*, ii, 352–3.

94 Livingstone, 'Scorpions', 56.

95 William of Poitiers mentions the Count of Maine, Earl Harold Godwinson and one of two Spanish royal brothers. Orderic claims the 'king of Galicia' was a candidate. *OV*, iii, 114–15.

96 The *vita* of Simon of Crepy mentions that King Alphonso of Spain and Duke Robert Guiscard were both 'disregarded' by William as suitable matches for either Adelheid or Adela. 'Vita beati Simonis comitis Crespeiensis auctore synchrono', *PL* 156, 1211–24 at 1215–16. See also Cowdrey, 'Count Simon', 253–4.

entered a monastic house with close ties to her family: St Léger de Préaux.[97] The same community provided Holy Trinity's first abbess, Matilda, who came to serve the foundation at Caen. Interestingly, Adelheid did not join her mother's foundation of Holy Trinity where her sister would be abbess. In 1070, Anselm of Bec sent Adelheid a series of Latin prayers and meditations, at her request, to focus her mind on 'everything that must be given up even while you have it'.[98] If Adelheid was the eldest daughter, she would have been about sixteen when she received Anselm's compositions. Prayers in her memory are requested in the mortuary roll of Holy Trinity, produced *c.* 1113. Thus, Adelheid disappears in 1070 and reappears in memoriam over forty years later. The necrology at Chartres cathedral records her death; William donated a 'costly' church tower to Chartres in her memory.[99] Bates suggest this was given after Adela's marriage to Stephen, when William would have been in the neighborhood of Chartres. If so, this suggests the terminus date of Adelheid's death was *c.* 1083. She would have been about twenty-six.

Daughter Mathilda, her mother's namesake, is the most difficult to trace. Prayers for her were requested on Holy Trinity's mortuary roll establishing the date of her death as before 1113. Other than her textual presence there and the Domesday entry mentioned above, no other trace of Mathilda the younger has been discovered. The Domesday evidence indicates that she spent significant time in England, at least enough to require the services of her own chamberlain, as 'Geoffrey, the chamberlain of the king's daughter, Mathilda, held land (from King William) for his service to her'. Her presence in Wessex may indicate she was at Wilton or Nunnaminster, the educational centers of royal English women but this can only be conjecture.[100] Nothing further is yet known about her.

CONCLUSION

Mathilda's approach to childrearing is difficult to discover within the confines of the brief details afforded us. Her maternal motivations for all of them, however, seem consistent; her children were placed into service of the Norman ducal house and, after the conquest, their nascent royal dynasty. From that perspective, Mathilda's support for Robert's rebellion seems contradictory.

97 *OV*, iii, 114–15.

98 *The Letters of Saint Anselm of Canterbury* trans. Walter Frohlich (Kalamazoo, MI, 1990–94), 92–94. See also *Epistolae: Medieval Women's Letters*, https://epistolae.ctl.columbia.edu/letter/383.html

99 *Cartulaire de Notre-Dame de Chartres*, ed. M. Lépinois (3 vols., Chartres, 1862), iii, 218. Bates, *William*, 418.

100 David Bates, 'William the Conqueror and Wessex' in *The Land of the English Kin: Studies in Wessex and Anglo-Saxon England in Honour of Professor Barbara Yorke*, ed. Alexander James Langlands and Ryan Lavelle (Turnhout, 2020), 517–37.

One can imagine nothing more damaging to the Norman dynasty's stability than civil conflict between members of the ruling family. Yet, Mathilda's experience of how a young heir might prove himself worthy of governing may have come directly from her parents' experience as discussed above. Furthermore, Mathilda had seen Robert's capacity for administration over the course of their rule together in Normandy. Her assessment of Robert was informed by years of associated governance in William's absence. Mathilda had an investment in her son's success as duke of Normandy and William's inability to allow Robert autonomy was damaging to his reputation. Even more, William repeatedly signaled that Robert's time had come to take the reins of the duchy only to seize them back or refuse funds for his administration. In the face of the staggering wealth of England now available to its royal family, William's financial conservatism must have appeared stingy. Perhaps Robert's frustration was shared by his mother. Given her possible assumptions about how a young heir might prove his mettle, Mathilda's encouragement of Robert's rebellion assumes a different cast. No evidence exists to support the notion that Robert was not capable of succeeding his father. Orderic was a biting critic of Robert Curthose, but he never denied that the duchy was his by right nor intimated that he was incapable of ruling it. If Mathilda believed that Robert could rule, this may have seemed the most expedient tactic to force William to accept his son's adulthood. The battle at Gerberoy led to an almost unthinkable result, at which point Mathilda pivoted and worked toward a reconciliation with equal energy and resolve. Thus, at another Easter court at Fécamp, the Norman dynasty was repaired in 1080. Mathilda did not live to see its final fissure.[101]

[101] It was left to Abbess Cecelia to negotiate the rift between her brothers. Gathagan, 'Maiden', 857.

APPENDIX

FULCOIUS OF BEAUVAIS, 'JEPHTHAH'

I came to see the wonders of which I had heard,
but more wonderful than those I had heard are the things I tell
At this time a queen lived; from the south she came:
Behold, two kings come again in this one king,
Father and son. Who? Solomon and David.
In whom? Pray tell? In King William. Who, pray?
That man is a David, 'strong in hand', as the English bear witness,
the same a Solomon, 'peacemaker', as the same bear witness.
He beats back, he withdraws, he heals where he wounds;
both peace and war obey him sympathetically.
they sing over again how much Jephthah's victory costs.
That is what William is doing, who does not know how to spare himself:
Jephthah would not spare his daughter, nor the king his life.
Let Jephthah's daughter not be passed over now improperly
Jephthah, about to wage battle, about to come back the victor, vowed that he would put on his dear altars
whatever he first met:
'Victory has vanquished the vow',
he says. First of all there had gone out, lest anyone is looking for more sadness,
carrying cymbals, bring grief through her joy,
his only daughter. As she sings, the daughter badly makes a fool of her father.
('Let Jephthah's daughter not be passed over now improperly')
When her father saw her, the pitiable man rent his clothes:
as he remembers his promise, he plainly forgets his prize, repeating:
'Oh, oh me! Daughter, you trap yourself and me.'
When she asks why the victor weeps, and he explains,
the maiden urged him not to act, but the pact is made,
and by her death she will let her people and her parent live.
('Let Jephthah's daughter not be passed over now improperly')
The only daughter begs 'send me away for three months, a breathing space,'
So she can grieve for her virginity and her life.

She brought together fine examples with collected dances
and, if he could, he would have brought together a thousand, when maidenly dances were joined in lovely meadows:
she produces a lament; a hundred songs reply:
('Let Jephthah's daughter not be passed over now improperly')
Since Jephthah was cast out, he heartily arms his heart;
since Jephthah was cast out, he has been disposed to war.
He was not an equal heir, since he is an unequal son.
But the Ammonites and the Israelites are disturbed:
there is no one to lead the Jews and bring them back;
among the Hebrews there is no one worthy of triumphs except Jephthah.
(Let Jephthah's daughter not be passed over now improperly)
First spurned, Jephthah was afterwards recalled;
they grant a cohort to the one they would not grant a consort.
Jephthah knew when he entered the battle, that the first
to come out would leave as a victim.
'I am the only daughter of my father and my wholly wretched mother.
I came out first; I entered the vow that he vowed.
Let him not consider anything of me, but let him pay the debt.'
('Let Jephthah's daughter not be passed over now improperly')

Translated by A. Orchard. Reprinted with permission from Elisabeth van Houts *The Normans in Europe* (Manchester, 2000), 132–3.

Original Latin text appears in M. Colker, 'Fulcoii Belvacensis epistolae,' *Traditio* 10 (1954) 245–6.

'Quae prius audieram ueni quod mira uiderem,
Sed prius auditis magis ammiranda reporto.'
Tempore uiueret hoc regina, ueniret ab austro.
Ecce duo reges hoc uno rege resurgunt,
Filius atque pater. Qui? Dauid cum Salomone.
In quo dic, precor. In Willelmo rege. precor, qui?
Ille manu fortis Dauid est testantibus Anglis,
Pacificus Salomon idem testantibus isdem.
Reicit et reuocat, quo uulnerat inde medetur.
Et pax et bellum parent concorditer illi.
Decantant Iepte quanti uictoria constet.
Id Willelmus agit, qui nec sibi parcere nouit.
Nec Iepte natae, nec rex uult parcere uitae.
Iam soboles Iepte non pretereatur inepte.
Prelia facturus Iepte, uictor rediturus,
Quod prius in caris occurrat sisteret aris
Vouerat, et 'uicit uotum uictoria' dicit.
Primitus exierat, ne plus quis tristia quaerat,

Cimbala portando, luctus per gaudia dando,
Vnica. dum psallit, male patrem filia fallit.
Iam soboles Iepte non pretereatur inepte.
Quod pater ut uidit, miserandus tegmina scidit.
Dum mernor est fidei, patet immemor esse trophei,
'Heu' geminans 'heu me, te, filia, decipis et me.'
Cur uictor plorat dum quaerit et ille perorat,
Virgo ne faciat monuit sed sponsio fiat.
Morte sua gentem uult et uixisse parentem.
Iam soboles Ieptae non pretereatur inepte.
'Menses tres, uitae spacium, 'petit unica mitte,'
Plangat ut aetatem simul haec et uirginitatem.
Cum collectaneis paradigmata grata choreis
Contulit, et mille, si posset, conferat ille,
Iunctis uirgineis per amoena uirecta choreis.
Profert lamentum, respondent carmina centum
(Iam soboles Iepte non pretereatur inepte):
'Iepte quod eiectus fuit, armat pectore pectus.
Iepte quod eiectus fuit, est ad bella receptus.
Heres non compar fuit, est quia filius impar.
Ast Ammonitae turbantur et Israhelitae.
Non est qui ducat Iudeos quique reducat,
Aptus in Ebreis non est nisi Iepte tropheis.'
Iam soboles Iepte non pretereatur inepte.
'Primum pulsatus, post est Iepte reuocatus.
Quem non consartem patiuntur bahere cohortem.
Iepte cum seiret quoniam eertamen iniret, Quod prius exiret quod uictima nouit abiret.
Vniea sum patris miseraeque per omnia matris.
Primitus exiui; uotum quod uouit adiui.
Nec quiequam uoluat pro me sed debita soluat.'
Iam soboles Iepte non pretereatur inepte.

Reprinted with permission from M. Colker, 'Fulcoii Belvacensis epistolae,' *Traditio* 10 (1954), 191–273 at 245–6.

6

FLESH

The real flesh of Christ and His Blood are offered on the Lord's table, eaten and are drunk, bodily, spiritually, incomprehensibly.

Lanfranc of Canterbury, *De corpore et sanguine Domini*

In her last charter, dated sometime before her death on November 2, 1083, Mathilda of Flanders constructed something along the lines of a will.

> I, Queen Mathilda give to Holy Trinity, Caen, a chasuble made in Winchester by Aldred's wife and the mantle made of gold cloth from my chamber to be made into a priest's cope, and also two golden book bindings which are in the shape of crosses, the hanging lamps engraved with emblems to be used before the altar, and the large candelabra made at St Lo; my crown and scepter, chalice and the vestment made in England, along with all my horse's accoutrements, and all my vases, except those I have already donated elsewhere during my lifetime. Quettou in Normandy and two houses in England I give to Holy Trinity.[1] All of this, therefore, I do with the approval of my lord king.[2]

1 Chibnall identified these two manors as Great Baddow and Umberleigh in England. The properties do not appear, however, in either set of surveys for Holy Trinity compiled after her death. In Domesday, these two manors are listed by name as manors of the queen. They only appear in a later charter for Holy Trinity, which Musset considered a forgery, but which Bates theorized was probably collated by the abbess and nuns at a later date. For description of the charter as a forgery, see Musset, *Les actes*, 111–12. For Bates' argument for a late copy made by Holy Trinity see *Regesta* (no. 62), 302. Chibnall, *Charters and Custumals*, xxv.

2 'Ego Mathildis regina do Sancte Trinitati Cadomi casulam quam apud Wintoniam operatur uxor Aldereti et clamidem operatam ex auro que est in camera mea ad cappam faciendam atque de duabus ligaturis aureis in quibus cruces sunt, illam que emblematibus est inscupta ad lampadam suspendendam coram sancto altari, candelabraque maxima que fabricantur apun Sanctum Laudum, coronam quoque et sceptrum, calicemque ac vestimentum quod operator in Anglia, et cum omnibus ornamentis equi atque omnia vasa mea, exceptis illis que antea dedero alicubi in vita mea. Chetehulmum in Normannia et duas mansiones in Anglia do Sancte Trinitati Cadomi. Hec ergo omnia concessu domini mei regis facio.' BNF 5650, folio 24r.

Mathilda's crown, scepter, saddle and bridle arguably demonstrate what she thought was essential to her identity. They represent her through her life's work: a consecrated queen, perennially on horseback, constantly active in the peripatetic governance of her realm. The chasuble made in Winchester could have been an example of the famous *opus Anglicanum*, representing the artistic bounty she commissioned as queen of the English. Alongside these important self-expressions, one phrase in particular stands out in the last document Mathilda commissioned. In the second line of the document, Mathilda insisted that 'the mantle of gold cloth from my chamber be made into a priest's cope'.[3] As I have shown in my previous chapters, Mathilda left very little to chance when it came to her documentary directives.[4] It would not have been unusual for her to specify how this rich cloth was to be used. The intimacy of this gift to clothe a priest during mass seems profound; an uncommon bequest enshrined forever in parchment. While modern conceptions of privacy differ somewhat from medieval, nevertheless, a queen's bedchamber did convey something apart. Mathilda drew a direct link from her chamber to clothing a priestly body.

Mathilda's favored gifts were almost always liturgical vestments and chalices. She employed goldsmiths, embroiderers and artisans for this purpose: Otto the goldsmith, Leofgeta, who made gold fringe, and the wife of Aldred, an embroideress, all held lands from Mathilda in exchange for their artistry.[5] Mathilda made good use of their labor. She gave to Saint-Évroul a chasuble made of gold and pearls, and a cope to be worn by the cantor.[6] She gave a cope to Marmoutier.[7] To Cluny, she gave a chasuble so stiff with gold that 'it could not be folded'.[8] She gave another chasuble to Chartres, for which we have no description.[9] She gave a gold chalice encrusted with jewels to the monks at Saint-Florent-de-Saumur.[10] And, in the her last charter recorded above, she gave Holy Trinity a chasuble made in Winchester. Donations of vestments and liturgical objects outweighed any other type of moveable gift Mathilda utilized.

Elite women's moveable wealth has been the focus of significant analysis in recent years. Women's gifts and patronage engaged cultural currency, identity

3 BNF 5650, folio 24r.

4 See Chapter Two: Hands, 63.

5 *DB* Essex 1, 11; *DB* Wiltshire 68, 86; *DB* Hampshire 6, 16.

6 *OV*, ii, 148–50.

7 Mathilda also 'built the beautiful refectory which still exists today, and through which one can feel the grandeur of she who had it built'. *Histoire de Marmoutier, inventaire des archives*, ed. Edmund Martène (Touraine, 1875), 329.

8 H.E.J. Cowdrey, 'Memorials of Abbot Hugh of Cluny (1049–1109),' Studi Gregoriani XI (1978), 45–109, at 64–5.

9 *Guibert of Nogent*, 186.

10 P. Marchegay, 'Chartres angevines des Xie et XIIe siècles', *Bibliothèque de l'École des chartes* 36 (1875), 413–4.

and spread religious innovation through new saints' cults.[11] Mathilda's gifts largely travelled in one direction – she used English wealth to patronize Norman recipients. Lucien Musset analyzed the moveable artistic gifts of the Norman aristocracy and came to the conclusion that their preferences were guided by individual taste and interests.[12] William the Conqueror, for instance, gave crystal vases to Saint-Denis that were apparently of the 'Arab school', perhaps representing some contact through his Norman relatives to the East.[13] Odo of Bayeux gave particularly lavish decorations to fit out his own cathedral at Bayeux, including two gold unicorns twenty feet high.[14] In the same way, Mathilda chose particular kinds of objects as expressions of her artistic preferences: liturgical vestments or chalices for the Mass. Other than her gifts to Holy Trinity, moreover, all the other donations of vestments and liturgical chalices were given to male monastic communities.

Mathilda was not the first queen to give vestments to a monastic community; nor was she the last.[15] Her predecessors, Queen Emma and Queen Edith, were active patrons though Emma's gifts were far more numerous than those recorded for Edith. Emma most often gave manuscripts like the famous Gospel book that includes her portrait. Her donations of deluxe books enriched Canterbury, New Minster at Winchester, London, Bury and York.[16] Vestments were not her gift of choice. Queen Emma did leave a record of two priestly garments: a cope with golden tassels given to Canterbury and a belt to Witgard of Augsburg.[17] Edith left record of giving at least one vestment, an amice, to the abbot of Saint-Riquier in France. However, the number and frequency of Mathilda's liturgical gifts seem to establish a regular pattern. Why might Mathilda, with all the wealth of England at her disposal, have chosen

11 For further reading on elite women's bequests of material objects, see *Moving Women Moving Objects (400–1500)*, ed. Tracy Chapman Hamilton and Mariah Proctor-Tiffany (Turnhout, 2019).

12 Lucien Musset, 'Le mécénat des princes normands au XIe siècle,' in *Artistes, artisans et production artistique au Moyen Âge*, ed. Xavier Barral Altet (Paris, 1987), 121–34 at 130.

13 Musset, 'Le mécénat,' 133.

14 V. Bourrienne, *Odon de Contreville, évêque de Bayeux* (Bayeux, 1900), 8–9. These objects existed at Bayeux until 1562.

15 Marguerite Keane, *Material Culture and queenship in fourteenth-century France: The Testament of Blanche of Navarre 1331–1398* (Leiden, 2016).

16 Stafford, *Queen Emma and Queen Edith*, 144.

17 Gervase of Canterbury, *Gesta Regum, Historical Works of Gervase of Canterbury*, Rolls Series, ed. W. Stubbs (2 vols., London, 1880), i, 56. Emma gave Ely an embroidered pall to drape each saint, and a cloth to cover the tomb of Saint Aethelryth; Stafford, *Queen Emma and Queen Edith*, 142. See also Valerie Garver, 'Weaving Words in Silk: Women and Inscribed Bands in the Carolingian World', *Medieval Clothing and Textiles* 6 (2010), 33–56 at 36; Maureen Miller, *Clothing the Clergy, 900–1200* (Ithaca, NY, 2014), 169–71.

to donate vestments and ornate objects crafted to adorn the altar? Why not deluxe manuscripts and gospel books, as her predecessor, Queen Emma, had, or her cousin Judith of Flanders? The answer might be found in the intimacy of her gifts, which reveal layers of meaning if one considers their context in the eleventh century.

Probably the most foundational theological dispute of Mathilda's lifetime centered on notions of real presence and the nature of representation concerning the Eucharist. The ideas of eleventh- and twelfth-century theologians are important for our discussion because the actors in this debate had direct links to Mathilda's court. They were intimately involved in both teaching and royal administration. The bishops and abbots who were engrossed in the controversy regarding personhood, representation, and mediation also had the final authority on documents produced for the royal house that were eventually ratified for the benefit of their monasteries.

Lanfranc was a significant presence at Mathilda's court from her earliest days as a young duchess: first abbot of St Stephen's Caen, then abbot at Bec and finally archbishop of Canterbury. He was also the most outspoken champion of 'real presence', that God, in the flesh, was on the altar table. Lanfranc's absorption with real presence would continue throughout his life. *Liber de corpore et sanguine Domini* (On the Body and Blood of Christ) was composed around 1063, just as Lanfranc took the reins of St Stephen's across the valley from Mathilda's Holy Trinity in Caen.[18] Lanfranc claimed the Body of Christ was present in the Eucharist sensually ('sensualiter') and that the 'true body and blood of our Lord Jesus Christ…are physically taken up and broken in the hands of the priest and crushed by the teeth of the faithful, not only sacramentally but in truth.'[19] His chief opponent, Berengar of Tours, considered the Eucharist to represent Christ's body, in memoriam, but denied that it miraculously *became* flesh on the altar.

Lanfranc's conclusions were deeply Aristotelian. According to the Aristotelian theory of substance, Christ's body displaced the bread that lay on the altar in real space.[20] The communicant, however, only saw the host. This illusion was a further miracle, according to Lanfranc, protecting those who would find bleeding flesh on the altar terrifying. To some of the faithful, however, Lanfranc claimed 'occasionally the mask dropped and pious eyes saw the very flesh itself'.[21] In Aristotelian fashion, the bread was merely a visual placeholder provided by God's mercy – with the appropriate physical

18 Sally Vaughn, *The Abbey of Bec and the Anglo-Norman State* (Woodbridge, 1981), 17–19.

19 Lanfranc, *Libre de corpore et sanguine Domini, PL* 150:234.

20 Kobialka, 'Staging Space/Place in Eleventh-Century Monastic Practices', in *Medieval Practices of Space*, ed. Barbara Hanawalt and Michal Kobialka (Minneapolis, MN, 2000), 34.

21 Kobialka quotes Lanfranc, 'Staging place/space', 134.

dimensions of bread – for the underlying truth of Christ's bleeding body. This holy body always occupied the space on the altar but was visible rarely and only to a few who had the piety (and stomach) for it. Seeing Christ's flesh on the altar was a miracle of uncovering – of revealing something already fully, completely present.

Lanfranc accused Berengar of the usual sins of the heretic – an adversary of the holy church, a sacrilegious oath violator – but Lanfranc also accused Berengar of treason.[22] According to Lanfranc, to theorize against Christ's real body and blood was to commit treason because the flesh of Christ was both sacramental and sovereign. To claim Christ was not real on the altar was to deny his body's sovereignty. Lanfranc's Eucharistic theories, Kathleen Biddick claims, 'are entangled in political theology' twining together the sacral and sovereign nature of the real presence.[23]

These theories closed the gap between reality (signified) and symbol (signifier), an alienation brought about, according to Augustine, by the fall of humankind.[24] Instead, scholars like Lanfranc and Anselm of Bec promoted the idea that things and objects could be the realization of form in matter. Lanfranc specified that the material objects on the Eucharistic table were themselves converted to the body of Christ *in their being* (emphasis mine).[25] He contested the distinction between mere objects and what they signified.[26] According to Bedos-Rezak, the cultural outcome of this debate changed the relation between the signifier and the signified 'so that an iconic representation might be seen as more real than empiric evidence'.[27] The object and the reality it signified were conflated; consequently the object was not merely *representative* of the signified reality but contained in itself its actual identity.[28] Thus the Eucharistic controversy pushed eleventh-century believers

22 Kathleen Biddick, 'What Does 'Deconstructing Christianity' Want? The Institutional Imaginary of the Incarnation' *the minnesota review* 80 (2013), 83–94 at 86–87.

23 Biddick, 'Deconstructing Christianity', 85.

24 Augustine, *De Doctrina Christiana*, ed. R.P.H. Green (Oxford, 1995), 24–5.

25 'We therefore believe that the earthly substances, which are divinely sanctified at the Lord's table through the priestly mystery, are ineffably, incomprehensible, miraculously transformed into the essence of the Lord's body…' ('Credimus igitur terrenas substantias, quae in mensa dominica per sacerdotale mysterium divinitus sanctificantur, ineffabiliter, incomprehensibiliter, mirabiliter, operante superna potentia, converti in essentiam dominici corporis…'). Lanfranc, *Libre de corpore et sanguine*, 234.

26 Ivo of Chartres used whole passages in his Decretum, as did Bernold of Constance. R.B.C. Huygens, 'Bérengar de Tours, Lanfranc et Bernold de Constance', *Sacris Erudiri* 16 (1965), 355–87.

27 Bedos-Rezak, 'Medieval Identity,' 1503.

28 Ibid.

to consider 'that signs could have intrinsic properties…to be extensions of their referents'.[29]

While no explicit evidence for Mathilda's participation in these theological exchanges exists, these concerns about mediation, signification and representation preoccupied the eleventh and twelfth century both in theological circles and more broadly within the court.[30] Theologians and teachers in this period were examining minutely the nature of personhood and representation as it touched theories of the Trinity, the sacraments and the Incarnation.[31] Yet elite theologians like Lanfranc were not only teachers who founded schools, but also courtiers.[32] Their careers demonstrate deep connections between cathedral, monastery and royal service. Lanfranc and Anselm of Canterbury produced much of their work while living in monastic houses, but their careers were ultimately bound up in the Anglo-Norman court. Theological debates and issues were not isolated from court circles. The lay nobility were deeply involved in doctrinal issues touching on the nature of the church, both spiritual and corporeal. Mathilda herself presided with William over ecclesiastical synods and councils, including the Easter council of Winchester featured in the next chapter, that established the primacy of Canterbury, Lanfranc's own pet project as archbishop.[33]

Scriptural exegesis and the hotly contested theories of the Eucharist deliberated by Lanfranc, Berengar and others swirled in and around eleventh-century Anglo-Norman royal circles.[34] Kobialka has argued that new forms of medieval representation in the liturgy followed these debates and were the result of the wholesale adoption of Lanfranc's theory. For instance, a flesh and blood monk representing Christ was suddenly featured at the Easter liturgy instead of a 'voiceover' from someone in the side aisle.[35] Likewise in all disciplines new representations were suddenly popular, even sculpturally in stone. Images of plants, animals, humans and monsters on Romanesque capitals in monasteries were part of the trajectory begun by the representation and

29 Bedos-Rezak, *When ego was imago*, 106–7.

30 Bedos-Rezak, 'Medieval Identity', 1492.

31 William J. Courtenay, *Covenant and Causality in Medieval Thought: Studies in Philosophy, Theology and Economic Practice* (London, 1984), see especially essays 2 and 7; Henri de Lubac, *Corpus mysticum: L'Eucharistie et l'Église au Moyen Âge* (Paris, 1949); Gary Macy, *The Theologies of the Eucharist in the Early Scholastic Age* (Oxford, 1984).

32 Bedos-Rezak, 'Medieval Identity,' 1502.

33 See Chapter Seven: Mouth, for Mathilda's synodal activity, 199–202.

34 At the Council of Rheims in 1049, Pope Leo IX denounced and made heretical many of Berengar's theories. A.J. Macdonald, *Berengar and the Reform of Sacramental Doctrine* (1930; rpt. edition, 1977). For tracts directed against Berengar, see Macy, *Theologies of the Eucharist*, 44–53.

35 Michal Kobialka, *This Is My Body: Representational Practices in the Early Middle Ages* (Ann Arbor, MI, 1999), 75–6.

embodiment of the absent body of Christ. The earliest examples were not, as Biddick and many historians have assumed, constructed at St Stephen's in Caen. They were constructed at Holy Trinity under Abbess Cecelia, Mathilda of Flanders' daughter.[36] The interior capitals analyzed so carefully by Maylis Baylé in her 1979 study were part of the ambitious building program completed under Cecelia and were the first figural capitals of their kind in the Anglo-Norman world.[37] These were artistic ripples that radiated from the definitive adoption of the doctrine of real presence and are suggestive of how aware – how closely bound up – Mathilda and her daughter were to this theological premise. There is every reason to believe that this deep attachment to Eucharistic theory was also something of an obsession for the women in Mathilda's family. The abbey of Corbie was the first site of radical Eucharistic theory that foreshadowed, and provided the basis for, Lanfranc's insistence on real presence.[38] In 831 Paschasius Radbertus, while he was abbot of Corbie, wrote the first work by the name *De Corpore et Sanguine Domini*, insisting on the real presence of Christ's body. Corbie was the dowry of Adela of France: Mathilda's mother and Cecelia's grandmother. As we have seen in Chapter One, Adela's attachment to Corbie was entrenched; she considered it hers even after it was alienated from her.[39] Adela lived to see Paschasius canonized in 1073 by Gregory VII, before her death in 1075. Thus, debates about real presence and the Eucharist encircled not just Mathilda, but her mother and daughter as well. Biddick claims that real presence was an orthodoxy that was 'an entangled phenomena in which sovereignty, bread, wine, body, flesh, precious metals, textiles, stone chisel, celibate clerics and texts intra-acted and produced exceptional grids of space and time'.[40] I would add into that mix royal women.

The presence of the laity through church dressings and furnishings and the role they played in the rites of the church have been explored by historians like Marguerite Keane, Nicola Lowe and Valerie Garver.[41] But it is

36 See Chapter Five: Womb, 161.

37 Baylé, *La Trinité*, 74–95 and Figures 50–115.

38 Owen Phelan, 'Horizontal and vertical theologies: "sacraments" in the works of Paschasius Radbertus and Ratramnus of Corbie', *Harvard Theological Review* 103:3 (2010), 271–89.

39 See Chapter One: Blood, 11–33.

40 Kathleen Biddick, 'Transmedieval mattering and the untimeliness of the Real Presence', Book Review Essay, *postmedieval: a journal of medieval cultural studies* 4 (2013), 238–52 at 241.

41 Keane, *Material Culture*; Nicola Lowe, 'Women's devotional bequests of textiles in the late medieval English parish church, *c.* 1350–1550', *Gender and History* 22:2 (2010), 407–29; Garver, 'Weaving Words', 33–56. See also Valerie Garver, *Women and Aristocratic Culture in the Carolingian World* (Ithaca, NY, 2009), especially section entitled 'Textile Work', 224–6.

within the specific context of eleventh-century Eucharistic debates and the resultant theories, propounded by members of Mathilda's court and family, that we should interpret her gifts of liturgical vestments to monasteries. It is suggestive that Mathilda would so often favor gifts in this form precisely during a period in which debates concerning presence and representation were raging. These circumstantial ties point to the logical conclusion that she was well aware of the debate even without definitive evidence. In this period, a new concentration on the clothing of priests is reflected by Gregory VII, Peter Damian and Mathilda's closest theological influences, Lanfranc and John of Avranches.[42] In parallel to this developing fascination with Eucharistic garments, prayers for vesting were proliferating throughout Europe, in missals both deluxe and quotidian.

Historians have demonstrated that, beginning in the Carolingian period, ministers at the altar rail enveloped themselves in finery, in stark contrast to their appearance in the world outside the Eucharistic space: a self-conscious attempt by the clergy to be literally 'clothed in righteousness'.[43] Their transformation from sinful men to celebrants, worthy to touch and serve the host, occurred through vesting, a parallel to the miracle of transformation of the Eucharist. Through the ritual of putting on gorgeous garments, they were made fit to serve Christ's body to the faithful: the food of the angels. During Mathilda's lifetime, liturgical raiment was scrutinized, analyzed and celebrated, notably in tracts written by Gregory VII. The vestments of Aaron and his sons – Old Testament high priests par excellence – were used as templates in eleventh-century commentaries on how clerics ought to dress while serving in God's temple.[44] One of the most famous of Aaron's accessories was his flowering rod, a relic of which had pride of place in Mathilda's relic inventory.[45]

Liturgical vestments were the focus of much attention in Mathilda's familiar clerical circles. In Lanfranc's regular letters to his friend John of Avranches, archbishop of Rouen, they debated which items the clergy should wear and when. John wrote describing a church dedication where the bishop wore his chasuble at the beginning of the ceremony, instead of donning it only at the moment the mass began. Lanfranc considered this 'extraordinary' and responded, shocked: 'I cannot remember ever having seen anything like

42 Archbishop of Rouen, John of Avranches, presided over the Easter court in 1077 when Cecelia, Mathilda's daughter, took the veil as an adult at Holy Trinity. Her career as abbess *de facto*, if not *de jure* seems to have begun at this moment. See Chapter Five: Womb, 145–67.

43 'Let Your priests be clothed with righteousness, and let Your godly ones sing for joy.' Psalm 132:9. See also Miller, *Clothing the Clergy*, 2–3.

44 Hamilton, *Sacred City*, 74.

45 See Chapter Three: Fingers, 77 and 83.

that.'[46] By his own admission, Lanfranc 'scrupulously observed' the vestment practices of the clergy as they performed rituals. 'I was present when St Leo himself, supreme bishop of the Holy Roman see, dedicated the church at Remiremont: everything which the rite had prescribed up to the mass was completed without a chasuble.' Lanfranc made reference to the many pontificals he had at his elbow; he conferred with these sources as the two men deliberated back and forth. He noted that they came from all over the world.[47] Lanfranc and John's correspondence may seem mind-numbingly arcane to us, but it demonstrates an intense awareness, even obsession, with liturgical vestments and objects and precisely how and when they should be used.

A final piece of evidence linking Lanfranc, real presence and liturgical vestments can be found in his letter to Pope Alexander II. Within it, Lanfranc speaks emotionally about a vestment Alexander had given him. Alexander gave him two palliums, or stoles, on a papal visit to Rome; the first was given to Lanfranc in his official capacity, as was typical from a pope to an archbishop. But the second pallium was a mark of love for his old friend Lanfranc that Alexander himself had regularly worn to celebrate Mass. Lanfranc wrote that this gift 'brings back the memory of your name to me'.[48] Lanfranc describes the pallium linking the two men in their efforts to do good.[49] The demonstrable sinew of this relationship, for Lanfranc, was the pallium. Lanfranc then pivots immediately, as if he himself had been reminded, to assure Alexander that the essay against the heretic Berengar was on its way as promised. A gift of a precious vestment, previously worn by his dear friend, now in his possession, fired the synapse that led Lanfranc to think of Berengar. The comment about Berengar follows directly from 'two men doing good' because in Lanfranc's mind, the physical manifestation of their connection was the liturgical vestment. That pallium steered Lanfranc's thoughts to real presence. The pallium Alexander had worn – then given for love of Lanfranc – does not simply represent the pope to Lanfranc; it partakes in his essence. Like Christ at the moment of transubstantiation, Alexander is not merely symbolized by the

46 *The Letters of Lanfranc of Canterbury*, ed. and trans. Helen Clover and Margaret Gibson (Oxford, 1979), 85.

47 *Letters of Lanfranc*, 87.

48 *Letters of Lanfranc*, 54.

49 Gibson's translation reads 'I say nothing of many other instances which in this respect are no different from these and bring back the memory of your name to me whenever I do anything good' but it should more properly be read as first person plural '... quaeque michi memoriam uestri nominis si quid boni bonifacio dulciter representant. Epistolam quam Berengerio scismatico dum adhuc Cadomensi cenobio praeessem transmisi paternitati uestrae sicunt precepistis transmittere curaui.' *Letters of Lanfranc*, 54–6. My thanks to Charlie Rozier for help with this translation.

pallium. Alexander, through the fabric he once wore on his body, is sensually present for Lanfranc as he writes.

Given the *mentalité* of eleventh-century churchmen regarding vestments, it is no surprise that the use of vesting prayers, invocations to be recited as the celebrant dressed in liturgical clothing, spiked in this period. Vesting prayers and rituals became necessary for the transformation of the priest. These prayers were recorded everywhere, not just at the wealthiest, most prestigious houses. Their high survival rate in missals is evidence of their saturation into clerical life.[50] The most basic prayer sequences asked for God's mercy for the celebrant and connected the vestments to cleanliness. More elaborate vesting sequences became a litany of the saints. One eleventh-century German version names up to two hundred saints, as the clergy surround the celebrant in a responsive plea for the aid and support of saints as he was clothed in priestly vestments.[51] This brings to mind the responsive nature of Mathilda's laudes, seen in Chapter Four, but also highlights the communal character of vesting. The donning of Eucharistic clothing was a communal priestly activity and, indeed, a necessity for a vestment so thickly embroidered with gold thread it could not be made to bend.

In concert with these notions, Peter Damian (d. 1072) was writing *Dominus vobiscum* at this precise time. In it, Damian posited that all the Christian faithful were present in the prayers of one hermit, even as he prayed alone in his cell. Damian insisted the pronoun used in prayer must always be plural, never singular; all Christians were present at the moment a solitary person opens her/his lips in supplication.[52] Damian's conception of the presence of all believers – the unity of the church through the invocation of one soul – dovetails with the reigning theologies of real presence. Just as all Christian believers were signified by one believer and were present in that prayer, physical objects could signify their patrons and partake of their essence. Peter Damian's theology provides further context for Mathilda's presence through her gifts of vestments.

Mathilda's inner motives and thoughts concerning these gifts may be unreachable. However, we can surmise a few things about her expectations. First, the audience for Mathilda's gifts was restricted to monastic communities and those present during the community's celebration of the Eucharist. In the case of renowned houses like Cluny or Chartres, visiting laity may have occasionally attended Mass, but the primary participants in the liturgy were the monastic community members themselves. Second, the vestments Mathilda commissioned for these occasions were easily recognizable. They

50 Miller, *Clothing*, 77.

51 Miller, *Clothing*, 79.

52 *The Fathers of the Church Mediaeval Continuation: The Letters of Peter Damian*, trans. Owen J. Blum, 255. See also *Dominus vobiscum*, *PL*:146, 231.

were usually heavily embroidered or covered with gold or silver, precious gems and ornaments. The cope for Saint-Évroul was gorgeously encrusted with gold and pearls. Her vestment for Cluny was so thick with gold thread it could barely be maneuvered to dress the priest. These were bespoke garments that she commissioned and evoked her as patron. Third, royal and ducal gifts attracted other donations. Monasteries saw their economic fortunes improve through the subsidiary gifts that came in the wake of royal favor. Therefore, a gift originating from the throne, in any form, would be a noted and welcome addition to monastic capital. Gifts of vestments from royal patrons were not hidden away in a closet. They were used precisely because they were so identifiable; they were advertised. Thus, they were a goad or an inspiration for others to give. Orderic describes the impulse of royal and noble Normans in response to Mathilda and William's gifts: 'the other barons of Normandy were inspired to do likewise, and vied with each other in the good work and competed in giving alms generously as befitted their rank'.[53]

Viewed against the backdrop of controversy regarding real presence, mediation and representation, Mathilda's celebrated gifts at the Eucharistic table did more than simply represent her, they participated in her essence: her person. Of Mathilda's donations to monastic houses, at least five of the six major houses she favored during her lifetime received vestments to be worn specifically for liturgical practice or objects explicitly given to be used in the Mass. Indeed, her last bequest, mentioned at the opening of this chapter, willed to Holy Trinity a garment from her own chamber to be made into a cope. This gift could only be worn by a male priest who performed the Eucharist even though the beneficiary was a female house.

The place Mathilda commanded at the Eucharist table was the result of a particular context. At a time when ideas about real presence were being stridently debated and received heightened attention in the linked circles of monastery, church and court, spectacular vestments given by a woman of the highest status and power, to clothe the body of a male priest during the Eucharistic celebration, invested the liturgy with her presence. Mathilda's propensity for vestments as gifts stands as evidence for her awareness of her own influence and princely rank. It would be impossible for Mathilda not to be cognizant of her status in regard to male monasticism. Mathilda's grants to monastic houses were very public affairs; other members of the nobility signed the charters that documented her gifts. The houses involved were careful to keep a record of these transactions for the sake of posterity and for legal purposes. As mentioned above, gifts from Mathilda could also stand as a signal to other members of the nobility that a monastery was worthy of gifts. Mathilda repeatedly used countergifts to her courtiers and her nobility as incentives to give to her favored houses. As we've seen in previous chapters,

53 *OV*, ii, 11.

she used these monetary enticements far more often than was typical and aggressively pressured her court to give.[54]

These liturgical gifts interleaved Mathilda into the all-male Eucharistic space at the very moment in doctrinal debate when her real presence might be consciously, radically, channeled through Eucharistic objects. Her identity as patron was explicit; Mathilda would have been identified by her gifts. Her cope or alb lay against the skin of the priest and formed a physical insertion between the body of the cleric and the physical stuff of Christ's body and blood.[55] This insertion clothed him in righteousness, making it possible for a fallen human to touch Christ. The bridge between fallen humanity and Christ was provided, explicitly and recognizably, by Mathilda of Flanders.

A queen's presence, indicated in cloth of gold almost too heavily embroidered to move, clothed the priestly body as his sleeves dragged across the altar to proffer the cup, the bread, to the monastic community. What might that have meant to the male monastic members of that house? A visceral awareness of the body: the body of Christ as embodied in the bread and the wine; the body of the believer who received it; the body of the community kneeling as one to receive the rite; the body of Christ 'broken for you'. All was mediated, literally and figuratively, by a royal woman. Her presence gleamed from cloth of gold enrobing the chest of the priest, radiated from the pearls on an embroidered sleeve; indeed, a woman present through a donated chalice, as he sipped the blood of Christ. When one envisions the physical reverberations of Mathilda's presence, the invasive nature of such gifts is striking. So is their intimacy: *sensualiter*, sensually present.

CONCLUSION

The queens who came after Mathilda of Flanders benefitted from the way she shaped patronage. Carrying on the tradition of her godmother, Matilda II also regularly gave liturgical vestments to monastic houses and even made them herself.[56] Ivo of Chartres asked Matilda II for a liturgical vestment directly, 'such a kind that is something fitting for a queen to give, and for a bishop to

[54] See Chapter Two: Hands, 63.

[55] Likewise, altar cloths formed a physical bridge between the elements of the Eucharist and stone or wood. These were consciously used at 'sites of grace' in the liturgy, that is, places where the Eucharist might come into contact with a physical surface. Church guilds in traditional parishes create altar cloths and liturgical vestments to this day. These guilds are primarily, if not exclusively, made up of women. For women's gifts of altar cloths, see Garver, 'Weaving Words', 33–56.

[56] Huneycutt quotes the *Vita Sanctae Margaretae*, which she translates in full in Appendix II, 161–78. Huneycutt, *Matilda of Scotland*, 127, and chapter 6.

wear while celebrating the Divine Offices'.[57] When she gave bells to the church at Chartres, Ivo responded that they would bring her memory to the faithful, at the very moment of transubstantiation.[58] Hildebert of Lavardin, bishop of Le Mans, who wrote poetry and prose to Abbess Cecelia, also found a patron in Matilda II.[59] In thanking her for a pair of altar candelabra, Hildebert declared that, while Matilda was not a priest, by providing elements for the Eucharistic table, Matilda II was also present at the altar 'when Christ is sacrificed'.[60]

These courtly writers made explicit what was, by the twelfth century, a commonplace. The idea that royal women participated in the mass by their presence through objects was no longer a radical one. Like other societal and cultural transformations addressed in this book, the Eucharistic theology of real presence was a cultural current Mathilda rode, participated in, and pushed along. Just as Mathilda of Flanders' vestments provided the bridge between an all-too-human priest and the divine reality of Christ's body, her donatory practice allowed for those who came after her. Established in a new world obsessed with Eucharistic theology, the signified and the signifier, the doctrinal meaning of liturgical vesting, and the universal church represented through a sole voice, Mathilda of Flanders established the queen's presence at the site of grace.

57 The full passage reads 'I ask also that, in order to impress the memory of your excellence more sharply on my mind, you send a chasuble or some other priestly garment to my smallness which is fitting for a queen to give and a bishop to wear in celebration of the divine sacraments. Farewell.' *PL* 162 ep.107 cols. 125–6.

58 'Whenever they are sounded to announce the hours, they touch the minds of the hearers renewing your memory in the hearts of individuals. Such memory is not to be valued lightly which blossoms again when the peerless host offered on the altar of the cross for our redemption is consecrated daily at the Lord's table by ministers of the new priesthood, when with heavenly hymns like sacrifices of the lips God is honored by the faithful, when an offended God is inclined to mercy by sinners beating their guilty breasts in the sacrifice of a contrite spirit. There is no doubt that they participate in these goods who offer the goods which they have in abundance to the ministers of God who lack them for his honor and love.' Hildebert of Lavardin, *PL* 162 epistolae, 142 columns 148–9. Text available online at *Epistolae: Medieval Women's Latin Letters.* https://epistolae.ctl.columbia.edu/letter/412.html

59 Gathagan, 'Maiden,' 840–57.

60 'You are also present when Christ is sacrificed, when he is buried; neither is celebrated without your service, since you prepared the lamps there where we believe in our hearts and confess with our mouths that the author of light is present. It does not matter that the service is different, which is celebrated with the same affection.' Huneycutt quotes Hildebert in *Matilda of Scotland*, 129. Hildebert of Lavardin, *PL* 171 epistolae 1.9, columns 160–2. Text available online at *Epistolae: Medieval Women's Latin Letters.* https://epistolae.ctl.columbia.edu/letter/416.html.

7

MOUTH

Her mouth has revealed wisdom; the law of clemency is upon her tongue

Odo of Cluny, *The Epitaph of Adelheid*

The upheaval of the conquest provided fertile soil for Mathilda of Flanders to expand the privileges and responsibilities of queenship. Amongst these developments was her participation in justice. Mathilda's judicial activity was truly woven throughout her reign. It consumed a significant portion of her time and was a defining factor of her queenship. That Mathilda acted as a royal judge is not a matter for debate; evidence is found in Domesday Book and the monastic chronicles surveyed below. The subject of this chapter is how she came to be there when previous English queens were not. The following discussion suggests that Mathilda drew from two sources that encouraged her to imagine herself as a judge: one practical and one ideological. The first was the legal praxis of Norman female abbatial authority with which she was familiar. In Mathilda's duchy of Normandy, some women – particularly abbesses – handed down verdicts in their own manorial courts. This stands in contrast to eleventh-century English courts that were based on the assembly of the hundred, shire or county. The English structure allowed less room for lordly women to create manorial courts over which they had control.[1] The second was the ideological foundation of the Ottonian empresses for whom Mathilda of Flanders was named. Ottonian traditions created a space for imperial women to preside over legal conflicts.[2] The imperial identity adopted by her mother may have predisposed Mathilda to assume prerogatives her English predecessors did not. Just as in earlier chapters, Mathilda can be found occupying unexpected spaces. This chapter shows her in the seat of justice.

1 English ecclesiastical courts could operate as private jurisdictions; archbishops like Dunstan of Canterbury and Ælfheah of Winchester sentenced offenders to corporal punishment. But they were episcopal, not abbatial courts, in which women did not preside as judicial authorities. Nicole Marafioti, 'Secular and Ecclesiastical Justice in late Anglo-Saxon England', *Speculum* 94:3 (July, 2019), 774–805.

2 MacLean, *Ottonian Queenship*; Wangerin, 'Ottonian Women,' 15–38.

Records of Mathilda's judicial activity can be found throughout contemporary documentary sources, including Domesday Book.[3] Domesday Book holds an understandably monumental place in the practice – and imagination – of medieval historians. It is the premier documentary source for landholding and lordship immediately after the Norman invasion. Though it was completed in 1086, after Mathilda's death, traces of her remain in the survey's entries. For example, in Hampshire:

> In Somborne Hundred William (the Balistarius, or William the Archer), held Compton. Aldred brother of Odo claims one virgate of land from this manor. He states that he held it in 1066, and he was dispossessed after King William crossed the sea. He established his right in front of the queen. Hugh de Port is witness to this and the men of the whole hundred.[4]

The short passage does not give away much but it demonstrates Mathilda's judicial role. After losing a virgate of land in Compton Aldred proved his claim to Mathilda's satisfaction. She decided in his favor, presiding over the case in front of the 'whole Hundred' of Somborne, in the county of Hampshire, where the case was brought before her.

Hundred courts were local assemblies that formed the backbone of the English communal experience of law. These assemblies were central to the idea that early English people – tenants, farmers, free peasants and lords – came together to seek justice and do the business of the region.[5] Assemblies in the seventh century had authority even to decide if kings should be granted the revenue they sought or the punitive measures they undertook.[6]

3 Studies of Domesday Book comprise what amounts to an historical sub-field. It is not my purpose to survey it here but recent comprehensive works include S. Baxter, J. Crick, C.P. Lewis and F. Thorn, *Making Domesday: The Conqueror's Survey in Context* (Oxford, 2021); *Domesday Now: New Approaches to the Inquest and the Book*, ed. David Roffe and K.S.B. Keats-Rohan (Woodbridge, 2019); Sally Harvey, *Domesday: Book of Judgment* (Oxford, 2014); David Roffe, *Decoding Domesday* (Woodbridge, 2007); David Roffe, *Domesday: The Inquest and the Book* (Oxford, 2000). For an overview of the field, see Stephen Baxter, 'The Domesday Controversy: a Review and a New Interpretation', *HSJ* 29 (2017), 225–93.

4 *DB* Hampshire, 48d. 'Aeldredus frater Ode calumniatur unam v(irgatam) terrae de hoc manerio et dicit se eam tenuisse die qua rex E(dwardus) fuit vivus et mortuus, et disaisitus fuit postquam rex W(illelmus) mare transiit, et ipse dirationavit coram regina. Inde est testis ejus Hugo de Port et homines de toto hundredo.' Printed in *English Lawsuits from William I to Richard I: Volume I*, ed. R.C. Van Caenegem (London, 1990), 57 (no. 35); Robin Fleming, *Domesday Book and the Law* (Cambridge, 1998), 157.

5 Nicholas Karn, *Kings, Lords and Courts in Anglo-Norman England* (Woodbridge, 2020), 72–4.

6 'If local assemblies refused to recognize that the king was entitled to receive the punitive fines he claimed in his legislation, these punitive fines would have no

Later hundredal assemblies also hosted the reading and dissemination of royal decrees and thus helped perpetuate royal ideology. When Mathilda and William came to power, they encountered a legal system that was quite different from Norman customs familiar to them. Shire and hundred courts were a product of the early English world long before the tenth century and, indeed, shaped justice from the sixth century on.[7] Over this most English of institutions, then, Domesday Book shows Mathilda presiding and handing down a verdict. Incidentally, her sentence repaired a loss Aldred experienced as a result of the conquest. Mathilda's activity here is also notable given that Somborne is just outside of Winchester, an important locus of royal power.

Another Domesday entry gives evidence for Mathilda's participation in the English judicial process when the claimants were members of the ecclesiastical elite. A case in Warwickshire between Bishop Wulfstan of Worcester and Archbishop Ealdred of York involved a large estate of about fifteen hides, approximately 1500 acres, and the income from it.

> Before 1066 Brictwin held 7 ½ hides in Alveston. Archbishop Ealdred (of York) had the full jurisdiction of this land, and the market rights and church tax, and all the other forfeitures except those four that the King has throughout his whole kingdom. His sons Leofwin, Edmer, and four others testify thereto, but they do not know from whom he held this land, whether from the church or from Earl Leofric, whom he served. They state however that they held it themselves from Earl Leofric, and could turn where they would with the land. Brictnoth and Alfwy held the remaining 7 ½ hides before 1066, but the County does not know from whom they held. Bishop Wulfstan however states that he established his claims to this land before Queen Mathilda in the presence of the four shires, and he has King William's writ for it, and also the witness of the County of Warwick.[8]

---

meaningful existence.' Tom Lambert, *Law and Order in Anglo-Saxon England* (Oxford, 2017), 137–8. It is worth noting that Somborne is just outside of Winchester, and that might make Mathilda's role more significant given that it was such an important locus of royal power.

7 Lambert, *Law and Order*, 243–50.

8 'Bricstuin T.R.E. tenuit in ALVESTONE vii hidis et dimidium. De hac terra habuit Eldred archiepscopi soca, et saca, et tol, et teim, et cerset, et omnias alias forisfacturas praeter eos illas iiii quas quam rex habebat per totum regnum. Hoc testantis filii ejus Lewin et Edmar et alii iiii sed nesciunt de quo an de aeclessia an de Comite Leuric cui seruiebat hanc terra tenuit. Dicunt tamen quod ipsi tenueret eam de Leeuric Comite, et quo volebant cuius terra poterant se uertere reliquis. Autre vii hide et dimidium tenuit Britnodet Aluui T.R.E. Sed comitat nescit de quo tenuerint. Wlstanus autem episcopus dicit se hanc terram deplacitasse coram regina Mathilde in praesentia iiii vicecomitatuum et inde habet breves regis W(illelmi) et testimonium comitatus Warwic.' *DB* Warwickshire Volume 23, 3–4. Van Caenegem, *Lawsuits*, 65 (no. 59); Fleming, *Domesday*, 250.

The record reveals a number of notable things. It presents a dispute between two high churchmen, not laymen as in the Somborne case, showing that Mathilda's involvement as a judge was not confined to the laity. The entry first notes Mathilda's previous public decision on Wulfstan's claim. Then the king's writ is mentioned as corroborating evidence to her ruling. Thus, the account shows an interplay of oral and textual evidence in the period. William's writ is pulled in as proof in the Domesday account but only after Mathilda's decision in Wulfstan's favor, which was witnessed by a significant crowd, is cited. Written evidence had weight, especially a royal writ, but a public oral judgement handed down by a queen was preferenced in the record. A crowd of witnesses was a great benefit for the successful party, and it was one which – in this period – still trumped written documentation. Thus, both Domesday entries surveyed above involve a crucial element that characterized Mathilda's judicial activity: it was performed in front of a multitude of participants and attendees. The brief texts of Domesday reveal that court proceedings drew crowds.

The medieval judicial court, it seems, was often overcrowded and noisy. Baldwin, the abbot of Bury St Edmunds, complained that some court hearings were attended by 'all the inhabitants of the land'.[9] His hyperbole is understandable. Eleventh-century English inquests sometimes combined different types of assemblies together resulting in massive crowds.[10] The local courts of the hundred and the county courts of the shire would often meet simultaneously to argue land disputes; criminal cases could also be included in these hybrid sessions. Like the organizational units of the hundred and the shire themselves, the tradition of meeting in concert was much older than the conquest. Great meetings of the Five Boroughs are described in English charters in Edward the Confessor's reign.[11] Constructions of jurisdictional organizations like the Five Boroughs were certainly created even earlier under the reign of Edmund in the 940s. Westminster Abbey assessed its rights before nine different hundreds together.[12] County assemblies could host seven or eight thousand people.[13]

The Warwickshire case above, indeed, shows evidence of an enormous mass of witnesses at the meeting of the four shires or sheriffdoms, 'iiii vicecomitatuum'. The 'Four Shires' refers to a central court location that bordered four

9 *Feudal Documents from the Abbey of Bury St Edmunds*, ed. D.C. Douglas (London, 1932), 3.

10 Fleming, *Domesday*, 13–15.

11 For the Five Boroughs, see David Roffe, 'The Danes and the making of the kingdom of the English', in *Nations in Medieval Britain*, ed. Hirokazu Tsurushima (Donington, 2010), 32–44.

12 For Westminster Abbey, see *Anglo-Saxon Charters: An Annotated List and Bibliography*, ed. Peter Sawyer (London, 1968), no. 1123.

13 Fleming, *Domesday*, 16.

medieval jurisdictions: Warwickshire, Gloucestershire, Worcestershire and Oxfordshire. A physical 'four shires stone' stood at the spot in the sixteenth century but there may have been four distinct 'shire stones' in the eleventh century that represented each shrievalty.[14] A series of conflicts between Abbot Baldwin, whose complaint is quoted above, and Bishop Herfast of Thetford played out in repeated hearings at the spot.[15] References to the Four Shires consequently found their way into charters drafted in response to their dispute. The Four Shires was an ancient open-air, English juridical space; a central location that touched all four hundreds at once and could accommodate a great crowd of people.

Ancient sites such as the Five Boroughs and the Four Shires had more than just capacity to recommend them. Aliki Pantos has shown that excavations of meeting sites had multiple features to accommodate related activities: a mound for pronouncements, a shallow, bowl-shaped earthen depression for debate and discussion, a twisted tree for a landmark to make the area recognizable.[16] Thus, such sites were campuses, if you will, of linked areas that served distinct purposes but formed a grouping in the landscape. Enclosure pens have also been found at some of them which denote market activity, too. More to the point, Pantos theorizes that the antiquity of these sites was the foundational attraction of them for later Anglo-Saxon leaders. They consciously chose assembly spaces that had a long history of ritual use even in pagan times.[17] While some ecclesiastical authorities cast pagan temples as places of evil that should be avoided,[18] English kings like Edmund and Edward the Confessor showed an 'intentional archaism' in continuing to call together their subjects at places with rich ritual traditions.[19] English authorities appropriated the primeval power of these locations to underscore their legitimacy, hoping to claim for themselves that early authority with which these sites were imbued. Holding assemblies and performing justice in these spaces, which were 'intimately connected with the control and cohesion of the community', linked these kings to the communal activity of the ancient past.[20] Of course, not all English assemblies were conducted at old pagan sites. In some areas purpose-built mounds were constructed new. 'Clean sites' like these were

14 Van Caenegem, *Lawsuits* (no. 59), especially at 65.

15 Van Caenegem, *Lawsuits* (nos. 9 and 10), at 24–32.

16 Aliki Pantos, 'The location and form of Anglo-Saxon assembly: some "moot points"' in *Assembly Places and Practices in Medieval Europe*, ed. Aliki Pantos and Sarah Semple (Dublin, 2004), 155–80, at 174.

17 Pantos, 'Anglo-Saxon assembly', 162–3.

18 Sarah Semple, 'Locations of assembly in early Anglo-Saxon England', in *Assembly Places and Practices in Medieval Europe*, ed. Aliki Pantos and Sarah Semple (Dublin, 2004), 135–54 at 151.

19 Pantos, 'Anglo-Saxon assembly', 174.

20 Ibid.

disassociated with the pagan past but they may have also been constructed because population patterns had changed and a new site was simply more convenient.[21] Yet, central sites on the archaic English landscape established an ideological link to other communal activity in the past. They were not neutral; they served the establishment. A very old assembly site underscored the authority of the ruler who called their subjects into session within its bounds.[22] Ecclesiastical mistrust of pagan sites only accentuated a sense of their supernatural power; it could be focused through them to inspire or reinforce the judgements given there. Like the early English kings before her, Mathilda channeled the ancient authority of ritual structures when she convened her court in such spaces.[23] Platformed on a venerable juridical site, used more or less continually from pagan times, she presided over the English people who were now hers to govern by right of conquest.

One might imagine for a moment how royal justice at these ancient places played out during Mathilda's reign. Occupying the same position as primeval pagan authorities, she would have looked out over a mass of people. Her own royal retinue beside her would have included at least one chamberlain, his clerks, and members of the queen's guard.[24] Royal officials brought their underlings and assistants, as did sheriffs.[25] English counties had an average of 128 jurors in each hundred, all of whom were required to attend.[26] Abbots and bishops like those mentioned in the cases above brought their households with them, and sometimes the entire monastic population of the abbey.[27] In attendance for both the defendant and the plaintiff would be as many witnesses and supporters as they could gather, ranging from the necessary players to the merely curious. Peasants, reeves, sheriffs, the newly minted Norman nobility, and their more desperate, displaced English counterparts all literally rubbed shoulders. Even allowing for some exaggeration on the part of contemporary sources, when property was under dispute it seems more was more. Multiple hundreds or shires packed into enormous crowds. Chroniclers described royal inquests in this period as a close approximation of the final

21 Pantos, 'Anglo-Saxon assembly', 173.

22 'In many ways, the function of such assemblies was to cement the social links which played an important part in the operation of Anglo-Saxon justice and administration.' Pantos, 'Anglo-Saxon assembly', 174.

23 Ryan Lavelle, *Places of Contested Power: Conflict and Rebellion in England and France, 830–1150* (Woodbridge, 2020).

24 Mathilda of Flanders employed at least four chamberlains in England. Humphrey, Reginald, Gerard and John appear in her charters as 'cameraria regina' and can also be traced through the land they held from Mathilda in Domesday.

25 C.P. Lewis, 'The Domesday Jurors,' *HSJ* 5 (1993), 17–44.

26 The jurors of the hundred provided crucial testimony in disputes. Lewis, 'Domesday Jurors', 18.

27 Fleming, *Domesday*, 15.

judgement for which Domesday Book was named. Relics of saints were held high for the swearing of oaths; compurgation and trial by ordeal meant that hot fires blazed and smoked to heat iron rods and to boil water. The incredible noise, the press of bodies from the throne's great barons to the modest freeholder, the arguments and heated denials, even the threat of violence barely suppressed; these were the features of eleventh-century law courts.[28] It was over this din and confusion that Mathilda of Flanders presided and handed down judgment. At the apex of this spectacle, the physical, human face of royal justice was sometimes hers.

Yet, changes in the role and jurisdiction of the hundred courts were in motion even as Mathilda presided over this crowded, clamorous arena. Those changes, moreover, can be linked to her Norman government. The hundred court was a distinctly English entity.[29] Ducal justice in Normandy, by contrast, was conducted by individuals; the duke, the duchess, or a justice appointed by them. Mathilda and William certainly utilized councils of nobles to help decide pleas but this was not a necessary element of the process. Ducal justice was operated by an individual even if the support of courtiers provided a helpful foil.[30]

Nicholas Karn has demonstrated that the new influx of Norman lords began to draw pleas and claims away from traditional English hundredal jurisdictional spaces into their own private manorial courts.[31] The business of the hundred was reduced and weakened as a result. The rise of manorial courts – ecclesiastical and secular – diminished the central place of hundredal meetings in the local landscape. Private courts presided over by an individual were not a feature of pre-conquest English justice.[32] This development has been seen as a direct result of the importation of Norman French expectations of how jurisdiction worked.[33] The establishment of Norman-style manorial courts would result in the hundred courts more regularly addressing

28 Fleming, *Domesday*, 16–17.

29 The hundred court was an important center not simply for justice, but for the organization of English local business of all sorts. Charles Insley, 'The Family of Wulfric Spot', in *The English and their Legacy, 900–1200: Essays in Honour of Ann Williams*, ed. David Roffe (Woodbridge, 2012), 115–28 at 121.

30 'When doing justice on offenders, then, the duke presided over the court and took the lead in making the judgement himself. He did not make that judgement alone, however. Others helped to find it and joined in it, thereby ensuring that the duke could not be accused of injustice. This was perhaps why the dukes, with the probable exception of Robert Curthose, do not seem to have experienced difficulties enforcing the sentences that they handed down. Even the greatest lords were apparently unable to resist their decisions.' Mark Hagger, *Norman Rule in Normandy, 911–1144* (Woodbridge, 2017), 494.

31 Karn, *Kings, Lords and Courts*, 101–26.

32 Karn, *Kings, Lords and Courts*, 72–4.

33 Karn, *Kings, Lords and Courts*, 125–6.

questions of jurisdiction, that is, who had the right to hear pleas as opposed to hearing the pleas themselves. There was, after the Norman invasion, a choice of venue for disputes and hearings. Manorial, lordly courts increasingly made claims for their private jurisdiction, notably over their own tenants, and siphoned this right away from traditional English courts.[34] Domesday Book reflects a vibrant hundredal court, like the assembly of the Four Shires, whose future was threatened by Norman French jurisdictional practice. It was the operation of justice by individuals, not hundreds, that would have been familiar to Mathilda as duchess.

Apart from the evidence of Domesday Book, examples of Mathilda's juridical activity were recorded in monastic accounts. One case concerning Abingdon Abbey is preserved in the abbey chronicle sometime between 1072 and 1073. The document frames a violent dispute between the 'barbarous' royal reeve of Sutton and the virtuous abbot as an encroachment on the abbey's rights. The narrative presents the case as a triumph for the abbey but the reality was more complex.

> A royal reeve from the manor of Sutton, in the neighborhood of this church, called Alfsi, has frequently and barbarously violated the old rights of the church in the plains and the woods, which were surrounded protectively by peasants, by often harassing men and beasts and forcing them to perform transport services for the king and by ordering to cut as many virgates as he wanted in the woods of Bagley and Cumnor. The abbot restrained his audacity with such a strong hand that from that time onwards no one followed the example of that man. In the first place, when the said reeve had demanded that oxen of the church should help in the transport of lead, requisitioned for the king's use, to the royal manor of Sutton, the abbot hit him with the stick he happened to be carrying, threw the lead onto the ground, and returned the oxen to the church. In the second incident, when the reeve returned from the wood of Bagley with heavy carts, the abbot seized the load of wood, and forced the reeve to flee on horseback, and to wade through the water near the mill adjacent to the bridge over the river Ock, wet up to his neck, because he avoided the bridge out of fear of the abbot. However, the man who had been hit went and complained to the queen, who was settled in those days at Windsor and weighed judicial matters in place of the king who was in Normandy, about the injury which he had suffered: the abbot, losing no time in preventing a royal inquiry, paid a sum of money to atone for what he had done to the royal official. He (the abbot) also put an end to tyrannical exactions by officials to the advantage of posterity, for in that royal assembly it was laid down after discussion and the testimony of numerous wise people, the church in Abingdon should in no way suffer this sort of exaction, but on the contrary, enjoy perpetual

[34] Karn, *Kings, Lords and Courts*, 126.

> freedom. This liberty which was then proclaimed is famous and freely defended until this day.[35]

The complaint of Abingdon is a glimpse into the competing rights and privileges of royal agents and local monastic lords as well as the age-old practice of doing violence with sticks. The abbey chronicle attempts to paint the abbot as a fearless victor in the case who ended injustice 'to the advantage of posterity'. The record shows him, however, scrambling to make amends quickly in order to avoid provoking Queen Mathilda. According to the record, the abbot hurriedly paid damages to the royal reeve to avoid Mathilda's involvement. Despite these evasive efforts he was brought before her royal assembly and his charge was read in court before Mathilda. After testimony and discussion, she eventually determined in the abbot's favor but not before the reader glimpses his panicked reaction to a day in Mathilda's court.

This was not the community's first encounter with Mathilda; the monks at Abingdon Abbey may have had good reason to fear Mathilda's displeasure. Abbot Ealdred, raised to the abbacy in 1066, was later implicated in a traitorous conspiracy against Norman rule and was deposed in 1071.[36] He remained in custody, held by Bishop Walkelin of Winchester, until his death. Ealdred's treason blackened Abingdon's reputation. In fact, at one time Mathilda demanded that the abbey hand over to her its most valuable items, perhaps as a punishment for their offenses. They offered what they thought would please her, but she was unimpressed. On her command, they tried again

35 'Cum interea praepositus quidam regiae villae Suttune, vicinae huic ecclesiae, Alfsi dictus, frequenter contra antiqua ecclesiae jura, planis et nemorosis locis, rusticorum vallatis, manu, barbare sese inferendo, homines et animalia ita passim exagitabat ut ab eis regalibus vectationibus summagia fieri exigeret, de nemoribus Bacheleia et Cumenora virgulta quantum volebat recidi juberet. Cujus ausum adeo viva manu tum abbas coercuit, ut ab eo tempore illius viri deinceps alter sectator non venerit. Nam primo, quadam vice dum plumbum, regio usui exquisitum, junctis ecclesiae bobus praepositus idem in curiam regis Suttune carreitare faceret, ipse baculo, quem abbas forte tenebat, non sine dedecore caesus, plumbum disjectum, boves reducti. Secundo, cum de silva Bacheleia onustis progrederetur rhedis, eadem onera abbas capiens, ipsum equo fugitantem prope molendinum contiguum ponti fluminis Eoche transvadare ad collum usque humectatum compulit, vitato timore abbatis ponte. Sed cum ab eo qui caesus fuerat, penes reginam, per hos dies Wildesore constitutam, querimonia de illata sibi injuria moveretur, quae regis vice, Normanniae degentis, justitiam rerum ingruentium impendebat, abbas nil moratus regium inde praevenit examen, et pecunia exsolvit quicquid in regis officiali fuerat commissum. Praeterea universis tyrannicum excussit exactum praefectorum posteris. Nam in concione illa regia, et rationatione et plurimorum testimonio sapientum, peroratum est nequaquam debere ecclesiam Abbendonensem hujusmodi sufferre exactum, quin libertate potiri perpetua. Ea itaque libertas tunc praeconata, hodie usque celebris libere defenditur.' Van Caenegem, *Lawsuits* (no. 12), 35.

36 His co-conspirator was Bishop Æthelwine of Durham.

harder and bitterly complained that they had to part with an exquisitely sewn gilded cassock, a very fine white set of robes with a matching cap as well, and a beautifully jeweled gospel book, covered in gold. With these, it seems, Mathilda was satisfied.[37] They, the monks complained, 'were their most precious possessions'.[38] Another notable feature of the Abingdon chronicle record was Mathilda's relative longevity, established as the source of royal justice in Windsor; 'settled' and weighing matters there as a permanent fixture.[39] William's absence in Normandy necessitated Mathilda's judicial activity 'in his place', but her authority there was unquestioned.[40]

The evidence outlined above shows Mathilda alone in the seat of royal justice. She also sat in judgment with William by her side. Together they presided at the royal court in England and the ducal court in Normandy over a broad range of legal disputes. In these joint ventures the documentary evidence shows the centrality of Mathilda's involvement in both the proceedings and the outcome. One of the most fascinating of these is the tangled story of a child switched at birth by his mother. The tiny imposter grew up to become the heir to significant properties in Normandy. The case is recounted by Rainald, a ducal chamberlain, who became a monk at the abbey of Jumièges, just as Abbot Adelelm above had once been. Recorded in a charter for the abbey, Rainald describes how a woman, Oringa, secretly replaced her own little boy who had died with another woman's child. Her husband, a ducal vassal named Stephen, was unaware of the substitution and assumed the child was his heir. One imagines the son was also completely unaware of his true identity. Oringa made covert but regular payments (ten sous a year) to the birth mother, named Ulburga.[41] Thus the little family lived in this state – Stephen, Oringa and their borrowed son – for years undisturbed. Eventually both Stephen and Oringa died. On Oringa's death, as one might expect, the payments stopped. Ulburga no longer received rent for her son. The boy was

37 *Chronicon of the monastery of Abingdon*, ed. J. Stevenson (2 vols., London, 1858), i, 485.

38 *Historia Ecclesie Abbendonensis: The History of the Church of Abingdon*, ed. and trans. John Hudson (2 vols., Oxford, 2002–07), ii, 224–5. Ealdred's successor was a royal favorite; Adelelm, a Norman monk from the ducal foundation at Jumièges. He performed diplomatic work in Scotland on behalf of Mathilda and William, indicating a significant level of favor and confidence in his abilities. The chronicle record does not name the abbot in the dispute above. It could have been during Adelelm's tenure but one imagines that a disagreement between a royal reeve and Abbot Adelelm, a trusted member of the Norman elite, might have been less violent.

39 '…per hos dies Windesore constitutam', Van Caenegem, *Lawsuits* (no. 12), 35.

40 '…quae regis vice, Normanniae degentis, justitiam rerum ingruentium impendebat', ibid.

41 According to the charter, Ulburga lived in the village of 'Merdiniacus', possibly Martigny, about 33 km southwest of Bayeux. *Regesta*, 530–3.

now a wealthy landowner thanks to his inheritance. He held multiple houses and property in and around Bayeux. Ulburga chose this moment to demand that her son be returned to her. She had not been paid since Oringa's death. Without the ten sous a year payment, she claimed, the arrangement was null and void. She wanted her son back. Oringa's family refused to part with their orphaned grandson whom they had known since a baby. The son may also have been unwilling to embrace the complete stranger who had made such a bargain. This unusual case made its way to the ducal court in Bonneville, where Mathilda and William, now also queen and king of England, heard it. It was decided that Ulburga should be required to undergo the ordeal of hot iron to prove her claim. Rainald records the outcome;

> King William and his wife Mathilda sent me, Rainald, their clerk, to Bayeux to witness the ordeal; William the archdeacon, now Abbot of Fécamp, Goselin the archdeacon, Robert of Lille, with his wife Albereda, Evremar of Bayeux, and quite a few other outstanding citizens went with me at the king's behest. When the ordeal was carried out in the little monastery of St Vigor, the woman reclaiming her son (Ulburga) was unharmed by the judgment of God, as I and the other named witnesses observed. And when the king learned this from me and the other witnesses, he laid claim to the estate of Stephen and gave it to the queen, who gave me, with the approval of the king, the houses and the twelve acres I mentioned before and the fields and all of Stephen's free holdings. Other things belonging to the same Stephen had already been given to the church of St John (London), which was the king's chapel, the king had already given to Thomas his cleric, not yet archbishop (of York).[42]

The purpose of Rainald's narrative was to prove his rights to Stephen's property; he donated it to the abbey of Jumièges.[43] The gift allowed for his entrance there

42 'Ad quod iudicium videndum misit me Rainaldum suum clericum rex Willelmus et Mathildis uxor eius Baiocas, et precepto regis ibi affuerunt mecum Willelmus archidiaconis, qui nunc est abbas Fiscannensis, et Godselmus archydiaconis et Rotbertus Insule, cum Albereda uxore sua, et Euremarus Baiocis et alii conplures ex melioribus hominibus civitatis. Quo iudicio portato in monasteriolo sancti Vigoris, fuit mulier illa que puerum reclamabat Dei iudicio illesa, mei vidente et prenominatis hominibus. Quod rex, per me audiens et per prefatos viros, accepit in suum dominium possessionem Stephani, et dedit eam regine, et regina dedit michi, concessu regis, domos et xii acras terre que iam predixi et ortos et omnis que habuerat Stephanus de suo alodio. Nam alias res eiusdem Stephani que pertinebant ad ecclesiam sancti Johannis, que erat capella regis, dederat iam rex Thome suo clerico, nondum archyepiscopo.' *Regesta*, 532. The text was translated by John Boswell. John Boswell, *The Kindness of Strangers: The Abandonment of Children in Western Europe from Late Antiquity to the Renaissance* (Chicago, IL, 1998), 447–8.

43 'Then I, Rainald, by the goodness of God, having adopted the order of St Benedict, petitioned Jumièges, and because I held (these things) in Bayeux by the grant and

as a monk.[44] But his rights to it were contested by Samson, another member of the royal household, who at one time was in favor with the queen and William. Rainald declares that he holds these properties directly from Queen Mathilda and, moreover, he has her approval for all of this. If Samson had any claim to it, Rainald asserts, the queen would have judged it so then because 'Samson was in favor with the king and queen at the time'.[45] In the latter half of the document, Rainald also reports that he has given some of the property he now holds from Queen Mathilda into the hands of two men who now have it from him in exchange for various services:

> To Geoffrey the cleric, surnamed the Masculine, I gave one field from the estate in return for his service; and another, yielding eleven sous a year, I gave to Evremar, in return for which he is to look out for my interest in court, if necessary, and whenever during the year I come to Bayeux he is to provide me, the first night, with wine and beer and good bread, according to custom, and to feed my horses, and – for this I have the witness of my lord, the queen – to advance me up to 100 sous in the city if I should need them. And a third field I gave to Vitale the clerk that he should serve me. And none of these men can sell the bequests to anyone but the abbot and monks of Jumièges, or without their permission. All these things which I have described can be verified by Vitale the clerk, who was with me through everything…[46]

seal of both King William and Queen Mathilda, I have been granted entrance in the same place.' ('Deinde ego Rainaldus, Dei bonitate veniens ad ordinem sancti Benedicti, Gemeticum petii, et quod Baiocis tenueram de rege Willelmo et Mathilde regina, eorum concessu et sigllio, eodem loco concessi, et quamdiu in clericali habitu fui quiete hec omnia et absque ullius calumpnia tenui.'). *Regesta*, 532.

44 'And if the right is granted in the place of St Peter's, Jumièges, they will have in peace all that I have said and given, because I had held it in peace when still a cleric, as I said before.' ('Et si loco sancti Petri Gemmetico rectum conceditur, quiete omnia que predixi et dedi habebit, quia quiete eam tenueram et in clericali habitu ut predixi'). *Regesta*, 532–3.

45 'Et tunc temporis bene erat Samson cum rege Willelmo et Mathilde, regina, qui illi facerent rectum de suis clamoribus si aliquid iuste clamaret.' *Regesta*, 533.

46 'Gauffredo clerico cognomento Masculo unum ortum dedi de prefato alodyo, ut inde serviret mihi, et alium Euremaro, xi solidos reddentem per annum. Pro quo idem Euremarus interesset meis placitis, si necesse fuisset, et quotiens venirem Baiocas per annum, preberet mihi de suo, prima nocte, vinum et cervisam et panem factitium per consuetudinem et victum equorum, et hoc testimonio REGINE domine mee. Et si opus haberem, acrederet mihi usque ad centum solidos in civitatem. Et tercium ortum dedi Vitali clerico ut inde mihi serviret. Et nemo istorum potest vendere ortos istos nisi abbati et monachis, neque alicui sine licentia ipsorum. Hec omnia que prescripsi bene novit ita esse Vitalis clericus qui in omnibus mecum interfuit …' *Regesta*, 533.

Rainald repeatedly names Mathilda, his queen and lord, as the guarantor of the property and the terms. Mathilda's activity and influence are also shown throughout the recitation of the strange case. Once Ulburga had proved she was the mother of the 'rented child', her son's rights to Stephen's property were nullified and the houses and estates came into Mathilda's hands. Mathilda's choice to distribute them to Rainald made him a wealthy man; her largesse gave him property that now included 'the houses and the twelve acres I mentioned before and the fields and all of Stephen's free holdings'.[47] Rainald's motive for providing minute details of the case and naming those involved was probably to assure that the arrangement would be remembered and supported. His repeated reference to Queen Mathilda was a form of surety; it elevated the agreement by giving it her imprimatur. Fortunately for us, his eye for detail allows a glimpse of the bizarre and almost incredible lengths to which a woman went to ensure she and her husband had an heir.

The case of Oringa's rented baby is demonstrative of Mathilda's share in the judicial process even when William sat beside her. She meted out justice with him, not as a passive observer, but as a participant in deciding on a verdict. This can be seen in other pleas. A report from Saint-Léonard of Bellême described Mathilda and William at their palace at Rouen, presiding together in a case that started as a tussle over the church offering, but eventually developed into a debate over ecclesiastical autonomy.[48] The canons of Saint-Léonard were supported by longtime ducal friend Roger of Montgomery. He invited the local bishop, Robert of Sées, to celebrate mass there. After the service, the bishop took hold of the offering and attempted to keep it. When one of the canons finally wrestled the funds away, the bishop flew into a rage and excommunicated the entire church and the canons in it. Roger, horrified on their behalf, sought justice from Mathilda and William. Roger claimed the canons of Saint-Léonard had never been subject to the bishop of Sées, and that the bishop was owed no part of their income, neither were they bound by his anathema. Mathilda and William both interrogated the claimants and questioned the 'old men' of the area who still remembered the grant of episcopal exemption for Saint-Léonard, made by Pope Leo IX.[49] After their fact-finding, Mathilda and William deputized a small group as a jury to give a verdict. Archbishop John of Rouen, Roger of Beaumont and a few other nobles '*plurus alias barones*' came to the decision that the canons of Saint-Léonard should be held free of all exactions.[50] Together, the plea records, Mathilda and William concurred

47 *Regesta*, 533. Boswell, *The Kindness of Strangers*, 448.

48 *Regesta* (no. 29), 183–7.

49 'antiquissi homines', *Regesta*, 185.

50 The document records Archbishop John of Rouen shruggingly making the point that he got no customs at all from many of the canons in his diocese. 'Dixit eciam Joh(anne)s archiepiscopus quasdam ecclesias in diocesi sua esse in quibus ipse nullam omnino consuetudinem haberet.' *Regesta*, 185.

with this judgement and allowed it to stand. The bishop of Sées had to make reparation and was warned that he himself would be expelled from the body of the faithful if he failed to do so. '*Guilelmus rex et Mahildis regina*' are paired together throughout the record of the case. They actively interrogated, arranged, deputized and dispensed justice as a couple; Robert and the canons presented their case 'in the palace and in the presence of the king and queen'.[51] Mathilda's authority, distinct from William's, is showcased in these records even as they preside together. Likewise in a confirmation of the rights of the abbey of Marmoutier, drawn up before Mathilda was crowned, William makes note of her standing, describing the grant made, '…in company with the most excellent Mathilda our wife (who) gives her own affirmation to the gift'.[52] In fact, Mathilda's judicial activity extended from before her coronation to the very last years of her life. In her final days in England, in the summer of 1081, Mathilda heard arguments at her palace at Winchester between Baldwin, the abbot of Bury St Edmunds, and Bishop Herfast of Thetford, who had been threatening the abbey with encroachments for many years. She, with William, granted Abbot Baldwin freedom for the abbey from episcopal interference from Herfast and his successors.[53]

Perhaps most notably, Mathilda presided with William over what was the most critical English ecclesiastical synod of the period; the primacy debate between Canterbury and York, held at the Easter court in Winchester, in 1072. The primacy synod was the first in a series of attempts to untangle a question of authority. Were the archbishops of York subject to the archbishops of Canterbury? Archbishop Lanfranc of Canterbury requested an oath of obedience from Thomas archbishop of York in 1070. After some hesitation, Thomas complied, but only with the caveat that his acquiescence should not be considered a precedent for later archbishops. Thomas and Lanfranc were friends who continued to converse and take counsel with each other throughout their lives.[54] But their successors reopened the issue with great hostility and it was said that, during periods of increasing antagonism, the competing archbishops would not appear in the same room together.[55] Innocent VI finally took charge of the issue in the fourteenth century and issued a final decision in favor of Canterbury in 1352.

51 'Ibi in palatio et in presentia regis et regina Anglorum, comes Rogerius conquestus est super Sagiensi episcopo quod ecclesiam sancti Leonardi sine causa excommunicare presumpsisset.' *Regesta*, 184.

52 'una cum precellentissima Mahilde sua uxore, proprio illud auctoramento firmavit…', *Regesta*, 627.

53 *Regesta* (no. 39), 201–9. Van Caenegem, *Lawsuits* (no. 9), 24–9. See also Thomas Arnold, *Memorials of St Edmunds Abbey* (3 vols., London, 1890–3), i, 347–50.

54 *Letters of Lanfranc*, no. 3, lines 83–143.

55 David Carpenter, *Struggle for Mastery: Britain 1066–1284* (London, 2003), 99.

In this first synodal hearing, by contrast, Pope Alexander II deferred judgement to the new Norman royal administration. The question was so foundational to England's ecclesiastical organization that Alexander considered Anglo-Norman royal jurisdiction more appropriate to decide the question. The debate between who had the right of primacy was an enormously important event for England and consequently the historiography surrounding it is vast.[56] The claims of Lanfranc and later archbishops have been the subject of examination, as was the torturous path the primacy debate took in later generations. Thus, the primacy synod Mathilda and William led would not be the last held on the matter; indeed, it was the first. A record of the proceedings can be found in extant charters that were products of the agreement.[57] Lanfranc himself also described the scene in detail in his letter to Alexander II, allowing us a peek into the workings of the hearing itself. Lanfranc famously called for and opened a copy of Bede's *Historia* as evidence that Canterbury had been Christianized first, and thus could claim primacy. But before that dramatic moment, a more private conference was held on Easter, April 8, 1072, at Winchester. This included only a small circle of stakeholders: Mathilda, William, Hubert the papal legate, Lanfranc, Thomas, and four bishops; Walkelin of Winchester, Wulfstan of Worcester, Herfast of Thetford and Remigius, formerly of Fécamp, the new bishop of Lincoln.[58] This small group of nine heard arguments and discussion in the royal chapel at Winchester Castle and came to an agreement in favor of Canterbury.[59] A document that resulted from this meeting, the Accord of Winchester, was autographed by the participants. Mathilda and William placed their signatures directly below the text of the diploma and the seven episcopal participants, with the papal legate, arranged their signatures beneath (Plate 5).[60]

The second charter from the primacy debate was produced on Pentecost, May 27 of that same year at Windsor. It was a formalization of the first and

56 Selected sources include Martin Brett, *The English Church Under Henry I* (Oxford, 1975); Frank Barlow, *The English Church 1066–1154: A History of the Anglo-Norman Church* (New York, NY, 1979); Sally N. Vaughn, 'Henry I and the English Church: The Archbishops and the King', *HSJ* 17 (2006), 133–57; Sally N. Vaughn, *Archbishop Anselm 1093–1109: Bec Missionary, Canterbury Primate, Patriarch of Another World* (London, 2012); James Raine, *The Historians of the Church of York and Its Archbishops* (Cambridge, 2012). Most recently, see Bridget K. Riley, 'Lost and found: Eadmer's *De reliquiis sancti Audoeni* as a cross-channel solution to the Canterbury–York dispute', *HSJ* 28 (2017), 15–38.

57 For a full description of both charters, see *Regesta*, 307–14.

58 Bishop Walkelin is the same bishop mentioned in the Abingdon case above who held the rebellious and deposed Adelelm, formerly abbot of Abingdon, in captivity.

59 Thomas, the archbishop of York, was excused from fealty to Lanfranc for his lifetime, but subsequent archbishops were not. Gibson, *Lanfranc of Bec*, 167–71.

60 Canterbury Cathedral Archive DCc-ChAnt/A/1. Printed in *Regesta,* 307–8.

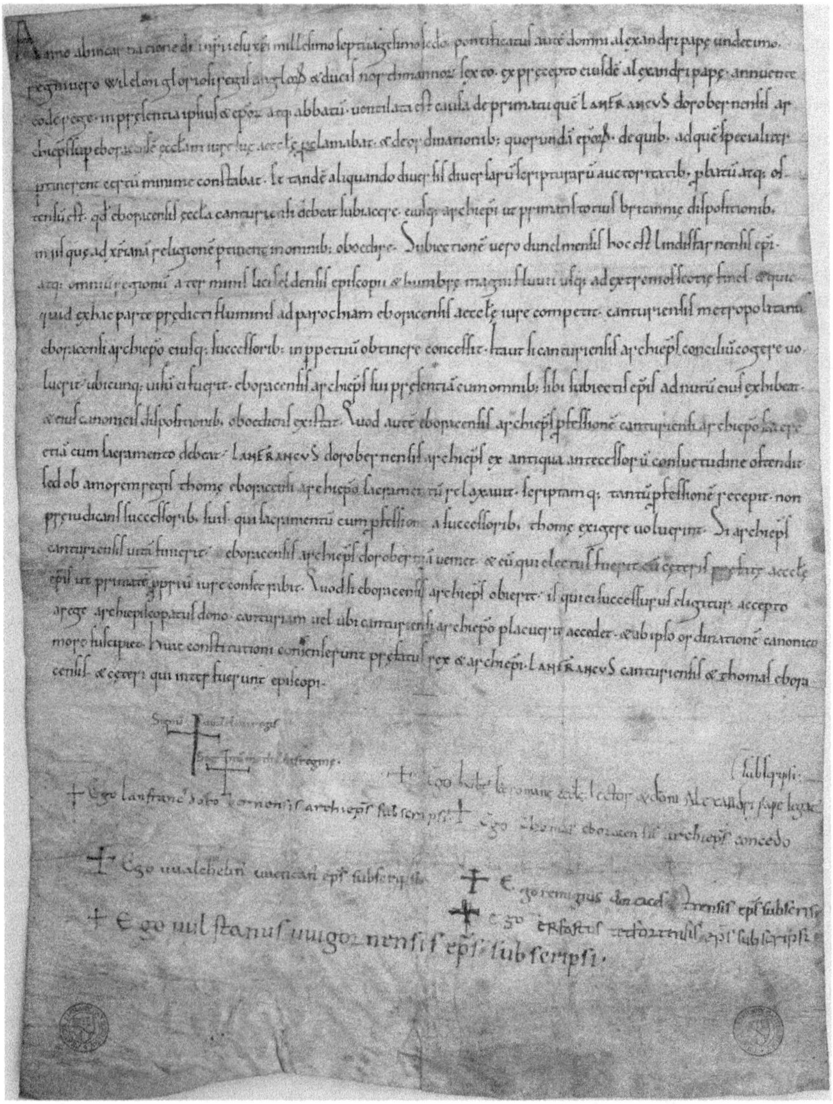

Plate 5. Accord of Winchester, Dated 8 April, 1072, showing autograph cross of Mathilda of Flanders, second from the left. Canterbury, Canterbury Cathedral Archive, DCc/ChAnt/A/1.

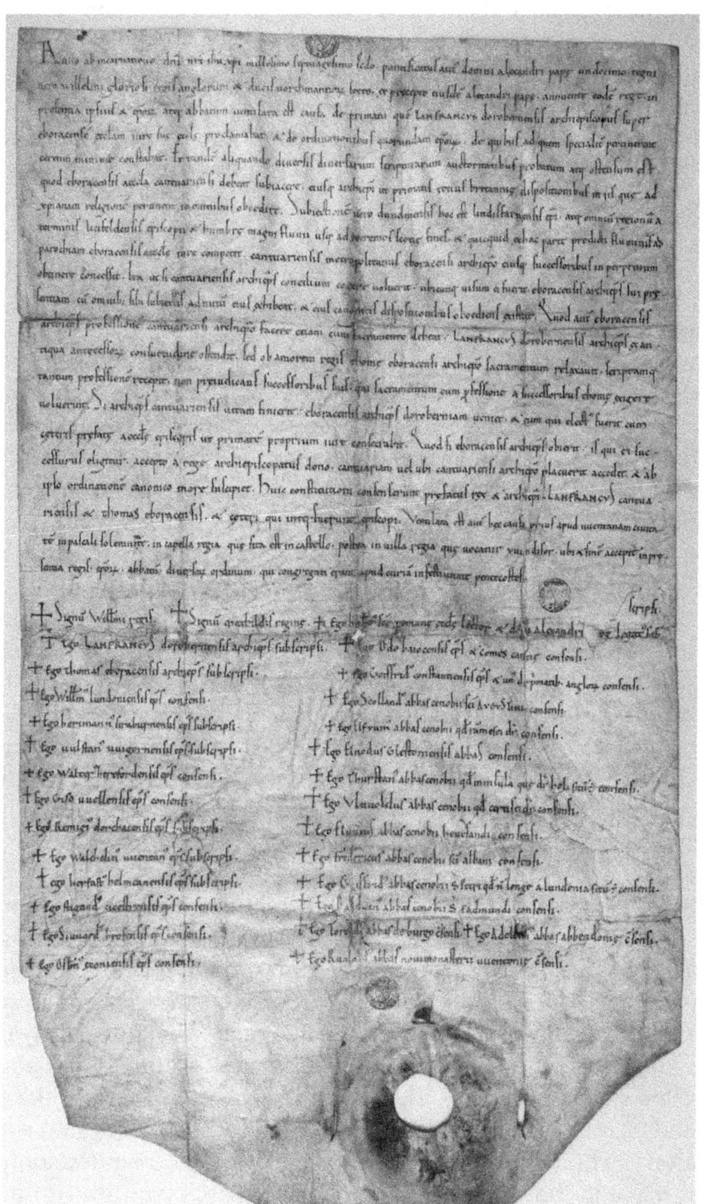

Plate 6. Accord of Winchester, Dated Pentecost, 27 May 1072, showing the non-autograph cross of Mathilda of Flanders, second from the left, placed slightly above the first line of signatories. Canterbury, Canterbury Cathedral Archive, DCc/ChAnt/A/2.

reflects the much larger audience in attendance at the public debate on primacy. The second version of the agreement included a long list of twenty-one additional attestors – all churchmen – arranged in non-autograph columns of thirteen lines (Plate 6). William, Mathilda, and the papal legate appear on the larger document represented by non-autograph signature crosses in one even horizontal line under the text, above the columns of ecclesiastical signators, including Lanfranc and Thomas.[61] Mathilda's cross is placed slightly above the rest in the line. The document was then sealed and disseminated throughout England. There remain many extant copies of this document and, as late as the eighteenth century, drawings of its seal were made and preserved in archives throughout England. This evidence supports the notion that it was carefully and thoroughly promulgated. No doubt the same hundredal assemblies over which Mathilda had presided, and many others across her kingdom, played a part in transmitting the document that so visibly exhibited her rank. She appeared over the ecclesiastical heads of her kingdom just as she had done in their courts. Mathilda participated in the symbolic act of issuing and signing the official, public decree that shaped England's ecclesiastical organization. She was intimately involved, moreover, in the architecture of the primacy agreement in its nascent form. Within the confines of the earlier meeting, hers was the only female voice. As the document was expanded into a more public and elaborate text, she maintained that position. On the physical parchment of the document, her name was above all others with William's, at the head of a community of signators composed entirely of bishops and abbots. She held pre-eminence over the leaders of England's most powerful churches and abbeys. The copies of the accord made their way all over her kingdom, like ripples out from the origination point of the synod. The Accord of Winchester was a physical manifestation – visible to all who received it, saw it, or heard it read out – of her precedence.

Mathilda once again appears where, to modern eyes, she should not be. The sole female participant – and the only lay person except William – in a crucial debate about the structure and organization of the English church. But as discussed in Chapter Four, Mathilda's anointing and coronation fitted her specifically for this purpose. She was a 'persona mixta'; her divinely ordained status made her position at the head of England's churches and abbeys not just possible but appropriate. The circumstances surrounding the primacy debate, and its outcome, are illustrative of her centrality. Both in the exclusive deliberations behind the scenes and the most public manifestations of the decisions made in those spaces, she took part in crafting royal administrative policy.[62] Viewing the evidence from another angle, Mathilda participated

61 Canterbury Cathedral Archive DCc-ChAnt/A/2. Text printed in *Regesta*, 311.

62 Just as Mathilda's experience here confirms, women's participation only in the 'private sphere' as opposed to the 'public sphere' of authority has long been debunked. See A. Saxonhouse, 'Introduction – Public and Private: The Paradigm's

whenever thorny problems were presented to the new Norman royal court. Her appearance in documentary evidence is unlike other queens before her. While Emma also appeared in charters with Cnut at the head of the ecclesiastical elite, the frequency and number of Mathilda's attestations and charter activity is remarkable. Her involvement in the documentary records that reflect the business of royal government is a defining factor of the new Norman royal government.[63] During her lifetime, throughout Normandy and England, Mathilda appeared in at least 141 extant charters and grants; more than any other person in the realm save William.[64] While the majority of these place her in Normandy, she attested to all the major diplomas issued in England during her lifetime.[65] Her presence in these documents reveals the physical spaces she inhabited; at the center of Anglo-Norman government, in the seat of royal justice and at the head of the church hierarchy of England.

The charter evidence confirms that Mathilda ruled differently than English queens but what of her judicial activity? Were there other English queens who were involved in judicial matters? A little more than one hundred years before Mathilda took the throne, Queen Ælfthryth (964–75) reigned with Edgar the Peaceable (959–75). She was described in contemporary tenth-century sources as a religious superior over every female monastic house in England, responsible for defending them all, something like a 'super-abbess'.[66] Andrew Rabin has shown that Ælfthryth embraced a judicial role as an advocate or *forespeca* for female religious.[67] She negotiated on behalf of the nuns who were her responsibility.[68] Her mediation as a royal woman was a privilege

Power', in *Stereotypes of Women in Power: Historical Perspectives and Revisionist Views*, ed. B. Garlick, S. Dixon and P. Allen (New York, NY, 1992), 1–9; T. Hillard, 'On the Stage, Behind the Curtain: Images of Politically Active Women in the Late Roman Republic', in *Stereotypes of Women in Power: Historical Perspectives and Revisionist Views*, ed. B. Garlick, S. Dixon and P. Allen (New York, NY, 1992), 37–64; J.B. Elshtain, *Public Man, Private Woman: Women in Social and Political Thought* (Princeton, NJ, 1981).

63 *Regesta*, 92–3; Bates, 'The origins of Justiciarship', 1–12.

64 *Regesta*, 93.

65 Mathilda appears in eight English diplomas but Bates warns that her relatively small number of acts in England can be 'misleading'. He has demonstrated that she appears in all the major English diplomas and that her position as an attestor in them – always immediately after William – is evidence of her centrality there. *Regesta*, 94.

66 *Regularis concordia Anglicae*, ed. Thomas Symons (London, 1953), 2. Simon MacLean, 'Monastic Reform and Royal Ideology in the Late Tenth Century: Ælfthryth and Edgar in Continental Perspective' in *England and the Continent in the Tenth Century*, 255–74.

67 Andrew Rabin, 'Female Advocacy and Royal Protection in Tenth-Century England: The Legal Career of Queen Ælfthryth', *Speculum* 84: 2 (2009), 261–88; Firth, *Early English Queens*, 142–5.

68 Rabin, 'Ælfthryth', 281; Firth, *Early English Queens*, 142–5.

offered especially to monastic communities. There are seven cases extant that document her work. In all of them Ælfthryth takes the part of monastic claimants and nearly all of them were women; the abbot of Bury St Edmunds was the only man among the seven parties she represented.[69] Ælfthryth's advocacy did not erase the boundary between royal justice and queenship; her special role as *forespeca* accentuated it. While she feminized a position that had been traditionally a masculine one, Ælfthryth 'became, in effect, a figure capable of mediating between the legal subject – especially the female legal subject – and masculine authority of her royal husband'.[70] Her voice was used to intercede on behalf of those under her protection but hers was not the voice of judgement itself. What Ælfthryth offered in these cases was mediation; an intervention that became an institutionalized adjunct to the royal court.[71]

Ælfthryth's formalized juridical activity is the first inkling of such a role for English queens. Mathilda's immediate predecessor, Queen Edith, is recorded on two occasions acting as an advocate. Both instances involved protecting the interests of widows. Like Ælfthryth, Edith is described in one of these cases as a *forespeca* concerning the dispute about a will.[72] By contrast Queen Emma, even at her most powerful, seems not to have participated in matters of justice. King Cnut's travels to Norway and Denmark required a council that maintained royal law in his stead, but this group did not seem to include Emma. His letter of 1020 instructed Earl Thorkell to uphold God's law in the king's absence 'with the power of us both' but Cnut refers to Thorkell, not to Emma.[73] There is no mention of the queen either in the body of the missive or in the address to the archbishops and nobles 'to whom I have entrusted the councils of all my kingdom'.[74] No evidence remains that links Emma to the exercise of royal justice. When early English queens are found in places of justice they provide examples of a different custom: queenly intercession.

Traditional models of queenly arbitration centered on intercession. A robust body of scholarship can be found on the queen's intercession, especially as it grew in popularity and formalization into the thirteenth century.[75] Fewer studies

69 Rabin, 'Ælfthryth', 273–7.

70 Rabin, 'Ælfthryth', 263.

71 '...this practice follows a long-standing royal tradition of intervening in disputes outside the king's jurisdiction in order to encourage settlements useful to the monarch.' Rabin 'Ælfthryth', 276.

72 Stafford, *Queen Emma and Queen Edith*, 158.

73 *English Historical Documents, Volume I*, ed. Dorothy Whitelock, 2nd, ed. (London, 1996), 459–60.

74 Whitelock, *Documents*, 460.

75 Studies of queenly intercession range broadly both chronologically and in terms of discipline: Yanay Israeli, 'Petition and response as social process: royal power, justice and the people in late medieval Castile (*c.* 1474–1504)', *Past and Present* 262 (2024), 3–44; Louise Tingle, *Chaucer's Queens: Royal Women, Intercession, and Patronage in England, 1328–1394* (London, 2020); Carolyn P. Collette, *Performing*

have been done for the central middle ages, but royal women's mediation served some of the same important purposes regardless of chronology. It allowed the king to be convinced that mercy was appropriate, even necessary, when his consort appealed to him. It provided a way for implacable kingly justice to keep up appearances of severity and save face while meting out a lighter sentence or forgiving rebels.[76] The intercession of the queen had unimpeachable biblical roots. The story of Esther was regularly featured as a model of queenly dignity.[77] Esther's rags-to-riches rise and her secret Jewish identity were compelling elements of the Old Testament story, but it was her intercession on behalf of her people that made for great drama. Esther was a medieval favorite and she became the pattern card for medieval queenship par excellence, second only to Mary the Queen of Heaven. By the twelfth century, moreover, Esther gained a permanent place in queenly inauguration rites.[78]

Esther-style mediation on behalf of supplicants was not simply a scripturally approved ideology; it was a lucrative income stream. Intercession with her royal husband became the basis for a significant source of revenue for queens. Ælfthryth received gifts and gold for her work as an advocate.[79] Edith received five marks of gold from the abbot of Ramsey to intercede for him.[80] Later queens saw this gratitude become institutionalized. Eventually intercessory proceeds were linked to 'the queen's gold'. This revenue was openly associated with the queen's intercession in the twelfth and thirteenth centuries.[81] It allowed for an expansion of the queen's finances without taxing the kingdom's treasury.[82] By the time of Henry II profits from royal advocacy were part of the queen's income.[83]

Polity: Women and Agency in the Anglo-French Tradition, 1385–1620 (Turnhout, 2006); *L' Intercession du Moyen Âge à l'époque moderne. Autour d'une pratique sociale*, ed. Jean-Marie Moeglin (Geneva, 2004); John Carmi Parsons, 'The Queen's Intercession in Thirteenth-century England' in *The Power of the Weak*, ed. Jennifer Carpenter and Sally Beth MacLean (Chicago, IL, 1995), 147–77.

76 Richard E. Barton, 'Making a clamor to the lord: noise, justice and power in eleventh- and twelfth-century France', in *Feud, Violence and Practice: Essays in Medieval Studies in Honor of Stephen D. White*, ed. Belle Tuten, Belle Stoddard and Tracey L. Billado (Farnham, 2010), 213–35.

77 Lois Huneycutt, 'Intercession and the High Medieval Queen: the Esther topos', in *The Power of the Weak*, ed. Jennifer Carpenter and Sally Beth MacLean (Chicago, IL, 1995), 130.

78 The Third English Ordo compares her to Esther, a 'partner in royal power'. *The Pontifical of Magdalene College*, ed. Henry A. Wilson (London, 1900), 96–8.

79 Rabin, 'Ælfthryth', 273–7.

80 Stafford, *Queen Emma and Queen Edith*, 181.

81 Kristen Geaman, 'Queen's Gold and Intercession: The Case of Eleanor of Aquitaine,' *Medieval Feminist Forum* 46:2 (2010), 10–33 at 17.

82 Geaman, 'Queen's Gold', 17.

83 Domesday claimed a marc of 'Queen's gold' taxed on every manor valued at over £100 payable to Mathilda, but it was not linked to intercession. Charles S. Taylor, *An Analysis of the Domesday Survey of Gloucestershire* (Bristol, 1889), 114.

Even after it became an unequivocal part of queenly expectations, however, a royal consort's presence in court was as a supplicant, though a singularly irresistible one. She entered into the king's legal arena, like Ælfthryth, on behalf of those fortunate enough to gain her ear. By its very nature her intercession was an enacted disruption; an interference in the force and proper exercise of law. Intercession was a break in law's practice even if codified and scripted.[84] The central middle ages saw an increase in this implicitly sanctioned interruption but it remained a disturbance of royal law in action. The queen's influence as an intercessor gained importance and frequency, and was even a source of revenue. Yet she remained outside formal authoritative legal praxis. Her intervention 'softened the king's anger'.[85]

Mathilda of Flanders, by contrast, left no evidence of intercession during her reign. Instead of mediating between royal justice and petitioners, she herself was the royal judge. Whether alone or with William, she was a full participant in royal adjudication of dispute resolution. Mathilda operated royal justice from a permanent court, as at Windsor where evidence shows she was 'established'. There was no divide between royal justice and Mathilda's influence, like there was for Ælfthryth. Neither was her juridical activity a disruption of the regular practice of 'kingly' justice – it was precisely the same justice. Instead of acting to temper the king's ire, Mathilda's own anger was to be avoided, just as the abbot of Abingdon attempted to do. His bid to circumvent her justice – and her displeasure – by rushing to pay off his accusers was in vain. When the possibility of Mathilda's anger loomed, the abbot did his best to evade it. Mathilda performed queenly justice that was equal in effectiveness to William's kingly version. In this arena, she set the pattern for later Anglo-Norman queens, as mentioned above; her daughters and granddaughters would also sit in judgement. If Mathilda of Flanders did not conform to traditional English queenly practice, what model might she have followed? As I noted at the beginning of the chapter, the customs of female abbatial jurisdiction in Normandy supplied a template.

The concept of spiritual jurisdiction was foundational to medieval justice. Increasingly under Mathilda and William's rule, moreover, ecclesiastical courts would mete out justice to professional religious – clerics, monks and nuns – at the expense of secular courts.[86] Abbatial participation in Norman justice is key to understanding Mathilda's judicial practice, because both abbesses and

[84] John Carmi Parsons, 'The intercessionary patronage of Queens Margaret and Isabella of France', *Thirteenth Century England, VI: Proceedings of the Durham Conference, 1995* (1997), 145–56.

[85] Parsons, 'Intercessionary', 157. Parsons quotes a fourteenth-century Franciscan exemplum, translated by Eileen Power. *Miracles of the Virgin Mary* trans. C.C. Swinton Bland (London, 1928), xiv.

[86] See Hagger, *Norman Rule*, 453–5; John Hudson, *The Oxford History of the Laws of England, Volume II, 871–1216* (Oxford, 2012), 258.

abbots had jurisdiction over their tenants that included judicial privileges.[87] The judicial function of abbesses has not received significant attention though there are recent valuable studies on women's abbatial power.[88] Recognizing and examining the judicial aspect of female abbatial authority has the potential to revolutionize modern conceptions about medieval women and law.[89] In Normandy, both the women's abbey of Montivilliers and Holy Trinity, Caen had jurisdiction over their tenants that included rights to 'blood justice' – *cum sanguine* – that is, over crimes of murder and violent assault.[90] At Mathilda's own foundation, the abbesses regularly meted out justice.[91] This is especially important for Mathilda's experience of judicial procedure as she herself arranged for her abbess to hold such judicial privileges.[92] The abbey's monastic properties in the city of Caen had a wide reach; the number of tenants who looked to the abbess for justice was notable. Furthermore, a later thirteenth-century manuscript provides undeniable evidence that the abbess of Holy Trinity had her own jail.[93] The prison was located in Ouistreham, a coastal town to the north of Caen. In a brief notice, issued in 1292, the 'Bailiff de Caen' appears before the Abbess of Holy Trinity and apologizes for removing a cleric from her jail in Ouistreham. The prisoner was accused of a violent attack, having drawn blood from his victim. The bailiff promises to return the criminal at once, as the abbess has jurisdiction over the prisoner.[94] The abbesses of Holy Trinity, then, were the judges responsible for sentencing and incarceration of not only their tenants in Caen, but those in the port of Ouistreham on the coast of Upper Normandy.[95]

87 Charles Homer Haskins, *Norman Institutions* (Harvard, MA, 1918), 28–9. See also Karn, *Kings, Lords and Courts*, 130–2.

88 See especially Jennifer C. Edwards, *Superior Women: Medieval Female Authority in Poitiers' Abbey of Sainte-Croix* (Oxford, 2019).

89 Laura L. Gathagan, 'Abbess, Judge, Jailor: Authority and Imprisonment at Holy Trinity, Caen', *Bulletin of the John Rylands Library* 99:2 (December 2023), 25–46. For 12th century developments, see Gary Macy, 'Abelard, Heloise and the Ordination of Abbesses', *JEH* 57:1 (2006), 16–32.

90 Edwin Hall and James Ross Sweeney, 'The "Licentia de nam" of the Abbess of Montivilliers and the Origins of the Port of Harfleur', *Bulletin of Historical Research* 52: 125 (1979), 1–8; Haskins, *Norman Institutions*, 28–9.

91 Louis Thomassin, *Vetus et nova Ecclesiæ disciplina, circa benefica et beneficiaries*, Part I, Book III, xlix, no. 4 (Mainz, 1787), 535. Also, Donald Hochstetler, *A Conflict of Traditions: Women in Religion in the Early Middle Ages, 500–840* (New York, NY, 1992), 154–5.

92 Gathagan, 'Abbess, Judge, Jailor'. The manuscripts specifically state the abbess of Holy Trinity had 'plenaria justicia' – full rights of justice – over the properties she held. John Rylands Library, Beaumont Charters Collection, MS. BMC 67, 68 and 71 (hereafter JRL, BMC).

93 JRL, BMC 66.

94 JRL, BMC 66. See Gathagan, 'Abbess, Judge, Jailor', 29–32.

95 Holy Trinity held significant portions of Ouistreham, including the right to first refusal on virtually everything the market had on offer. The busy commercial town was a seaport with all the attendant possibilities for crime and graft. JRL, BMC 63.

The laconic tone of the document regarding the abbess's prison indicates this was nothing out of the ordinary and thus raises a number of questions. The center of the abbey's jurisdiction was in Caen. Did the abbesses also have facilities to imprison malefactors there? How many other abbesses across northern Europe ran their own prisons? While there is yet no textual evidence to corroborate it, an archaeological analysis of the abbey grounds of Montivilliers suggests that the abbesses there had a prison located within the monastic complex in the later Middle Ages.[96] A wooden torture device was also found at the site of the prison.[97] Canon law forbade torture of monastic adherents or professional religious. Thus, the prisoners who suffered the use of such a mechanism were likely lay people arrested and held by the abbess at her prison at Montivilliers.[98] Further investigation of monastic imprisonment by abbesses is outside the remit of this chapter, but sufficient for the purposes at hand is the evidence that Mathilda herself was deeply involved in the furtherance and extension of her abbesses' juridical entitlements.[99] Mathilda supported her nuns as they fought for jurisdiction against competing juridical authorities in the city of Caen, including the abbot of St Stephen's across town.[100] Mathilda brought her royal status to bear on debates about the nuns' jurisdiction.[101] Thus Mathilda's own experience of abbatial justice allowed for a thorough understanding of how female authority engaged the law. Female abbatial justice was demonstrably different than royal justice. But in her own court the abbess was judge.

Mathilda's significant engagement with female abbatial authority suggests that this was a familiar paradigm to her. The Norman exemplar of lordship in her duchy featured jurisdictional rights of lords over the pleas and claims of their dependents. Transported to England, the Norman French model would later encroach upon and dilute traditional English hundredal assemblies. This trend would not find its fullest expression in Mathilda's England; the twelfth century saw the dominance of local manorial courts. Yet its contrast with hundredal English structures can already be seen in the

96 Francoise Yvernault, 'Les bâtiments de l'abbaye de Montivilliers au moyen âge', *Bulletin de l'association Montivielliers, Hier, Aujourd'hui et Demain* (MHAD) 9 (1997), 41–51.

97 Yvernault, 'Les bâtiments de l'abbaye', 49.

98 Gathagan, 'Abbess, Judge, Jailor', 43–5.

99 These are outlined in BNF 5650, 18v–20r, dated sometime before 1081, an update of Holy Trinity's great foundation charter BNF 5650, 1r–8v. Printed in Musset, *Les Actes*, 28–30 and 199–200; *Regesta*, 271–86.

100 William handed over ducal lands to the abbess and nuns to save St Stephen's from losing significant property to them. The three charter versions tracing out this dispute are BNF 5650, folios 15r–16v, and AD Calvados, Cartulaire de Saint-Étienne, entrée 1996–135, folios 23r–24v. Musset, *Les Actes*, 52–7 and *Regesta*, 297–301.

101 Mathilda's acquisition of land and jurisdiction for the nuns – literally in the monks' backyard– would ignite the dispute mentioned above. BNF 5650, folios 15r–16v.

eleventh century. Norman lords, abbatial and secular, had brought their own jurisdictional expectations to England. As mentioned above, the new Anglo-Norman approach to ecclesiastical courts in particular confirmed their special judicial privileges. The conquest changed ideas about how law was practiced and where. Lord-dependent relationships became the determinant factor of where pleas were held and who had the right to hear cases.[102] Jurisdiction followed the contours of lordship in a new way. Unlike the communal courts of hundreds and shires, Norman-style lordly courts could more easily be directed by a woman and, indeed, they were. English courts of hundred and shire did not allow for women's participation as dispensers of justice. An abbatial court – presided over by an abbess – was a Norman-style lordly court that featured a woman in the seat of abbatial justice.

Women's abbatial justice was also a distinctly Ottonian model.[103] Previous chapters of this book have illustrated how Mathilda of Flanders' Ottonian pedigree especially influenced her choices. The quote at the head of this chapter is taken from Adela's own commissioned version of the *Epitaph of Adelheid*; the passage explicitly claims justice as one of Adelheid's prerogatives.[104] Adelheid's daughter Mathilda, who became the renowned Ottonian princess-abbess of Quedlinburg, demonstrated how justice was a woman's prerogative in an Ottonian context. She was in charge of imperial affairs when her nephew, Otto II, was on campaign. She convened assemblies 'of all the nobility as one' regularly in his absence.[105] During one such assembly, when Mathilda of Quedlinburg was absent from her monastery, trouble arose. Otto's sister Liutgard, who was being educated at Quedlinburg, was abducted. Abbess Matilda sent armed men to retrieve her and either kill or capture the perpetrators, but these attempts failed. So, the abbess once again convened an assembly and demanded the presence of both the kidnappers and Liutgard. They came. Before the 'great multitude', the criminals begged forgiveness, penitent and barefoot, and Liutgard was returned.[106] Abbess Mathilda exacted recompense and Liutgard was returned to Quedlinburg. This episode would have been well understood both by the abbesses of Holy Trinity and Mathilda of Flanders herself. Abbess Mathilda was a judge who

102 Karn, *Kings, Lords and Courts in Anglo-Norman England*, 150–1.

103 Laura Wangerin, 'Representation of Ottonian Women: Politics and Sanctity in the Tenth Century' presented at IMC Leeds, 2014. Many thanks to Dr. Laura Wangerin for an early, unpublished draft of this article. See also Phyllis Jestice, *Imperial Ladies of the Ottonian Dynasty: Women and Rule in Tenth-Century Germany* (London, 2018).

104 Sean Gilsdorf, *Queenship and Sanctity: The 'Lives' of Mathilda and the 'Epitaph' of Adelheid* (Washington, DC, 2004).

105 *Ottonian Germany: The Chronicle of Thietmer of Merseburg*, ed. and trans. David Warner (Manchester, 2001), 180–1.

106 Warner, *Thietmer of Merseburg*, 181.

commanded troops and wielded – at least metaphorically – a sword. One imagines she may also have had a prison.[107]

Moving back further in time, St Mathilda of Saxony (sometimes called Matilda of Rengelheim) was Adelheid's mother-in-law, the first Ottonian queen and the mother of the Ottonian dynasty; Otto I was her son. She also founded Quedlinburg, the Ottonian necropolis. Her reputation for juridical involvement is reflected in two biographies of her life that attest to her reputation for imposing justice.[108] Her name continued to be synonymous with justice even in Dante's time; there is good evidence that she was the 'Matelda' who acted as his spirit guide in the *Divine Comedy*. Historians have emphasized links between Dante's choice of Matelda in his works and ruling mothers, daughters, and markedly, his concern for justice.[109]

Thus, two strands – Ottonian identity and an experience of Norman legal practice – encouraged Mathilda to reorient the expectations of and approach to queenly justice in England. Mathilda had the models of the Ottonians from which to draw. Furthermore, she was accustomed to Norman legal praxis that accommodated lordly women as abbatial judges; indeed, the abbesses of her own foundation had this right of jurisdiction. Mathilda also had opportunity. As Simon MacLean has argued for the Ottonian queen, Gerberga, the provisionality of the Anglo-Norman dynasty made Mathilda more powerful, not less.[110] The Norman Conquest resulted in a new cross-channel kingdom that demanded joint rule. Mathilda seized the possibilities that circumstance accorded her and carved out a new kind of queenship: sacral, lordly, juridical.

Before Mathilda, English royal women did not direct justice; in her queenship, England saw something wholly innovative. Ælfthryth's early adoption of advocacy for nuns and abbesses was mirrored in the *Regularis Concordia*, promulgated during her reign. It recorded the queen's responsibility for women's religious houses, placed especially under her guardianship. Yet, the explicit connection drawn by the *Regularis* translated into an intercessory role for English queens. The royal women who immediately preceded Mathilda – Queen Edith and Queen Emma – likewise left no records of directing royal justice. Circumstances outside of their control may have also compromised both Edith and Emma's ability to step into the judicial role that Mathilda chose. Both queens were vulnerable in ways Mathilda was not. Queen Edith was exiled from court by Edward the Confessor, almost

[107] For lives of the Ottonian Empresses, see Gilsdorf, *'Lives' of Mathilda and the 'Epitaph' of Adelheid*.

[108] Gilsdorf, *'Lives'*, 71–87 and 88–127.

[109] Jo Ann Hoeppner Moran Cruz, 'Dante's Matelda: Queen, Saint, and Mother of Emperors' *Viator* 47:3 (2016), 209–44.

[110] MacLean, *Ottonian Queenship*, 94. For a full expression of this argument, see Chapter One: Blood, 11–33.

certainly as a prelude to divorcing her. Her reinstatement against his will was a triumph in her retelling but their continued childlessness made her vulnerable.[111] Her powerful natal family, the Godwines, were the source of her strength and also her weakness. When King Edward turned against them, she fell too. Edith, moreover, was herself the subject of legal inquiry; she was implicated in the murder of Gospatric, an enemy of her brother, Tostig. She also took a compurgation oath on her deathbed to prove her innocence against charges of adultery.[112] Moving back chronologically to Emma, she was active politically and, during her second marriage to Cnut, a crucial part of the diplomatic process that allowed the success of his rule. But in both of her marriages, Emma was a second or even third wife. Cnut did not repudiate his first union with Ælfgifu of Northampton even as he and Emma were joined in marriage and crowned together. Emma's status as queen was weakened by this previous union.[113] Yet even apart from the vagaries of Edith and Emma's particular queenly fortunes, the development of English courts, based on the hundred and the county, allowed no place for women as judges. Norman legal processes featured manorial courts, including abbatial courts run by women, instead of the English hundredal structure. Mathilda's experience as duchess in Normandy influenced her expectation that women could operate the levers of justice. As queen, her assumption of judicial authority over court proceedings, both secular and sacred, can be seen as a natural outgrowth of Norman practice.

CONCLUSION

Mathilda's work at the head of jurisprudence changed the prerogatives of queenship in England. In the next two generations after her reign, a queen's exercise and influence in the judicial branch of government was not unusual. Mathilda's successors, Queen Matilda II of Scotland and Queen Matilda of Boulogne, each sat in justice and claimed royal authority alone.[114]

111 *Life of King Edward who lies at Westminster*, 2nd edition, ed. Frank Barlow (Oxford, 1992); Stafford, *Queen Emma and Queen Edith*, 21–2.

112 Stafford, *Queen Emma and Queen Edith*, 118.

113 Emma insisted that Ælfgifu was a concubine, but nevertheless, Cnut continued to rely on her to rule Norway with their son, Swein.

114 Matilda of Scotland also presided in her court over a case for Abingdon Abbey; *History of the Church of Abingdon*, ii, 168–169 also printed in Van Caenegem, *Lawsuits*, (no. 189). She notably ruled on the drawing of boundaries of a hundred itself. Karn, *Kings, Lords and Courts*, 82–3. Queen Matilda of Boulogne (Queen Matilda III) ruled in the context of the 'Anarchy', the civil war between Empress Matilda and Stephen of Blois. Thus, her experience as an English queen might be considered singular. See Heather Tanner, 'Queenship: office, custom, or ad hoc? The case of Queen Matilda III of England (1135–1152)', in *Eleanor of Aquitaine: Lord and Lady*, ed. Bonnie Wheeler and John Carmi Parsons (New York, NY, 2002),

Mathilda's youngest daughter, Adela of Blois, did the same as countess, presiding over judicial matters in her comital court.[115] By the twelfth century, moreover, abbatial jurisdiction over crimes had expanded as Nicholas Karn has shown.[116] The royal English nunneries of great wealth and influence – Barking, Shaftesbury, Wilton, Reading – eventually had abbatial courts in England that followed the Norman model; they dispensed justice to their tenants and the religious in their care into the thirteenth century.[117] But this was not originally an English model of justice. Mathilda's innovations in royal justice had long-term effects on queenship, and arguably on women's abbatial authority, in England. Mathilda's juridical activity over newly conquered England also had great significance on a symbolic level.

Robin Fleming has theorized that legal cases reflected in Domesday's entries were ritualized re-enactments of the Conquest. In the context of the court, without force of arms, the Norman victory over the English population was repeatedly revisited.[118] In a thousand juridical decisions Norman mastery was codified. If one imagines the law court as a restaging of the conquest, as Fleming asserts, Mathilda's position at its head has a martial quality. Just as the ship she commissioned, the *Mora*, represented Mathilda on the shores of Hastings, her conquest over England was demonstrated each time she handed down a verdict. She was never on a battlefield, but her law court was a place of compulsion and coercion, supported by the implicit threat of royal punishment. Mathilda and her Normans assumed she had the right to drive the legal machinery of English royal justice. The fair copies of the Accord of Winchester reflect this truth. As the documents traveled throughout her kingdom, they acknowledged her legitimacy as a judge over England. The privilege was affirmed each time she sat at the head of a court or synod and handed down a decision. For Mathilda of Flanders the seat of justice was a place both symbolic and authentic, where the law was 'upon her tongue'.

133–58. For Eleanor of Aquitaine, see Ayaal Herdam and David J. Smallwood, 'The queen from the south: Eleanor of Aquitaine as a political strategist and lawmaker', in *Strategic Imaginations: Women and the Gender of Sovereignty in European Culture*, ed. Anke Gilleir and Aude Defurne (Leuven, 2020), 159–80.

[115] LoPrete, *Adela of Blois*, Appendix 'Itinerary and Register of Sources', 439–534.

[116] Particularly under Henry I, the idea that a hundred might not simply be an administrative unit of financial management but exist as a property of monastic community or lay lord developed broadly. See Karn, *Kings, Lords and Courts*, 84–98.

[117] Under King Stephen, the abbess at Barking insisted on her right to negotiate pleas and collect 'murdrum and danegeld' without the interference of royal agents. Karn, *Kings, Lords and Courts*, 96–7.

[118] Fleming, *Domesday*, 17.

8

CORPSE

Where there is a corpse, there the vultures will gather.

Matthew 24:28

Mathilda of Flanders died on November 2, 1083. Her illness must have lasted only a matter of months as she was active in mid-July of that year.[1] According to Orderic Vitalis, she fell ill sometime in September and her condition rapidly declined.[2] It is possible that Abbot Baldwin of Bury St Edmunds treated her as he was in Caen at the time. If so, he was unable to improve her health.[3] Orderic reported that her death was mourned for many days in Normandy and England. Both Orderic and William of Malmesbury indicate she was celebrated with a lavish funeral.[4]

Mathilda was interred at Holy Trinity, Caen just as she intended, her body placed between the choir and the altar.[5] Orderic attests that many archbishops, bishops and abbots were present for the ceremony, as well as monks, nuns and 'a great throng of poor people'.[6] Mathilda was set beneath an elaborate black Tournai marble monument covered in gold and jewels, decorated with a golden effigy. Orderic records her epitaph, carved in gold, which celebrates her bloodline, her piety and her foundation of Holy Trinity (Plate 7).[7] After

1 See Chapter Two: Hands, 66–8.

2 *OV*, iv, 44–5.

3 Baldwin was the royal physician who had also served Edward the Confessor. He appears as a signator in charters in Caen at this time. *Regesta*, no. 64.

4 William of Malmesbury, *GR*, i, 503.

5 Parsons theorized that Mathilda's burial arrangements may have influenced the next two generations of Anglo-Norman queens. While church dedications to the Trinity had fallen out of fashion, Matilda of Scotland founded Holy Trinity Aldgate where she intended to be buried. Matilda of Scotland's niece, Queen Matilda of Boulogne, linked herself to Holy Trinity Aldgate by burying two of her children there. She also employed its prior as her confessor, in line with her aunt's example. John Carmi Parsons, '"Never was a body buried in England with such solemnity and honour": the burials and posthumous commemorations of English queens to 1500', in *Queens and Queenship in Medieval Europe*, ed. Anne Duggan (Woodbridge, 1997), 317–37 at 330.

6 *OV*, iv, 44–5.

7 For full text of the epitaph, see Chapter Five: Womb, 145.

Plate 7. Mathilda of Flanders' tombstone of black Tournai marble, placed in the choir of Holy Trinity, Caen.

her death, her daughter Abbess Cecelia and the nuns further celebrated her: 'Mathilda the Queen whose works declare the probity of her deeds and the nobility of her life'.

> Here, too, after a life of blessed works, devotion, and virtue, was this queen buried, even as she had requested beforehand, so that in death she might adorn with her bones the chapel that she had embellished with her love while alive.[8]

Likewise, her last bequest to Holy Trinity, recorded in Chapter Six, continued her lifelong pattern of lavishing resources on the abbey she planned and constructed.[9]

The consequences of Mathilda's loss were felt at court immediately. Robert Curthose left Normandy after his mother's death and would not return until his father died in 1087. Mathilda was clearly the link that held them together; once she was gone, their relationship dissolved. Chroniclers of the period were explicit about the effect of Mathilda's absence. William of Malmesbury claimed her husband's grief was deep and long-lasting. Her death so affected William that he 'abandoned pleasure of every kind'.[10] The chronicler wrote of their love for each other, their depth of feeling and constancy. Even if this was hyperbole, Mathilda's centrality to the Anglo-Norman royal family was made manifest by her death. One is tempted to wonder how the bitterness between her sons – Robert, William Rufus and Henry I – might have played out differently had Mathilda lived.[11] Her husband William's challenges between 1083 and 1087 must have felt more acute without the partnership that featured Mathilda's talented and capable governance.[12]

Surrounded by the Caennaise community she founded – with her own daughter to lead it – no doubt Mathilda expected her body would lie in peace. Instead, her tomb was repeatedly disturbed. The premise of this book is that Mathilda embodied conquest; that she used her bodily presence consciously in a variety of contexts to signal her identity and legitimacy. Yet Mathilda's corpse demonstrates a reverse: in death she had no agency. Her remains were used to variously embody corruption and exploitation, absolutism and even

8 Daniel Sheerin, 'Sisters in the Literary Agon', in *Women Writing Latin, Volume 2*, ed. Laurie Churchill, Phyllis R. Brown, Jane E. Jeffrey (New York, NY, 2002), 93–131, at 119.

9 See Chapter Six: Flesh, 171–2.

10 William of Malmesbury, *GR*, i, 500–3.

11 Cecelia seems to have occasionally taken on the role of mediator between her brothers, but only to protect her abbey. Gathagan, 'Maiden', 854–7.

12 For William 1084 was a relatively peaceful year on the political front but the dynastic crisis worsened. In 1085–6, William struggled with the outbreak of renewed conflict in Maine and the very serious threat of invasion by the Danes. Bates, *William*, 451–9.

provide a backdrop for a critique of religious repression, as demonstrated below. Even those who should have safeguarded her, moreover, removed valuables from her tomb. Scientists of the 'modern' age could not resist the urge to examine her remains.

On May 8, 1562, the abbey of Holy Trinity was invaded by Calvinists during the First War of Religion ostensibly in response to the corruption of the Catholic church. Calvinist rioters burned the relics that Mathilda had gathered with such care and intention and attacked her tomb.[13] Mathilda of Flanders' jeweled effigy was destroyed, and the gold and gems stripped and carted away.[14] Only the Tournai marble slab, originally brought from her home in Flanders at her death, remained. The abbess of Holy Trinity, Anne de Montmorency, barely convinced the iconoclasts to leave Mathilda's body undisturbed. In some reports, Mathilda's bones were scattered and Abbess Anne had to collect them.[15] The trauma of that scene was imaginatively depicted by Pre-Raphaelite artist Sir John Everett Millais (Plate 8).[16] The nuns of the community stand in rows behind their abbess, horrified at the desecration of their foundress; some scream and faint. The rabble surrounding the tomb strip the entire abbey of its treasures – even the tapestries on the walls are being cut down. The crowd moved aside Mathilda's stone effigy and are busy looking into her coffin for valuables – a deluxe illuminated gospel book is thrown to the side. One man picks gold thread out of Mathilda's heavily embroidered shroud. The abbess stands above the fray looking on desperately. One looter, recalled to his senses, carefully hands her Queen Mathilda's sapphire ring, the traditional emblem of episcopal authority. Mathilda's dead hand is held up from the sepulcher in the background, having just been relieved of it.

13 See Chapter Three: Fingers, 75–104.

14 'The May 1562 iconoclasts were not deterred by the weeping nuns, including their abbess, kneeling before them.' Pierre Carel, *Histoire de la ville de Caen sous Charles IX, Henri III et Henri IV* (Paris, 1887), 19. For the year 1562, de la Rue's entry reads, 'It was then that the tombs of King William and his wife Queen Mathilde were broken and desecrated, with the epitaphs and carved tomb effigies with which they were decorated. The sectarians carried their hatred against the images to the point of destroying the statues of the seven Liberal Arts, which adorned the portal of the College of Arts. It has been claimed that they took them for saints.' Gervais De la Rue, *Nouveau Essais Historiques sur La Ville de Caen et son Arrondissement, contenant Mémoires d'antiquités locales et annales militaires, Politiques et Religieuses de la ville de Caen et de la Basse-Normandie* (Caen, 1843), 375.

15 De la Rue, *Essais*, 41–2.

16 *The Disentombment of Queen Matilda* was drawn in 1849 by Millais for a patron, Mrs. Brockbank, 'in reference to the "Lives of the Queens of England" by Agnes Strickland', according to the inventory of his works. John Guille Millais, *The Life and Letters of Sir John Everett Millais, President of the Royal Academy*, 3rd edition (London, 1905), Appendix: 'Black and White Drawings'. Not paginated (398).

Plate 8. *The Disentombment of Queen Matilda*, Sir John Everett Millais, Permission, The Tate.

Millais's depiction was invented but was based on the violence of 1562 when the churches of Caen were systematically looted and robbed by Protestant rebels. By 1563, Abbess Anne's powerful father, the Constable of France – also named Anne – helped craft the Edict of Amboise, which forgave the crimes of the iconoclasts but only allowed the practice of Protestantism privately, at home.[17] The destruction of Mathilda's tomb was repaired and her Tournai stone was once again laid down on the top of a raised sepulcher.

Despite Millais' artistic license, Holy Trinity actually suffered very little property damage in the Protestant assault. Complaints against the looters were to be lodged with the civic authorities. Maylis Baylé found that unlike other churches targeted by Protestants, Holy Trinity did not report damages to the royal authorities.[18] Abbess Anne de Montmorency herself may have led to the mob sparing the queen's body, contenting themselves with her gold and jewels; Anne's own mother was a well-known Protestant sympathizer.[19] Yet the Abbess Anne betrayed her royal founder: Anne gave her father, Constable of France, Queen Mathilda's sapphire ring the following year when he visited Caen with Charles IX.[20] The symbol of Mathilda's episcopal authority – an object of profound importance to the abbey's own autonomous identity – disappeared forever.[21] Many years later however, in 1707, Mathilda's tomb was repaired and enriched anew. Abbess Gabrielle-Françoise Fronlay de Tessé re-established a new black marble mausoleum erected for Queen Mathilde over her Tournai marble slab.[22] Her body lay beneath in its coffin in splendor once more.

The second disruption of Mathilda's tomb was carried out during the French Revolution. In 1793, Revolutionary soldiers once again attacked Holy Trinity, as they did almost all royal tombs in France, as a symbol of religious monarchy. They tore down the mausoleum and took away everything of value but did not realize the marble slab underneath the ornate mausoleum hid Mathilda's remains. They never moved the slab or dug beneath it. This stroke

17 According to the Edict of Amboise, public Protestant worship was permitted on the estates of nobility with rights of high justice.

18 Baylé, *La Trinité*, 15 and 20.

19 de la Rue, *Nouveau Essais*, 375. See Joan Davies, 'The Montmorencys and the Abbey of Sainte Trinité, Caen: Politics, Profit and Reform', *JEH* 53:4 (2002), 665–85.

20 Davies, 'Montmorencys and the Abbey of Sainte Trinité', 682.

21 These vows were enshrined in London, British Library, MS. Harley 3661. Davies has demonstrated, however, that the de Montmorency abbesses were committed to the enrichment of their own family above all. Davies, 'Montmorencys and the Abbey of Sainte Trinité' at 675 and 682.

22 Abbess Francoise de Froulay de Tessé also commissioned La Bataille d'Auvray to produce the *Catalogue of Abbesses*, now Caen, Musée de Beaux-Arts, Mancel 80. It was the last manuscript produced for Holy Trinity.

of good fortune meant that Mathilda's body was undisturbed.[23] There was no one left at the abbey in 1793 to prevent the plunder or to rebuild Mathilda's mausoleum. In the previous year, 1792, the community at Holy Trinity was dissolved. Almost 900 years after Mathilda founded Holy Trinity, the final group of nuns and their last abbess, Marie Aimée Doulcet de Pontecoulant, were expelled from the grounds of the abbey. Abbess Marie Aimée died in 1806 and was buried in the graveyard at St Giles, outside the abbey church she had ruled. With these last sisters of Holy Trinity, the institutional memory – and the whereabouts of their founder – was apparently lost.

Through the years that followed, Mathilda's body lay hidden, forgotten but safe. Holy Trinity was a storage bunker, an armory, a prison and lastly a shelter for the homeless and destitute.[24] Somewhat ironically, given Holy Trinity's charitable function, it was this last conversion which eventually caused a local outcry, and a renewed 'interest in Holy Trinity's prestigious past was reborn'.[25] The mystery of Mathilda's body became a matter of significance to local authorities. The first search for Matilda's coffin began in March 1818 but was unsuccessful.[26] The matter was taken up again a year later in 1819; Count de Montlivault, the Prefect of the department of Calvados, searched again with Spencer Smythe, the bishop of Bayeux.[27] Smythe discovered Mathilda's body contained in a leaden box, precisely under the spot where her monument once stood, inside a stone coffin, 'five feet four inches long, by eleven inches deep, and varying in width from twenty inches to eleven'. Queen Mathilda had not moved as the abbey around her had repeatedly transformed.

After the discovery of her coffin in 1819, it was opened yet again, this time to confirm that Mathilda's body was still inside:

> Within this coffin was a leaden box, soldered down; and, in addition to the box, the head of an effigy of a monk, in stone, and a portion of a skull-bone filled with aromatic herbs, and covered with a yellowish-white membrane, which proved, upon examination, to be the remains of a linen cloth. The box contained various bones, that had belonged to a person of nearly the same height as Matilda is described to have been. No doubt seemed to remain but that the desideratum was discovered. The whole was therefore carefully replaced; and the prefect ordered that a new tomb should be raised, similar to that which was destroyed at the revolution; and that the original slab, with the epitaph, should be laid on the top…[28]

23 De la Rue, *Essais*, ii, 41; Baylé, *La Trinité*, 24–5.

24 Baylé, *La Trinité*, 23.

25 Baylé, *La Trinité*, 23.

26 A detailed account of the proceedings can be found in the *Journal Politique du Département du Calvados*, for March 21, and May 6, 1819.

27 Dawson Turner, *Account of a Tour in Normandy, Volume 2* (Caen, 1818), Letter XXV, 20–4.

28 Turner, *Account of a Tour in Normandy*, Letter XXV, 204–5.

Mathilda's Tournai stone slab was recovered at St Stephen's abbey, where it was acting as a paving stone.[29] It was returned to the top of Mathilda's coffin. She was placed back under her black marble headstone, but not before her body was given a gynecological and obstetric examination.

Dr. Pierre-Chorin Dominel, a surgeon in Caen and member of the Revolutionary government, accompanied the antiquarian Léchaudé d'Anisy to the opening of Mathilda's tomb. D'Anisy was a scholar and professional antiquarian who had, in Nicholas Vincent's words, 'Unfortunately begun as an admirer and aficionado of all things documentary, Norman and medieval… (but) could not resist the temptation to proceed from admiration to collection, and from collection to outright theft'. [30] D'Anisy's predatory practices are somewhat visible in his conduct in 1819; together he and Dominel removed the lead box that held Mathilda's remains and took it from the abbey grounds. They opened the lead casket, probably in Dominel's lab at the hospital. Dominel proceeded to measure Mathilda. The men examined her skeleton, focusing particularly on her pelvis and pubic bones. The resultant report discussed her height and the width of her pelvic opening. Dominel suggested that Mathilda was under 4 feet tall and expressed fascination at her ability to deliver so many children. Dominel and d'Anisy's gynecological examination of Mathilda promulgated the notion that she was tiny, an idea that persists today. But their attention to and manipulation of her pelvic and pubic bones in the name of science give a somewhat voyeuristic impression. After the examination, Mathilda was placed back in her leaden box and it was welded shut. She was reinterred under her mortuary slab in the abbey church of Holy Trinity. The original slab was laid on a new tomb designed and commissioned by Count de Montlivault. He directed that:

> …the original slab, with the epitaph, should be laid on the top, that copies of the former inscription, stating how the queen's remains had been re-interred by the abbess, in 1707, should be added to two of the sides; that to the third should be affixed the ducal arms of Normandy; and that the fourth should bear the following inscription: 'This tomb containing the mortal remains of the illustrious Foundress of this Abbey, overthrown during civil strife and moved for a long series of years, was restored, in accordance with the wishes of the friends of religion, antiquity and the arts, 1819. Casimir, Comte de Montlivault, Counselor of the State, Prefect. Léchaudé d'Anisy, Director of the Hospital.[31]

Dominel and d'Anisy were the first to examine Mathilda in the name of obstetrics but not the last. On October 10, 1959 Jean Dastugue and Michel Boüard opened Mathilda's grave again. The report of that examination was published by Dastugue

29 Baylé, *La Trinité*, 24, n. 49.

30 Nicholas Vincent, *Norman Charters from English Sources: Antiquaries, Archives and the Rediscovery of the Anglo-Norman Past* (London, 2013), 71.

31 Turner, *Account of Normandy*, Letter XXV, 204–5.

in 1960. He showed that the inventory of Mathilda's bones still accorded with Dominel's report: five of her ribs, the nearly complete sacrum, the left hip bone, her broken left femur, the lower three quarters of the right femur, the left tibia, and an incomplete right tibia. Overall, claimed Dastugue, the bones had a 'very feminine appearance'.[32] Dastugue's process had all the trappings of modern science. He measured each bone meticulously and reported his results. His focus repeatedly returned to Mathilda's pelvis; he decided her rib bones were 'not particularly interesting'.[33] He ignored the sacrum, though he identified a significant anteversion; femoral anteversion is an inward rotation of the femur or thighbone. In other words, Mathilda's knee was markedly twisted inward relative to her hip. Dastugue might have expanded on this interesting finding – the anomaly could have affected how Mathilda experienced riding a horse or even walking – had he not been distracted by Mathilda's pelvis.

According to his documentation, Dastugue made a plastic reproduction of Mathilda's pelvis because only half of it was intact. He frequently manipulated it and marveled at how beautifully it fit into the sacrum. The penultimate section of the report is entitled, 'Evaluation of Obstetric Characteristics'. After reconstructing Mathilda's pelvis, Dastugue had quite a few suppositions to report. Her pelvis area was poorly developed – only 9.45 cm wide – whereas the average for a safe delivery, according to the midwives Dastugue cited, was 10 cm. This poor measurement was compensated by Mathilda's 'large transverse and, especially, oblique diameter' – the most crucial obstetric dimension: that is, the opening width of her pelvis. 'It is therefore probable that despite this only somewhat 'fair' pelvic ring, Mathilda must not have had any difficult or obstructed pregnancies.'[34] Mathilda's 'relatively numerous' successful pregnancies were a mystery that he had now solved.[35] Dastugue's report closed with a brief determination of Mathilda's overall stature which he estimated at about five feet. Dastugue re-enclosed Matilda's remains in a glass box which was then filled with inert gas. His report was placed inside of it. It is unclear whether Dastugue's plastic pelvis was also included with Matilda's remains.

Finally, Sir John Dewhurst, physician to Queen Elizabeth II, published a precis in 1981 on the subject of Mathilda's height but did so in a gynecological journal. It is evident from his publication that his area of interest was also Mathilda's pelvis.[36] After relaying the remarkable staying power of Dominel's

32 Jean Dastugue, 'Anthropologie régalienne: Mathilde et Bérengère', *Bulletin des anthropologists de Basse-Normandie* 4:3 (1979): 67–80.

33 Dastugue, 'Anthropologie régalienne', 69.

34 Dastugue, 'Anthropologie régalienne', 70.

35 '...Queen Mathilda must not have had any real dystocias and we should not be surprised by her relatively numerous maternities.' Dastugue, 'Anthropologie régalienne',70.

36 Sir John Dewhurst 'A historical obstetric enigma: how tall was Matilda?', *Journal of Obstetrics and Gynaecology* 1:4 (1981), 271–2.

original height estimation – 4 foot 2 inches – Dewhurst corrected the record.[37] In fact, Mathilda was five feet tall, just as Dastugue had reported. In his two-page brief, Dewhurst spent a full page estimating the width of Mathilda's pelvis in relation to recorded data of nineteenth-century women's pelvic dimensions. He concluded that at five feet tall, her obstetric abilities would indeed allow for a large family of children.

Mathilda's corpse offered a blank canvas for those who wished to project their assertions onto her. The Calvinists in 1562 reanimated her to demonstrate a corrupt popish church. Characterized by bits of bone and dust – relics of false saints – her abbey represented the manipulation of a credulous populace.[38] In 1793, the hostility directed at her – and all other royal tombs in the period – reflected the animus of revolutionary soldiers toward absolutism and the 'divine right' of royalty. Driven by the same resentment, the Revolutionary army burned irreplaceable monastic manuscripts and documents throughout Normandy. Dominel and d'Ainsy – the revolutionary and the thief – removed Mathilda from Holy Trinity after she had been discovered, and pored over her remains in the name of 'scientific' curiosity.

In 1894, Millais's drawing of Mathilda's disentombment carried his condemnation of women's repression. The scene incites the viewer to pity the nuns in the work, who draw the viewer's eye; one nun is unable to contain her emotion and she looks to be on the verge of collapse. Through the nuns' repressed emotions, erupting into something like hysteria when Mathilda's casket is uncovered, Millais demonstrated the unnaturalness of the celibate life.[39] Millais was particularly hostile to the sexual repression of women; the 'disorder of the senses' he portrays in the sketch expressed his negative views toward women's claustration.[40] Thus, Millais used Mathilda's body to level a critique of female repression. Millais was a member of the Pre-Raphaelite Brotherhood whose tenets included the embrace of nature and human sexuality.

In turn, Sir John Dewhurst in the 1980s used Mathilda's measurements to discuss royal pregnancies and births. He did not disrupt her tomb or unearth

37 Dewhurst cites numerous authors that accepted Mathilda's small stature. These included David C. Douglas, *William the Conqueror: the Norman Impact upon England* (Berkeley, CA, 1964), 370; John Gillingham, 'William I, 1066–1087' in *The Lives of the Kings and Queens of England*, ed. Antonia Fraser (London, 1977), 20–6 at 21. Dewhurst 'A historical obstetric enigma', 272.

38 The political authorities in Caen turned a blind eye to the destruction because the stolen gains would fund the war. Carel, *Histoire de la ville de Caen*, 27–8.

39 'Millais's preoccupation with the enclosed nun as the visible form of the "disorder of the senses" created by the repression of female sexuality continues throughout the 1850s.' Herbert Sussman, 'The Pre-Raphaelites and the "Mood of the Cloister"', *Browning Institute Studies* 8 (1980), 45–55. My thanks to Kevin Sheets for this reference.

40 Sussman, 'Pre-Raphaelites', 48.

her body, but he celebrated the work of Jean Dastugue, especially his creation of a plastic replica of Mathilda's pelvis, 'an added bonus'. It allowed modern men to determine her pelvic measurements with more exactitude.[41]

The introduction of this book provided a justification of its unusual structure based on medieval and modern approaches to queenly power; a woman's royal body was central to its conception. Here in Mathilda's final chapter, her body is once more pulled back into frame. Preoccupation with it persisted across centuries.[42] The community at Holy Trinity also celebrated their queenly founder with a reference to her body, as she 'adorn(ed) with her bones' their choir. Unlike the saintly remains she collected for them, Mathilda's own body was never considered holy. Yet it was a relic of Holy Trinity's foundation miracle – the Norman Conquest. Even after the vicissitudes of the Calvinists, the French Revolution, and nineteenth-century antiquarians, however, Queen Mathilda's body endures as the only 'relic' that remains today at Holy Trinity.[43] The stone abbey itself, her final resting place, still stands commandingly on the landscape in modern Caen after almost a thousand years. It is a testament to Mathilda's influence and power reaching back to the eleventh century.

CONCLUSION

Mathilda of Flanders ruled at a pivotal moment in European history, yet historians of the nineteenth century nearly succeeded in obscuring her. The antiquarians who first examined the texts of the conquest set the tone for how she was approached. Steeped in their own nineteenth-century perspective, they seem to have squinted against the truth as they pored over eleventh-century documents and preserved them. Perhaps in a world where women could not inherit or make choices about their future, a queen such as Mathilda –

41 Dewhurst 'A historical obstetric enigma', 272.

42 The obstetrical details of historical queens in history are regularly a source of fascination in the medical community. For instance, Catherine de Medici's difficulty in conceiving has gained attention from the medical community as has the medical explanation for Anne Stuart's many stillbirths. Caroline de Costa, 'The long barren years of Catherine de Medicis: A gynecologist's view of history', *Obstetrics and Gynaecology Magazine* 12:3 (Spring 2010), 55–7. For Queen Anne Stuart's diagnosis of Antiphospholipid Syndrome (APS) an autoimmune disease that causes pregnancy loss, see A. Tincani, G. Fontana and C. Mackworth-Young, 'The history of antiphospholipid syndrome', *Reumatismo* 74: 4 (2022), 144–50.

43 Somewhere deep beneath the abbey choir, her daughter Cecelia also sleeps, but her tomb is now covered by the eighteenth-century additions to the monastery. 'Another remarkable tomb in this church was that of Abbess Cecelia, daughter of William the Conqueror: she was in the choir of nuns; but it was covered without any opening by the new work done in this part of the old church.' De la Rus, *Essais de Caen*, 45.

actively wielding authority over men and women in every area of royal governance – was impossible to countenance. Instead, Victorian historians of queenship, like Agnes Strickland, attributed to Mathilda the creation of the Bayeux Tapestry; Strickland considered embroidery a suitable employment for a medieval queen.[44] The narrative sources of the eleventh century – which rarely mentioned Mathilda – made it possible to ignore and obviate her.

In this book, I've used documentary sources, architecture, and the objects she commissioned and collected, to uncover the reality of Mathilda of Flanders. Her active rule helped form a new polity, the Anglo-Norman realm, the creation of which would affect medieval Europe for hundreds of years. She imported to England a version of queenship unique to her, crafted by her lived experience, within this nascent political entity. Earenfight describes 'a daily act of reconstruction and interpretation situated in a zone of multiple and overlapping cultures, in which personality and temperament have some degree of influence over a queen's ultimate expression of her own unique practice of queenship'.[45] In Norman England, Mathilda's unique practice of queenship was robustly public. It was characterized by an unapologetic embrace of both new and traditional institutions: military lordship, royal justice, monastic foundation and ecclesiastical reform, documentary initiatives and cultural networks. Mathilda can be seen governing in documents and charters, articulating her identity in architecture, expressing her authority through innovative custom-made liturgies, handing down juridical sentences, and weighing in on the most fundamental theological issues of her day.

Mathilda's practice of active public queenship also recalls early Ottonian royal women. Simon MacLean has noted that the earliest Ottonian queens, specifically Queen Mathilda of Saxony and Queen Edith, were more prestigious than the men they married; they were already royal. As a result, Ottonian queens retained stronger links to their natal courts and families. Their networks, moreover, were utilized not just by the queens themselves but by their royal husbands. Carolingian queenly models of royal domesticity – as passive keepers of the throne's dignity – were replaced by a more active model for Ottonian queens.[46] The resemblance between Mathilda of Flanders' position and that of the Saxon queens is noteworthy. Mathilda's

44 Agnes Strickland, *Lives of the Queens of England, From the Norman Conquest: With Anecdotes of Their Courts, Now First Published from Official Records and Other Authentic Documents, Private as Well as Public* (12 vols., London, 1840–1848) i, 35. That characterization remains stubbornly entrenched even today. As recently as 2018, posters advertising the Bayeux Tapestry Museum in Normandy pictured Mathilda hard at work with her needle.

45 Earenfight, 'Persona of the Prince', 14.

46 MacLean argues this contrast is related to the Carolingian practice of marrying non-royal aristocratic women; their status did not allow for such a powerful role. MacLean, *Ottonian Queenship*, 16.

natal networks were crucial to Norman success; they made the conquest of England possible. At the most crucial moment of their political life, Mathilda's family neutralized the single political entity that might have threatened their invasion: the king of France.

Another Ottonian equivalent in the development of a more robust version of queenship was its political context. MacLean demonstrates that early Ottonian queens lived in '…a multi-polar world of shifting frontiers, whose kingdoms had soft and insecure political centers, and whose rulers competed not only against rival members of their own families, but to be considered royal at all'.[47] The Ottonian milieu corresponds to the struggle for legitimacy experienced by the early Anglo-Norman dynasty. MacLean's case for the increased power of Ottonian ruling women 'emphasizes this provisionality, this lack of certainty, as an important reason for the emergence of so many powerful queens'.[48] I would argue that Mathilda benefitted from a comparable extemporization.

Unlike the English queens who came before her, Mathilda ascended to a throne that her own ship had helped to win. The royal blood that already flowed in her veins was crowned again in Westminster in 1068. The mother of nine children, pregnant in full view of the court, Mathilda's rule over England and Normandy was made explicit at her royal inauguration and given formal assent by her newly subject people. Her part in the Norman Conquest, however, only commenced with her laudes. Pacification of England and continued good governance of England and Normandy would consume the rest of her days. Evidence of her own sense of identity remains in her final gift to Holy Trinity, the foundation she brought to life with such energy and care: her crown, her scepter, her horse's harness. These were the accoutrements of a queen's life lived in the public sphere.

Mathilda's ability to meet the challenges of her new cross-channel kingdom and exploit its gifts, I would argue, sprang from her consciousness of her own peerless bloodline. Her self-confidence was no doubt formed in her natal court of Flanders as the only daughter; her Ottonian sense of prerogative was encouraged by her mother. Once married, she outranked her husband. As duchess of Normandy, she wielded power with ease, quickly becoming central to Norman ducal governance.[49] Mathilda worked tirelessly for the success of the Norman Conquest, tying her monastic house and her daughter's future

47 MacLean, *Ottonian Queenship*, 18.

48 Ibid.

49 Mathilda's charter activity shows her participating in governance from the time of her marriage, c. 1052–3. Eleanor Searle first observed almost forty years ago that Norman rule was based exclusively on family relation: the gender of any given family member was not a consideration. Mathilda is an example of that truism. Eleanor Searle, *Predatory Kinship and the Creation of Norman Power, 840–1066* (Davis, CA, 1988).

to an enormous gamble. When it was accomplished, she stepped into the highest possible place of authority without hesitation and remade the practice of queenship in England. The new version of queenly rule she created was fit for a Norman Conquest queen. Mathilda was a Flemish cosmopolitan with a Norman's ruthlessness and an Ottonian's dynastic sensibility.

The current study has centered on a body metaphor to reveal Mathilda of Flanders through her acts, working against a relational approach that too narrowly defines her. For while she was a daughter, wife and mother, Mathilda was the ruler of the Anglo-Norman realm, a builder of monasteries and warships, a judge and patron. I've also shown the ways Mathilda herself used embodiment: a concept central to the eleventh-century world in which she lived. She commissioned and created objects that carried her into spaces barred to her: behind the monastic altar at the Eucharist, on the shores of England at the invasion. Furthermore, her awareness of her own body, and the messages it conveyed, were an important element of her queenship. This was true when she was pregnant – as she was at her coronation and on the eve of the conquest – but also throughout her life. In the 1070s, when Mathilda was 'settled' in Windsor hearing legal petitions, or in 1081, presiding over the Four Shires, she was not an intercessor but the embodiment of royal justice herself. Thus, with her hands, Mathilda endowed religious orders and commissioned warcraft. With her crowned head, she asserted authority. With her mouth, she dispensed justice. In a world where authority is so often assumed to be masculine, Mathilda of Flanders – as patron, judge and queen – embodied power.

SELECT BIBLIOGRAPHY

MANUSCRIPT SOURCES

Caen, Archives de Calvaldos, Cartulaire de Saint-Étienne de Caen, entrée 199 (cote provisoire).

Caen, Archives de Calvaldos, *Journal Politique du Département du Calvados*, for March 21, and May 6, 1819.

Caen, Musée de Beaux-Arts, Mancel 80

Canterbury Cathedral Archives DCc–ChAnt/A/1

Canterbury Cathedral Archives DCc–ChAnt/A/2

London, British Library MS Cotton Vitellius E. XII

Manchester, John Rylands Library, Beaumont Charters Collection, MS. BMC 67, 68 and 71.

Oxford, Bodleian Library MS E Museo 93

Paris, Bibliothèque National de France, MS. Lat 5650

PRINTED PRIMARY SOURCES

Actes des comtes de Flandre, ed. F. Vercauteren (Brussels, 1937).

Actes et documents anciens intéressant la Belgique, ed. Charles Duvivier (Brussels, 1898).

Aelfric's Catholic Homilies, Second Series, Text, ed. Malcolm Godden (London, 1979).

Les actes de Guillaume le Conquérant et de la Reine Mathilde pour les abbayes Caennaises, ed. Lucien Musset (Caen, 1967).

Les Annales de Saint Pierre de Gand et de Saint-Amand, ed. Philip Grierson (Brussels, 1937).

The Anglo-Latin satirical poets and epigrammatists of the twelfth century, ed. Thomas Wright (2 vols., London, 1872).

Anglo-Saxon Charters: An Annotated List and Bibliography, ed. Peter Sawyer (London, 1968).

Anglo-Saxon Chronicle, ed. Charles Plummer (2 vols., Oxford, 1892–9).

Annales monasterii de Wintona, Winchester Annals, ed. H.R. Luard (London, 1865).

Augustine, *De Doctrina Christiana*, ed. R.P.H. Green (Oxford, 1995).

Bede, *Liber hymnorum, rhythmi, variae preces*, ed. J. Fraipont (Turnhout, 1955).

Berengar of Tours, *De Sacra Coena*, ed. A.F. Vischer and F.T. Vischer (Berlin, 1834).

Cartulaire de l'abbaye Sainte-Croix de Quimperlé, ed. Léon Maitre and Paul de Berthou, 2nd, ed. (Rennes, 1902).

Cartulaire de l'abbaye de la Saint Trinité du Mont de Rouen, ed. A. Deville (Rouen, 1840).

Cartulaire de Notre-Dame de Chartres, ed. M. Lépinois 3 vols. (Chartres, 1862).

Charters and custumals of the Abbey of the Holy Trinity, Caen: Part I the English estate, ed. Marjorie Chibnall (Oxford, 1982).

Charters and custumals of the Abbey of the Holy Trinity, Caen: Part II the French estates, ed. John Walmsley (Oxford, 1994).

The Chronicle of Battle Abbey, ed. and trans. Eleanor Searle (Oxford, 1980).

Chronicon of the monastery of Abingdon, ed. J. Stevenson (2 vols., London, 1858).

'Chronica monasterii guatinensis', MGH *SS* 14.

The Chronicle of John of Worcester, ed. and trans. P. McGurk (Oxford, 1998).

Das Register Gregors VII, MGH, *Epistolae Selectae*, ed. Erich Caspar (Berlin, 1920–3).

Decrees of the Ecumenical Councils, Volume One, ed. Norman P. Tanner (Georgetown, DC, 2016).

The Deeds of God through the Franks: a translation of Guibert de Nogent's Gesta Dei per Francos, ed. and trans. Robert Levine (Woodbridge, 1997).

Encomuim Emmae Reginae, ed. and trans. Alistair Campbell (London, 1949).

English Historical Documents, Volume I, ed. Dorothy Whitelock, 2nd ed. (London, 1996).

English Lawsuits from William I to Richard I: Volume I, ed. R.C. Van Caenegem (London, 1990).

Epistolae: Medieval Women's Latin Letters, ed. Joan Ferrante (Hosted by Columbia University), https://epistolae.ctl.columbia.edu/letter/50.html

Études sur le règne de Robert le Pieux, 996–1031, ed. Christian Pfister (Paris, 1885).

The Fathers of the Church Mediaeval Continuation: The Letters of Peter Damian, trans. Owen J. Blum (Washington D.C., 2014).

Feudal Documents from the Abbey of Bury St Edmunds, ed. D.C. Douglas (London, 1932).

Fulcoius of Beauvais, 'Certe si fortis' and 'Tempore quae nostro', in *Mélanges Julien Havet; Receuil de Travaux D'Érudition dédiés à la memoire de Julien Havet, 1853–1893*, ed. M.L. Delisle (1895; repr. Geneva, 1972).

Gesta episcoporum Cameracensium, MGH, *SS* VII, ed. L.C. Bethmann (Hannover, 1846).

Gesta Guillelmi of William of Poitiers, ed. and trans. R.H.C. Davis and Marjorie Chibnall (Oxford, 1998).

Gesta Normannorum Ducum of William of Jumièges, Orderic Vitalis and Robert of Torigni Volume II, ed. and trans. Elisabeth M.C. van Houts (Oxford, 1995).

Gesta Regum, Historical Works of Gervase of Canterbury, ed. W. Stubbs (2 vols., London, 1880).

Guitmund of Aversa, 'De corporis et sanguinis Jesu Christi veritate in Eucharistia', ii, *PL* CXLIV: cols. 1449–50.

Hildebert of Lavardin, 'Epistolae', *PL* CLXII, 148–9.

Hildebert of Lavardin, 'Versus ad Ceciliam abbatissam Cathomi' in *Carmina Minora*, ed. Alexander Brian Scott (Berlin, 2002).

Histoire de Marmoutier, inventaire des archives, ed. Edmund Martène (Touraine, 1875).

Historia Ecclesie Abbendonensis: The History of the Church of Abingdon, ed. and trans. John Hudson, 2 vols. (Oxford, 2002–7).

Historiae Dunelmensis Scriptores tres: Gaufridus de Coldingham, Robertus de Graystanes, Etc Willielmus de Chambre, ed. J. Raine (London, 1839).

The Homilies of the Anglo-Saxon Church, ed. Benjamin Thorpe (London, 1844).

Hubert Guillotel: Actes des ducs de Bretagne (944–1148), ed. Philippe Charon, Philippe Guigon, Cyprien Henry, Michael Jones, Katharine Keats-Rohan and Jean-Claude Meuret (Rennes, 2014).

Lanfranc, 'Libre de corpore et sanguine Domini', *PL* CL: 234.

The Leofric Missal, 1: *Introduction, Collation Table, and Index*, ed. Paul Hayward; 2: *Text*, ed. Nicholas Orchard (Woodbridge, 2002).

Letters and Charters of Gilbert Foliot, ed. A. Morey and C.N.L. Brooke (Cambridge, 1967).

The Letters of Lanfranc Archbishop of Canterbury, ed. and trans. Helen Clover and Margaret Gibson (Oxford, 1979).

The Letters of Saint Anselm of Canterbury, trans. Walter Frohlich (Kalamazoo, MI, 1990–4).

Liber de officiis ecclesiasticis of Jean d'Avranches, ed. D. Johannis (Rouen, 1679).

Liber secundus miraculorum S. Adalardi, MGH *SS*, XV, 862–5.

The Life and Letters of Sir John Everett Millais, President of the Royal Academy, ed. John Guille Millais, 3rd edition (London, 1905).

Life of King Edward who lies at Westminster, ed. Frank Barlow, 2nd edition (Oxford, 1992).

Livy, *Ab Urbe Condita*, ed. Robert Seymour Conway and Stephen Keymer Johnson (Oxford, 1935).

Manuel de Diplomatique, Diplomes et chartes, ed. Arthur Giry (Paris, 1894).

Memorials of St Edmunds Abbey, ed. Thomas Arnold (3 vols., London: 1890–3).

Methodius, The Symposium: a treatise on chastity, trans. Herbert Musurillo. (Westminster, MD, 1958).

Milo Crispin, 'Vita beati Simonis comitis Crespeiensis auctore synchrono', *PL* CLVI, 1211–24.

The Missal of Robert Jumièges, ed. H.A. Wilson (Woodbridge, 1994 reprint).

Missale ad usum insignis et praeclarae ecclesiae Sarum, ed. Frances Henry Dickinson (Princeton, NJ, 1891).

Opera Diplomatica et Historica: ex editione et cum notis et supplemento Johannis Francisci Foppens, ed. Aubert Le Mire (4 vols., Louvain, 1723–48).

Orderic Vitalis, *The Ecclesiastical History of Orderic Vitalis*, ed. Marjorie Chibnall (6 vols., Oxford, 1990).

The Pontifical of Magdalene College, ed. H.A. Wilson (London, 1910).

Recueil des actes des ducs de Normandie de 911 à 1066, ed. Marie Fauroux (Caen, 1961).

Recueil des actes de Philippe Ier, Roi de France, ed. Origo M. Prou (Paris, 1908).

Recueil des Rouleaux Des Morts; VIIIe siècle vers 1536 (2 vols., Paris, 2005).

Regesta Regum Anglo-Normannorum: The Acta of William I (1066–1087), ed. David Bates (Oxford, 1998).

Regesta Regum Anglo-Normannorum, ed. H.W.C. Davis, C. Johnson, H.A. Cronne and R.H.C. Davis, 4 vols. (Oxford, 1913–69).

Regularis concordia Anglicae, ed. Thomas Symons (London, 1953).

Symeon Libellus de Exordio, ed. David Rollason (Oxford, 2019).

Translatio Balthildis anno 833, trans. Gaston Duchet-Suchaux in *Le tresor des saints de Chelles*, ed. Jean-Pierre Laporte (Chelles, 1988), 156–61.

Two Chartularies of the Priory of S. Peter at Bath, ed. W. Hunt (London, 1893).

Vetus et nova Ecclesiæ disciplina, circa benefica et beneficiaries, ed. Louis Thomassin (Mainz, 1787).

Wace, *The History of the Norman People: Wace's Roman de Rou*, trans. Glyn S. Burgess (Woodbridge, 2004).

William of Malmesbury *Gesta Regum Anglorum: The history of the English kings*, ed. and trans. R.A.B. Mynors, R.M. Thompson and M. Winterbottom (2 vols., Oxford, 1998–9).

SECONDARY SOURCES

Abbot, Judith. 'Political Strategy in the Coronation of Queen Matilda', paper presented at the 1990 Meeting of the Haskins Society Conference, abstract published in the *Anglo-Norman Anonymous* 9 (1991), 5.

Adair, Penelope Ann. '"Ego et Uxor Mea": Countess Clemence and Her Role in the Comital Family and in Flanders', PhD dissertation (University of Santa Barbara, CA, 1993).

Airlie, Stuart. 'Private Bodies And The Body Politic in the Divorce Case Of Lothar II', *Past & Present* 161:1 (Nov 1998), 3–38.

Alexiou, Margaret and Peter Dronke. 'The Lament of Jephthah's Daughter: Themes, Traditions, Originality', *Studi Medievali* 12 (1971), 819–69.

Armstrong, Dan. 'The Norman Conquest of England, the Papacy, and the Papal Banner', *HSJ* 32 (2020), 47–72.

Ayloff, Sir John. 'The Body of the King of Edward I', *Archaeologia* 3 (1770).

Baker, Rev. E.P. 'St Oswald and his Church at Zug', *Archaeologia* 93 (1949), 105–6.

Baptist, Edward E. *The Half Has Never Been Told: Slavery and the Making of American Capitalism* (New York, NY, 2014).

Barlow, Frank. *The English Church 1066–1154: A History of the Anglo-Norman Church* (New York, NY, 1979).

———William Rufus, 2nd edition (New Haven, CT, 2000).

Barthélemy, Dominique. 'Le concile de paix tenu à Caen (1035/1042)', *Annales de Normandie* 71 (2021/1), 37–53.

Bates, David. *Normandy before 1066* (New York, NY, 1982).

———'The origins of Justiciarship', *ANS* 4 (1982), 1–12.

———*William the Conqueror* (Stroud, 2001).

———*William the Conqueror* (New Haven, CT, 2016).

———'William the Conqueror and Wessex', in *The Land of the English Kin: Studies in Wessex and Anglo-Saxon England in Honour of Professor Barbara Yorke*, ed. Alexander James Langlands and Ryan Lavelle (Turnhout, 2020), 517–37.

Baxter, Stephen. 'The Domesday Controversy: a Review and a New Interpretation', *HSJ* 29 (2017), 225–93.

Baylé, Maylis. 'La Trinité de Caen,' *Congrès archéologique de France* 132 (1978), 22–58.

———*La Trinité de Caen: sa place dans l'histoire de l'Architecture et du Décor Romans* (Paris, 1979).

———'Les relations entre massif de façade et vaisseau de nefen Normandie avant 1080', *Cahiers de civilization médiévale*, 34: 135–6 (1991), 225–35.

Bedos-Rezak, Brigitte Miriam. 'Medieval Identity: A Sign and a Concept', *American Historical Review* 105: 5 (2000), 1489–1533.

———*When Ego Was Imago: Signs of Identity in the Middle Ages* (Leiden, 2011).

———'Semiotic Anthropology: The Twelfth-Century Approach', in *European Transformations: The Long Twelfth Century*, ed. Thomas F.X. Noble, and John Van Engen (Notre Dame, IN, 2012), 426–67

Beech, George. 'Queen Mathilda of England (1066–1083) and the Abbey of La Chaise-Dieu in the Auvergne', *Frühmittelalterliche Studien* 27:1 (1993), 350–374.

———*Was the Bayeux Tapestry made in France? The Case for St Florent of Saumur* (New York, NY, 2005).

Belliart, Michel. 'Les Miracles de saint Adalhard de Corbie en Flandre (vers 1075)', *Revue du Nord* 102: 436 (2020), 641–52.

Bethell, Denis. 'The making of a twelfth-century relic collection', in *Popular Belief and Practice,* ed. C.J. Cuming and Derek Baker (Cambridge, MA, 1972), 61–72.

Biddick, Kathleen. 'What Does "Deconstructing Christianity" Want? The Institutional Imaginary of the Incarnation' *minnesota review* 80 (2013), 83–94.

———'Transmedieval mattering and the untimeliness of the Real Presence', *postmedieval: a journal of medieval cultural studies* 4 (2013), 238–52.

Biddle, Martin. 'Seasonal Festivals and Residence: Winchester, Westminster and Gloucester in the Tenth to Twelfth Centuries', *ANS* 8 (1985), 51–72.

Bland, C.C. Swinton. *The Autobiography of Guibert, Abbot of Nogent-sous-Coucy* (London, 1925).

Blough, Karen, ed. *A Companion to the Abbey of Quedlinburg in the Middle Ages* (Leiden, 2022).

Bobrycki, Shane. 'The Royal Consecration Ordines of the Pontifical of Sens from a New Perspective', *Bulletin du centre d'études médiévales d'Auxerre* 13 (2009), 131–42.

———'The flailing women of Dijon: Crowds in Ninth-Century Europe', *Past & Present* 240:1 (April 2018), 3–46.

———*The Crowd in the Early Middle Ages* (Princeton, NJ, 2024).

Boldrick, Stacey. 'An Encounter between Death and an Abbess: The Mortuary Roll of Elisabeth 'sConincs, Abbess of Forest (Manchester, John Rylands Library, Latin MS 114)', *Bulletin of the Rylands Library* 82:1(2000): 29–48.

Boswell, John. *The Kindness of Strangers: The Abandonment of Children in Western Europe from Late Antiquity to the Renaissance* (Chicago, 1998).

Boüard, Michel de. 'La Reine Mathilde', *Les Amis de Bernay: Société Historique et Archéologique* 26 (1989), 13–29.

Bouchard, Constance Brittain. 'The Carolingian Creation of a Model of Patrilineage', in *Paradigms and Methods in Early Medieval Studies*, ed. C. Chazelle and F. Lifshitz (New York, NY, 2007), 135–51.

Bourrienne, V. *Odon de Contreville, évêque de Bayeux* (Bayeux, 1900).

Boutmey, André. 'Trois oeuvres inédites de Godefroid of Reims', *Revue de moyen âge latin* 3 (1947), 335–66.

Bozóky, Edina. 'Introduction' in *Hagiographie, idéologie et pouvoir au Moyen Âge. L'écriture de la sainteté, instrument politique*, ed. Edina Bozóky (Turhout, 2012), 1–10.

———'Les reliques, le prince et le bien public', in *Le Prince, Son Peuple et Le Bien Commun: De l'Antiquité tardive à la fin du Moyen Âge*, ed. Joëlle Quaghebeur, Hervé Oudart and Jean-Michel Picard (Rennes, 2013), 203–15.

———'Hagiography, Relics and Secular Politics in Western Europe, 6th–13th Centuries', in *Hagiography and the History of Latin Christendom, 500–1500*, ed. Samantha Kahn Herrick (Leiden, 2019), 272–94.

Brunel, Ghislain. 'Chartres et chancellaries épiscopales du Nord de la France au IXe siècle', in *À propos des actes d'évêques: Hommage à Lucie Fossier*, ed. Michel Parisse (Nancy, 1991), 238–42.

Buc, Philippe. *The Dangers of Ritual: Between Early Medieval Texts and Social Scientific Theory* (Princeton, NJ, 2001).

Bukofzer, Manfred. 'The Music of the Laudes', in Ernst Kantorowicz, *Laudes Regiae: A Study in Liturgical Acclamations and Mediaeval Ruler Worship* (Berkeley, CA, 1946), 188–222.

Callebaut, Dirk. 'Ename and the Ottonian west border policy in the middle Scheldt region', in *Exchanging Medieval Material Culture: Studies on archaeology and history presented to Frans Verhaeghe*, ed. K. De Groote, D. Tys and M. Pieters (Brussels, 2010), 217–43.

Carel, Pierre. *Histoire de la ville de Caen sous Charles IX, Henri III et Henri IV* (Paris 1887), 19.

Caroli, Martina. 'Bringing saints to cities and monasteries: *translationes* in the making of a sacred geography (ninth–tenth centuries)' in *Towns and their*

Territories between Late Antiquity and the Early Middle Ages, ed. G.P. Brogiolo, N. Gauthier and N. Christie (Leiden, 2000), 259–74.

———'A woman's body for the empire's salvation: the translatio of Queen Bathild's body and the crisis of the year 833,' in *Relics, Identity, and Memory in Medieval Europe*, ed. Marika Rasanen, Gritje Harnnann, and Earl Jeffrey Richards (Turnhout, 2016), 91–113.

Carpenter, David. *Struggle for Mastery: Britain 1066–1284* (London, 2003).

Carter, Michael. 'The Relics of Battle Abbey: A Fifteenth-Century Inventory at the Huntington Library, San Marino,' *The Journal of Medieval Monastic Studies* 8 (2019), 309–43.

Cartwright, Charlotte. 'Before She Was Queen: Matilda of Flanders and the Use of Comitissa in the Norman Ducal Charters', *HSJ* 22 (2010), 59–82.

Chaix, Valerie. Les chœurs cloisonnés du monde anglo-normand dans la seconde moitié du XIe siècle', in *Ars auro gemmisque prior: mélanges en hommage à Jean-Pierre Caillet* (Zabrege, 2013), 241–9.

Charruadas, Paulo. 'Principauté territoriale, reliques et Paix de Dieu. Le comté de Flandre et l'abbaye de Lobbes à travers les Miracula S. Ursmari in itinere per Flandriam facta (vers 1060)', *Revue du Nord* 2007/4 (no. 372), 703–28.

Chibnall, Marjorie M. 'The translation of the relics of St Nicholas and Norman historical tradition', in *Piety, Power and History in Medieval England and Normandy*, ed. Marjorie Chibnall (Farnham, 2000), 33–41.

Christianson, Karen Ann. 'Female Leadership and Male Submission the Order of Fontevraud in Twelfth-Century France', PhD thesis (University of Iowa, 2009).

Church, Stephen D. 'The Date and Place of King John's Birth together with a Codicil on His Name', *Notes & Queries* 67.3 (2020), 315–23.

Clanchy, Michael. 'Did Mothers Teach Their Children to Read?' in *Motherhood, Religion, and Society in Medieval Europe, 400–1400*, ed. Conrad Leyser and Lesley Smith (Farnham, 2001), 129–53.

Cleaver, Laura and Andrea Worm, ed. *Writing History in the Anglo-Norman World: Manuscripts, Makers and Readers, c. 1066–c. 1250* (York, 2022).

Colker, Marvin L. 'Fulcoius of Beauvais: Poet and Propogandist,' in *Latin Culture in the Eleventh Century*, ed. M.W. Herren, C.J. McDonough, R.G. Arthur (2 vols., Turnhout, 2002).

Collette, Carolyn P. *Performing Polity: Women and Agency in the Anglo-French Tradition, 1385–1620* (Turnhout, 2006).

Constable, Giles. *The Letters of Peter the Venerable* (2 vols., Cambridge, MA, 1967).

Cooper, Mariah. 'A Female King or a Good Wife and a Great Mother? Seals, Coins, and the Epitaphic Legacy of the Empress Matilda', *HSJ* 32 (2020), 149–62.

Corbet, Patrick. *Les Saints Ottoniens: Sainteté Dynastique, Sainteté Royale Et Sainteté Feminine Autour de l'An Mil* (Freiburg, 1986).

Courtenay, William J. *Covenant and Causality in Medieval Thought: Studies in Philosophy, Theology and Economic Practice* (London, 1984).

Cowdrey, H.E.J. 'Bishop Ermenfrid of Sion and the Penitential Ordinance following the Battle of Hastings,' *JEH* 20 (1969), 225–42.

———'Memorials of Abbot Hugh of Cluny (1049–1109),' *Studi Gregoriani* XI (1978), 45–109.

———'The Anglo-Norman Laudes Regiae', *Viator* 12 (1981), 37–78.

———'Count Simon of Crépy's monastic conversion,' in *Papauté, monachisme et théories politiques. Volume I: Le pouvoir et l'institution ecclésiale* (Lyon, 1994), 253–66.

———*The Register of Pope Gregory VII: An English Translation* (Oxford, 2002)

———*Lanfranc: Scholar, Monk, Archbishop* (Oxford, 2003).

Dale, Johanna. *Inauguration and Liturgical Kingship in the Long Twelfth Century: Male and Female Accession Rituals in England, France and the Empire* (York, 2019).

Davies, Joan. 'The Montmorencys and the Abbey of Sainte Trinité, Caen: Politics, Profit and Reform', *JEH* 53:4 (2002), 665–85.

Defries, David. 'The Emergence of the Territorial Principality of Flanders, 750–1050', *History Compass* 11: 8 (2013), 619–31.

Dekker, Kees. 'Pentecost and Linguistic Self-Consciousness in Anglo-Saxon England: Bede and Aelfric', *The Journal of English and Germanic Philology* 104:3 (July, 2005), 345–72.

De la Rue, Gervase. *Essais Historiques sur la ville de Caen et son arrondissement* (2 vols., Caen 1820).

———*Nouveaux Essais Historiques sur la ville de Caen et son Arrondissement, contenant Mémoires d'antiquités locales e annales militaires, Politiques et Religieuses de la ville de Caen et de la Basse-Normandie* (Caen, 1843).

de Lubac, Henri. *Corpus mysticum: L'Eucharistie et l'Église au Moyen Âge, étude historique* (Paris, 1949).

Dessaux, Nicolas. 'Les enjeux politiques et religieux des translations de reliques a Lille au XIe siecle' *Revue du Nord* 102: 436 (2020), 489–509.

DeVries, Kelly. 'Count Baldwin V of Flanders: Broker of Eleventh-Century Power', in *Military Cultures and Martial Enterprises in the Middle Ages: Essays in Honour of Richard P. Abels*, ed. John D. Hosler and Steven Isaac (Woodbridge, 2020), 81–98.

Dickinson, F.H. 'The Sale of Combe', *Somerset Archaeological and Natural History Society Proceedings* 22 (1876), 106–13.

Dockray-Miller, Mary. *The Life and Books of Judith of Flanders* (Burlington, VT, 2015).

Douglas, David C. 'The Ancestors of William Fitz Osborn', *EHR* 59 (1944), 62–79.

Drewer, Lois. 'Jephthah and his Daughter in Medieval Art: Ambiguities of Heroism and Sacrifice', *Insights and Interpretations: Studies in Celebration of the Eighty-Fifth Anniversary of the Index of Christian Art*, ed. Colum Hourihane (Princeton, NJ, 2002), 35–59.

Dumézil, Bruno. 'Les attributs du pouvoir et la compétition pour le pouvoir: armes et titulatures au VIe siècle,' in *Genre et compétition dans les sociétés occidentales du haut Moyen Âge (IVe–XIe siècle)*, ed. Sylvie Joye and Régine Le Jan (Turnhout, 2018), 79–92.

Dunbabin, Jean. 'What's in a name? Phillip, King of France', *Speculum* 68: 4 (1993), 949–68.

Earenfight, Theresa M. 'Without the Persona of the Prince: Kings, Queens and the Idea of Monarchy in Late Medieval Europe', *Gender & History*, 19: 1 (2007), 1–21.

——'Raising Infanta Catalina De Aragón to be Catherine, Queen of England', *Anuario de Estudios Medievales* 46:1(2016), 417–43 at 422.

Edwards, Jennifer C. *Superior Women: Medieval Female Authority in Poitiers' Abbey of Sainte-Croix* (Oxford, 2019).

Ellis, A.S. 'Biographical Notes on the Yorkshire Tenants Named in Domesday Book,' *Yorkshire Archaeological and Topographical Journal* 4 (1877).

Elshtain, J.B. *Public Man, Private Woman: Women in Social and Political Thought* (Princeton, NJ, 1981).

Engels, L.J. *Dichters Over Willem De Veroveraar; Het Carmine de Hastingae prelio* (Gorningen, 1967).

Firth, Matthew *Early English Queens, 850–1000 Potestas Reginae* (London, 2024).

Fleming, Robin. *Domesday Book and the Law* (Cambridge, 1998).

Fößel, Amalie. *Die Königin im mitteralterlichen Reich: Herrschaftsausübung, Herrschaftsrechte, Handlungsspielräume* (Stuttgart, 2000).

Foreville, Raymonde. 'L'École de Caen au XIe siècle et les origines Normandes de l'Université d'Oxford', in *Etudes médiévales offertes à M. le Doyen Augustin Fliche* (Paris, 1952).

Foulon, Jean-Hervé. 'The foundation and early history of Le Bec', in *A Companion to the Abbey of Le Bec in the Central Middle Ages, 11th–13th Centuries*, ed. Benjamin Pohl and Laura L. Gathagan (Leiden, 2019), 11–38.

Fradenburg, Louise Olga, ed. *Queenship and Sovereignty* (Edinburgh, 1992).

Frolow, A. *La relique de la Vrai Croix: Recherches sur le developpement d'un culte* (Paris, 1966).

Ganshof, F.L. *La Flandre Sous Les Premiers Comtes* (Brussels, 1949).

Garnett, George. 'Coronation and Propaganda: Some Implications of the Norman Claim to the Throne of England in 1066: The Alexander Prize Essay', *Transactions of the Royal Historical Society*, 36 (1986), 91–116

——'The Third Recension of the English Coronation *ordo*: the Manuscripts', *HSJ* 11 (1998), 43–71.

——*Conquered England: Kingship, Succession, and Tenure, 1066–1166* (Oxford, 2007).

Garver, Valerie. *Women and Aristocratic Culture in the Carolingian World* (Ithaca, NY, 2009).

——'Weaving Words in Silk: Women and Inscribed Bands in the Carolingian World', *Medieval Clothing and Textiles* 6 (2010), 33–56.

Gathagan, Laura L. '"Mother of heroes, most beautiful of mothers": Mathilda of Flanders and royal motherhood in the eleventh century', in *Virtuous or Villainess? The Image of the Royal Mother from the Early Medieval to the Early Modern Era*, ed. Ellie Woodacre and Carrie Fleiner (London, 2016), 37–63.

——'You conquer countless enemies, even as a maiden: The Conqueror's daughter and Holy Trinity, Caen', *History: The Journal of the Historical Association* 103 (2017), 840–857.

——'Introduction' with Heather Tanner and Lois L. Huneycutt in *Medieval Elite Women and the Exercise of Power, 1100–1400: Moving beyond the Exceptionalist Debate*, ed. Heather Tanner (New York, NY, 2018), 1–18.

——'Audi Israel: Apostolic Authority in the Coronation of Mathilda of Flanders', *ANS* 43 (2021), 89–104.

——'Family and Kinship in the Age of William the Conqueror', in *The Cambridge Companion to the Age of William the Conqueror*, ed. Benjamin Pohl (Cambridge, 2022), 143–62.

——'Abbess, Judge, Jailor: Authority and Imprisonment at Holy Trinity, Caen', *Bulletin of the John Rylands Library* 99:2 (December 2023), 25–46.

——'Mathilda of Flanders: The Innovator', in *English Consorts: Power, Influence, Dynasty: Volume I*, ed. Aidan Norrie, Carolyn Harris, J.L. Laynesmith, Danna R. Messer and Elena Woodacre (New York, NY, 2023).

——'The Trappings of Power: the Coronation of Mathilda of Flanders' *HSJ* 13 (1999), 21–39.

Gazeau, Véronique. 'Le temporel de l'abbaye de Saint-Pierre de Préaux au XIe siècle', *Cahier des Annales de Normandie: Recueil d'études en hommage à Lucien Musset* 23 (1990), 237–53.

——'Notices biographiques des abbés de Saint-Étienne de Caen à l'époque ducale', *Annales de Normandie* 32 (2002), 93–105.

——*Normannia monastica (Xe–XIIe siècle): Princes normands et abbés bénédictins et Prosopographie des abbés bénédictins* (2 vols., Caen, 2007)

Gazeau, Véronique and Jacques Le Maho, 'Les origins du culte de saint Nicolas en Normandie', in *Alleorigini dell'Europa: il culto di San Nicola tra Oriente e Occidentel*, ed. Gerardo Cioffari and Angela Laghezza (Bari, 2010), 153–60.

Geaman, Kristen. 'Queen's Gold and Intercession: The Case of Eleanor of Aquitaine', *Medieval Feminist Forum* 46:2 (2010), 10–33.

Geary, Patrick J. *Furta Sacra: Thefts of Relics in the Central Middle Ages* (Rev. Edition, Princeton, NJ, 1978).

——*Phantoms of Remembrance: Memory and Oblivion at the End of the First Millennium* (Princeton, NJ, 1994).

Gibson, Margaret. *Lanfranc of Bec* (Oxford, 1978).

Gierson, P. 'The Translation of Relics of St Donatian to Bruges', *Revue bénédictine* 49 (1937), 29–61.

Gilsdorf, Sean. *Queenship and Sanctity: The "Lives" of Mathilda and the "Epitaph" of Adelheid* (Washington, DC, 2004).

Godden, Malcolm. 'Biblical Literature: The Old Testament', in *The Cambridge Companion to Old English Literature*, ed. Malcolm Godden and Michael Lapidge (Cambridge, 1991), 214–33.

Grant, Lindy. *Architecture and Society in Normandy 1120–1270* (New Haven, CT, 2005).

Green, Judith. *The Aristocracy of Norman England* (Cambridge, 1997), 28–30.

Greenway, Diana E. 'The False Institutio of St Osmund', in *Tradition and Change: Essays in Honour of Marjorie Chibnall*, ed. Diana Greenway, Christopher Holdsworth and Jane Sayers (Cambridge, 1992), 77–102.

———*Saint Osmund: Bishop of Salisbury 1078–1099, and founder of the Cathedral at Old Sarum* (Much Wenlock, 1999).

Greer, Sarah. *Commemorating Power in Early Medieval Saxony: Writing and Rewriting the Past at Gandersheim and Quedlinburg* (Oxford, 2021).

Gretsch, Mechthild. *English Benedictine Reform* (Cambridge, 1994).

Grodecki, Louis. *L'Architecture Ottonienne* (Paris, 1958).

Hagger, Mark. *Norman Rule in Normandy, 911–1144* (Woodbridge, 2017).

Hall, Edwin and James Ross Sweeney, 'The "Licentia de nam" of the Abbess of Montivilliers and the Origins of the Port of Harfleur,' *Bulletin of Historical Research* 52: 125 (1979), 1–8.

Hallam, Elizabeth M. 'Monasteries as "War Memorials": Battle Abbey and La Victorie', *Studies in Church History* 20 (1983), 47–57.

Hamilton, Louis I. *A Sacred City: Consecrating Churches and Reforming Society in Eleventh-Century Italy* (Manchester, 2010).

Hare, Michael. 'Kings, Crowns, and Festivals: the Origins of Gloucester as a Royal Ceremonial Centre', *Transactions of the Bristol and Gloucestershire Archaeological Society* 115 (1997), 41–78.

Harvey, Sally. *Domesday: Book of Judgment* (Oxford, 2014).

Haskins, Charles Homer. *Norman Institutions* (Cambridge, 1918).

Head, Thomas and Richard Landes. *The Peace of God: Social Violence and Religious Response in France Around the Year 1000* (Ithaca, NY, 1992).

Herrick, Samantha Kahn. 'Introduction', in *Hagiography and the History of Latin Christendom, 500–1500*, ed. Samantha Kahn Herrick (Leiden, 2019), 1–10.

Herrmann-Mascard, Nicole. *Les Reliques des saints: Formation coutumière d'un droit* (Paris, 1975).

Hicks, Leonie V. *Religious Life in Normandy, 1050–1300: Space, Gender and Social Pressure* (Woodbridge, 2007).

———'Magnificent Entrances and Undignified Exits: Chronicling the Symbolism of Castle Space in Normandy', *JMH* 35:1 (2009), 52–69.

Higham, Nicholas J. 'Constantinus, Germanus and fifth-century Britain,' *EME* 22:2 (2014), 113–37.

Hillard, T. 'On the Stage, Behind the Curtain: Images of Politically Active Women in the Late Roman Republic', in *Stereotypes of Women in Power: Historical Perspectives and Revisionist Views*, ed. B. Garlick, S. Dixon and P. Allen (New York, NY, 1992), 37–64.

Hippeau, Celestine. *L'abbaye De Saint-Étienne De Caen, 1066–1790* (Caen, 1855).

Hochstetler, Donald. *A Conflict of Traditions: Women in Religion in the Early Middle Ages, 500–840* (New York, NY, 1992).

Hoeppner, Jo Ann and Moran Cruz. 'Dante's Matelda: Queen, Saint, and Mother of Emperors', *Viator* 47:3 (2016), 209–44.

Hollister, Warren and Amanda Frost. *Henry I* (New Haven, CT, 2003).

Holmes, L.L. and G. Harbottle. 'In the Steps of William the Conqueror: Neutron Activation Analysis of Caen Stone', *Archaeometry* 45, 2 (2003) 199–220.

Hourlier, Jacques. 'Les Sources Écrites de l'Historie Montiose Anterieure à 966', *Millénaire Monastique du Mont Saint-Michel 2: Vie montoise et rayonnement intellectuel*, ed. Raymond Foreville (Paris, 1993).

Hudson, John. *The Oxford History of the Laws of England, Volume II, 871–1216* (Oxford, 2012).

Huneycutt, Lois L. 'Intercession and the High Medieval Queen: the Esther topos', in *The Power of the Weak*, ed. Jennifer Carpenter and Sally Beth MacLean (Chicago, IL, 1995), 126–46.

———*Matilda of Scotland: A Study in Medieval Queenship* (Woodbridge, 2003).

Huygens, R.B.C. 'Bérengar de Tours, Lanfranc et Bernold de Constance', *Sacris Erudiri* 16 (1965), 355–87.

Huyghebaert, Nicholas. 'Les Femmes laïques dans le vie de religieuse des XIe et XIIe Siècles dans le province ecclésiastique de Reims', in *I laici nella "societas christianan" dei soceli XI e XIII, Miscellanea del Centro di Studi Medioevalia* 5 (Milan, 1968), 381.

———'Adela van Frankrijk, Gravin van Vlaanderen, Stichteres Van de Abdij Van Mesen (ca. 1017–1079)', *Ipres Kwartier* Vol 158: 3 (1979), 67–126.

Huynes, Jean and Paul Marchegay. 'Translation des reliques de saint Florent, de Roye à Saumur', *Bibliothèque de l'école des chartes* 3(1842), 475–98.

Insley, Charles. 'The Family of Wulfric Spot' in *The English and their Legacy, 900–1200: Essays in Honour of Ann Williams*, ed. David Roffe (Woodbridge, 2012), 115–28.

Iogna-Prat, Dominique.'Le lieu de culte dans l'Occident médiéval entre sainteté et sacralité (IXe–XIIIe siècles)', *Revue d'Histoire des Religions* 4 (2005), 463–80.

Israeli, Yanay. 'Petition and response as social process: royal power, justice and the people in late medieval Castile (*c.* 1474–1504)', *Past and Present* 262 (2024), 3–44.

Jackson, Richard A. *Ordines coronationis Franciae: texts and ordines for the coronation of Frankish and French kings and queens in the Middle Ages* (Philadelphia, PA, 1995).

Jacobson, Howard. *A Commentary on Pseudo-Philo's Liber Antiquitatum Biblicarum: With Latin Text and English Translation* (Leiden, 1996).

Jaeger, Stephen. *The Envy of Angels: Cathedral Schools and Social Ideals in Medieval Europe, 950–1200* (Philadelphia, PA, 2011).

Janssen, Sam. 'A Pattern of Alternating Interests: The Peace of God in the Archdiocese of Reims in the First Half of the Eleventh Century', in *Episcopal Power and Personality in Medieval Europe, 900–1480*, ed. Peter Coss et al. (Turnhout, 2020), 203–22.

Jestice, Phyllis G. *Imperial Ladies of the Ottonian Dynasty: Women and Rule in Tenth-Century Germany* (Cham, 2018)

Jones, C.W. 'The Norman Cult of Sts. Catherine and Nicholas, saec. IX', in *Hommages à André Boutemy*, ed. G. Cambier (Brussels, 1976), 222–3.

Kantorowicz, Ernst. 'The Quinity of Winchester', *The Art Bulletin* 29: 2 (Jun 1947), 73–85.

———*The King's Two Bodies* (Princeton, NJ, 1957).

Karn, Nicholas. *Kings, Lords and Courts in Anglo-Norman England* (Woodbridge, 2020).

Keane, Marguerite. *Material Culture and Queenship in fourteenth-century France: The Testament of Blanche of Navarre 1331–1398* (Leiden, 2016).

Kidd, Judith A. 'The Quinity Reconsidered', *Studies in Iconography*, 7/8 (1981), 21–31.

Klein, Stacy. *Ruling Women: Queenship and Gender in Anglo-Saxon Literature* (Notre Dame, IN, 2006).

Kobialka, Michal. *This Is My Body: Representational Practices in the Early Middle Ages* (Ann Arbor, MI, 1999).

———'Staging Space/Place in Eleventh-Century Monastic Practices' in *Medieval Practices of Space*, ed. Barbara Hanawalt and Michal Kobialka (Minneapolis, MN, 2000).

Koziol, Geoffrey. 'Monks, Feuds and the Making of Peace in Eleventh Century Flanders', *Historical Reflections / Réflexions Historique* Vol. 14, No. 3 (Fall 1987), 531–49.

———*Begging Pardon and Favor: Ritual and Political Order in Early Medieval France* (Ithaca, NY, 1992).

Kreins, Jean-Marie *Histoire du Luxembourg: des origines à nos jours* (Paris, 2007) 10–20.

Laleman, M.C. 'Het stenen verleden. Een beknopt overzicht van bouwactiviteiten, bouwkundige ontwikkelingen en monastieke architectuur', in *Gand & Blandinium: de Gentse abdijen van Sint-Pieters en Sint-Baafs*, ed. G. Declerqc (Ghent, 1997), 115–46.

Lambert, Tom. *Law and Order in Anglo-Saxon England* (Oxford, 2017).

Landes, Richard. 'L'accession des Capétiens: une reconsidération selon les sources aquitaines', in *Religion et culture autour de l'an Mil. Royaume capétien et Lotharingie: Actes du Colloque Hugues Capet 987–1987*, ed. Dominique Iogna-Prat (Paris, 1990).

Lauer, P. 'Les translations des reliques de saint Ouen', *Bulletin philologique et historique du Comité des travaux historiques et scientifiques*, ed. Dominique Iogna-Prat (Paris, 1921), 119–36.

Lazowski, Christophe. 'La "mise en scène" d'une théologie eucharistique: la procession anglo-normande des Rameaux' in *Liturgie, pensée théologique et mentalités religieuses au haut Moyen Âge: Le témoignage des sources liturgiques* (Munster, 2016), 127–60.

Lee, Becky R. 'Men's Recollections of a Women's Rite: Medieval English Men's Recollections Regarding the Rite of the Purification of Women after Childbirth', *Gender and History* 14 (2002), 224–41.

Legg, J. Wickham. 'The Queen's Coronation Ring', *Archaeological Journal* 54 (1897), 1–9.

Le Jan, Régine. 'Le couple aristocratique au haut Moyen Âge', *Médiévales* 65 (2013), 33–46.

L'Estrange, Elizabeth. *Holy Motherhood: Gender, Dynasty and Visual Culture in the Later Middle Ages* (Manchester, 2008).

Letouzey-Réty, Catherine. 'Écrit et gestion du temporel dans une grande abbaye de femmes anglo-normande: la Sainte-Trinité de Caen (XIe–XIIIe siècle)', PhD dissertation (3 vols., Université de Paris I Panthéon-Sorbonne, 2011).

——'Les abbesses de la Trinité de Caen, la Reine Mathilde et l'Angleterre', *Annales de Normandie* 69: 1 (2019), 57–69.

——'Memory and Documentary Culture at Holy Trinity Abbey, Caen in the eleventh–twelfth centuries', in *Gender, Memory and Documentary Culture, c. 900–1300*, ed. Laura L. Gathagan and Charles Insley (Woodbridge, 2025), 254–70.

Lewis, C.P. 'The early earls of Norman England,' *ANS* 13 (1991), 207–23.

——'The Domesday Jurors,' *HSJ* 5 (1993), 17–44.

Leyser, Karl. *Rule and Conflict in Early Medieval Society: Ottonian Saxony* (Bloomington, IN, 1979).

Lifshitz, Felice. 'The migration of Neustrian relics in the Viking Age: the myth of voluntary exodus, the reality of coercion and theft', *EME* 4:2 (1995), 175–92.

Livingstone, Amy. *Out of Love for My Kin: Aristocratic Family Life in the Lands of the Loire, 1000–1200* (Ithaca, NY, 2010).

——'Pious women in a "den of scorpions": the piety and patronage of the eleventh-century countesses of Brittany', *Historical Reflections / Réflexions historiques* 43:1 (2017), 45–61.

——*Medieval Lives, c. 1000–1292 AD: The World of the Beaugency Family* (London, 2019).

LoPrete, Kimberly A. *Adela of Blois: Countess and Lord, c. 1067–1137* (Dublin, 2007).

MacLean, Simon. 'Making a difference in tenth-century politics: King Aethelstan's sisters and Frankish queenship', in *Frankland: The Franks and the World of the Early Middle Ages. Essays in honour of Dame Jinty Nelson*, ed. Paul Fouracre and David Ganz (Manchester, 2008), 167–90.

——'Monastic reform and Royal Ideology in tenth-century England: Æthelfryth and Edgar in Continental Perspective', in *England and the Continent in the Tenth Century: Studies in Honour of Wilhelm Levison (1876–1947)*, ed. David Rollason and Hannah Williams (Turnhout, 2010), 255–74.

——'Cross–channel marriage and royal succession in the age of Charles the Simple and Athelstan (c. 916–936)' in *Medieval Worlds. Comparative and Interdisciplinary Studies* 1:2 (2015), 26–44.

——*Ottonian Queenship* (Oxford, 2017).

Macy, Gary. *The Theologies of the Eucharist in the Early Scholastic Age* (Oxford, 1984).

———'The ordination of women in the early Middle Ages', *Theological Studies* 59 (2000), 481–507.

———'Abelard, Heloise and the Ordination of Abbesses', *JEH* 57:1 (2006), 16–32.

———*The Hidden History of Women's Ordination: Female Clergy in the Medieval West* (Oxford, 2007).

Marafioti, Nicole. 'Secular and Ecclesiastical Justice in late Anglo-Saxon England', *Speculum* 94:3 (July, 2019), 774–805.

Marchegay, Paul. 'Chartes Angevines des onzième et douzième siècles', *Bibliothèque de l'École Des Chartes* 36 (1875), 381–441.

Martindale, Jean. 'Monasteries and castles: the priories of St-Florent de Saumur in England after 1066', in *England in the eleventh century: proceedings of the 1990 Harlaxton symposium*, ed. Carola Hicks (Stamford, 1992), 135–56.

Mason, Emma. *The House of Godwin: the History of a Dynasty* (London, 2004).

Macdonald, A.J. *Berengar and the Reform of Sacramental Doctrine* (1930; rpt. edition, 1977).

McCartney, Elizabeth. 'Ceremonies and privileges of office: queenship in late medieval France', in *Power of the Weak: Studies on Medieval Women*, ed. Jennifer Carpenter and Sally-Beth Maclean (Urbana, IL, 1995), 178–219.

McClain, Aleks and Naomi Sykes. 'New Archaeologies of the Norman Conquest', *ANS* 41 (2019), 83–101.

Medici, Maria Terea Guerra. 'For a History of Women's Monastic Institutions: The Abbess: Role, Functions and Administration', *Bulletin of Medieval Canon Law* 23 (1999), 35–65.

Mégier, Elisabeth. 'Christian Historical Fulfilments of Old Testament Prophecies in Latin Commentaries on the Book of Isaiah (ca. 400 to ca. 1150)', *The Journal of Medieval Latin* 17 (2007), 87–100.

Mersch Katharina Ulrike. 'Quedlinburg Abbey's Medieval History in Ever-Changing Political and Religious Frameworks: A Survey', in *A Companion to the Abbey of Quedlinburg in the Middle Ages*, ed. Karen Blough (Leiden, 2022), 15–46.

Miles, Laura Saetveit. *The Virgin Mary's Book at the Annunciation: Reading, Interpretation and Devotion in Medieval England* (Cambridge, 2020).

Miller, Maureen. *Clothing the Clergy: Virtue and Power in Medieval Europe, c. 800–1200* (Ithaca, NY, 2014), 169–71.

Moeglin, Jean-Marie, ed. *L' Intercession du Moyen Âge à l'époque moderne. Autour d'une pratique sociale* (Geneva, 2004).

Mureşan, Dan Ioan. 'Ego Wilhelmus victoriosus Anglorum basileus: Les circonstances de la synthèse impériale anglo-normande', *Annales de Normandie* 69:1 (2019), 107–64.

Musset, Lucien. 'Autour des origines de Saint-Étienne de Fontenay,' *Bulletin de la société des antiquaires de Normandie* 56 (1963) 11–41.

———'L'Exode des reliques du diocèse de Sées au temps des invasions normandes,' *Bulletin Société historique et archéologique de l'Orne* 88 (1970), 3–22.

———'La Reine Mathilde et la fondation de la Trinité de Caen (Abbayes-aux-Dames)', *Bulletin de la Societé des antiquaires de Normandie* 21 (1984), 191–210.

——'Les contacts entre l'Église normande et l'Église d'Angleterre de 911 à 1066', in *Les Mutations socioculturelles au tournant des XIe–XIIe siècles*, Comité international des études anselmiennes (Paris, 1984), 67–84.

——'Le mécénat des princes normands au XIe siècle', in *Artistes, artisans et production artistique au Moyen Âge*, ed. Xavier Barral Altet (Paris, 1987), 121–34.

——'Les translations de reliques en Normandie (IXe–XIIe siècles)' in *Les Saints dans la Normandie Médiévale*, ed. Pierre Bouet and François Neveux (Caen, 2000), 97–108.

Nash, Penelope. *Empress Adelheid and Countess Matilda: Medieval Female Rulership and the Foundations of European Society* (London, 2017).

Nelson, Janet L. 'The Rites of the Conqueror', *ANS* 4 (1981), 117–32.

——*Politics and Ritual in Early Medieval Europe* (London, 1986).

——'Early medieval rites of queen-making and the shaping of medieval queenship', in *Rulers and Ruling Families in Early Medieval Europe: Alfred, Charles the Bald, and Others*, ed. Janet L. Nelson (Farnham, 1999), 301–15.

Nicholas, David. 'Of Poverty and Primacy: Demand, Liquidity, and the Flemish Economic Miracle, 1050–1200' *American Historical Review* 96: 1 (1991), 17–41.

——*Medieval Flanders* (London, 1992).

——*Trade, Urbanisation, and the Family: Studies in the History of Medieval Flanders* (London, 1996).

Noizet, Hélène. *La fabrique de la ville: Espace et sociétés à Tours, IXe–XIIIe siècle* (Paris, 2007).

O'Brien, Conor. 'Moses, Aaron, and the Abbacy of Wearmouth-Jarrow in 716', in *All Roads Lead to Rome*, ed. Jane Hawkes and Meg Boulton (Turnhout, 2019), 105–14.

Occhiato, Giuseppe. 'Roberto de Grandmesnil, un abate "architetto" operante in Calabria nell'XI secolo', in *Calabria bizantina. Testimonianze d'arte e strutture di territorio. Atti dell'VIII e IX Incontro di Studi Bizantini, Reggio Calabria 1985–89*, ed. Soveria Mannelli (Catanzaro, 1991), 129–75.

Oksanen, Eljas. *Flanders and the Anglo-Norman World, 1066–1216* (Cambridge, 2012).

Omont, Henri. 'Epitaphes metriques en l'honneur de differents personnages du XI siecle composées par Foulcoie de Beauvais archidiacre de Meaux', *Mélanges Julien Havet* (Paris, 1895), 211–36.

Pantos, Aliki. 'The location and form of Anglo-Saxon assembly: some "moot points"' in *Assembly Places and Practices in Medieval Europe*, ed. Aliki Pantos and Sarah Semple (Dublin, 2004), 55–180.

Parkes, Henry. *The Making of Liturgy in the Ottonian Church: Books, Music and Ritual in Mainz, 950–1050* (Cambridge, 2015).

Parsons, John Carmi. 'The Queen's Intercession in Thirteenth-Century England', in *The Power of the Weak*, ed. Jennifer Carpenter and Sally Beth MacLean (Chicago, IL, 1995), 147–77.

———'The intercessionary patronage of Queens Margaret and Isabella of France', *Thirteenth Century England, VI: Proceedings of the Durham Conference, 1995* (1997), 145–56.

Pearse, Roger. 'Life of Saint Cuthman (BHL 2035)', translation available Open Source, https://archive.org/details/cuthman-life-bhl-2035/page/12/mode/2up

Peltier, Henri. 'Saint Adalard, Abbe de Corbie: son rôle politique et administrative', in *Corbie Abbaye Royale*, ed. Louis Gaillard and Joseph Daoust (Lille, 1963), 61–94.

Phelan, Owen. 'Horizontal and vertical theologies: "sacraments" in the works of Paschasius Radbertus and Ratramnus of Corbie', *Harvard Theological Review* 103:3 (2010), 271–89.

Pick, Lucy. *Her Father's Daughter: Gender, Power and Religion in the Early Spanish Kingdoms* (Ithaca, NY, 2017).

Pohl, Benjamin. *Dudo of Saint-Quentin's Historia Normannorum: Tradition, Innovation and Memory* (York, 2015).

———'Processions, Power, and Public Display: Ecclesiastical Rivalry and Ritual in Ducal Normandy', *Journal of Medieval Monastic Studies* 6 (2017): 1–49.

Pohl, Benjamin and Elisabeth van Houts. 'History and memory,' in *The Cambridge Companion to the Age of William the Conqueror*, ed. Benjamin Pohl (Cambridge, 2022), 244–71.

Poncelet, Albert. 'Sanctae Catharine virginis et martyrs translatio et miracula rotomagensia saec. XI', *Analecta Bollandiana* 22 (1903), 423–38.

Power, Eileen. 'Introduction,' in *Miracles of the Virgin Mary*, trans. C.C. Swinton Bland (London, 1928).

Rabin, Andrew. 'Female Advocacy and Royal Protection in Tenth-Century England: The Legal Career of Queen Ælfthryth', *Speculum* 84: 2 (2009), 261–88.

Ragnow, Marguerite. 'The Worldly Cares of Abbess Richildis: Power, Property, and Female Religious in 11th-Century Anjou', PhD dissertation (2 vols., University of Minnesota, 2006).

Raine, James. *The Historians of the Church of York and Its Archbishops* (Cambridge, 2012).

Räkel, Hans-Herbert. 'Geschichte mit allen Registern', *Archiv für Kulturgeschichte* 64.1 (1983), 41–62;

Reilly, Lisa. *The Invention of Norman Visual Culture: Art, Politics, and Dynastic Ambition* (Cambridge, 2020).

Richard, Jean-Claude. 'Les "miracula" composés en Normandie aux XIe et XIIe siècles', PhD dissertation (L'École des Charters, 1975).

Ridyard, Susan J. '*Condigna Veneratio*: Post-Conquest Attitudes to the Saints of the Anglo-Saxons', *ANS* IX (1987), 179–206.

Riley, Bridget K. 'Lost and found: Eadmer's *De reliquiis sancti Audoeni* as a cross-channel solution to the Canterbury–York dispute', *HSJ* 28 (2017), 15–38.

Roche, Thomas. 'Holy Trinity Caen's List of Losses', *HSJ* 26 (2014), 123–40.

Roffe, David. *Domesday: The Inquest and the Book* (Oxford, 2000).
———*Decoding Domesday* (Woodbridge, 2007).
———'The Danes and the making of the kingdom of the English', in *Nations in Medieval Britain*, ed. Hirokazu Tsurushima (Donington, 2010), 32–44.
Rolland, P. 'La première église Saint-Donatien à Bruges', *Revue belge d'archéologie et d'histoire de l'art* 14 (1944), 101–11.
Ruprich-Robert, Victor. *L'église Ste-Trinité (ancienne Abbaye-aux-dames) et l'église St-Étienne (ancienne Abbaye aux Hommes) à Caen* (Caen, 1864).
Sassier, Yves. *Hugues Capet: Naissance d'une dynastie* (Paris, 2018).
Saxonhouse, A. 'Introduction – Public and Private: The Paradigm's Power', in *Stereotypes of Women in Power: Historical Perspectives and Revisionist Views*, ed. B. Garlick, S. Dixon and P. Allen (New York, NY, 1992), 1–9.
Scheck, Helene. 'Queen Mathilda of Saxony and the Founding of Quedlinburg: Women, Memory, and Power', *Historical Reflections* 35:3 (2009), 21–36.
Schulmeyer-Ahl, Kerstin. *Der Anfang vom Ende der Ottonen Konstitutionsbedingungen historiographischer Nachrichten in der Chronik Thietmars von Merseburg* (Berlin, 2009).
Schwennicke, Detlev. *Europäische Stammtafeln: Stammtafeln zur Geschichte der Europäischen Staaten, Neue Folge* (16 vols., Marburg, 1978–1995).
Schulze, Hans K. and Günter W. Vorbrodt. *Das Stift Gernrode* (Böhlau, 1965).
Searle, Eleanor. *Predatory Kinship and the Creation of Norman Power, 840–1066* (Davis, CA, 1988).
Semple, Sarah. 'Locations of assembly in early Anglo-Saxon England', in *Assembly Places and Practices in Medieval Europe*, ed. Aliki Pantos and Sarah Semple (Dublin, 2004), 135–54.
Shadis, Miriam. *Berenguela of Castile (1180–1246) and Political Women in the High Middle Ages* (New York, NY, 2009).
Shahar, Shulamith. *Childhood in the Middle Ages* (London, 1990).
Sheerin, Daniel. 'Sisters in the Literary Agon', in *Women Writing Latin, Volume 2*, ed. Laurie Churchill, Phyllis R. Brown, Jane E. Jeffrey (New York, NY, 2002), 93–131.
Smith, Julie A. 'The Earliest Queen-making Rites', *Church History* 66 (1997), 18–35.
Spear, David S. 'William Bona Anima, abbot of St Stephen's of Caen, 1070–1079', *HSJ* 1 (1989), 51–60.
Stafford, Pauline. 'Judith, Charles the Bald and England', in *Charles the Bald, Court and Kingdom*, ed. M. Gibson and J. Nelson (Oxford, 1981).
———'Emma: The Powers of the Queen', in *Queens and Queenship in Medieval Europe*, ed. Anne Duggan (Woodbridge, 1997), 3–26.
———*Queen Emma and Queen Edith: Queenship and Women's Power in Eleventh-Century England* (London, 2011).
Stanton, Robert. *The Culture of Translation in Anglo-Saxon England* (Cambridge, 2002).

Stover, Jos. 'Beschouwingen bij een "bouwschool". Vorstelijke elementen aan elfde-eeuwse kerken in Normandie', in *Bouwen en duiden: studies over architectuur en iconologie*, ed. E. den Hartog and R.J. Stover (Canaletto, 1994), 53–77.

Swanton, Michael. *Anglo-Saxon Prose* (London, 1975).

Tabuteau, Emily Zack. *Transfers of Property in Eleventh-Century Normandy Law* (Chapel Hill, NC, 1988).

Tanner, Heather. 'Queenship: office, custom, or ad hoc? The case of Queen Matilda III of England (1135–1152)', in *Eleanor of Aquitaine: Lord and Lady*, ed. Bonnie Wheeler and John Carmi Parsons (New York, NY, 2002), 133–58.

———*Friends, Enemies and Allies: Boulogne and Politics in Northern France and England, 879–1160* (Leiden, 2004).

Taylor, Charles S. *An Analysis of the Domesday Survey of Gloucestershire* (Bristol, 1889).

Thompson, Kathleen. 'Being the Ducal Sister: the role of Adelaide of Aumale', in *Normandy and its Neighbors, 900–1250. Essays in honour of David Bates*, ed. David Crouch and Kathleen Thompson (Turnhout, 2011), 43–59.

Tingle, Louise. *Chaucer's Queens: Royal Women, Intercession, and Patronage in England, 1328–1394* (London, 2020).

Tinti, Francesca and D.A. Woodman, ed. *Constructing History across the Norman Conquest Worcester, c. 1050–c. 1150* (York, 2022).

Trân-Duc, Lucile. 'Le culte des saints en Normandie (IXe–XIIe siècle): Enjeux de pouvoir dans les établissements bénédictins du diocèse de Rouen', PhD dissertation (2 vols., Université de Caen, 2006).

Turner, Dawson. *Account of a tour in Normandy: undertaken chiefly for the purpose of investigating the architectural antiquities of the duchy* (2 vols., London, 1820).

Tuten, Belle Stoddard. 'Holy Litigants: The Nuns of Ronceray d'Angers and their Neighbors, 1028–1200', PhD dissertation (Emory University, 1994).

———'Disputing Corpses: Le Ronceray d'Angers versus Saint-Nicolas d'Angers, ca. 1080–1140' *Medieval Perspectives* 10 (1995), 178–88.

Tyler, Elizabeth M. 'Crossing Conquests: Polyglot royal women and literary culture in eleventh-century england,' in *Conceptualizing Multilingualism in England, 800–1250*, ed. Elizabeth M. Tyler (Turnout, 2011), 171–196.

———*England in Europe: English Royal Women and Literary Patronage, c. 1000–c. 1150* (Toronto, 2017).

———'German imperial bishops and Anglo-Saxon literary culture on the eve of the conquest: The Cambridge Songs and Leofric's Exeter Book', in *Latinity and Identity in Anglo-Saxon Literature*, ed. Rebecca Stephenson and Emily V. Thornbury (Toronto, 2016), 177–201.

Ugé, Karine. *Creating the Monastic Past in Medieval Flanders* (York, 2005).

Van den Bremt, An and Geert Vermeiren. 'Archeologisch vooronderzoek op het Sint-Pietersplein en aan de Tweekerkenstraat', *Handelingen der Maatschappij voor Geschiedenis en Oudheidkunde te Gent* 58 (2004), 23–58.

Vanderputten, Steven. *Monastic Reform as Process: Realities and Representations in Medieval Flanders, 900–1100* (Ithaca, 2017).

van Deusen, Nancy. 'Laudes regiae: In Praise of Kings. Medieval Acclamations, Liturgy and the Ritual of Power', in *Procession, Perfomance, Liturgy and Ritual: Essays in Honor of Bruce R. Gillingham*, ed. Nancy van Deusen (Ottowa, 2007), 83–118.

van Houts, Elisabeth. 'The Ship list of William the Conqueror', *ANS* X (1987), 176–9.

———'Historiography and Hagiography at Sant-Wandrille: the "Inventio et Miracula Sancti Vulfranni"', *ANS XII* (1989), 233–51.

———'Latin Poetry and the Anglo-Norman court, 1066–1135: the "Carmen de Hastingae proelio"', *JMH* 15:1 (1989), 39–62.

———'Women and the Writing of History in the early Middle Ages: Abbess Matilda of Essen and Aethelweard,' *EME* 1:1 (1992), 54–68.

———*The Normans in Europe* (Manchester, 2000).

———'The Echo of the Conquest in the Latin Sources: Duchess Mathilda, her daughters and the Enigma of the Golden Child', in *The Bayeux Tapestry: Embroidering the Facts of History*, ed. Pierre Bouet (Caen, 2004), 135–55.

———'Edward and Normandy,' in *Edward the Confessor; the man and the legend,* ed. Richard Mortimer (Woodbridge, 2009), 63–76.

———'The Fate of the Priests' Sons in Normandy with special reference to Serlo of Bayeux', *HSJ* 25 (2013), 57–105.

———'Queens in the Anglo-Norman/Angevin realm 1066–1216', *Vorträge und Forschungen* 81 (2015), 199–224.

Vaughn, Sally N. *The Abbey of Bec and the Anglo-Norman State* (Woodbridge, 1981).

———'Henry I and the English Church: The Archbishops and the King', *HSJ* 17 (2006), 133–57.

———*Archbishop Anselm 1093–1109: Bec Missionary, Canterbury Primate, Patriarch of Another World* (London, 2012).

Vezzoni, Maria. 'Alexander II and the Normans: Borders as Instruments of Dialogue and Compromise', in *Borders and the Norman World: Frontiers and Boundaries in Medieval Europe*, ed. Dan Armstrong, Áron Kecskés, Charles C. Rozier and Leonie Hicks (Woodbridge, 2023), 127–47.

von der Nahmer, Dieter. '"Fortuna atque mores": Widukind I 25 und zur Bedeutung dieser Paarformel für die Rerum gestarum Saxonicarum libri tres', *Studi Medievale* 53.1 (2012), 313–56.

Walsh, Christine. *The Cult of St Katherine of Alexandria in Early Medieval Europe* (Farnham, 2007).

Wangerin, Laura. 'Holy relics, authority, and legitimacy in Ottonian Germany and Anglo-Saxon England,' *HSJ* 27 (2016), 15–38.

———'The governance of Ottonian Germany in historiographical perspective', *History Compass* 15:1(2017), 1–10.

———*Kingship and Justice in the Ottonian Empire* (Ann Arbor, MI, 2019).

———'Ottonian Women, Textual Memory and Dynastic Legitimacy', in *Gender, Memory and Documentary Culture c. 900–1300*, ed. Laura L. Gathagan and Charles Insley (Woodbridge, 2025), 145–62.

Ward, Emily Joan. 'Anne of Kiev (*c.* 1024–*c.* 1075) and a reassessment of maternal power in the minority kingship of Philip I of France', *Historical Research* 89: 245 (2016), 435–53.

Ward, J.C. 'Royal Service and Reward: the Clare Family and the Crown, 1066–1154', *ANS* 11 (1989), 261–5.

Warner, David A. *Ottonian Germany: The Chronicon of Thietmar of Merseburg* (Manchester, 2001).

———'Reading Ottonian History: The Sonderweg And Other Myths', in *Challenging the boundaries of medieval history: the legacy of Timothy Reuter*, ed. Patricia Skinner (Turnhout, 2009), 81–114.

———'Comparative approaches to Anglo-Saxon and Ottonian coronations', in *England and the Continent in the Tenth Century: Studies in Honour of Wilhelm Levison (1876–1947)*, ed. David Rollason and Hannah Williams (Turnhout, 2010), 275–92.

Welton, Megan and Sarah Greer, 'Establishing just rule: the diplomatic negotiations of the dominae imperiales in the Ottonian succession crisis of 983–985', *Frühmittelalterliche Studien* 55 (2021), 315–42.

Williams, Ann. *The English and the Norman Conquest* (Woodbridge, 1995).

———*The World Before Domesday: The English Aristocracy 900–1066* (London, 2011).

Williams, John R. 'Godfrey of Rheims, a Humanist of the Eleventh Century', *Speculum* 22 (1947), 29–45.

———'Cathedral Schools of Rheims in the Eleventh Century', *Speculum* 29 (1954), 661–77.

Wilmart, Dom A. 'Les reliques de saint Ouen à Cantorbéry', *Analecta Bollandiana* LI (1933), 285–92.

Wolf, Gunther. 'Königinnen-Krönungen des frühen Mittelalters bis zum Beginn des Investiturstreits', *Zeitschrift der Savigny-Stiftung für Rechtsgeschichte* 107:76 (1990), 62–88.

Wood, Ian. 'Germanus, Alban and Auxerre', *Bulletin du centre d'études médiévales d'Auxerre* 13 (2009), 123–9.

Yarrow, Simon. *Saints and Their Communities: Miracle Stories in Twelfth-Century England* (Oxford, 2006).

Yvernault, Françoise. 'Les bâtiments de l'abbaye de Montivilliers au Moyen Âge', *Bulletin de l'association Montivielliers, Hier, Aujourd'hui et Demain* (MHAD) 9 (1997), 41–51.

INDEX

GENDER IN THE MIDDLE AGES

I *Gender and Medieval Drama*, Katie Normington, 2006

II *Gender and Petty Crime in Late Medieval England: The Local Courts in Kent, 1460–1560*, Karen Jones, 2006

III *The Pastoral Care of Women in Late Medieval England*, Beth Allison Barr, 2008

IV *Gender, Nation and Conquest in the Works of William of Malmesbury*, Kirsten A. Fenton, 2008

V *Monsters, Gender and Sexuality in Medieval English Literature*, Dana M. Oswald, 2010

VI *Medieval Anchoritisms: Gender, Space and the Solitary Life*, Liz Herbert McAvoy, 2011

VII *Middle-Aged Women in the Middle Ages*, edited by Sue Niebrzydowski, 2011

VIII *Married Women and the Law in Premodern Northwest Europe*, edited by Cordelia Beattie and Matthew Frank Stevens, 2013

IX *Religious Men and Masculine Identity in the Middle Ages*, edited by P.H. Cullum and Katherine J. Lewis, 2013

X *Reconsidering Gender, Time and Memory in Medieval Culture*, edited by Elizabeth Cox, Liz Herbert McAvoy and Roberta Magnani, 2015

XI *Medicine, Religion and Gender in Medieval Culture*, edited by Naoë Kukita Yoshikawa, 2015

XII *The Unspeakable, Gender and Sexuality in Medieval Literature, 1000–1400*, Victoria Blud, 2017

XIII *Popular Memory and Gender in Medieval England: Men, Women, and Testimony in the Church Courts, c. 1200–1500*, Bronach C. Kane, 2019

XIV *Authority, Gender and Space in the Anglo-Norman World, 900–1200*, Katherine Weikert, 2020

XV *Female Desire in Chaucer's* Legend of Good Women *and Middle English Romance*, Lucy M. Allen-Goss, 2020

XVI *Treason and Masculinity in Medieval England: Gender, Law and Political Culture*, E. Amanda McVitty, 2020

XVII *Holy Harlots in Medieval English Religious Literature: Authority, Exemplarity and Femininity*, Juliette Vuille, 2021

XVIII *Addressing Women in Early Medieval Religious Texts*, Kathryn Maude, 2021

XIX *Women, Dance and Parish Religion in England, 1300–1640: Negotiating the Steps of Faith*, Lynneth Miller Renberg, 2022

XX *Women's Literary Cultures in the Global Middle Ages: Speaking Internationally*, edited by Kathryn Loveridge, Liz Herbert McAvoy, Sue Niebrzydowski and Vicki Kay Price, 2023

XXI *Women and Devotional Literature in the Middle Ages: Giving Voice to Silence. Essays in Honour of Catherine Innes-Parker*, edited by Cate Gunn, Liz Herbert McAvoy and Naoë Kukita Yoshikawa, 2023

XXII *Female Devotion and Textile Imagery in Medieval English Literature*, Anna McKay, 2024

XXIII *Premodern Masculinities in Transition*, edited by Konrad Eisenbichler and Jacqueline Murray, 2024

XXIV *Financing Queenship in Late Fifteenth Century England*, Michele L.C. Seah, 2025

www.ingramcontent.com/pod-product-compliance
Lightning Source LLC
LaVergne TN
LVHW020507100826
845148LV00003B/715
9781837654895